People, Places, and Belonging

Deepening
Our Sense of Community
and Identity

People, Places, and Belonging

William Marsiglio

Aevo UTP
An imprint of University of Toronto Press
Toronto Buffalo London
utorontopress.com

© William Marsiglio 2025

ISBN 978-1-4875-5145-2 (Cloth)   ISBN 978-1-4875-5146-9 (EPUB)
                                 ISBN 978-1-4875-5148-3 (PDF)

All rights reserved. No part of this publication may be reproduced, stored in or introduced into a retrieval system, or transmitted in any form or by any means (electronic, mechanical, photocopying, recording, or otherwise) without the prior written permission of both the copyright owner and the above publisher of this book.

Library and Archives Canada Cataloguing in Publication

Title: People, places, and belonging : deepening our sense of community and identity / William Marsiglio.
Names: Marsiglio, William, author
Description: Includes bibliographical references and index.
Identifiers: Canadiana (print) 20240448626 | Canadiana (ebook) 20240448693 | ISBN 9781487551452 (cloth) | ISBN 9781487551483 (PDF) | ISBN 9781487551469 (EPUB)
Subjects: LCSH: Community life. | LCSH: Group identity. | LCSH: Place attachment – Social aspects. | LCSH: Place attachment – Psychological aspects.
Classification: LCC HM761 .M37 2024 | DDC 307 – dc23

Cover design: Kathleen Lynch / Black Kat Design
Cover image: Gettyimages.ca / cnythzl

We wish to acknowledge the land on which the University of Toronto Press operates. This land is the traditional territory of the Wendat, the Anishnaabeg, the Haudenosaunee, the Métis, and the Mississaugas of the Credit First Nation.

University of Toronto Press acknowledges the financial support of the Government of Canada, the Canada Council for the Arts, and the Ontario Arts Council, an agency of the Government of Ontario, for its publishing activities.

To all the environmentalists who relentlessly dedicate themselves to protecting our planet and its people because earth is ultimately humanity's most precious place and only home – at least for the foreseeable future.

Contents

List of Illustrations   viii

Preface   x

Introduction   1

PART ONE: THE BASICS OF PLACE   31

1 Framing Properties   33
2 Types of Places   61

PART TWO: KEY PLACE PROCESSES (*CART*)   121

3 Attachments   123
4 Rituals   140
5 Transitions   176
6 Claims, Control, and Decision-Making   211

PART THREE: CONSTRUCTIVE PLACEMAKING   251

7 Cultivating Place Consciousness to Enrich Society   253
Epilogue: A Placemaking Roadmap for the Future   313

Notes   327
Index   351

Illustrations

Photos

1 Gainesville Health & Fitness, Gainesville, Florida x
2 George Floyd Memorial, Minneapolis, Minnesota 1
3 Aerial view of various naval vessels around the beaches of Normandy 33
4 Kenneth Niedermeier, Armando Niedermeier-Rubio, and Hannah Rubio strolling through a street in San Miguel de Allende, Guanajuato, Mexico 61
5 Tile mural celebrating the story of *Kamome*, the lost Japanese boat, created in 2023 by artist Harley Munger 123
6 Aerial photograph capturing the Hajj – the annual Muslim pilgrimage to the Kaaba in Mecca, Saudi Arabia 140
7 Volunteers with Aguilas del Desierto during one of its regular organized searches to rescue or recover migrants along the United States–Mexico border 176
8 Azovstal Plant, Mariupol, Ukraine, after the Russian invasion and devastating bombing 211
9 Damanhur, federation of spiritual communities, northern Italy; annual photo of the Spiritual *Popolo* in the Open Temple 253
10 View of Earth as seen by the Apollo 17 crew traveling toward the moon 313

Models

1 *CART* social processes affecting place consciousness 120
2 Ethical placemaking in five social domains involving *CART* processes 262
3 *CART* social processes 315
4 *MEAL* life skills 320

Preface

Photo 1: Gainesville Health & Fitness, Gainesville, Florida, owned by Joseph D. Cirulli. (Photo courtesy of Joseph D. Cirulli)

We usually associate our lasting memories, good and bad, with specific places. One way we reconstruct poignant memories for the benefit of others and ourselves is to put them into story form. Our meaningful life stories – the ones we tell family, friends, and people with whom we seek intimacy – are often situated in places.

Place-based tales can foster the reconstruction of memories of a childhood home, an exhilarating vacation spot, a setting where tragedy and trauma were endured, a site that yielded profound personal insight, a place that housed festive times, and more. Most stories capture memorable social exchanges, but some are firmly rooted in our personal impressions of a place's unique features independent of any human activity. Some stories focus on a specific event in a specific place at a specific time. Alternatively, sentimental stories can summarize a string of enduring memories of relatively unremarkable experiences that occurred in a place over many years. While we often share significant place-based experiences with others, we sometimes experience special moments in solitude, away from public scrutiny. Whether we experience a meaningful place largely for the social aspects or for its nonsocial attributes, as a noteworthy singular moment or an effect over an extended period, in a shared or a solitary context, our lived experience confirms that place matters. We usually recognize this intuitively on some level, yet we are enlightened when we explore the nuances of what this means for us and the larger social landscape. This book is designed to deepen our understanding of that sentiment and inspire us to leverage that knowledge to improve the quality of places and of our lives.

As a scholar trained in the social sciences, my professional instinct has been to reflect on the social dimensions of people's experiences with place. However, in recent years I've also expanded my appreciation for how the nonsocial properties of the built and natural environments surrounding us influence our mind, body, heart, and soul. The seeds for this intellectual awakening took root decades ago in my everyday life due to my fondness for such simple things as tropical landscapes, mountain ranges, sunny skies, vaulted ceilings, open floor plans, extra-large windows, and walls painted in light violet shades. These attributes magnify the effects of place, thus deepening my place attachments and uplifting my mood. Mostly, I've been fortunate because I've been able to expose myself in a timely way to the elements of place that appeal to me. Sometimes this means that I invest my time, labor, and money into making places personally more enticing. Regrettably, many people are far less fortunate, having limited resources and sway to affect how a place looks or feels to them.

This book accentuates the idea that issues related to personal empowerment, civic engagement, and social and environmental justice implicate how we relate to places and each other. Such relations are affected by our relative position in the privileged hierarchies of social class, race and ethnicity, gender, sexual identity, physical and mental (dis)ability, and age that alter the odds that we will encounter certain life opportunities or constraints.

Writing this book has afforded me the occasion to consider how my placed-based memories shape the way I see myself and the world. Moreover, I've been able to reflect on how places have affected my physical, emotional, and psychological well-being. Thus, I augment my narrative with personal anecdotes while also including numerous pop culture references to underscore the dynamic relations between people, places, and our sense of group belonging.

Ironically, I did some of the reading and writing for this book at the main facility of Gainesville Health & Fitness (GHF), a special place in my life for more than thirty-six years. Joe Cirulli, the owner of GHF and a friend, launched this business in 1978 and has made countless architectural design decisions at his three facilities throughout the years that enhance members' physical workouts, quality of life, and social networks. He's incorporated structural design features such as open floor plans, massive exterior windows, indoor and outdoor lounges and patios, a juice bar, an outdoor fitness pavilion, steam and sauna rooms, therapeutic pools, a recovery lounge, and much more. These and other aspects of the built environment improve members' emotional states while in the company of others. Additional programmatic initiatives afford members options to participate in assorted small-group exercise sessions that promote a sense of group belonging. One of the core values guiding Joe's design decisions is his commitment to build an inviting fitness environment where people of all ages, abilities, and backgrounds can gather to focus on their health and fitness. I, like thousands of others, have benefited greatly because Joe's mission is to not only address members' physical needs but the desires of many to find peace of mind in a welcoming "third place" away from home and work. Writing this book has deepened my appreciation for just how vital this place has been in providing me and others with valuable opportunities to meet and spend quality, productive time with like-minded friends and family.

In addition to my personal and pop culture examples, I selectively refer to a wide range of scholarly sources to reinforce my main ideas. However, my intention is not to develop an elaborate theory about the concept of place. Instead, my primary purpose is to weave themes from various disciplines into a coherent, accessible message that encourages the public to think more clearly and passionately about place and opportunity. In the process, it is crucial to reflect on the interconnections among the places we frequent, our significant relationships with others, and our capacity to improve the places that shape our lives. Although I trust that the well-versed place studies professional will find something of value in the way I've framed my narrative, my principal commitment is to the "street reader" – the person who has limited or no experience wading through the interdisciplinary literature related to place.

That said, I'm indebted to several anonymous expert reviewers who urged me to expand my frame to say more about such topics as collective memory, architecture, community development, mental mapping, ethics, and more – which I did. Responding to their feedback was a stimulating challenge in writing an interdisciplinary book for a broad audience. Prior to launching this project, I had only a passing familiarity with topics associated with place studies. Most notably, I had considered place issues when studying aspects of fathering and men's youth work in communities. During the current project, I likened my exhilaration from exploring and integrating new substantive fields (for me) to the endorphin rush I get when playing Word Fresh, a Peak brain training phone app. A user has ninety seconds to form as many words as possible from a 5 x 6 box of thirty letters. A successful finger swipe over a string of chosen letters identifies a usable word while replacing them with new letters and repositioning other affected letters into a reconfigured slate. This transitional moment triggers a pleasing sensation, providing the user a fresh opportunity to create additional words. Similarly, as I encountered diverse perspectives and concepts while working on this book, I was able to see new opportunities and sharpen my conceptual framing of people's relationships to places.

Over the past few years, I have also immensely enjoyed working closely with twenty inspirational University of Florida undergraduate students throughout this project's evolution. They have each in their own way helped me mold a fragmented set of ideas into a published book with a focused message advocating a deeper *place consciousness* and ethical, constructive *placemaking*. Although I expand on these terms in the text, suffice it to say here that I want to convey the value of being acutely aware of how places affect us and of being thoughtful and engaged in how we try to cultivate places that promote more positive outcomes for ourselves and others. I emphasize how our heightened place consciousness includes being cognizant of how our identities and social status influence our experiences with places. While many of my students were pursuing a degree in sociology, others were involved in environmental studies, history, political science, psychology, urban planning, women and gender studies, and other fields. This eclectic cadre of assistants amplified my interdisciplinary writing mission and inspired me to think more deeply about how people with varied identities and backgrounds navigate places. In practical terms, they served as perceptive arbiters of my ideas, vignettes, photos, personal and cultural examples, conceptual framing, and storytelling while providing excellent assistance with substantive research, editing, proofing, and brainstorming. Some even worked with me on developing a new course, People, Places, and Belonging, that I taught for the first time in Fall 2023. The prepping and teaching of that course refined my thinking and revealed students' stories about how an assortment of places mattered to them and how they've tried to change them. I express my profound gratitude to the following student assistants who played a pivotal role in making this project intellectually challenging, personal, and fun: Mariana Alemany, Mailys Angibaud, Emmaleigh Annas, Skylar Bailey, Jay Blaske, Kiara Cazares, Nicole Cecil, Mary DiFresco, Sydney Engstrom, Emma Heidelberg, Lauren Manso, Megan Meehan, Zachary Pipping, Gloria Ponce, Camille Rendon, Dahlia Salman, Sami Sumer, Ian Tajalli, Brittany Teeples, and Garrison Wells. Thank you!

I'm especially appreciative that Jodi Lewchuk, my acquisitions editor, has been a literary coach in my corner for more than four years. She enthusiastically embraced my earlier book *Chasing We-ness: Cultivating Empathy and Leadership in a Polarized World* and then immediately understood how my *People, Places, and Belonging* project had the potential to be a natural sequel that expanded my ideas about group belonging as well as empowerment, civic engagement, and social and environmental justice. Her championing both projects reinforced my conviction that promoting healthy we-ness and constructive placemaking are worthwhile personal and collective endeavors. As usual, Jodi was instrumental in helping me streamline my message about the overarching place-based themes organizing the current book – cultivating deeper place awareness and mobilizing informed, ethical action to enrich places. Finally, I also requested and was fortunate to secure the same incredible copy editor, Dr. Emily Reiner, who assisted me on my previous book. I highly value her keen eye for nuance in tone and substance; she's gifted in gently prodding me to improve my thinking and narrative. She is the most meticulous copy editor one could imagine. Ultimately, I claim responsibility for the wording of my message, but I owe much to Dr. Reiner for her conscientious and friendly support throughout the editing process.

Introduction

Photo 2: George Floyd Memorial, East 38th Street and Chicago Avenue, Minneapolis, Minnesota. A sea of flowers and tributes next to the convenience store Cup Foods. (Andrew Morse for Alamy Stock Photos)

"I can't breathe!" These were the words that George Floyd, a Black man, repeatedly uttered in distress as he was slowly murdered by a white police officer in front of pedestrians in Minneapolis, Minnesota on May 25, 2020. Over the next year, millions of people watched the graphic videos showing Floyd lying on his chest with his neck being crushed into the street by officer Derek Chauvin's knee. Chauvin sustained this position for nine minutes and twenty-nine seconds while two other officers helped restrain Floyd.

In the immediate aftermath and for months thereafter, thousands flocked to the site of the gruesome tragedy. It included the Cup Foods and Pawn Shop, adjacent shops and buildings, and the streets near the intersection of East 38th Street and Chicago Avenue. The area, which was later named "George Floyd Square," quickly became a high-profile *place* steeped in symbolism. It was flooded with protesters, murals, flowers, statues, placards, photographs, and other material displays of support and outrage. The area organically transformed into a social venue for public grieving and a base for political activism. This place honored the man who was brutally killed by the police while reminding the global community that America, despite some ignorant assertions to the contrary, is still haunted by systemic racism.

Throughout the 2020–1 period leading up to and after Chauvin's murder trial, various stakeholders, including local business owners, the mayor and city commissioners, the police, residents, and Black Lives Matter (BLM) activists debated how the murder site and the adjacent public space should be used. The stakeholders were busy doing what social scientists call "place-work" or "placemaking" as they struggled to reconcile the competing definitions of this place.[1] Numerous instances of vandalism by those who disapproved of the memorial also occurred, yet most who were involved in the placemaking saw this place in a fresh light. The previously banal street corner now holds importance for people near and far in a visceral, profoundly different way. In symbolic and practical terms, George Floyd Square morphed into a dynamic piece of city landscape that broadcasts a collective voice for racial justice and police reform. Whether that voice will continue to be expressed and heard, only time will tell.

Events like these remind us too that, like fish in water, we are immersed in a place every moment of our lives. But unlike fish, we consciously sense our surroundings, realize when we feel "at home" or "out of place," and respond accordingly. The small collection of onlookers who took video that fateful night and pleaded unsuccessfully with the police to stop using excessive force will forever see this place with tainted, sad eyes. The onlookers initially entered the commercial and residential intersection in hopes of fulfilling everyday pursuits, unaware that their definition of this place would rapidly shift into a crime scene and memorial site where they reluctantly "chose" to bear witness to a travesty. Presumably, testifying in the spring of 2021 in the widely watched Chauvin murder trial solidified the witnesses' shared experience of observing police brutality and murder firsthand. Now, they share an unwanted identity as emotionally distraught witnesses swept up by the long, turbulent history of American racism.

Defining Place

The term "place" is one of those common yet abstract words that people use loosely. Over the years, scores of philosophers, social theorists, and other thinkers from diverse disciplines have offered alternative, often elaborate, ways to think about place. I selectively explore some of that thinking in Chapter 1. For now, let's establish a basic understanding of how I use the term in this book.

A place can generally be thought of as part of a bounded physical entity, but it is far more than just a geometric configuration. It is not simply another name for space. Places include social and symbolic elements, and they vary widely in form, scope, impact, and susceptibility to change. We are surrounded by and immersed in places. When we look at things in a specific way by focusing on and comparing the different layers of a place, we'll see that some places are nested inside others.

None of us live our lives in a vacuum, and even if we did, we might be tempted to classify that vacuum as a special type of place. We learn to differentiate places by interpreting how they fit into the social terrain and facilitate social life. Although some theorists perceive places as fluid processes,[2] the everyday person typically imagines borders that demarcate one place from another. In addition, Yi Fu Tuan, the renowned geographer who wrote one of the seminal books on place in 1977, *Space and Place: The Perspective of Experience*, viewed place as "essentially a static concept."[3] He believed that "if we think of space as that which allows movement, then place is pause; each pause in movement makes it possible for location to be transformed into place."[4]

Although Tuan's framing makes sense intuitively, we can qualify it a bit by acknowledging that place represents pauses that we can discern and, in effect, choose to distinguish. Technically, at the subatomic level, all matter is in motion or transition, so space itself is continually moving and it affords opportunities for objects to move within its borders as well. Thus, all places are in motion, but we do not in a practical sense observe that motion. Ultimately, whatever borders we perceive are permeable and subject to change. At various moments, we attend to places, "seeing" them as real and assigning meaning to them. On some level, we recognize that places affect us as well as others.

When we consciously compare different types of places, we enhance our ability to discern any specific place and to assess how we value it. Usually tagged with a name (home, church, park, courthouse, factory, farm, the border, neighborhood, nation), a place fosters an opportunity for personal and social expression. Some labels are broad descriptors (urban area, blue-collar factory, the South). Other labels are more specific (New York City, Ford Motor Company plant, Louisiana).

A place is where social life happens. We express and contest our identities in place. We live our emotional highs and lows in places that matter to us. We make personal and political choices about the places we choose to frequent and control. And we design places to reflect our values and interests. In sum, our embodied experiences occur in diverse places that shape how we see and express ourselves, forge a sense of group belonging, interact with our communities, and assert our claims over places meaningful to us. This eclectic understanding of place is extended too when we consider the views of Edward Relph, another of the early geographers to write about place: "Place, both as a concept and as phenomenon of experience, therefore has a remarkable capacity to make connections between self, community, and earth, between what is local and particular and what is regional and worldwide."[5]

The characteristics of a place, and how we interpret them, can affect us in myriad ways, sometimes unwittingly. Aspects of a place can alter our sense of safety, privacy, independence, relevance, curiosity, and authenticity. More broadly, they affect our well-being and the health of the groups to which we belong; they are intimately linked to the activities that occur in place.

Place is closely connected to the physicality of space which includes the geometry of an area where natural and manufactured objects reside. It is in place that objective realities (the sights, smells, sounds, tastes, and tactile sensations of a place) converge with narrative fictions (the symbol-rich stories we tell and listen to about a place). This coming together of objective and subjective realities fosters an ambience that permeates individuals' perceptions of a place and the social life that emerges from it. We experience that sensation in our mind, body, heart, and soul. Place contributes to who we become socially by helping us form memories, and with our consequential mix of social characteristics and memories, we also construct place.

In grand terms, then, a place has personal significance because we assign meanings to it that are shaped by historical, cultural, and social forces that transcend the moment and circumstances. For example, today when people of Jewish descent visit Auschwitz, the Nazi concentration camp, their shared sense of a cultural, ethnic, and religious we-ness or group belonging with other Jewish people, dead and alive, is usually intensified. Even though most current visitors were not present for the atrocities Auschwitz prisoners endured, the memorial's physical remnants that define this place and time, as well as the stories that bring to life the tragedies of the Holocaust, are powerful triggers for visitors to embrace their Jewish heritage. Even those without Jewish heritage may find themselves appreciating the depths of their common humanity once they set foot in the camp.

The types of places we encounter are molded by the institutions, norms, and customs of the local, national, and global landscapes we navigate. One historian, Wilfred McClay, laments how aspects of globalization and modern telecommunications have profoundly distorted our sense of place:

> Our actual and tangible places seem less and less important to us, more and more transient or provisional or interchangeable or even disposable. The pain of parting becomes less, precisely because there is so little reason to invest oneself in "place" to begin with. Sometimes it almost seems as if we are living like plants without roots, drawing our sustenance not from the earth beneath our feet but from the satellites that encircle us and the computer clouds that feed and absorb our energies.[6]

Irrespective of how we perceive and feel about the consequences of our fast-paced, high-tech world, or if we even recognize these processes, the historical landscape that enables and constrains how we see ourselves and act in various places is woven into our experiences. Our self-perceptions and experiences are shaped, in part, by the organization of residential communities; our exposure to the latest developments in AI, pharmacology, and cosmetic surgery; our use of social media; and the political forces that shape public discourse.

With the passage of time, we continually build, sustain, redefine, and sometimes destroy or walk away from places, both literally and metaphorically. Initiatives to change aspects of place, both formal and informal, stem from personal, grassroots, and professional human activity. On the personal front, we can expand the meaning of our home, especially as adults. We might, for example, alter our residential property in practical ways by childproofing rooms to make them safer for our new toddler or we can make other adjustments to accommodate our elderly parents whom we've invited to live with us because of their failing health. In the latter scenario, the meaning of the place we call home changes for both us and our parents. The extended family setting now resembles a caregiving site with new rights and obligations.

At the grassroots level, we can join forces with our neighbors to start a neighborhood watch program. In addition to organizing a protocol for how neighbors should monitor the area, we might persuade officials to tear down a crack house or an abandoned building, organize more frequent police patrols, strategically mount "neighborhood watch" signs, and put in additional street lighting. Part of our plan might also include efforts to initiate an outdoor neighborhood block party to improve our sense of community and communication networks.

Meanwhile, some of us in our professional lives work in architecture, landscape architecture, interior design, urban design, community development, environmental advocacy, or in a related field that enables us to fashion diverse types of public places into "quality places." Mark Wyckoff, an expert on planning, design, and construction, describes a quality place as one in which "people want to live, work, play and learn."[7] Such a place will attract people who express having a "strong sense of place" toward it. In other words, one goal of placemaking from a community development perspective is to create a place that people perceive as desirable.

But the process of creating a desirable place – the ideal expression of thoughtful placemaking – is a messy process, especially when viewed from a community or global perspective. It involves a host of actors, often with competing special interests, whose contributions align them with governments, businesses, activist groups, and building professions, as well as others.[8] Unfortunately, high quality, inclusive placemaking is a complex process that is too often neglected. Sarah Williams Goldhagen, a renowned critic of architecture and design and author of the provocative book *Welcome to Your World: How the Built Environment Shapes Our Lives*, sounds the alarm about the need for more thoughtful, professional placemaking by those who produce our built environment: "Wherever we look – at infrastructure or urban areas or suburban settlements; at landscapes or cityscapes or individual buildings, the bottom line is boring buildings, banal places, and hoary landscapes."[9] Goldhagen disabuses us of the notion that thoughtful design is a "discretionary luxury." As she convincingly argues, design matters, because

> every day, children around the world, especially underprivileged ones, are robbed of opportunities for social advancement and

self-actualization. One large part of the reason why is that they live in unhealthy or cognitively dulling habitats and attend school in buildings that put a drag on or literally undermine attention, motivation, and effective learning. Every day, millions of people fail to find comfortable, inviting, well-designed streetscapes, buildings, parks, and plazas where they can simply escape the stresses of daily life or share the easy company of others. Every day, the least privileged members of our society return to inhospitable, decrepit, soul-deadening homes ... The world is literally littered with places that were built on the cheap and violate practically everything we now know about what makes for salutary, enriching environments.[10]

Although everyday people, and even building professionals, are often oblivious to the unconscious ways the built environment affects our moods and behavior, the evidence is mounting that the built environment affects our health, cognitive abilities, and our efforts to establish and cultivate communities.

Just as we recognize that generic places like prisons, sports stadiums, doctors' offices, and playgrounds are linked to broad understandings of what happens in a designated type of space, some places promote a more distinct meaning for those who encounter them. George Floyd Square, for example, is viewed by many as a "truth spot" for those concerned about racial justice. This spot, and the activist energies that emerged from it, highlights demands for policing reform.

A truth spot, according to sociologist Thomas Gieryn, is a place that facilitates an account or claim of truth that is "discovered or manufactured, where it is displayed and celebrated, where it gets enacted and reproduced, where it is contested or obscured."[11] In *Truth Spots: How Places Make People Believe*, Gieryn unpacks how aspects of place contribute to our willingness to embrace a specific claim about reality. As he notes, "Places are not idle backdrops – they have agency and exert a force of their own on the direction and pace of knowledge and belief, on what becomes true."[12]

Yet, when treated as social constructs, places do not exist outside of human thought and activity. In some respects, we seem to inject places with agency by assigning meaning to them. We allow ourselves to be shaped by the forces that operate within the physical confines of a place. As conscious beings, we can reflect on aspects of a place to make sense of our socially constructed world. We do so while processing the countless messages about place that define our everyday reality. Just as humans are hardwired to seek attachment, our physical attributes compel us to create and navigate place. Ultimately, how we interpret and react to a place is shaped by our social experiences before and during our social encounters in that place. Thus, place and social life are a part of a dynamic feedback loop. Our personal and social realities are affected by the very places that we collectively help to fashion.

We have much to gain by examining how aspects of place are intimately tied to how we experience a sense of group belonging. In an earlier book, *Chasing We-ness*, I focused on how our desire to experience a sense of group belonging or "we-ness" affects our lives. I outlined three expressions of we-ness or group belonging that can inform our understanding of place: deep dyadic, ideational, and spontaneous. I also proposed opportunities to develop a series of what I labeled *MEAL* life skills (Mindfulness, Empathy, Altruism, and Leadership) that can help us cultivate healthy forms of we-ness.

Each expression of we-ness enables us to feel connected to something larger than ourselves. Deep dyadic we-ness occurs when we develop an interpersonal bond and mutual awareness of our affinity with someone such as a family member, friend, or coworker. Our sense of we-ness in this case influences our perceptions about our rights and obligations in the relationship. When we experience ideational we-ness, we embrace ideas and beliefs that define a broader thought community. These perceptions often symbolize a type of collective consciousness or identity (feminism, veganism, LGBTQ+, Trumpism, white nationalism, etc.) that we share with others, many of whom we do not know. We may sometimes also experience a type of intergenerational bond that cements our sense of group belonging and humanity as well as our commitment to those from different generations. Spontaneous we-ness is the most fleeting and least consequential form of we-ness. It represents our momentary awareness that we share something of symbolic value with someone else (cultural heritage, alumni status, sports team fandom, common personal trait, or zodiac sign). Although the least significant, our spontaneous expressions of we-ness can trigger more consequential forms of we-ness.

We usually realize these forms of we-ness as we go about our daily lives in one or more of the following social domains: primary groups, community and civic groups, thought communities, leisure/sports, and work. The activities in these domains generally unfold in some sort of place. Often, the way we express each form of we-ness is affected by how we interpret and encounter the diverse properties that distinguish a place and give it meaning for us.

Our Roadmap to a Better Place

Now that you have a basic understanding of how I'm thinking about place and we-ness, let me clarify my intentions for this multilayered, interdisciplinary book that builds on the powerful and pervasive process of we-ness. I initially sketch a socially informed roadmap to deepen our appreciation for dynamic and complex settings and the ways place matters in our personal and public lives. Guided by this roadmap, I then demonstrate how we can leverage a heightened place consciousness to both individually and collectively engage in more ethical and constructive placemaking in diverse settings.

I show how applying *MEAL* life skills and our understanding of four key place processes involving Claims, Attachments, Rituals, and Transitions (*CART*) can help us promote personal empowerment, civic engagement, and social and environmental justice. To achieve these objectives in ways that advance the greater good, we must base our initiatives on sound ethical principles. Thus, I highlight the five principles of Beneficence, Autonomy, Social and environmental justice, Inclusive collaboration, and Nonmaleficence (*BASIN*) to guide our placemaking. Consistent with the geographical image of a basin as an area of land where flowing surface water converges into a single spot, we can think of these ethical principles as merging into a consistent philosophy that respects and enhances our varied relationships to place. I chose these guideposts by integrating widely accepted ethical principles and methods of moral decision-making commonly associated with the fields of health care and community development.[13]

By honing our awareness of what place is and how it matters in its many forms, we can more readily identify thoughtful placemaking strategies to cultivate a healthy placed-based social landscape, one that encompasses our natural and built environments. Moreover, by improving our personal place consciousness, we will be better positioned to work collaboratively with others on placemaking initiatives that vary in type and scale.

While I switch the order slightly relative to how I address them in the text, I use the acronym *CART* to refer to these four place processes. I demonstrate how the *MEAL* life skills can be used to enhance our Attachments, encourage supportive Rituals, smooth out Transitions, and allow us to manage with less conflict and more social justice the Claims we and others make concerning places. Thus, the *CART* processes structure the places where people demonstrate their *MEAL* life skills. Simply put, we express mindfulness somewhere, we show empathy to others in various settings, we are altruistic to others who are situated in a place, and we demonstrate leadership in a place-based context. The *CART* processes shape the social ecology for developing *MEAL* life skills and these skills, in turn, provide us with human, social, and cultural capital that enables us to enhance our place consciousness and placemaking abilities.

This approach is premised on the notion that our embodied minds and activities are situated in socially constructed places that also have diverse properties that influence our thoughts, feelings, and actions, sometimes unconsciously. Furthermore, we can more fruitfully promote personal well-being and the common good when we appreciate how our relationship to place is intertwined with our need for group belonging and a sense of we-ness. Thus, I illustrate the varied ways our experiences with place are tied to the three expressions of we-ness. In a related manner I demonstrate the value of applying the *MEAL* life skills to navigating place issues. I root my examples in the five social domains noted above and in the various types of public and private places I delineate that often facilitate expressions of we-ness.

In some respects, my use of the phrase "place consciousness" extends Relph's classic description of "sense of place." For Relph, a sense of place is the "ability to grasp and appreciate the distinctive qualities of places."[14] I, too, see those qualities as essential to our ability to express place consciousness. However, I emphasize not just our *capacity* to think and feel these things about place, but our *predisposition* or tendency to accentuate place qualities as part of our everyday life experience and wide-awake consciousness. In other words, when we refine and deepen our place consciousness it becomes a more integral part of who we are as a person. We engage more fully with and filter our understanding of our surroundings by being aware of how this place or that place affects us in the moment and beyond. That awareness reflects our attentiveness to both the properties of a place and the social dynamics that give that place meaning for us and others. The stronger our place consciousness, the more we come to understand our embodied life experience through a place-based lens that transcends any particular place. Writing this book has heightened my own place consciousness in every social domain of my life; I trust that reading it will do the same for you.

Understanding and enhancing the connections between we-ness and place is consistent with Jenny Odell's thinking in *How to Do Nothing: Resisting the Attention Economy*. Odell, an artist and writer, is worried about how our growing receptivity to social media and other distractions minimizes our face-to-face encounters in real time. This drift in our awareness habits, as well as how we prioritize and manage aspects of our lives, tends to isolate us. It also increasingly dilutes our attention from the things that should matter to us. Drawing on her own experiences as a longtime resident of Oakland, California, as an artist, and as a bird lover, Odell challenges people to adopt a more ecological perspective to their surroundings. Like me, she asks that people pay closer attention to how context matters for them and others in various ways. She stresses that "if we want to relearn how to care about each other, we will also have to relearn how to care about place."[15] She also hints at the intersection of we-ness and place when commenting on creating an ideal social network that would move us beyond the attention economy:

"This social network would rehabilitate the role of time and location in our everyday consciousness. It would offer the places where we are right now as the incubation spaces for the empathy, responsibility, and political innovation that can be useful not just here, but everywhere."[16]

Place Matters

Place matters – for better or worse. Our relationship to our physical surroundings informs our embodied, lived experiences. Characteristics of a place, often paired with social conditions and personal attributes, can activate our self-awareness, motivating us to react to life circumstances in our own individual ways. Our place-based experiences can shape our identities and how we relate to others.

Goldhagen, coming from a design perspective, animates our vision of place as consequential by referring to places as "action settings." She reminds us that "buildings and interiors and streetscapes and landscapes are all *action settings*, places shaping what people do and think and how they engage with one another. Every action setting is composed of what we have been calling affordances, meaning spaces and objects that afford certain actions."[17] The affordances endemic to a place generate socially meaningful informational cues about what we might or should do in an action setting. They also foster practical opportunities for us to act according to social expectations. For example, a worksite that supports a high quality, onsite fitness facility provides employees with potentially appealing options. Employees might establish a mutually rewarding sense of we-ness by becoming workout buddies who commit to an early morning, lunchtime, or after-work fitness ritual. Throughout the book I retain Goldhagen's term, action setting, but my approach to place accentuates how it often serves as an environment for *inter*action.

The symbolic meanings we associate with a place or action setting personally affect us. They can, and often do, influence our ability to feel a sense of group belonging and comfort from our relationships. Our natural urge to feel a part of something bigger than ourselves can be cultivated when our social life unfolds in places that enable us to feel connected to others and at peace with ourselves. On a personal level, when we feel at home in a physical setting, whether it be the woods, a playground, a city or neighborhood block, a house of worship, a sports stadium, or somewhere else, we're more likely to feel authentic. When this occurs, we often feel empowered. We assert ourselves, acknowledge our vulnerabilities, take calculated risks, and are more receptive to bonding with others. Thus, our positive orientation to a place lays the foundation for our personal development. It helps us pursue options that enable us to realize healthy social relations and productive forms of we-ness.

The cultural critic and feminist, bell hooks, vividly captures this sentiment in *Belonging: A Culture of Place*.[18] In this series of essays, she intimately reflects on her experience growing up as a Black girl in the hills of Kentucky, leaving as a young woman, and then returning to the region to live as a middle-aged adult. Her life's journey inspired her to appreciate how her personal development as a Black woman in America was grounded in her relationship to nature, the Appalachian life, farming, and the politics of place. As she developed a deeper appreciation of her connection to the land, bell hooks embraced finding a way to establish a sense of belonging while coping with how the politics of race and class intersect with place. She ultimately rediscovered the rural homeplace that had provided the lasting foundation to her life's perspective. Her relations with family and friends from the area deepened her sentiments for the places that mattered to her.

Environmental psychologists have devoted much time and energy to exploring versions of the sort of connection bell hooks writes about. They call the experience "place attachment." While commentators differ a bit on how they interpret it, one working definition is that "place attachment and meaning are the person-to-place bonds that evolve through emotional connection, meaning, and understandings of a specific place and/or features of a place."[19] We can be attached to all sorts of places ranging from homes, downtown urban venues, landscapes, a country, and more.

Unfortunately, we may also sometimes feel at home with a place that eventually leads us down a self-destructive, unethical path.

Some places, then, bring out the worst in us. When a gang member is hanging out in a pool hall or an abandoned house that they view as their homeplace, it may provide them a sense of community, but it will also encourage them to make lifestyle decisions that will increase their chances of dropping out of school, doing jail time, getting hurt, hurting others, and dying prematurely.

Our negative response to features of a place can contribute to us feeling detached from other people. In other words, aspects of a place, separate from or in combination with the unique attributes of the other people present, can sometimes disrupt our peace of mind and sense of belonging. As a result, we can feel outside our comfort zone, alienated, or threatened. When we discover ourselves in such a place, we typically struggle to be ourselves and to build meaningful relationships with others. We feel emotionally inhibited, unable or unwilling to let our guard down or display empathy.

The complex and potentially adverse implications of how a place and place attachment can affect us are poignantly captured by Tara Westover in her acclaimed memoir, *Educated*. Living a reclusive life at the foot of Buck's Peak in rural Idaho, Westover was raised and casually homeschooled by ultraconservative, Mormon, survivalist parents. She describes how she was forced to spend much of her childhood doing risky manual labor alongside her father and brothers in a junkyard family business while also being subjected to domestic abuse. Her memoir vividly recounts how she forged a sense of dyadic we-ness with family members and a form of ideational we-ness steeped in Mormon teachings. The land and her father's massive junkyard served as distinct places where both forms of we-ness and their related rituals materialized. Ultimately, she acted on her youthful yearnings to experience life beyond the mountain by enrolling in and graduating from Brigham Young University and earning a PhD from Cambridge. She achieved all of this without ever earning a high school diploma! Yet, despite these improbable accomplishments, she continued to mull over the origins and meaning of her childhood self and family circumstances: "That person, or that likeness of one, had belonged. I was *of* that mountain, the mountain that had made me. It was only as I grew older that I wondered if how I had started is how I would end."[20]

Westover's memoir illustrates how aspects of a place can feed our frustration, discomfort, and anger while forging our innermost core. These aspects can sometimes even agitate us enough to forge bonds with other like-minded people in the setting. Think of how natural disasters often elicit heroic and cooperative behaviors, even from complete strangers. Or imagine the countless sites where people mobilize to challenge injustices while struggling to deal with the dire circumstances of their physical and social settings. Evidence that place matters is revealed by our propensity to create historic landmarks out of places that mark social protest. For example, the Edmund Pettus Bridge (which, facing strong opposition, activists have tried to rename the John Lewis Bridge) in Selma, Alabama, is a vivid place-based reminder of the infamous "Bloody Sunday" confrontation between civil rights demonstrators and the police on March 7, 1965.[21] More than half a century later, activists still gather there to solidify their commitment to achieving racial justice.

The fight to rename this bridge illustrates that throughout history and around the world politicized conflicts have erupted over the meaning of a place and the activities that have transpired therein. For instance, the Middle East region is home to such long-standing, well-publicized controversies about holy sites and politicized ethnic lands. Most notably, the Israelis and Palestinians are wedded to their competing place-based visions that generate distrust and violence. The Israel-Hamas war, triggered by Hamas's vicious surprise attack on Israel on October 7, 2023, which then led to Israel's relentless bombing of Gaza, is the latest manifestation of this long-standing deadly feud over the respective meanings of Israel and Palestine.[22] Unfortunately, thousands have died in this and other regions of the world because ethnic groups' religious ideologies are fundamentally anchored to rigid, politicized beliefs about specific places.

Today in the United States, we have plenty of our own controversies about places that are tied to our troubling legacy of genocide, slavery, and environmental recklessness. Indigenous reservations, Southern plantations, the US–Mexico border, LGBTQ+ bars, and the "cancer alley" in Louisiana are merely a handful of the countless places central to our heated debates about social and environmental justice issues. The way we frame debates about places like these highlights how we think about our identities and preferred groups. How inclusively do we define the groups to which we belong? How and to what extent does our concern about place influence our life choices? What rights do we wish to extend to those we either want to include or exclude from our group? As our society becomes increasingly diverse and wrestles with competing perspectives on equality and equity, these sorts of questions about place become more critical to us on a personal and public level.

Some of the meanings we collectively assign to places are transformative because their ramifications extend beyond our individual orbits. They generate public discourse, shape our social worlds, and even alter the cultural landscape at times. In both mundane and profound ways our everyday life experiences with these meanings are intertwined with the ongoing project of memory construction. As philosopher Janet Donohoe describes in *Remembering Places: A Phenomenological Study of the Relationship between Memory and Place*, our encounters with place often contribute to place-based collective memories shared by a group.[23] That pool of memories reinforces the collective identities we use to define our sense of self. Such memories also remind us that they are interwoven with our experience of place, which "is always intersubjective. Place is part of the structure of intersubjectivity," our mental ability to communicate by sharing symbolic meanings with each other.[24] Granted, the term "collective memory" has its shortcomings because it is often portrayed as having "capacities that are in fact actualized only on an individual level" – by individuals.[25] In other words, we do not literally share ideas as computers share CPU; our minds are not physically linked – at least not yet in 2024. Memory is ultimately generated by separate individuals. Yet, the abstract phrase "collective memory" compels us to take stock of how our unique experiences are also representative of our shared encounters with and reflections on place.

Remembering the past, which is inextricably connected to place, is a critical part of our humanity as social beings. Thus, our experiences with place are filtered by a structured social process and storytelling norms that shape our memories and representations of place as well as our identities.[26] Sociologist Eviatar Zerubavel, well known for his writings on the sociology of time, extends this thinking by explaining how we are embedded in "mnemonic communities," groups that influence our memories by shaping our habits of mind and how we come to value certain things like family, education, self-reliance, community service, and more. In these communities we are exposed to "mnemonic traditions" and "mnemonic socialization" that guide our experience with remembering and forming collective memories.[27] Although matters of place are not explicitly central to his sociocultural framework of time, Zerubavel notes that the "constancy of place" in the form of our physical surroundings helps us to stabilize our memories.

Collective memories and identities often motivate us to value places from the past, present, or the projected future and engage in placemaking activities. Thus, individually and as group members, we write history when we construct, reinforce, or challenge the prevailing meanings and purposes that define a place. How we relate to a place that means something to us often affects our self-image. Sometimes our place-based identities are connected to the we-ness we forge with others directly and intimately. Other times we are part of a broader, more diffuse group while we are anchored to a place.

An intriguing connection between place and person is depicted in the many stories bell hooks shares about her relationship with rural life and her "backwoods kin." In one story, she describes her disappointment about her family's move when she was a young girl from their home in the Kentucky hills to a neighborhood in town:

> In my child's mind rural life was synonymous with belonging in nature, freedom, adventure, safety; city life was about containment, restricted movement, and overdeveloped dangerous landscape. The fearlessness and awe I experienced as a child belonging in nature imbued me with a power and confidence I soon lost in the city where I felt invisible, powerless, and lost. In the isolated, underpopulated, rural environment of the Kentucky hills, there had been no persistent sense of threat or danger – no need for a child to be endlessly told to be careful, to always be on guard. In the world of the city danger was everywhere.[28]

While the types of activities bell hooks pursued individually and with her family in a Southern, rural setting gave her unique opportunities to develop her personality and life skills, living in a segregated neighborhood in town gave her others. Visiting her grandmother who lived in a white neighborhood, for instance, forced her to endure "racist white folks who taunted and jeered at us," which led to her "post-traumatic growth."[29]

The experiences that environments provide to people can be difficult to change. Revamping the spirit and public perception of a neighborhood, town, or city often depends on leaders stepping forward to propose and implement significant social change. A leader's new vision of a place requires residents to accept the prospect that change is needed in how they perceive and participate in their community.

In the short and long term, our individual and shared attachments can produce varied outcomes. To borrow *Star Wars'* message about "The Force," the energies that give meaning to places can do so in ways good and bad. Just as the Jedis' approach to the Force was to cultivate the "light" energy for places, those who allied with the Empire were compelled to promote the dark side. Ultimately, we must find ways to encourage people to develop, individually and collectively, a consciousness about place that generates outcomes consistent with social and environmental justice as well as individual well-being.

Exploring Place

This book, following Gieryn's lead, pivots on the assumption that place matters. It makes a difference in how we see ourselves, live our lives, and interact with our communities. Our physically embodied experiences with place help shape who we are and who we want to be. Our embodied sense of self can influence the extent to which we interpret places as ones where we feel at home or not at home. In addition, our embodied sense of self often affects the choices we make about the places we choose to frequent, and how we want to design certain places to reflect our values and interests.

The gravity of these claims underscores the significance of paying attention to place. They also align with those of Jeff Malpas, a philosopher and author of *Place and Experience: A Philosophical Topography*. Malpas asserts that there is "no possibility of understanding human existence – and especially human thought and experience – other than through an understanding of place."[30] In addition, my advocacy for ethical placemaking is grounded in the reality described by David Seamon in his elaborate theoretical work, *Life Takes Place: Phenomenology, Lifeworlds, and Place Making*. A professor of architecture, Seamon reminds us that, "For good or bad, whether we realize it or not, we are all always emplaced, and some emplacements facilitate wellbeing while others fester unkindness, distress, or outright despair. Who we are contributes hugely to what we become, but how we are emplaced also matters."[31] Thus, identifying how place-based forces affect our wellbeing can improve our encounters with place, and in the process, our relations with each other and ourselves.

My approach deepens our understanding of place by emphasizing how our search for we-ness and meaning is intimately tied to how we navigate the places of consequence to us. Developing insights about how dimensions of place influence our efforts to belong can enrich our well-being and expand our options to feel connected to others. Elsewhere, I've written about how the competing life philosophies of libertarianism and communitarianism shape our approach to we-ness and social life more generally.[32] Here, I extend those ideas to consider how our individual and collective decisions about embracing and navigating certain types of places are related to how we express a sense of group belonging. Many of the healthy interpersonal bonds that define and empower us are expressed in different types of places.

A Three-Part Book

Our journey begins with Part 1, comprised of Chapters 1 and 2, which builds the foundation of place. Here I clarify my basic thinking about place and how I frame its relationship to our lives and the groups to which we belong. In Chapter 1, I outline the consequential properties of place that affect how we think, feel, and act. I begin by selectively introducing a series of place properties I initially developed with colleagues Kevin Roy and Greer Litton Fox to explain fathers' involvement with their children.[33] I adapt, supplement, and expand some of the properties to sharpen our thinking about how social life, embedded in a place, can either foster or restrict the production of we-ness, and how expressions of we-ness influence the way places are constructed and experienced.

I also highlight how place is embodied. To this end, I accentuate how the physical realities of our corporeal existence make a difference in the way we experience a place and the people associated with it.

A key feature of this discussion is to show how our interactions situated in place incorporate both cooperative and competitive elements. On occasion we work collaboratively with others as we interact with them in a particular place. Some of our exchanges may involve working together with others to alter aspects of a place (workplace, community, school setting) so that it will reflect our shared expectations about what a place should represent. But we also struggle sometimes to convince others to accept our ideas on what the place should be like.

I use Chapter 2 to outline a simple typology of the different types of places that are most significant in our lives and influence our well-being. These are labeled nature, homes/dwellings (broadly defined), communities (including community groups) and beyond, public space, sites that involve the exchange of goods and services, institutions, key landmarks and ceremonial locations, leisure spots, transport vehicles and hubs, and the metaverse (the 3D virtual reality world that goes beyond the mobile internet).[34] This typology highlights the types of places that have implications for our quality of life and civic engagement, as well as social and environmental justice. Moreover, these places are often connected to how we develop and express a sense of group belonging. I specifically consider how the COVID-19 pandemic and our polarized political landscape have influenced our need to feel a sense of belonging and altered the way we navigate certain places.

My analysis is informed by landscape architecture professor Lynne Manzo's work on place. Whether we are keenly aware of it or not, our life unfolds as "experience-in-place." Manzo extrapolates four themes related to experience-in-place from interviews she conducted. These themes are linked to the places participants refer to as significant, and include:

a) instances in which people experience changes to their identity;
b) moments that involve pleasures associated with either privacy, introspection, or reflection;
c) bridges that link the present to the past; and
d) opportunities for people to experience a sense of safety, threat, or belonging.[35]

While Manzo focuses on how these themes are related to individuals' personal experiences, the circumstances she highlights can be expanded to consider their relevance for how people share experiences and manage we-ness. Let's start with the places that foster personal transformations in identity. These places can be group sites where people collaboratively help each other to alter their identities and behavior. This description reminds me of an all-male event held in the Jacksonville Jaguars' football stadium that I attended as a researcher more than twenty years ago. It was sponsored by the Promise Keepers, a male-oriented, Christian-based organization that seeks to inspire participants to be godly men as husbands, fathers, and leaders. Founded in 1990 by a former University of Colorado football coach, Bill McCartney, the social movement has coordinated many revival-type gatherings of men in massive stadiums throughout the country. At the one I attended, I witnessed more than forty thousand men bonding, physically and emotionally, as they celebrated their love for Jesus Christ. One impressive practice called for men to come forward to the stadium floor if they were prepared to embrace a new, or renewed, identity as a follower of Christ. They were afforded the chance to declare their commitment to Christ in this very public setting with other men.

Although football stadiums have logistical advantages in holding such large events, the symbolism of men forging bonds to create a faith-based form of we-ness in these masculine venues is worth thinking about. The men are asked to be vulnerable before God and in the presence of their fellow Promise Keepers. Together they are charged with the responsibility of holding each other accountable to live life with integrity. I witnessed firsthand how these traditionally masculine places motivate men to self-reflect and create both personal and group-based identities as men of faith. Their perceptions of being manly demand that they be accountable to other men. They are expected to express their Christian manhood by forming a masculine type of dyadic we-ness and ideational we-ness as part of a spiritual brotherhood.

Smaller group settings that foster personal reflection and transformation in identity, such as meditation retreats and support groups of all types, can similarly motivate participants to build a spirit of we-ness when they are attached to a consequential place. This type of *esprit de corps* permeated a psychodrama retreat I once attended in the late 1980s in a large, remodeled home in New York State. Psychodrama therapy is action-oriented and encourages participants to role-play events from their past. In my case, strangers quickly became intimate friends over the extended weekend. They shed their self-protective masks to bare their souls during captivating group therapy sessions in a facility designed to host such events. The calming ambience of the place was enhanced by its seclusion on a wooded mountaintop. On this special weekend, eight inches of snow blanketed the trees and retreat center, adding to the tranquil yet invigorating effect. The open layout of the main gathering room, accentuated by an extended bank of large windows, created a sensation that we were part of a blended world of natural and constructed realities. In addition, the food prep and dining areas gave participants ample opportunity to collaborate in the preparation and sharing of meals. The chemistry that I experienced with my fellow participants, and the we-ness I built with the group as a whole, encouraged me, as well as others, to be more introspective and vulnerable. I came to trust many people there more quickly than I had ever done before or since.

Thirty-six years later, I still vividly recall many details about this retreat, including how a rugged, bearded Vietnam vet dramatically disclosed the darkness that had tormented him for more than twenty years. He struggled to cope with his horrific memories of placing body bags on planes. This man's fiancée had persuaded him to come to the retreat; she demanded that he confront his trauma before she would plan a wedding. Prior to the retreat, he had not been able to do this on his own or in her presence. But, guided by a gifted facilitator, and supported by the rest of the group who physically surrounded him in the "circle of trust" during his therapy session, this man embarked on a remarkable transformation. He had arrived at the retreat a rigidly comported, stoic guy. In looks and demeanor he resembled the stereotypical manly man. However, by the final day his identity makeover had produced a much gentler, vulnerable man. He was at ease lying down on pillows as new acquaintances massaged his back and feet with his head cuddled in his partner's lap during other participants' sessions. This man, like the rest of us who attended, became more self-aware and emotionally healthy, in part, because of the mix of characteristics associated with the place and its people.

While a retreat provides a serious, yet relaxed place for individuals like this former soldier to reflect on and deal with psychological anguish, some places create more casual opportunities to help people bridge the divide between the past and present. For example, high school and college reunions staged on campus offer former students a chance to reflect on their younger selves. When former classmates collectively reconstruct memories of their younger selves in a carefree setting, it can help them to resurrect or strengthen the sense of we-ness they forged years ago. School facilities may trigger deep emotions that remind people what their lives were like before they amassed their adult responsibilities. The physical surroundings can reignite the powerful bonds former classmates cherished or sought to establish when they were younger.

Finally, places can prompt us to experience instinctive and powerful feelings. Although Manzo emphasizes threats, safety, and belonging in this regard, I'm most interested in belonging. However, our desires to belong are often intertwined with our desires for safety as well as our fears about suffering. We see this clearly with members of white nationalist groups. People who join these groups, searching for brotherhood, often take this path because they are full of uncertainty and fear.[36] They worry that they, as well as others like them, are losing their grip on the conventional world that has been tailored to serve their best interests. This power, as they see it, is being stolen by persons of color and women. Their loss of power also means that they have less sway in shaping the various everyday places associated with work, school, leisure, neighborhoods, and so forth, where they would like to claim their privileges and express their traditional identities.

Although many places exist without rising to the level of a person believing them to be significant, I'll focus primarily on those places that matter at a given point in time to at least two people. Those individuals who are invested in a place may have complementary or competing views of it. For example, we see the wide range of views among those who are affected by the gentrification of urban landscapes. I highlight how people shape the meaning of a specific place through their encounters and interpretations of it and the people who are associated with it. Our interpretations are often driven by how we compare one place to another. Thus, we can experience life in real time in one place while our perceptions of place and ourselves are being shaped by how we imagine other places. Those alternative places can be similar or quite different.

In Part 2 (Chapters 3–6), I discuss the four interrelated social processes I've labeled *CART* (Claims, Attachments, Rituals, and Transitions) that shape how we engage with places. Becoming aware of how these processes operate is critical to the larger enterprise of promoting ethical, constructive placemaking. I defer my discussion of claiming until the end because it is the most controversial and politically volatile.

I begin by examining the nature of our attachment to places. Numerous scholars have theorized that humans develop attachments to places,[37] and although the definitions vary, they tend to emphasize the "idea of bonding or affective connection."[38] Like our interpersonal ties, our attachments to a place can be both complex and meaningful to us as well as others. Many of our place attachments implicate our real or symbolic relationships with friends, family, neighbors, colleagues, and similarly minded people. Our attachments to places, many of which incorporate our bonds with people, provide us with opportunities to form both individual and collective identities. They also enable us to nurture forms of deep dyadic and ideational we-ness. What types of attachments do we develop to places that are consequential to our memories and sense of group belonging? What are the forces related to group belonging that either promote or discourage our attachments to places and the people associated with them?

Our place attachments are often strengthened by our everyday activities. So, I consider how we perform countless rituals and routines, some mundane, others vital, that link us to distinct types of places. The properties of a place can encourage us to embrace rituals and routines in ways that have special meaning for us: these activities help us appreciate how places enable us to develop our interpersonal bonds and sense of we-ness to others. Historically, social movements and religions have facilitated rituals and routines that shape how we see and react to places. Most recently the BLM, #MeToo, LGBTQ+, Never Again MSD, Occupy Wall Street, and environmental movements have given people powerful opportunities, some place-based, to coalesce around social and environmental justice issues. The symbolic messages that breathe life into social movements and religions often reflect the commitments people express to themselves, to each other, to sacred entities, and toward certain places. We should ask, then: What features of place-based rituals and routines encourage people to assign meaning to a place and strengthen their sense of we-ness? Alternatively, how does enhancing our sense of we-ness promote rituals and routines that alter the meanings we assign to the places of interest to us? Finally, how do rituals enhance our desire and ability to engage in placemaking?

These questions are especially timely owing to the impact of COVID-19 and our increasingly polarized political landscape. This disruptive combo has markedly influenced our cultural norms, social exchanges, and identities. Consequently, I pay close attention to how place-based rituals and routines have been affected by the pandemic and our polarization. We all witnessed a range of disturbing images of angry and emotionally distraught individuals coping poorly in various public settings during the pandemic. The most widely publicized displays have involved medical facilities, schools, retail stores, restaurants, airports and airplanes, political rallies, vote counting sites, and more. The politicized pandemic triggered fundamental changes to how many people think about and act in public places. That transformation is partly grounded in the convictions we have about the groups to which we belong. Thus, we need to ask: To what extent and how do rituals and routines reinforce our sensitivity to specific places that are most directly affected by the pandemic and our tribal politics? How have the pandemic and our politics influenced our need to feel a sense of belonging? Now that we have transitioned beyond the most intense months and years of the pandemic, how have these developments altered the way we navigate certain places? How has our sense of we-ness led us to modify our rituals and routines in these places? How has social media offered us new and more mobile ways to realign ourselves to place and provide us with the means to pursue a sense of we-ness differently? And how does being physically alone intensify our feelings of isolation and alter the way we spend time in private places?

Next, I consider the circumstances, including COVID-19, that lead us to change over time how we see and respond to a place. In addition, I highlight how transitional aspects of a place can have implications for our everyday experiences and significant life course events that affect our quality of life.

A place is defined by a fluid mix of characteristics, including its physical, social, and symbolic dimensions. Given enough time, places typically change. Similarly, our perceptions of a place can change with or without significant changes to a place's physical profile. Sometimes these changes are profound. When a place changes it can provoke us to alter our individual and group identities as well as our way of life. The changes can also result from the way we express our identities. What are the processes, then, that transform a place and alter the way we feel about and react to it? How do those changes affect us personally? Alternatively, how do our actions significantly change the places that matter to us? In both cases, the place-based transformations that alter our actions or are produced by our actions are frequently related to our transitions within and between places. Thus, the elements of time and mobility become key features that link aspects of place with our need for group belonging and we-ness. How do our desires and decisions about moving from one place to another influence our own and others' placemaking? How are the transitional moments we experience in and between places affected by the attributes of a place and our interpretation of them?

Lastly, I attend to how places, and the attachments people have to them, stir social conflicts and people's desires to claim and control their surroundings. Conflicts emerge in places big and small, ranging in scale from family homes to nation-states. While some conflicts are political in nature, many fall outside the scope of politics. Irrespective of the type of place or conflict, motivating people to embrace a shared understanding of a place can be a weighty endeavor. Unfortunately, securing a compromise is increasingly a monumental achievement.

The January 6, 2021, insurrection at the US Capitol underscores this reality on a grand scale. Many see the Capitol as a beacon of democracy that was unjustly attacked by those who disrespected the time-honored ritual of the peaceful transfer of power at this site. The insurrectionists, on the other hand, are convinced that an illegitimate government was being installed against the public's wishes. Thus, they claim that they had a right to take over the Capitol because it is the "people's house." The tribal mentality was on full display during this event and in the subsequent months during the congressional investigation into the circumstances related to the insurrection. Both interpretations of the insurrection signal that we need to consider how our sense of group belonging influences the way we try to challenge or cooperate with others to forge an acceptable image for a place. More generally, how do characteristics of a place affect our willingness to work in concert with or in opposition to others who wish to bring about change or sustain the status quo? On a global scale, similar types of questions emerge about national leaders' responsibilities to negotiate a collective understanding of how best to protect specific places like rainforests, oceans, rivers, as well as the planet more generally.

We end our journey with Part 3 where I highlight placemaking opportunities in the five social domains (primary groups, communities and community groups, thought communities, leisure/sport, and work). We need to develop options that enable us to cultivate a healthier place consciousness and create more appealing places that enrich our lives. We can start by seeing how the *MEAL* life skills are relevant to this mission. Specifically, they are vital for building forms of we-ness that can foster collaborative efforts that lead to desirable outcomes at all levels of the place-based social landscape, from the home to the global stage. When we are inspired by healthy forms of we-ness, and grounded in them, we are likely to make better and more equitable decisions about the places we value.

Identifying creative and ethically sound strategies to promote placemaking is a crucial step in this process. As noted earlier, our placemaking initiatives need to be guided by our understanding of how our placed-based experiences are interwoven with and affected by the *CART* processes associated with claims, attachments, rituals, and transitions. Additionally, we need to apply the *BASIN* ethical principles (beneficence, autonomy, social and environmental justice, inclusive collaboration, and nonmaleficence) to our placemaking. To honor these principles, we must listen to and incorporate the diverse voices of individuals and groups who have a vested interest in a place, including those who are disadvantaged. In addition, I recognize the three principles Goldhagen champions when she challenges us to adopt a more informed approach as we physically build our environments: building efforts should be *designed*; professionally trained designers should be intimately involved in the process; and these professionals should be trained to be *aware of environmental aesthetics* and *experiential design*.[39] Although the main purpose of using these building principles is to help people feel more engaged and comfortable with their environments, the principles can also create affordances that provide people with opportunities to bond with others in healthy ways – which is what I emphasize.

When we consider placemaking options, we must also consider the full range of places and processes that significantly affect our personal well-being and sense of belonging in each of the five social domains I discuss. Ideally, we should resist the temptation to focus only on the most newsworthy and consequential places that involve territorial disputes, public events, residential and commercial districts, or major national landmarks that dominate public and political discourse. No doubt these are vital, but we need to consider places of all sizes and relative importance because the effects that places have on us emerge from a complex web involving our natural, built, and social landscapes. Places outside the public spotlight still contribute to our personal well-being and facilitate our belonging to various types of groups. When we are well grounded in meaningful places, however small or seemingly insignificant politically, we are more likely to invest our energies into collaborative efforts to ensure that others also feel connected to places that enrich their lives. When we have homes and feel at home in them and the surrounding neighborhood, we are more apt to experience personal growth, engage in civic activities, and contribute to social and environmental justice causes.

PART 1

The Basics of Place

Places are socially constructed. So, in this initial section, I ask: What key place properties distinctly shape our life experience in the places that matter to us? By reflecting on the consequences of place properties, we deepen our appreciation for the differences between places in their form and impact on our lives. Additionally, we broaden our understanding of the place landscape by identifying and describing the places that most affect how we see ourselves, afford us opportunities to develop a sense of we-ness with others, and alter our personal and social well-being.

Ideally, the insights we glean from considering these issues will inspire us to heighten and refine our place consciousness. Armed with this quality of mind, we can grasp more fully how we live every moment of our lives as embodied human beings navigating fluid and complex places. In practical terms, understanding the basic features of the place landscape reveals a roadmap for discovering how we can best improve the quality of those places and enhance our well-being.

1
Framing Properties

Photo 3: Aerial view of various naval vessels around the beaches of Normandy in northern France that took part in Operation Neptune in June 1944 during World War II. (John Parrot, Gettyimages)

In the early morning hours of June 6, 1944, over 150,000 Allied troops readied themselves as best they could for the Normandy Campaign and Operation Neptune, the largest amphibious invasion in history. But few, if any, fully fathomed what they would confront on the five beaches of northern France. In the dramatic moments before, during, and immediately after the surprise D-Day attack, the troops could not see how this legendary battle would shift the course of world history, including the collapse of the Nazi regime. While many sensed that the mission was vital, few fully appreciated its magnitude as a turning point in World War II. With time, the public also celebrated the Normandy beaches as a truth spot that honors valor, sacrifice, political freedom, and patriotism. This sentiment is reinforced knowing that roughly four thousand men lost their lives fighting for a free world at this site.

People often imagine the typical beach in an idealized way. Set against a horizon that boasts a rising or setting sun, a beach's essence is captured by the splendor of timeless ocean waves rhythmically dancing over shorelines. The marriage of these physical forces creates a welcoming place that fosters meditative moments, family fun, romance, friendly games, and exercise. But the young men who stormed the Normandy beaches on foot and in their support vehicles experienced the beach much differently when the boat ramps were lowered. The Allies' elaborate training sessions on England's beaches during the preceding weeks could not simulate the chaos and carnage they endured on that unforgettable day. Still, when given the signal, the men thrust themselves into the turbulent waters that led to a killing zone. This was especially the fate of those who landed on Omaha Beach in the initial deployment of troops.

Russell Stover, a former member of the 116th Infantry Regiment, US 29th Infantry Division, is one of many to offer a firsthand account of the formidable obstacles the men faced landing on the beach:

> The ramp went down and we leaped out, into waist-deep water and three-foot waves. Some lost their footing, some their weapons. We had more than two hundred yards to go to the high water mark. Some engineers were working to our left. There was only one tank ahead

and to the left but it wasn't firing or moving. There were no "instant fox holes" either; there wasn't one crater for cover ... It was very obvious to me that many plans were going wrong. There was a boat burning to our right, heading back out. We waded through the surf and floating debris ... Reaching the sand, I tried to run, but found it was very difficult, my impregnated pant legs were filled with water. The extra weight took its toll and about half way in I fell to the sand exhausted. I thanked the Good Lord for the smoke that still covered the bluffs. A shell had started a grass fire. If not for that smoke, we would not have made it in. Recovering, I started running again. The man to my right didn't follow, I think he was our first casualty.[1]

Similar to Stover's story, other men's heart-wrenching accounts of the atrocities they experienced on D-Day are supported by documentary footage. The opening scenes of the blockbuster movie *Saving Private Ryan* also graphically depict the brutality that unfolded on those beaches. Even though nearly twenty-five years have passed, I vividly remember being mesmerized as I watched those scenes at the movie theater. Unsurprisingly, then, former soldiers decades removed from participating in that legendary battle also retained the haunting images of countless dead bodies floating in the water, others mangled and ripped apart by mines and artillery shells, and expansive pools of bloody beach water. The effects of those visual cues were augmented by deep memories of the sounds and smells of war up close: machine-gun fire, bullets whistling nonstop through the air, the booming noises of the big guns launching ordnance from ships, fallen soldiers' desperate and painful cries for help, the stench of wounded and burning bodies, and much, much more.

Survivors also tell us about how saltwater triggered excruciating pain as it poured into the open wounds of soldiers as they lay helpless on the beach. One tank operator shares his hesitancy to follow a superior's order to get his tank onto the beach. His initial resistance reflected not his fear, but rather his compassion. He could not drive his tank without running over soldiers who lay dead or dying on the beach. Ultimately, he followed the order. When faced with the inevitable choice to run over a man, he carefully sought to maintain the soldier's dignity by trying to run over only his legs, waiting to turn until he had cleared the soldier to minimize the damage.

For most men who lived through the experience, the trauma they associated with the Normandy beaches began before their boots ever touched the water and sand. Packed like sardines in small boats on turbulent seas, many wrestled with intense seasickness. On their way to battle, men were scared, dizzy, weak, and many vomited repeatedly. Ironically, many of these disoriented young men, trapped in a stew of vomit, were eager to regain control over their vulnerable bodies by "escaping" this hellish floating vessel as quickly as possible – despite knowing that the beach would be a far more dangerous place. It is difficult to grasp how these men dealt with this kind of physical distress while simultaneously being forced to summon the resolve to storm a treacherous beach where injury and death were distinct possibilities.

Those units of sick, tired, and frightened men ran separately, yet together, with their comrades into harm's way. They did so with their physical senses and survival instincts on high alert. Their collective consciousness as soldiers and sailors also pushed them to stay alive and advance. As their time on the beach painfully ticked away, the seeds of meaning they assigned to this place took root. They leaned into their personal and shared understanding of what the battle on the beach represented for them and others.

In dramatic fashion, the men's stories illustrate how we rely on our embodied experiences to construct memories: these memories render social places out of the encounters we have with physical realities. The stories of Normandy just happen to be some of the most graphic examples of this process. They clearly demonstrate that our life experiences are mediated by our bodies in socially constructed places. What we see, hear, smell, taste, and feel with our senses makes a difference in how we define a place. But the stories also reveal how the D-Day men built a shared understanding of that time and place that went beyond their individual physical sensations. Their socially constructed sense of we-ness pumped life into the Normandy beaches during and after the fighting, putting into context how the deaths happened in service to a noble and collective goal.

Normandy has been portrayed as a site where the epic struggle between the forces of good and evil was waged. The series of events connected to the build-up of D-Day, as well as its aftermath, illustrate how some places are often nested inside of others. This nesting is driven by the overlapping forces of time and place. Looking to the past, the beaches represent places embedded in a larger set of places in England relevant to the planning and execution of the invasion, including the troops' final journey by sea to where the D-Day fighting took place. In other words, a wider lens reveals that the operation involved a more expansive sense of place than just the beaches. Looking beyond D-Day, the message of hope that grew out of what transpired on the beaches of northern France spread throughout *all of France* and, ultimately, to the rest of Europe. Over time, D-Day helped the French, and Europeans more broadly, reclaim their homelands and rekindle their shared images of what their land and the places therein meant to them. People who lost their freedom and were forced to live with distorted images of their homelands because of the Nazi occupation were able to reconstruct their vision of those places. Many across Europe deepened their appreciation for the places that enabled them to forge their national and regional identities. Although the public's attention has waned recently, for many decades the stories and footage of Operation Neptune have helped to shape the public's perception of those beaches and the men who stormed them.[2]

Jeff Malpas's philosophical perspective on the relationship between human experience and place offers us a useful frame to consider what unfolded in the Normandy campaign. Building on the work of the twentieth-century French novelist Marcel Proust, Malpas centers his thinking about place on what he labels "Proust's Principle." Specifically, Malpas emphasizes the "place-bound identity of persons." In other words, "the identity of persons is inextricably bound to place, and not merely to place in some general, abstract sense ... but also, as consequence to those *particular* places, multiple and complex though they may be, in and through which a person's life is lived." Who we are in our own eyes, then, is directly tied to our experiences in specific places. But Malpas goes further by noting that we are not simply tied to places. Rather, "the very possibility of the appearance of things – objects, of others, and of self – is possible only within the all-embracing compass of place – *it is in place, and in relation to our own being-in-place, that the world begins.*"³

The beaches of Normandy enabled the Allied forces to articulate their identities as soldiers and their sense of we-ness as members of their respective units and armies. Each soldier who survived, physically injured or not, was forced to deal emotionally and psychologically with the horrors they experienced. Yet, while each struggled to carve out their own coping strategy, they did so, at least in the immediate aftermath of the fighting, realizing that they shared a haunting experience with the other living members of the fighting force.

Philosophically, place empowers us to be human; without place we could not exist. It enables us to express our individuality, our humanity, and our social ties. More broadly, all social experience is intertwined with elements of place that allow us to exist and to do what we do – live by experiencing life amidst our surroundings.

Embodied Place

Every time we breathe, think, feel, or act, we do so in place. Sometimes we express our human capacity to process time and place self-consciously. As we do this, we are mindful of some of our personal circumstances, including, at times, our physical surroundings. We may also be aware of our bodies and how our physical form structures the way we see, process, and respond to places and the objects contained therein. This type of mindfulness allows us to consider how our physical senses give us feedback about the features of the place we're experiencing.

Many philosophers, including Mark Johnson, have accentuated the importance of the body-place connection. Johnson observes in *The Body in the Mind: The Bodily Basis of Meaning, Imagination, and Reason*:

> As animals we have bodies connected to the natural world, such that our consciousness and rationality are tied to our bodily orientations and interactions in and with our environments. Our embodiment is essential to who we are, and to what meaning is, and to our ability to draw rational inferences and be creative.⁴

By extension, our embodiment connects us to others, real and imagined, who are also embodied as they navigate, or are perceived to navigate, places.

One way to think about embodiment is to consider how we experience place by using what Aristotle identified as our five primary senses (sight, sound, smell, taste, touch). We use these senses (and others) by focusing on the myriad stimuli generated by the material world. While much of this information processing occurs subconsciously, we are sometimes clearly aware of our sensory efforts to interpret our worlds.

In 1909, the Baltic-German zoologist Jakob von Uexküll adapted the German word for environment, *umwelt*, to highlight the perceptual worlds that are accessible to different types of animals.[5] Because animals, including humans, have different abilities to sense their environments, each species, and even every member of that species, will have a different umwelt. Now, more than a century later, Ed Yong, the Pulitzer Prize–winning science writer, has deftly reimagined Uexküll's initial observation. In his enlightening book *An Immense World: How Animal Senses Reveal the Hidden Realms around Us*, Yong assumes the role of adventure guide as he meticulously describes how a cornucopia of common and exotic animals use their specialized senses to engage with their physical environments. Although he devotes most of his attention to the wider animal kingdom, he selectively reveals humans' capabilities to discern their own surroundings. Juxtaposing us to other species – the tick in one noteworthy instance – he acknowledges that while our perceptual tools may have more to offer in some instances, "our Umwelt is still limited; it just doesn't *feel* that way. To us, it feels all-encompassing. It is all there is *to* know. This is an illusion, and one that every animal shares."[6] Moreover, when we compare our individual sensory skills to those that belong to other species, we recognize that we often come up short: some animals can sense sounds, colors, vibrations, and more that escape our grasp.

As they do for all animals, our uniquely configured senses reveal or restrict the world we perceive. So, too, individuals may have distinctive sensory advantages or disadvantages compared to others. The person who is blind, in contrast to the sighted person, has an umwelten devoid of visual cues, but one that may be more enriched by the sounds and smells that accompany various places. As Yong notes, "the senses transform the coursing chaos of the world into perceptions and experiences – things we can react to and act upon … They turn stimuli into information."[7]

Although I do not focus extensively on our physical capacities to sense the materiality of a place, we should be aware of the umwelten subtext that shapes how we interact with the places that matter to us. The sighted city dweller gathers visual information because they can see and label unsightly and beautiful areas and the people they deem to be either dangerous or safe. Those visual images can perhaps provoke fear or joy: feelings that could either drive them to avoid or embrace a place, stay inside or go outside, make a decision to flee the city to pursue a "safer" life in the suburbs or look forward to remaining at their current location. In contrast, the person whose umwelt does not feature visual imagery must rely on other senses to draw conclusions about the place they are visiting or call home. Thus, the person without a sense of sight cannot see the dangerous activities that are occurring in their community, yet their sense of hearing and smell may be heightened and still provide them useful signals to detect potential danger.

An important sense that Aristotle ignored, *proprioception*, represents our ability to be aware of our own body. This sense compels us in many situations to react to a place based on our perceptions of how others see and respond to our embodied characteristics. Thus, another way to think of embodiment requires us to focus on the intersection between the cultural forces that socially define our bodies in both positive and negative ways and our discernable physical attributes. Irrespective of whether our assumptions about the meanings that others assign to our bodies are accurate or not, they can alter how we navigate a place and our potential social exchanges therein. For example, assume you are a young American woman and are surrounded by others who expect you to act like a typical female by shaving your leg and armpit hair to accommodate traditional gender norms. You may feel anxious when you interact with others who "police" you on American beaches, in locker-rooms, or even at family gatherings in your own home.

Think too about how our fear for our physical safety may be heightened as we walk in a neighborhood at night that we deem to be unsafe. Part of our fear is likely shaped by our own self-perceptions and experiential knowledge related to our bodies: our age, race and ethnicity, sexual and gender identity, physical stature and abilities, and more. We filter our embodied reality through the cultural messages that reveal to us whether we are acceptable in others' eyes. Those assessments are based on prevailing ideologies that define our relative standing on various social hierarchies that separate the stigmatized from the privileged. If we are a woman, we may feel vulnerable because we've internalized fears based on our beliefs about how rape culture is manifested on the streets. Or, if a physical disability requires that we use a wheelchair, we might worry that others will see us as an easy "mark" while we're traveling the city on our own.

These diverse examples illustrate the multilayered complexity of the process by which we make sense of our lives as we navigate places as embodied beings. The philosopher Janet Donohoe captures this sentiment by noting that "Place, memory, and body function as palimpsests, written upon repeatedly from differing perspectives at different moments with different salient themes and values layered one upon the other."[8] Thus, not only is place one of the factors that goes into our understanding of ourselves, it is a prominent feature in how we build memories with others as members of groups in our shared social landscape.

Because I am most concerned with the connection between place and we-ness, I highlight how places create opportunities for embodied individuals to negotiate or contest a sense of group belonging. Broadly speaking, those activities are guided by cooperative energies that encourage people to support one another, or competitive juices that pit individuals and groups against each other. For example, community residents who suspect that their bodies are being exposed to toxins released by a nearby chemical plant can mobilize themselves to create a local activist group to protest the chemical company's practices. The group may even bring a legal suit against the company. For many, it is their embodied experiences that motivate them to share their body-centered concerns with other community members. As they share their tragic stories, they forge collective memories and a collective identity that are both embodied and place-based.

Properties

If we are to delve deeply into the various types of places that affect us most, we should explore some of the key properties or features that distinguish them. Doing so allows us to sharpen our understanding of how places and people intersect. Such insights also enhance our ability to do effective placemaking in the social domains that are related to our quality of life and social justice issues. Ultimately, the more we know about the aspects of place that set them apart from one another, the more we can tailor our placemaking to specific settings.

Those who study the concept of place have put into play a wide range of considerations that enable us to think about place in myriad ways. As a social scientist, my inclination is to introduce ten key properties (physical conditions, organic/digital, symbolic meaning, social structural, shared power, public/private, institutional and cultural conditions, level of stability, gendered attributes, and discourses) associated with place that are also relevant to our experiences with group belonging. The properties I discuss represent key attributes of the place landscape that enhance our understanding of how different aspects of a place affect us. Places that appear to be similar at first glance because they share a similar label, such as household, school, or community, can also differ dramatically because of the properties that uniquely define and differentiate them. Keep in mind that while I delineate the ten properties separately, their effects on how we experience a place frequently overlap. In addition, the properties I present are not meant to be an exhaustive list, but they all matter.

Physical Conditions

Any type of place has *physical conditions* associated with it including the natural and human-made boundaries that delimit it. A place's physicality can be assessed by considering its level of openness or its exposure to nature. Although a neighborhood typically has streets and other land-based markers to differentiate it from adjacent property, it is more open than the neighborhood church or school. All three can be viewed as places, but the structure of both the church and school is more physically restrictive than a neighborhood's open space. Still, gated neighborhoods, especially those with formidable walls, gates, electronic security, and guards, limit a neighborhood's practical and perceived openness. This explains how our sense of openness is multifaceted when applied to a place.

The amount of space associated with a place can vary as well. Think of the different feelings of confinement you can experience when you are in a car, bus, or train versus a home or office building. Each of these places may represent a site where we regularly have discussions with our family, friends, and coworkers, but a car is clearly the most restrictive. The car (and often a bus and train to a lesser degree) provides no physical privacy whereas a house and most office buildings have multiple rooms that can usually offer people an opportunity to get away from others and experience some semblance of privacy.[9] This is most important when people feel distressed or are simply looking for some alone time. If we're full of fear, anger, or sadness, it is far more difficult to hide those feelings from our companions in a car than it would be if we have the option to isolate ourselves in a separate room instead.

As someone who loves the outdoors and has lived for years in both cloudy-cold and sunny-hot climates, I'm particularly sensitive to how climate conditions associated with a place can alter our personal and group experiences. The most significant conditions include variations in temperature, precipitation, topography, light/darkness, and extreme weather events. These physical conditions can alter how we engage in different social activities and how we establish and maintain our sense of we-ness. Imagine you're an elderly person living in a house in Rochester, New York, the snowiest large American city where an average of 102 inches of snow falls each year.[10] You would be more likely to depend on your neighbors' goodwill to help you keep your driveway and sidewalk clear of snow than someone living in a snow-free city. Recall the moving stories of how folks in Buffalo came to each other's aid during the record-breaking blizzard in December 2022.[11]

More generally, climate conditions can encourage us to be more outgoing or reclusive. Extreme cold may limit the time we spend outside on our property or elsewhere, but intense heat can keep us inside too. Alternatively, these extreme conditions may compel us to seek refuge with others who can provide us with heat or air conditioning if we are financially unable to secure these privileges ourselves. This assumes, of course, that we are connected to others. Unfortunately, many of us are isolated from close contacts and exposed to extreme conditions that can lead to horrific outcomes as a result. We saw this occur in July 1995 in Chicago during an unprecedented heat wave that accounted for over seven hundred Chicagoans perishing within a week, many at home. In *Heat Wave: A Social Autopsy of Disaster in Chicago*, urban sociologist Eric Klinenberg concludes that a combination of forces accounted for such a high fatality rate.[12] The institutional abandonment of poor neighborhoods and the large number of isolated seniors in those neighborhoods were pivotal in causing this tragedy. On the flip side, nice weather can foster outdoor neighborly time that includes walks, casual chores, and porch sitting, all of which may create opportunities for us to see and talk to our neighbors. In short, climate conditions can influence our motivations and opportunities to be neighborly or needy, establishing a sense of we-ness in either case.

The human-made physical features of a place can be just as significant in shaping our options to develop and sustain our sense of we-ness. Much has been written about how developers and home builders of the twentieth century altered how our neighborhoods and houses are designed in ways that inadvertently dampened the flow of social life.[13] Building houses with garages in the front reduces sidewalk strolls, neighbors' socializing, and kids' outdoor free play. Likewise, placing single homes on large parcels of property without sidewalks or front porches limits people's contact with their neighbors. We've also limited our options to socialize with our neighbors because we've built tracks of suburban homes in places that discourage walking to a central shopping area.

The new urbanism movement has experimented with more neighborhood-friendly alternatives for people, but this design philosophy only affects a relatively small number of people. In addition, as sociologist Ray Oldenburg argues in *The Great Good Place: Cafés, Coffee Shops, Bookstores, Bars, Hair Salons, and Other Hangouts at the Heart of a Community*, we have lost far too many of our convenient options to build community because the number of "third places" are rapidly declining. These social sites are "public places that host the regular, voluntary, informal, and happily anticipated gatherings of individuals beyond the realms of home and work."[14] The loss of places like these that were embedded in the community reduces that number of convenient and public options to nurture a sense of we-ness.

If we apply a wider lens to human-made physical features that change how we relate to each other, we can consider the barriers on our southern border that received so much media coverage during the Trump administration. The optics of the "wall" accentuate the "us" against "them" sentiments. But those optics simultaneously downplay how the image of America as a physical place and a moral beacon of hope is also part of our national heritage that many of us have internalized. Our nation historically has been a destination for persons who feel threatened in their native countries and communities or are looking for a brighter future.

In September 2017, the much-publicized wall was amplified by the French artist JR's creative photographic artwork, focusing attention on the US–Mexico border in Tecate, California. JR's installation included a sixty-five-foot-tall image of a Mexican baby boy, Kikito, that was pasted to plywood and mounted on a huge section of scaffolding. JR had recently photographed the adorable boy standing in his crib at his house on the hillside overlooking the display. The image of Kikito was positioned on the Mexican side of the international divide with the boy's fingertips seemingly resting on top of the border wall as he appeared to be innocently and playfully looking over it toward America. The precious, yet provocative, image went viral, generating public recognition of the site and JR's work. After JR posted the site's coordinates on Instagram, people from both the US and Mexico flocked to see the image. Once there, people on both sides began to mingle, exchange pleasantries through the perforated panels of the wall, and even swap phones to take selfies with each other. JR was most impressed with the fact that his installation enabled people to connect: "The fact that you went there, and you tell me that people exchanged their phones through the fence and it created interaction between people that would never talk, for me, that's the most amazing part of the project."[15] A spontaneous form of we-ness and temporary placemaking emerged at the site, which easily morphed into a meeting place for people to express their humanity.

One of the most memorable days was when JR arranged for long tables to be positioned so they appeared to extend through both sides of the wall. The tables had images of two large eyes displayed on them, with one on each side of the wall. An aerial view of the structure and of the festive atmosphere created a dramatic visceral effect of two communities apart, but together. That day, Americans and Mexicans, with the support of border patrol agents, cooked and shared a meal while celebrating their open-minded ability to cultivate a sense of we-ness.[16] JR's work reminds us that imaginative, artistic energies can inspire people to see and feel places in a fresh light. Art and music can bring people together in new ways to appreciate a powerful sense of we-ness that might otherwise go unrealized.

Historically, we are most accustomed to experiencing a place, such as a border wall or locations where we carry our everyday activities, in its physical sense. Physical conditions help to define settings, like the one where people gathered to interact with JR's project and respond to each other. In recent years, however, we are increasingly sharing time in digitally constructed places. These alternative places position us in a virtual reality that is not directly dependent on physical conditions and what we typically define as reality. In other words, we spend more time engaged with 3D virtual reality that is informed by, but seemingly separate from, our real-world experiences. In this reality, we are not having the same type of embodied experiences interacting with people on the border or anywhere else that would be grounded in or affected by physical conditions.

Organic/Digital

An *organic/digital* distinction draws our attention to the extent to which the place in which we are participating is natural, a part of what we commonly describe as "real" life, something organic that has physical, tangible features. The more we depart from this physical world, the more immersed we become in a virtual reality environment that we created ourselves or that was created for us. We can loosely view this distinction as binary, but it is more accurate to think of this place property as existing on a continuum that ranges from exclusively part of our physical life experience to a total immersive involvement in a digitally rendered simulated environment.[17] As I describe more fully in Chapter 2, big tech companies and other smaller businesses, including game developers, are guiding us toward what has been labeled the metaverse – a technologically driven new world where virtual reality (VR) and augmented reality (AR) will shape our embodied experiences. In the future, we will spend more of our time in a digital place and gain more experience with transitioning back and forth between the organic and digital worlds.

We can develop a more nuanced appreciation of the digital features of place by exploring how professional groups who manage digital systems, and everyday users of digital technologies, engage with place-based digital media to shape their sense of place and experiences with it. In her incisive book *The Digital City: Media and the Social Production of Place*, Germaine Halegoua, a film and media studies professor, reveals the intriguing complexities associated with contemporary digital placemaking, especially in urban environments. With an eye on the process of "re-placeing" – the remaking of place over time – Halegoua develops a broad theoretical framework to interrogate the "discursive, cultural, and political practices of (re)doing place with digital media."[18] In doing so, she casts a wide net that covers place-relevant digital technologies and practices that are relevant to "smart cities," local digital infrastructure projects, and users of navigation technologies and social media. Halegoua is one of a growing cadre of interdisciplinary researchers who study how modern digital technologies are affecting our sense of place,

place attachments, and placemaking. I'll integrate her ideas when I address transitional processes associated with place in Chapter 5, and then again in the concluding chapter when I showcase placemaking themes for the future. The digital side of place, either as a property to define a place or as a medium to produce and experience it, will become increasingly critical for understanding how we perceive and experience place, considering the unique affordances that our rapidly changing technological landscape is generating.

Symbolic Meaning

Whether we are navigating organic or digital worlds, we assign *symbolic meaning* as social creatures to the specific places that grab or compete for our attention. We even have impressions of generic and specific places that we've never experienced. This happens because we internalize public discourses that reinforce the meanings associated with places and the impressions we have of them. Consequently, most of us have ready-made impressions of places like "the projects," playgrounds, nursing homes, dentist offices, and prisons, to name several obvious ones.

The meanings we embrace and attribute to places vary widely. Most commonly, we see a familiar or projected place as sacred/profane, safe/risky, child-/adult-focused, fun/boring, happy/sad, work/play, poor/affluent, informal/formal, emotionally warm/cold, cooperative/competitive, and so on. Our impressions encourage us to make decisions about whether we want to spend time in a place. They also affect how we interact with others in those places as well as those who are not physically present. For example, we can use digital technologies to produce and share self-images that are meant to convey to others our sense of place and place-based identity.

Social Structural

The places that bring us together can be characterized by the *social structural* features that organize our relative roles. This condition offers us clues about individuals' relative knowledge, rights, obligations, privileges, and access to resources. It locates people in a system that enables some people to have a more privileged stake in a place than others. One key aspect of this property deals with the relative control we have in making decisions about a place, including the types of claims we can realistically make regarding it. Are we in charge of calling the shots and coordinating our actions on our own terms, or are we expected to appease others and follow preexisting norms?

Shared Power

Our ability to collaborate with others to effect change is connected to how we and others collectively relate to a place. Depending on the circumstances, we have varying degrees of *shared power* to alter place conditions to our liking. Our shared knowledge, financial means, social capital, political status, and physical presence are some of the more significant assets we can leverage on behalf of our group to negotiate our claims to be present in certain places and to modify them.

Humans' thirst for power throughout the ages has been anchored in the desire to control not just people, but places. Ruthless despots like Genghis Khan, Queen Isabella I and King Ferdinand II, Joseph Stalin, Benito Mussolini, Adolf Hitler, Vladimir Putin, and countless others have exerted their will over places and people near and far. They coerced or ensnared others to enlist them in their power campaign and to carry out their ambitions to define places according to their selfish desires. But a form of "power over" others is not the exclusive province of the ruthless, rich, or famous. It also represents an orientation adopted by everyday people in their place-based lives. Think of the abusive husband and father who perceives himself as the "king of his castle" as he asserts his unrelenting control over his family. We see a different form of power, "power with," when we consider the courageous efforts of the miners, factory workers, and others who fought to build unions so they would have a voice in the demanding, dangerous places where they made a wage.

Moving forward, we need to explore how social ties affect the way power is used to define certain places. Most importantly, how much and in what forms do we collaboratively contribute to influencing those places that matter most to us – our home, neighborhood, worksite, country, and the planet? How much autonomy and sway do we have in collaborating with others to improve our chances of shaping a place to our liking? Those who are committed to their collective identities, such as environmentalists, community activists, union members, and white nationalists, assume that they have some collective agency to determine the fate of places that matter to them.

Public/Private

Our perceptions of place give us clues as to what part of ourselves we feel comfortable showing to others. The notion of a place being relatively *public* or *private* is an important feature in this regard. This matters most when we consider personal issues central to how we spend time in a place. We have all dealt with situations that require us to differentiate between our public and private selves. While some of us are extraordinarily transparent, revealing ourselves as an open book to others in public and private places alike, many others make calculated decisions to protect themselves from scrutiny. They act in a more reserved, introspective manner in public settings. Many parents, for example, tailor their discipline tactics based on whether they are in a public or private setting. Not wanting to appear inappropriate or abusive, they may suppress their anger and wait until they are alone with their children (or only other family members) before they either physically or verbally respond to their children's misdeeds.

A pervasive and poignant example my female students frequently share with me involves their complaints about the way their boyfriends interact with them when they are alone versus when they are together in public around the boyfriend's male friends. Driven by fears of being emasculated in front of their "bros," many college-age men are much less affectionate, nurturing, and accommodating to their partners in a public setting. Instead, they are too often inconsiderate, controlling, and confrontational. This dynamic reveals the contrasting visions of expressing we-ness among bros as compared to with their romantic partner. The phrase popularized by young people, "bros before hoes," captures this disturbing pattern.

Although we generally agree on which places are relatively public or private, some places can be framed as a kind of "interstitial space" that includes both public and private features.[19] For example, the brothels in Nevada, first legalized in 1971, provide one intriguing type of setting that can be characterized in this way. A 1980 Supreme Court ruling and the actions of the Nevada legislature in 1987 have provided additional guidance outlining the conditions needed to sanction public spaces for commercialized sex work. The zoning laws restrict brothels to counties with populations of less than 400,000 and they cannot be within four hundred feet of a school or place of worship. Yet, within the "private" confines of the brothel, patrons are afforded the opportunity to engage in a wide range of fluid sexualities and gendered performances.

Institutional and Cultural Conditions

Institutional and cultural conditions can play a critical role in determining the types of options we believe we have for navigating a place. What are the policies, rules, protocols, and norms that govern the expectations others have of us when we're associated with a place? Are the guidelines restrictive or empowering? Do they encourage us to trust others and cooperate or do we feel pressured to be secretive and protective in a setting? Places like schools, medical facilities, prisons, military barracks and war zones, sports locker-rooms, outdoor neighborhood block parties, and therapy sessions are a handful of useful examples. When we think of places like these, we should consider how the formal and informal mechanisms that guide our behavior can affect our experiences of feeling connected to others in those places. Are there cultural forces that constrain or enhance our chances to develop a sense of we-ness in a place?

Level of Stability

As noted earlier, place and time are fundamentally related. Together, they influence our perception of a place's *level of stability*. With time, the conditions or properties that distinguish a place often change. Over time, people also revise their perceptions about the defining characteristics of a place. Some places are significantly more stable than others, exemplified by how some communities retain their basic profile over decades whereas others undergo significant changes due to war, natural disaster, gentrification, or an economic downturn that leads to boarded-up buildings and higher crime rates. Another common type of place shift over time is one I've experienced several times firsthand. An untouched wooded area, often one that serves recreational purposes, is developed for residential or commercial use. Several years ago, a big nature area stood less than a half-mile from my house. It offered my son and me exciting opportunities to do off-road biking when he was younger. We "claimed" it as our personal wooded playground. But the land has since been cleared and turned into residential neighborhoods. Now some of his friends live there. Our fading memories remain, but the riding trails are long gone, and we no longer claim this space as ours because it was transformed into a different place.

A place's level of stability can be affected by how the people involved with each other, and associated with a specific place, develop a mutual commitment inspired by the place. When people feel united by principle and purpose, they can challenge those with the power to institute basic changes that can affect a place's appearance, the inclusion or exclusion of certain types of people, the type of permissible activities, and so forth. This was vividly displayed in the media coverage of everyday Ukrainians forming military brigades and taking to the streets to fight Putin's invading army.

We can also see how principle and purpose are vital to the thriving anti-gentrification movement in Puerto Rico. In recent decades, especially since Hurricane Maria devastated the island in September 2017, grassroots activists have intensified their protests over coastal gentrification initiatives that support the tourism industry and are funded by foreign investments. Environmental groups like In Defense of Our Beaches have challenged the government's efforts to open up coastal areas to unfettered resort and tourism construction that many believe undermine local communities' sense of identity and well-being.[20] Slogans like "gringos go home," "Yankees go home," and "beaches belong to the people" express the growing frustration that many local residents share. The development projects, often located in rural coastal areas with fragile mangroves and wetland ecosystems, are being launched because legislative changes (Acts 20 and 22, collectively referred to as Act 60) enacted in 2012 in Puerto Rico provide huge tax benefits for foreign investors, mostly Americans with no personal ties to the places they buy and develop.[21]

Political leaders promote the investment and development practices as a way to pump much needed capital into the financially strapped colony, but the economic changes are also fundamentally changing the communities and ecosystems of the coastal regions. Foreign companies and individuals are buying properties in poor neighborhoods and typically build luxury hotels and Airbnbs in these beachfront areas. In the process, land developers displace low-income people, many of whom have lived for generations in the same neighborhood. The rising real estate prices are also preventing Puerto Ricans living off the island from returning to their homeland, many of whom fled the country because of Hurricane Maria. The activist collective #AbolishAct60 labels this transactional economic process "predatory" gentrification. One man who had been a longtime resident of a gentrified area offers an emotional, personal account of the foreign investment trend:

> If they remove us, Puerta de Tierra will die ... I lived there. For fifty-four years, I lived on that corner. Look at it now: a building, a new housing project for the rich. I was born there, and I can't go in there. Because we're Black and poor they're abusing us, you know? And it isn't fair to be displaced by economic interests.

Another woman, feeling victimized by what she and many others see as a modern iteration of colonialism, expresses her sense of place about a different gentrified area:

> When you've lived thirty years in the same place, you establish a relationship with the community. Twenty-one families had to leave the La Ferreteria building. You can't come there with a colonizer's mentality, thinking that people don't live here or that the people that did can be discarded with an eviction letter thinking they'll just find some other place.[22]

In addition to the housing crisis, another practical consequence of the foreign gentrification of Puerto Rico is that the new owners often make public access to the beaches more difficult. In some cases, public access is virtually impossible. This practice is occurring even though by law every beach must have public access. Highly visible protests challenging the de facto privatization of the beaches have emerged throughout the country, with some achieving temporary success by shaping land use practices in specific instances. The movement has recently received more mainstream attention because Bad Bunny, the internationally acclaimed Puerto Rican rapper and singer, and other celebrities from the island have publicly spoken out on the gentrification issue. They have also infused the movement with more passion, hope, and resources. In May 2022, Bad Bunny funded and released a YouTube documentary video featuring his song "El Apagón – Aquí Vive Gente" ("The Blackout – People Live Here") that celebrates the country and is raising public awareness of how outsiders are at the crux of the gentrification dilemma.[23]

Overall, the circumstances in Puerto Rico showcase how various stakeholders, including local residents, members of the Puerto Rican diaspora (largely in the US), foreign investors, local business owners, politicians, real estate professionals, construction companies, and social media influencers are competing to both define the meaning of places associated with the island and establish their claims to those places. Debates that incorporate messages linked to foreign investment, gentrification, local control, individual and community identities, environmental impacts, statehood proposals, and more illustrate how a complex set of overlapping issues can frame how people experience their sense of place and implement placemaking strategies. Perceptions about the stability of Puerto Rico are intimately tied to local residents' efforts to mobilize their historical, cultural, and national sense of we-ness as members of this unincorporated territory of the US.

To understand the intersection of place and people's sense of group belonging, we must recognize those basic changes that occur in a place. Equally important, however, is dissecting how people's sense of we-ness is implicated. Do expressions of ideational or dyadic we-ness inspire changes to a place? How does a place's lack of stability prompt people to bond and generate the social capital needed to cultivate a collaborative social response?

Gendered Attributes

Our approach to studying place can also explore how *gendered attributes* make a difference. The more we see ourselves and the world around us through a gendered lens, the more relevant this property is likely to be for us. If, for example, we are susceptible to gender stereotypes, then we may uncritically perceive daycare centers, yoga studios, construction sites, football stadiums, and the like as gendered places. When this occurs, our openness to and style of pursuing we-ness is likely to be affected. We may only feel comfortable aligning ourselves with others and forming a sense of we-ness with those who we believe embody our gendered expectations. For example, a traditional male working on a construction site may refuse to respect and cooperate with a female coworker who challenges traditional feminine stereotypes. Consequently, these coworkers are unlikely to form any sort of we-ness in this place, although they might have collaborated in a different place, say, as chaperones on a church mission trip to help disaster victims.

People's attitudes about gender are not the only factors that can influence how we feel about places; sometimes gendered characteristics of the places matter, too. Some places, including cities, are organized in gendered ways that adversely affect women's well-being. Guided by assumptions that anchor feminist geography, Leslie Kern demonstrates in her provocative book *Feminist City* how the urban environment is a gendered world largely constructed by male urban planners and developers. Kern's basic premise is that the built urban environment, combined with the social forces generated by a patriarchal culture, constrains women's practical opportunities to thrive in the city. As she notes,

> A geographic perspective on gender offers a way of understanding how sexism functions on the ground. Women's second-class status is enforced not just through the metaphorical notion of "separate spheres," but through an actual, material geography of

exclusion. Male power and privilege are upheld by keeping women's movements limited and their ability to access different spaces constrained.[24]

Kern's analysis is informed by both the expanding body of research produced by urban feminists who emphasize intersectional themes of race, class, gender, and sexuality, and by her rich firsthand accounts of navigating major cities like London, New York City, and Toronto throughout her life. She deepens our appreciation for how urban cities reinforce traditional masculine practices and norms. For example, public transit systems are often designed in ways that are not family-friendly and penalize individuals who have safety concerns or make frequent stops to fulfill caregiving responsibilities like escorting kids to and from school and daycare. In addition, many transit systems are difficult to use with baby strollers. They also extract further financial costs from riders (mostly women) who have frequent stops associated with caregiving responsibilities.[25]

We can also appreciate how gender is related to place by following the line of thinking that Daphne Spain, an urban and environmental planning expert, set forth when she provided her detailed sociohistorical analysis more than three decades ago in *Gendered Spaces*.[26] She revealed how gendered spaces, in what she labeled "spatial institutions" (homes, schools, and workplaces), have restricted women's access to consequential knowledge throughout history, which has, in turn, helped to perpetuate gender inequalities. The spatial designs that have dominated these three social institutions have limited gender integration, with the most persistent patterns occurring in the labor force. She notes, for example, that women are much more likely to work in "open floor" settings, whereas men's jobs are more likely to be "closed door." Although this discrepancy continues to narrow with the passing of time, women typically still have less control over their workspace than do men. Women have less privacy, are more likely to be interrupted, and less likely to be exposed to information sharing that can enhance their work status. Thus, gender composition and how a place is physically configured can influence gender dynamics and the perception of a place. As Spain asserts, "spatial relations exist only because social processes exist. The spatial and social aspects of a phenomenon are inseparable."[27]

Discourses

Finally, each of the preceding properties can be affected by various place-based *discourses*. A discourse gives us a framework to make sense of specific places. It reveals and integrates knowledge, values, and beliefs that allow us to depict our place-based realities in ways that make sense to us. At any point in time, there are often competing discourses that provide us with alternative views of a place and what is supposed to happen there. The one we adopt is designed to serve our best interests, at least as we see them. Some of the most obvious place-based discourses are grand in scope; they affect how we see nation-states or the entire world.

Today, ardent environmentalists picture the earth as being under assault by the effects of the extraction and burning of fossil fuels. Their discourse demands that we take drastic action to confront and minimize climate change.[28] They perceive the earth as a fragile place and conclude that all people living today have a vested interest in it, as do our descendants. In contrast, deniers of the human-caused climate crisis see the earth as a resilient place that we can control and bend to our will.

Relatedly, the biosphere consciousness shapes one of the most critical discourses related to how we think about place and our relationship to it. The biosphere represents the roughly forty miles ranging from the bottom of the ocean to the upper atmosphere that contains an impressive mix of geochemical processes and living organisms crucial to all life on earth. In *The Empathic Civilization: The Race to Global Consciousness in a World in Crisis*, social and economic theorist Jeremy Rifkin argues that we are gradually moving toward a unifying biosphere consciousness that encourages us to appreciate more fully our existence in and contribution to a larger ecological system. When we see the world through an ecological lens, we recognize how all life forms are intertwined with countless geochemical processes that enable planet earth to support life. This perspective expands our conception of place, reminding us that we are immersed in a complex, global web of diverse organic and inorganic elements.

This view of life, and our sense of responsibility to planetary health, inspired the controversial Biosphere 2 experiment conducted in southern Arizona decades ago. Heralded as the biggest and longest self-sustaining ecological study ever undertaken, eight biospherians lived in a 150-million-dollar, three-acre closed ecological facility between 1991 and 1993.[29] It contained thousands of species of plants and animals, various "terrestrial and aquatic/marine areas based on major biomes as well as a farm and human habitat with kitchen crew rooms, recreation space, laboratories and workshops."[30] That initial session was followed by another eighteen-month stint with a different small team of biospherians. The project was originally executed to study the viability of human beings surviving inside a closed ecological system, with an eye on eventually supporting human life in a distinctly different type of place – outer space.

Despite being adversely affected by outside politics regarding how the project should be managed, the unique experiment illustrated the powerful bonds humans can express when they are forced to rely on their environment in an intimate way. Mark Nelson, one of the original biospherians, reflected on his twenty-five-year-old memories to express an insider's account of living in this novel environment. In *Pushing Our Limits: Insights from Biosphere 2*, Nelson candidly assesses what he and his team members experienced as they responded to power struggles outside the airlocked facility that raised tensions among those living inside. Nelson notes:

> We continued working unselfishly with one another. Whenever we feasted, partied, or enjoyed a rare delicacy like a cup of coffee from the rainforest trees, tensions magically melted away. We'd relax and enjoy a temporary truce from group tensions. We acted mindfully in Biosphere 2, understanding that its teeming life was keeping us alive and healthy. We took care of her needs with tender loving care. She was our third lung and lifeboat. Some of us thought Biosphere 2 was the ninth biospherian.[31]

Waxing poetic about a place symbolizing a high-profile engineering achievement, Nelson portrays a strained, yet symbiotic relationship between the research team and the environment that was essential to their health. Thus, he envisages an intimate, special bond between people and place, while also signaling how the bonds between the research team were enhanced when their personal exchanges heightened their ties to the place that was their "lifeboat." Mirroring how astronauts' breathtaking photos of the earth from space in the late 1960s altered the public consciousness and discourses about our relationship to the planet – the "Outerview Effect" – Nelson emphasizes that the "Innerview" perspective he and his teammates developed from their unique living circumstances can be of similar consequence:

> We lived with, took care of, and were nurtured by a living system – a miniature biosphere. All the while, we received communications and listened to news of developments between the rest of humanity and the planetary biosphere. As our connections with our world deepened, we became acutely aware of the jarring contrast between how we lived inside the biosphere and what was happening outside it. We'd hear of ecological degradation, mindless pursuit of technological advance, and short-term profit, regardless of the damage inflicted.[32]

The innerview captures our capacity to be fundamentally attached to an ecologically grounded place that nurtures us and is subject to either the negative or positives effects of our placemaking. Ideally, then, the innerview should motivate us to strengthen our place consciousness so that we make environmentally healthy decisions when navigating the places that matter to us.

Throughout history, we have increasingly generated discourses that extend beyond nature to account for city life. One of the more consequential public discourses about place has helped to differentiate the meaning of the work sector from home life – the public from the private – and, by extension, the traditionally perceived separate places for men and women. The gendered discourse that prevailed centuries ago, linked as it was to the transition from an agrarian to an industrial economy and then to a postindustrial one, justified the city's masculine infrastructure and ethos as noted earlier. In practical terms, this is because men have always dominated the field of urban planning. Consequently, their vision has disproportionately shaped the urban landscape and our conventional understandings of the activities that men and women should pursue there. Historically, urban areas have been cast as places that are unsafe for women, especially those unaccompanied by male chaperones. City designs and expectations have also channeled women toward retail shops and children's play areas if they exist.

Other discourses are more limited in scope, but still valuable. They target the most immediate places affecting us. They inform our impressions about our homes and neighborhoods, places for leisure, and worksites. Those impressions often overlap with concerns about personal, business, and governmental power. To what extent do we have the right to determine what goes on inside our homes? Businesses? Communities?

In the mid-twentieth century, Americans altered the discourse about family privacy and the home. The public, medical community, and legislators took a more aggressive position that something needed to be done to protect children and other family members from abuse – even if it occurred in the privacy of the American home.[33] The home became a place open to government scrutiny even though the norm supporting family privacy still shapes the prevailing discourse about our domestic lives. Similarly, the gender-related discourses that shape workplace behavior and politics began to emphasize accountability. In recent decades, the public and legislators have redefined the workplace by ushering in official policies that discourage sexual harassment. The stereotypical masculine norms that once permeated workplaces from boardrooms to construction sites are no longer as readily acceptable. Although implementing the formal policies is often cumbersome, fraught with controversy, and not always successful, the discourses that guide our perceptions of the gender and sexual politics of workplaces have undergone some revision.

2

Types of Places

Photo 4: Kenneth Niedermeier, Armando Niedermeier-Rubio, and Hannah Rubio strolling through a street in San Miguel de Allende, Guanajuato, Mexico. This international romantic couple met as part of the TLC reality TV show *90 Day Fiancé: The Other Way*. (Photo courtesy of Kenneth Niedermeier)

Kenneth (Kenny) and Armando entered the public spotlight and became fan favorites as romantic partners on season two of the TLC reality TV show *90 Day Fiancé: The Other Way*.[1] This show is a spinoff of the original *90 Day Fiancé* launched in 2014 that profiles international romantic couples who have applied for or received a US K-1 visa. The visa is designed to circumvent the difficulties associated with partners committed to one another who live in different countries. It enables an American citizen's fiancé who lives outside the United States the chance to come to the US for a ninety-day period to coordinate and execute their marriage plans. If the couple does not get married within that timeframe, the foreigner must leave. But the premise for the spinoff is that Kenny, an American who was living in St. Petersburg, Florida, would need to leave the country to be with Armando and his young daughter who reside in Mexico. Thus, it was Kenny who uprooted his life by quitting his job, selling his home, and leaving his four adult children and a grandchild to explore romance in a foreign land.

Having met through an online support group for gay fathers in 2016, Kenny had visited Armando in Mexico before moving there permanently to live with him. Ultimately, they moved into an apartment and community that was a fresh start for each of them. But it was only Kenny who was embarking on a new life adventure in a different country whose language he did not speak. Although Kenny was open to the challenge of living in Mexico if it meant that he could fulfill his romantic dreams, he immediately experienced culture shock. He struggled with appreciating how stop signs are randomly hung, buying food from street vendors, contemplating going to an unimpressive hospital, dealing with Mexican currency to make store purchases, living in a relatively rundown area, needing to drive forty minutes to get to a bank, manually flushing toilets in restaurants, being targeted with homophobic slurs in public, and more. Thus, place, represented most broadly in the form of Mexico's Latin American culture that permeated the local settings, generated new meanings for Kenny, and Armando too. In addition, place properties including physical conditions, symbolic meanings, discourses, public/private distinctions, and others prompted Kenny and Armando to recognize that their dyadic we-ness would evolve in response to their challenging place-based circumstances. But at the same time, place played a more positive role when Kenny orchestrated his marriage proposal in front of family and friends at a Mexican beach setting that they shared fond memories of from a previous visit. They eventually married in May 2021.

The original *90 Day Fiancé* series and its many spinoffs indirectly underscore the basic challenges that stem from our inability to be physically in two places at once. That physical limitation affects how we experience place. Fortunately, modern communication technologies, including texting, video messaging, and virtual reality enable romantic couples living apart the chance to find creative ways to sustain their relationship. But as Kenny and Armando would confirm, nothing can replace being together in person. Like Kenny and Armando, couples who live in different countries and claim different citizenships are often frustrated by their circumstances. But partners living in very different types of places within the same country can also experience frustrations that result from living apart. They not only have to navigate the physical distance between them, but some couples must deal with being partnered to someone who lives in a decidedly different cultural setting. Think of the urbanite who is partnered with the rural inhabitant, or the person who resides in a deep blue state and city who is romantically involved with someone who lives in a red state and community. Such couples are likely to find that their divergent place-based circumstances complicate their romantic relationship, especially when they visit each other or consider an arrangement that would have one of them move to the other's location.

Most of us, irrespective of our relationship status, transition repeatedly from place to place as part of our normal flow of daily activities. The types of meaningful places we frequent include natural settings, homes, communities, worksites, public spaces, retail stores, leisure spots, and many others. These places afford us distinct opportunities to pursue our personal interests, express our identities, and fulfill the expectations others have of us. They include the sites where we pursue our hopes and dreams and chase a sense of we-ness with those who matter most to us. We experience some places sporadically or only engage with them temporarily, others represent more permanent fixtures in our lives. In either case, our lives can be enriched by the change of scenery and the varying types of people, objects, resources, options, and responsibilities we encounter as we experience whatever different places have to offer. Places enable us to experience personal growth. However, when transitioning between places we are also forced to make tradeoffs and sacrifices concerning what we can experience at a specific point in time. These tradeoffs occur whether our transitions are compelled or voluntary. Our residential moves often have the most profound impact on us. They typically offer a new set of challenges, sometimes reminding us that we must now forego special place-based amenities that had previously shaped how we thought, felt, and behaved.

Just as aspects of place matter in varied ways for all types of romantic couples, including Kenny and Armando, place matters to us irrespective of our relationship status, age, race, ethnicity, social class, gender or sexual identity, religious views, or any number of attributes that we use to define ourselves and others. And places come in many forms as well. To deepen our understanding of how they matter to us, we must appreciate the wide range of places that influence our lives. And when we fully grasp the breadth of places, we enhance our ability to engage in effective, collaborative place-making in various contexts.

A Typology

We can turn to an endless number of criteria to differentiate the types of places that influence how we experience dimensions of social life. Thus, the typology I outline here should not be viewed as fundamentally more valuable than other approaches scholars have used to conceptualize place. Rather, it distinguishes some of the key types of places that are most relevant to how we experience group belonging.

Although my discussion focuses primarily on places with significant social meaning that are located aboveground, I selectively acknowledge places that are part of what Robert Macfarlane, the acclaimed landscape writer, categorizes as the "underland." These sites include both the natural spaces and built environments that are located beneath or inside the earth's outer surface (caves, bomb shelters, mines, waste storage facilities, subway systems, catacombs, vaults). The subterranean Temples of Humankind in the Italian Alps, which I profile in Chapter 7, provide a riveting example of a socially significant underground place. According to Macfarlane, much of what has taken place historically in the underland is designed to achieve one of three tasks: "to shelter what is precious, to yield what is valuable, and to dispose of what is harmful."[2] All three of these tasks are typically shaped by competing or cooperative social forces. Grounded in a masterful narrative and remarkable experiential storytelling, Macfarlane reveals the complex and compelling intersections between such concepts as space, place, environmentalism, geology, nature, technology, culture, and social life. His insights about these intersections inform my own interdisciplinary approach to place aboveground. Finally, my selections of types of places relate to the four themes that Lynne Manzo highlights related to the moments when places tend to be significant to people.

Nature

Throughout my childhood, I lived in a house that was a stone's throw away from a large, densely wooded area. It gave me countless adventure opportunities to navigate the rocky creek on foot, hike the hilly terrain, build mud forts, climb trees, play chasing games, and engage in fanciful play that simulated military missions. This was especially true during the colder months when my mother was not worried that poison ivy would threaten me. Sometimes I played on my own, other times I explored nature with neighborhood friends.

Unfortunately, my parents never nurtured my love for the woods. Ironically, my father had spent much of his childhood in the rural outdoors. One distinct memory he was fond of sharing was of him walking one and a half miles daily as a boy to fetch buckets of clean water for his family. Later, he was too busy working at his factory job or recovering from his labor-intensive work to venture into the woods with me. As for my mother, her lukewarm attitude toward the outdoors was probably her reaction to being forced as a poor young girl to work endless hours on her family farm in rural Pennsylvania, often without shoes. In due course, despite the lack of guidance, I generated my love for and connection to nature on my own terms.

For me, and others, nature offers peaceful moments for reflective solitude. These experiential moments prepare individuals to establish healthy forms of we-ness. Although I didn't recognize it as a child, when I spent alone time in the woods (without a cell phone), I was developing my imagination, sense of curiosity, and self-confidence. Regrettably, by the time I completed college, much of the woods were cleared to expand the town's hospital and create parking lots. Thus, I never had the chance to introduce my own sons to the same patch of woods that had been my personal playground.

My experience reveals the dynamic nature of place, illustrating the risk we take in growing attached to a place. There are no guarantees that a place that we come to cherish, whether it be part of nature or the built environment, will continue to be available to us in the future in its current form or at all. Places change and our access to them can change as well. Just as we can be saddened when our primary relationships end from death or circumstance, we can experience a sense of loss when we no longer have access to a place, or it is transformed in ways that disappoint us.

As an adult, I've nurtured moments of dyadic we-ness with either my friends or family while white-water rafting, camping, hiking, and mountain biking. One of my distinct expressions of we-ness came roughly ten years ago when, for the first time, I took my then seven-year-old son, Phoenix, off-road biking early one morning in a state park packed with wildlife. On that venture, we deepened our bond with each other and nature by sighting forty-four deer in several hours. Many of our amazing encounters positioned us within "talking" distance of these wild animals as we rode by. They typically stood still, sometimes even allowing us to stop to "speak" to them. As that magical morning unfolded, we increasingly felt like the deer had gifted us with a compact that allowed us to ride the trails and explore their natural habitat if we treated them respectfully. I suspect our emotions on that day, in that place, were a microcosm of the awe-inspiring sensations Jane Goodall, the renowned primatologist, felt when the apes she studied accepted her into their secluded homeplace in the thick jungle of Tanzania.

Over the years, many have lamented how industrialization has unleashed economic and technological forces that have eroded our bonds to nature. Early on, the brutal forces of colonialism also reconfigured the natural landscape by disrespecting Indigenous peoples' perceptions of and claims to their ancestral lands.[3] Unfortunately, the persons who immigrated to what became the United States, and their descendants, have not shown the same reverence for nature as the Indigenous peoples they displaced. They have been less inspired to incorporate nature as a basic and significant place in their daily lives.

These trends blemish our history, but our social traditions also reveal that the American public since the mid-nineteenth century has been receptive to preserving segments of "our" natural lands. This vision has been formalized by a series of presidents, beginning with Abraham Lincoln. In 1864, Lincoln pushed through the Yosemite Grant Act that gave California land to set aside for "public use, resort, and recreation." That decision reinforced the public sentiment that national lands were special places that represented a public good. Next, Ulysses S. Grant declared the first national park (Yellowstone) in 1872. Then in 1906, bolstered by his close relationship and three-day camping excursion with John Muir, the famous naturalist and founder of the Sierra Club, Theodore Roosevelt made good on his conservationist tendencies by signing the Antiquities Act. The Act gave the government the authority to protect natural, historic, and scenic features of public lands. Woodrow Wilson then made his contribution in 1916 that reaffirmed nature as a public good when he created the National Park Service. In 1933, Franklin D. Roosevelt signed an executive order that further legitimized the preservation of nature for "scenic and scientific importance." That directive allowed fifty-six national monuments and military sites to be part of the National Park Service. These presidential actions, and some less consequential ones that followed, shaped the public discourse about national lands while structuring opportunities for people to experience these places for themselves.

Unfortunately, during the 1800s and 1900s racial prejudice often dictated how the initiatives that were intended to preserve nature, and supposedly provide people access to it, were developed and promoted. Writing in the journal *Social and Cultural Geography*, one team of researchers examined how the contemporary "slow violence" (a form of harm that plays out over many years and is structural in origin)[4] occurring in public parks is historically linked to how bigoted and powerful conservationists like Madison Grant, Theodore Roosevelt, and John Muir sought to preserve their own self-interests:

> The white elite defined, built, and managed public parks by displacing, excluding, and criminalizing the Indigenous, the poor, people of color, and immigrants. As such, many of today's park injustices, such as inequitable park availability and quality, gentrification, and non-visitation of people of color, originated from the beginning of the public parks in the nineteenth century and have been sustained ever since.[5]

Today, the racialized legacy of the national park system is evidenced by the relatively low visitation rates for persons of color.[6]

Notwithstanding these historical concerns about accessibility, our national and state park system reflects our increasingly proactive approach to experiencing nature. Today, we often feel like we must go out of our way to experience nature directly because of our busy lives and extensive human-made surroundings. To connect with nature, many of us need to make a specific plan. Sometimes it even requires us to organize a getaway vacation from the hustle and bustle of work and, often, our city living. This limited and regimented approach to communing with nature can have grim consequences for us personally and the social system more generally.

I came to appreciate more fully one of the outcomes of this historical shift when I listened years ago to Richard Louv, a journalist, give a talk about his provocative book *Last Child in the Woods: Saving Our Children from Nature-Deficit Disorder*. Louv's thesis is that recent cohorts of children suffer from what he labels a "nature-deficit disorder" because they are disconnected from nature. In the United

States, the insatiable demand for more and more urban and suburban construction projects reconfigures countless fields and wooded landscapes. So, too, the rise in parental concerns about "stranger danger" and kids' proclivity for more and more screen time have led to youth spending far less time exploring and playing in nature. Parents have augmented this pattern by relying heavily on modern tech to entertain their children. And as social psychologist Jonathan Haidt documents in his insightful 2024 book, *The Anxious Generation: How the Great Rewiring of Childhood Is Causing an Epidemic of Mental Illness*, Gen-Z youth in the United States, and elsewhere too, are spending inordinate amounts of time using smartphones and social media and are being raised in an overprotective child-rearing culture.[7] According to Louv, the downward generational shift in children's exposure to nature profoundly disrupts children's mental and emotional health. I agree, but we must also emphasize that children's disconnection from nature alters their chances to develop a nature-based form of we-ness with others who matter to them. Experiencing and celebrating nature with our friends, family, and even strangers not only shapes our personal development, it compels us to adopt a more ecological approach to our social and physical environments. In other words, if we are attuned to nature – if we celebrate nature as a life-affirming place – we will understand more clearly the complex ecology that surrounds us. When we are connected to nature, we are more apt to understand the interrelationships between ourselves and other people, animals, and the physical elements that make up our surroundings.

Compared to earlier generations, our contemporary information technologies position us differently toward nature. We can now easily access remarkable YouTube videos that take us deep into nature preserves and wilderness settings around the world. Those images can expand our appreciation for the global ecology of life. These exposures extend viewers' perspectives and can even inspire some to trek to the profiled places to experience them in the flesh. But video images can also prove to be "adequate" substitutes, deterring some from feeling the need to experience places in person. We may be more aware of the global ecology than our predecessors were, yet have far less regular and direct experience in nature. As a result, we spend less time sharing nature with others and developing our sense of dyadic we-ness in nature settings.

Folks who run various community groups and youth camps understand this message. For example, GROW HUB (Growing Real Opportunities to Work – Harvest of Urban Business) is a thriving nonprofit Gainesville nursery launched in 2016, designed to connect people with nature by "cultivating, empowering and assisting disabled adults for sustainable living through education, training and job opportunities."[8] The nursery and garden are situated on eighty acres of forested land that provide the employees, volunteers, and patrons a tranquil place to commune with nature while experiencing a sense of we-ness as participants in this endeavor.

Boy Scout leaders, 4-H Club supervisors, youth ministers, and others have talked to me about their efforts to exploit aspects of nature to help kids develop self-confidence, people skills, and healthy life habits. Carlos, a thirty-three-year-old pastor who works extensively with youth and takes boys on camping excursions, says that

> There's something about just being out in the outdoors around an open fire that gets people talking … it's like everybody's an open book. Somebody mentions something about their childhood or what they've been through, and this person over here will chime in and go, "yeah, I know what that's like" and blah blah blah. There really is a dynamic to that. That's the kind of stuff that goes on when they're just pulled out of their environment.

The environment Carlos alludes to is one saturated with communication technology that fosters more superficial, less interactive forms of leisure for kids. As a result of these camp circumstances, kids have a greater chance to establish a deep dyadic tie with a camp buddy.

Another thoughtful commentary comes from a thirty-four-year-old youth worker, Joseph, who works with at-risk and troubled youth. As Joseph recalls, when he was a boy, his great-grandfather, a "full-blooded Cherokee Indian," spent a lot of time teaching him the ways of the woods. Thus, it was a good fit for him when, early in his career, he had a chance to supervise delinquent kids in an outdoor alternative juvenile detention camp. He speaks highly of what he was able to accomplish with kids who participated in the challenging camp that he describes as having "no bars ... no fences. They're just deep in the woods." As he described the camp rituals and routines, I reflected on my less impressive early childhood days roaming the woods. Joseph's kids were forced to be much more creative because they had to build their own wooden sleeping structures with primitive tools. They were required to

> cut down pine trees, take a big blade, skin the bark off, bleach them out, sink them in holes ... The only thing the camp provided was a wooden platform as a floor on blocks and a piece of the big tarp that went on as the roof ... They had to do that all together and they had to figure out what design, how many poles they'd have to cut, what size.

This work in the woods necessitates that the kids develop teamwork skills and a willingness to cooperate. A sense of we-ness is also reinforced by the camp rules for dealing with inappropriate behavior. When a counselor calls out a kid for causing trouble, the entire group must stop whatever they're doing, and everyone comes together on the ground to form a circle. Each person in the group has a chance to share their ideas about the circumstances and how it is affecting them. Ultimately, the person with the problem speaks. During this time, no one in the group is allowed to move until everyone believes that the person understands what they did wrong. Joseph emphasizes that the instigator needs to "make some type of commitment to the group." This program weaves expectations about personal responsibility into a large mosaic of the kids developing a group identity. The push to create that group mentality is meant to hold everyone accountable to each other. The woods, as a place, limits distractions and offers the kids basic life challenges that can help them mature.

While Joseph wholeheartedly supports this group-based disciplinary philosophy for the kids, he laments that this process has on occasion forced counselors and kids alike to sit for up to six or seven hours before things are resolved. He's endured freezing cold and rain, swarming mosquitoes, late nights until 3 a.m., and circumstances that forced everyone to sleep "dirty and smelly" because they weren't yet free to take a shower during their designated time slot. Despite their annoyance, the counselors knew that their decision to suffer alongside the kids showed the youth that they were committed to honoring their inclusive sense of we-ness they had established deep in the woods.

Joseph persuasively portrays the benefits for many youths when they participate in this type of wilderness therapy or nature-based style of behavior modification, yet some observers have challenged the effectiveness of such programs.[9] Recent reports of abuse and death have generated closer public scrutiny. Thus, while nature as a place has potential to provide youth productive opportunities to grow as part of a group endeavor, a nature setting by itself will not lead to positive results without a responsible professional staff to implement a program.

Whether it is adults helping young people to appreciate more deeply their relationship to nature or adults personally expressing a style of mindfulness that opens up their minds to embrace their ecological surroundings, individuals who have a mindfulness practice will be better positioned to feel connected to their immediate ecosystem. Being self-aware can lead individuals to be more sensitive to how their natural environments affect them and vice versa.

Some cultural geographers, as well as other naturalists, have promoted the idea of bioregionalism as a timely concept that can enlighten people on the natural places that give meaning to their lives. Much like the relationship many Indigenous people forge with the land, seeing the world in a way consistent with bioregionalism connects people to where they live. Jenny Odell astutely summarizes this position by noting that it is

> first and foremost based on observation and recognition of what grows where, as well as an appreciation for the complex web of relationships among those actors. More than observation, it also suggests a way of identifying with place, weaving oneself into a region through observation of and responsibility to the local ecosystem.[10]

Odell frames her comments by emphasizing the process of "rendering," which is akin to paying attention to aspects of one's surroundings with a heightened sense of awareness. We often learn to see aspects of the world and our relation to them differently: "When the pattern of your attention has changed, you render your reality differently. You begin to move and act in a different kind of world."[11] Moreover, with time, your new vision of reality becomes second nature to you. When this occurs, you become more sensitive to absorbing certain types of information from your surroundings even though you may not be fully conscious of your perspective in the moment. Nonetheless, when we undergo this transformation, our place consciousness evolves and becomes more nuanced.

Social theorist Jeremy Rifkin writes about a similar, but more global version of this bioregionalism perspective, calling it the biosphere consciousness.[12] While the definition of the biosphere partly relies on spatial criteria, we can think of the entire biosphere as a place – one that encompasses the earth and makes it a viable life-producing planet. Rifkin believes we are moving toward a heightened awareness of the interconnectivity between all life forms and the geochemical processes that sustain the earth. His conclusion is supported by the trend of theorists and other scientific experts in various fields increasingly adopting systems-oriented perspectives. In addition, there has been a growth in collaborative learning paradigms that encourage youth and others to recognize their carbon footprint. This type of biosphere consciousness can foster ideational we-ness and a more inclusive perspective on humanity.

Home, Dwelling, and Everyday Life

Long ago, before we learned how to build increasingly sophisticated structures to protect ourselves from nature's elements, we were connected to our surroundings in a distinctly different way. For much of our time roaming the earth, we found places to shelter in caves, rock formations, and tree canopies, or we used geological and plant materials to create primitive structures. As our ancestors began to settle for extended periods of time in one place and in larger groups, the concept of home found its way into their consciousness and became part of their socially constructed worlds. Today, the term "home," like the word "place," is a commonly used word with diverse meanings for everyday people and scholars alike. With that being said, connecting home with place can get a bit muddled conceptually.

As we consider the value of "home" for understanding "place," it is worthwhile to dig into the commentary by Peter Somerville. Writing in the *International Journal of Urban and Regional Research*, Somerville suggests that home is a socially constructed, ideological construct with both emotive and cognitive elements. We can look at the concept of home as having seven different dimensions with the following signifiers: shelter, hearth, heart, privacy, roots, abode, and paradise.[13] Thus, when we think of home we're likely to tap into our concerns about the materials used to build it, the warmth and physical coziness our bodies derive from it, the emotional sense of security linked to love and happiness, the control over our boundaries, a source for our identity, the physical presence of where we stay, and all the positive features about what it ought to be like.

Some of these features are illustrated by how Armando's father responded to Kenny when they first met in Mexico. Consistent with stereotypes of some Mexican men, Armando's father was reluctant to accept that his thirty-one-year-old son was gay and engaged to be married to another man. When the couple first visited the father at his house with other family members present, the father sequestered himself inside while everyone else mingled outside. After Armando's mother finally persuaded her husband to come out to greet their son and to meet Kenny for the first time, he was extremely reserved and curt, spending less than a minute outside. Despite his reticence, he did shake Kenny's hand and, more importantly, he quickly made eye contact with Armando and then Kenny as he said, "esta es tu casa" (this is your home) before turning to go back inside. These four simple yet symbolic words conveyed the father's willingness to connect his son and his fiancé to a meaningful homeplace that he claimed and shared with his family.

While each of the dimensions Somerville outlines are relevant to framing home as a type of place, the shelter, privacy, roots, and abode dimensions are most clearly connected to home as a tangible place. The privacy dimension alludes to a home having a sort of territoriality associated with it that grants the person occupying the home the right to determine who gets to enter, stay, or leave. We can extend the notion of privacy to the land directly connected to the home.

In a cultural context, the Western view of land and home contrasts sharply with the Indigenous conception of land and home because the former recognizes the value of property rights.[14] Over the years we've also been exposed to the property theme through gendered references to the home, such as "a man's castle," or "a woman's place." References like these remind us that home is often a negotiated place that includes people coming to terms with a form of place-based we-ness that involves individuals abiding by gendered and social class norms. Homeplace can produce profound displays of competitive jockeying by the involved parties who are eager to stake their claim to how the place should be conceived and maintained. They can assert these claims while they live there as well as when one or more of the parties leaves the location.

John Brinckerhoff Jackson, the renowned pioneer in landscape studies, offers a relevant observation about households with potential implications for domestic negotiations. He refers to the "vernacular concept of a space" when distinguishing between the typical working-class and middle-class home.[15] Jackson suggests that compared to the middle-class home, the spaces in working-class homes are less likely to have a singular function or "inherent identity." In other words, occupants are more likely to share space and engage in a wide range of activities in the various rooms. Consequently, residents define rooms based on what activities occur there. Presumably, this type of dynamic functionality results in more opportunities for family members to challenge each other on how they use spaces and seek to define domestic places. In addition, the working-class house is perceived to offer a less formal and more fluid approach toward incorporating hospitality. As Jackson notes, vernacular space represents "a common ground, a common place, a common denominator which makes each vernacular neighborhood a miniature common-wealth."[16] In this context, familiar nonresidents are likely to have greater access to another person's dwelling space and are able to enter and navigate the space more freely. This image of the working-class homeplace situates it more squarely as part of a communal neighborhood. Presumably, participants in these settings are more likely to develop a place-based type of we-ness that reinforces their mutual commitments to one another as neighbors and friends who are prepared to share.

Although the home dimension labeled "roots" elicits an image of a person having a sense of belonging anchored to a physical homeplace, we can extend this idea to capture how a person sees their home as an opportunity to express a gendered identity. One scholar who studies the home as a gendered environment suggests that "in contemporary consumer culture, the home is presented as an important site of self-expression for both women and men. The 'feminine' worlds of fashion, beauty and the home are being opened up to men, acquiring new centrality and changing status within the culture."[17] Based on fieldwork in Spanish and British households, Sara Pink's *Home Truths: Gender, Domestic Objects and Everyday Life* illustrates the gendered and performative aspects of home decoration and what she calls, "home creativity" – a multisensory activity with long-lasting effects that cover the "embodied experiences and production of sound, smell and texture in the home."[18] How individuals decorate and manage the home can be viewed as part of a symbolic narrative that is designed to express feminine and masculine self-identities. In addition, Stephen Vider's *The Queerness of Home: Gender, Sexuality, and the Politics of Domesticity after World War II* provides a historical account of how proponents of lesbian feminist architecture, beginning in the early 1970s, began to reimagine domestic living spaces to make them more consistent with their political values and their openness to separatist communities.[19] These types of home-based initiatives represent a form of domestic placemaking that I explore further in Chapter 7.

Focusing on the abode dimension, we realize the physical and social setting where we sleep is a significant place that typically affects us directly and continuously. This place also represents somewhere for us to interact with family, fulfill our daily rituals, and take care of our basic hygiene needs. The fortunate see this place as their haven and respite from the hectic world. They hold this place near and dear to their hearts. In contrast, the less fortunate often experience the homeplace as stressful. They are swamped with demanding responsibilities or are forced to deal with physical, emotional, and psychological abuse from those in their immediate orbit. In their eyes, they're trapped by their circumstances and see this homeplace as a living hell. Consequently, they feel like they have little shared or personal control over their life choices at home. Technically, they may be free to leave, but they see no viable option to relocate. In their mind, staying and enduring their suffering is their only practical alternative, other than resorting to an extreme reaction – murder or suicide.[20] Unfortunately, these are too often the experiences that plague youth who are part of the LGBTQ+ community and have parents or other resident family members who stigmatize and mistreat them because of their sexual and gender identities. They live in a house that is not a home.[21]

Andrew Ross, a professor of social and cultural analysis at New York University, sharpens how we think about housing both as a place and a national crisis. In *Sunbelt Blues: The Failure of American Housing*, Ross takes us into the intimate spaces that make up the infamous fifteen-mile Route 192 corridor in Osceola, Florida, located just south of Disney.[22] In addition to offering a critique of the larger system that has created and perpetuated our housing crisis, his observations and interviews with "moteliers" are telling. Moteliers' backstories vary, but they typically involve taking refuge in motels for extended periods of time (sometimes years) because they can't afford to sign a rental contract or buy a home. As a result, they find themselves compromising to keep a roof over their heads, and in many instances, their children's heads as well. With no good options, some choose to perceive their motel room as their home; others reluctantly see themselves as temporarily homeless. Government agencies also play an official role in defining different types of moteliers as homeless. The federal government explicitly labels children living in these conditions as homeless. But the formal definitions for adults are less rigid. Thus, adults are less likely to be defined as officially homeless. Ultimately, how individuals define themselves will affect their self-esteem and their perceptions of both the motel and the room they occupy. Because many moteliers frequently switch hotels or rooms in the same hotel, it further complicates attempts to understand their orientation toward their living quarters. For those dealing with difficult circumstances by living in motels or out on the streets, many may experience a sense of placelessness.

As restrictive as some homeplaces may feel to those living under such dire conditions, some places where people sleep have even tighter restrictions. This becomes apparent when we distinguish between the institutional and noninstitutional dwellings that shelter us while we sleep and carry out other practical tasks. Prisons and concentration camps, what sociologists refer to as total institutions (because the staff control all aspects of people's lives), offer a place for people to sleep and eat, but those who live there are confined against their wishes. This distinction illustrates that some homeplaces have voluntary occupants and others are populated with people who have no say in the matter. The same discrepancy is evident in how people experience retirement homes, psychiatric facilities, and refugee camps; some are there voluntarily and others against their will.

Unfortunately, social scientists have spent little time exploring the social circumstances related to sleeping, inside or outside of a home environment.[23] There's much talk these days about food insecurity but little discussion about "sleep insecurity." Ideally, when we prepare ourselves to go to sleep, we want to feel safe and secure. Unless we are situated in a physically dangerous place like a concentration camp, prison, war zone, or a home with an abuser who is a threat to us, we typically feel at ease to drift into our vulnerable, unconscious sleep state. Yet, LGBTQ+ youth who are stigmatized by members of their resident family may still feel uneasy about going to sleep even though they do not necessarily fear being physically attacked in their house. Their trauma often reflects their anxiety and fear over being emotionally, not physically, abused. Still, many homeless LGBTQ+ youth report being physically abused while living with their families.[24] Most of us take for granted the place circumstances that enable us to transition from being wide-awake to entering our sleep state. But when we mistrust our surroundings and the people in them, our insecurities are accentuated. This should come as no surprise because we are at our most vulnerable when we are asleep.

I'm reminded of my own encounter with sleep insecurity in late August 1990 when a mass murderer terrorized the University of Florida and the Gainesville community, killing five students over a three-day period. It immediately became national news and a topic of class discussions. The events also left me, and most everyone else in the city, feeling vulnerable and threatened. I no longer perceived my condo as a safe place to sleep. I went so far as to arrange obstacles as noise "alarms" on the stairs that lead to the only pathway to my upstairs bedroom. I also positioned my largest kitchen knife next to my bed for weeks. This experience gave me a glimpse of what many people living in the most crime-laden communities must feel when they turn out the lights each night for bed.

The noninstitutional places are those we are more likely to think of as a conventional home. The home setting marks the private sphere of our lives and is distinct from the public places where we invest much of our time away from home. Oddly, distinctions between the private homeplace and a more public housing unit can get quite messy. Before their passing, my parents lived in a small brick home for roughly forty-eight years and then moved together into an assisted living facility ten miles away. They considered the home that they purchased to be their real home where they raised their two kids. However, they eventually resigned themselves to accept that their new facility and the individual unit comprised of several rooms that provided them with their private space was their new, less intimate, "home." They felt more confined and monitored, but their long-term marriage reinforced their shared sense of we-ness as a couple. This allowed them to expand their symbolic definition of home to include the assisted living unit. To be clear, because my father was suffering from vascular dementia, he most likely considered home to be whatever dwelling allowed my mother to be by his side, yet their shared place-based experiences over many years most likely cemented his emotional connection to his wife.

The previous examples have at least one thing in common: they refer to a sleeping environment that has some sort of structure with a roof, floor, and walls. Collectively, we can think of them as a type of dwelling. But what about the homeless who are living on the street or in the woods? They too must find a place to sleep, sometimes alone, other times with family, friends, or strangers nearby. These places range from the very private (a secluded spot deep in the woods) to the very public (a park bench in the middle of a busy city). While some homeless people stick to a regular site for an extended timeframe, others move from place to place, experiencing a form of roaming placelessness. Presumably, spending more consecutive overnights in the same spot can prompt a homeless person to develop an attachment to the place and, in a provisional sense, see it as home.

Communications professor David Purnell shares a keen insider's perspective on what it was like for him to be homeless three times in different urban settings. His intimate storytelling reveals that his interactions with other homeless people represented one of the key strategies for his "accomplishing place" or creating "homelike places within public spaces."[25] One of Purnell's periods of homelessness landed him in a city park where he learned powerful life lessons through his primarily nonverbal, but also verbal, interactions with other homeless people. He notes that "Together, our community, built purely upon trust, engaged in place-work." Purnell clarifies how this place-work helped to "transform public park benches and patches of grass into private beds, thus fulfilling our desire for a homelike place." His connections with the other homeless individuals emerged organically at first and were then reinforced through repetition:

> The group trip to and from the soup kitchen soon became a daily routine, and I could always count on a round of Checkers with my new companion after our communal meal ... I had a home, one that was complete with a bed (bench), food and "family." Without interaction, however, none of this would have been possible.

Purnell's ability to create a place for himself in the park environment depended on him developing an informal semblance of we-ness with the others who co-existed with him in this public place.

Although Purnell, a single man, had it tough during his homeless stints, sharing the homeless experience with other family members, especially vulnerable small children, can further complicate a homeless person's life experience. The Pulitzer Prize–winning *New York Times* investigative journalist Andrea Elliott brilliantly brings to life the myriad obstacles and intense frustrations that poor urban families confront when they navigate home insecurity. In *Invisible Child: Poverty, Survival, and Hope in an American City*, Elliott showcases her eight years of immersive reporting in New York City on a young girl, Desani, who was twelve years old when they meet in 2012, and her blended family that includes two married parents and a set of eight siblings.[26] As she achieves insider status, Elliott's rendering of this family's heart-wrenching story illustrates each of the *CART* processes of claims, attachments, rituals, and transitions without naming them. All these processes are intertwined with this poor family's vital and continuous struggle to secure a stable homeplace. While Desani and her family realize that the essence of a home is much more than a place, the transitions into and out of numerous physical living arrangements deeply affect the family.

Another example of the homeless family dynamic was captured brilliantly on the big screen by Will Smith and his son Jaden in the 2006 movie *The Pursuit of Happyness*. The Smiths effectively portrayed the perils that happened in real life to Chris Gardner, an unemployed salesman who eventually became a stockbroker and millionaire. Gardner was a homeless father who struggled to protect and nurture his son as the pair struggled to make it on the San Francisco streets for nearly a year before the father's professional success. Impressively, whether they were spending nights in a BART train station restroom, a homeless shelter, or occasionally a hotel room, the father and son sustained their precious familial bond as they did innovative place-work along their journey.

While Gardner exhibited tremendous resolve and creativity in altering his family circumstances, most homeless families do not produce a Hollywood ending. Still, many homeless people exhibit resilience while surviving without a typical residential arrangement. I'm reminded of two homeless men (Jensen, aged 22, and Austin, aged 32) whom I interviewed for a study focused on fathering and family health. These men, who affectionately referred to themselves as "brothers" despite having no family tie, shared a tent on and off for over a year at a site called "tent city," relatively near the downtown area of Gainesville, Florida. They impressed me with how they managed their personal lives despite moving in and out of dwellings, ultimately living in tent city by the time they talked to me. Their shared troubles as homeless fathers helped them to bond as they dealt with their difficult circumstances. Jensen had two closely spaced infant children with a woman during his homeless period and Austin had three kids of his own. While Jensen's partner spent several months with him in the tent city during her pregnancies, she found other accommodations when it came time to give birth and take care of her daughter and son. Because they were homeless, Jensen and his partner initially placed their daughter into foster care; she was then sent to live with the mother's second cousin out of state. With the second pregnancy, Jensen was proactive and arranged for his partner to move into a local shelter a week before the baby was due. They took a bus to the hospital for the birth. After several days, the mother and child returned to the shelter where Jensen would go to hold his son outside the building because the shelter policy did not allow him to go inside.

All things considered, Jensen and Austin were in pretty good spirits despite living in a tent away from their children. They were frustrated though that they didn't have a suitable homeplace to be hands-on dads. Austin emphatically asserted that he had never taken his son to the tent city because it is "dirty" and he felt inclined to "keep a knife on you ... cus you got a lot of homeless people out there." Jensen and Austin were both frustrated with the shelter's policy of not permitting fathers to stay with their partners and children unless the father is listed on the birth certificate. This policy illustrates how place-based stakeholders can institute regulations that influence how homeplaces are perceived and used.

Communities and Beyond

For the homeless, the distinction between home and community may be a bit muddled. By not having a specific and stable dwelling to call home, the most transitory homeless individuals may lean toward identifying with a larger, loosely bounded place like a community or region. The homeless, as well as others, can use these nondwelling versions of places to frame their sense of place as it relates to notions of having a home. This type of awareness can still enable people to grasp how they fit into the larger ecological context that includes their physical, social, and cultural surroundings. Whether a person is homeless or not, they can juggle different levels of place awareness and place attachment and be affected by them all.

Many Americans, especially those who spend years and years in the same location, have some sense of place and attachment related to their town or city. In *Chasing We-ness*, I described in detail how my sense of we-ness and place were shaped by growing up in Jeannette, Pennsylvania, a small, working-class town twenty-six miles east of Pittsburgh. That place, defined by its ethnically mixed population of working-class laborers and sports enthusiasts, is symbolic of other communities across the country that are uniquely defined by features of the local economy, attributes of the residents, and signature historical and weather events. Jeannette's character emerged over decades of ethnic immigration and business development, most notably glass production, beginning in the late 1800s. Like many other cities in the rust belt, Jeannette experienced dramatic economic, cultural, and population decline that started during the last quarter of the twentieth century. That decline also began to erode the town's place-based, spirited sense of we-ness.

Unlike the organic development that put Jeannette on the map and in the hearts of the locals, a fundamentally different and planned approach created the "town" of Celebration, Florida, in 1994. The town (technically a subdivision of the city of Kissimmee) was supposedly built in honor of Walt Disney, who had sketched plans for his dream city that would complement Orlando's famed Walt Disney World. Established in Disney's backyard, Celebration (often referred to as "The Bubble") is a meticulously designed community with a nine-page laundry list of strict rules for homeowners.[27] In the early days, Celebration attracted residents by using a marketing message that promised occupants a safe, tidy, close-knit community ambience as well as a location near Disney. One of the story lines Disney's publicity professionals developed for their marketing package tried to create a nostalgic sense of communal heritage:

> There once was a place where neighbors greeted neighbors in the quiet of summer twilight. Where children chased fireflies. And porch swings provided refuge from the cares of the day. The movie house showed cartoons on Saturday and there was one teacher who always knew you and had a special something that they thought you'd have. Remember that place? Perhaps from your childhood or maybe just from stories. It held a magic all its own. The special magic of an American hometown.[28]

The Bubble: A Documentary Film about Celebration, Florida, produced in 2013, highlights key cultural aspects of this community of roughly nine thousand. It also profiles numerous residents, allowing us to hear their voices as they describe what the community means to them. Most residents value the small-town spirit that has been preserved over the years. Many have moved to the city and stayed there as a result. But Celebration also provides an excellent example of how a place can be assigned different meanings depending on whether we consider the insider or outsider perspective. One of my student research assistants for this book, a Floridian who spent time visiting Celebration during her youth, put this community on my radar. Her view, like that of others who lived outside "The Bubble," was that the place was overly restrictive and eerily like the town depicted in the 1998 movie *The Truman Show*, starring Jim Carrey. That perspective was also shared by some who lived there and left.[29] However, other young people who had been raised in Celebration were quick to point out that they enjoyed growing up there.

A more working-class type of planned residential environment is facilitated by what human development professors Sonya Salamon and Katherine MacTavish label the "mobile home industrial complex." This system is aided by the "manufacturers, the home financers, trailer-park owners and operators, and the municipalities where the parks are located." In *Singlewide: Chasing the American Dream in a Rural Trailer Park*, Salamon and MacTavish draw on their three case studies of mobile home parks in Illinois, New Mexico, and North

Carolina to explore the social ecology of these arrangements.[30] They reveal how the insider and outsider perspectives affect mobile home residents' experiences in the park and larger community. Many living outside the park stigmatize it and the individuals who live there; many who live inside the park are aware of these negative perceptions but do not necessarily share the sentiments. In addition, the researchers challenge the motto "We Build Communities," often touted by that industry:

> A community, it is clear, is more than a grouping of homes, even if the homes are clustered close together. As underlined by the trailer-park case studies, those who live in a place because they are landless and where they lack basic rights or input to park governance find that disenfranchisement in particular undermines engagement with neighbors or attachment to place. A place to live, not a community, is what trailer-park developers actually build or manage. The lack of a sense of community may to a certain extent account for the behavior of a small group of residents in each site that helps bolster the trailer-trash stereotype for all housed in these land-lease parks.[31]

Although trailer park residents are far less likely to develop a sense of community than residents who live in places like Celebration, residents in both places are aware of the outsider gaze that casts aspersions on them. Whereas Celebration residents probably perceive the stigma as a sign of outsiders' misguided resentment, many trailer park residents assume that outsiders are snobby and ill-informed.

Public perceptions can also shape the images of the communes and small intentional communities that have emerged organically in the United States and elsewhere around the world. According to the Foundation for Intentional Community (FIC), these arrangements are defined as "a group of people who have chosen to live together or share resources on the basis of common values."[32] In the US, the 1960s and 1970s is typically seen as the most visibly distinct time period in which people experimented with different forms of communal living. Although precise estimates are impossible to produce, some who have studied the scene suggest that there were between two and three thousand communes during this time. According to the FIC, the most recent documented estimate is roughly 1,200 as of 2016. Historically, the stereotypical public perceptions of these diverse community living arrangements have been that people who participated were at least unconventional, and in some instances, were assumed to be involved in multiple-partner sexual relationships and doing lots of drugs.[33] Although intentional communities are still poorly understood by many, and viewed as a form of fringe living by some, people today are probably more likely to perceive them as being closer to the mainstream than before.

One expert, Yvonne Daley, author of *Going Up the Country: When the Hippies, Dreamers, Freaks, and Radicals Moved to Vermont*, shared her insights about the intentional community movement over the past sixty years in a 2021 interview with *Forbes Magazine* editor Russell Flannery. Commenting on the 1960s and 1970s, Daley indicates that:

> Although American communards worked to raise food, shared parenting and household tasks, shared financial responsibility and upkeep, the rules and organization were often lax, leading many to fail simply because there was no governing body, not enough discipline or consequence when someone did not do their part. Also, for some, drugs and sex were more important than work.[34]

She adds, however, that in contemporary times, "older people of all sorts are moving into intentional communities all over the country for shared responsibility, companionship, and entertainment under the general rubric of co-housing." According to Daley, there are roughly two hundred co-housing arrangements in the country that are "a more independent and formalized form of communal living." A few notable examples of established places in the US include the EcoVillage Ithaca in New York and the Living Tree Alliance in Vermont.[35] Both of these communities have well-established guidelines for how members are expected to contribute to and be involved with the community. In addition, an analysis of the placemaking activities associated with the recently launched Hitzacker/Dorf intentional community in Germany offers insights about what happens behind the scenes in the early stages of creating one of these communities.[36]

Whether we call intentional communities communes, cohousing, ecovillages, coliving, or student co-ops, they each represent a unique system that brings people together to be part of a community in a shared place. Members can include either the people who initiated the project or those who joined the community after it was established. In the final chapter, I describe Damanhur, a unique and dynamic intentional community in the Italian Alps that emerged more than forty years ago and continues to thrive today, with some of the original members still participating.

The preceding examples represent just a few of the many ways the public face of communities is portrayed and internalized. Some additional standard portraits include the big urban city, inner-city project, midwestern farm town, small fishing community, liberal arts college town, middle-class suburb, wealthy resort community, blue-collar factory town, and small Southern rural town. While each of these places is distinguished by its own objective features, how we subjectively see and experience these places is also filtered through the perspectives we use to engage with the world. These standpoints are often related to our gender, race, ethnicity, social class, and sexual orientation. In addition, our experience with the diverse types of community environments is shaped by the discourses structuring what is expected of us because others perceive us to be certain types of people frequenting or living in these places. We can see this clearly in Leslie Kern's personalized, feminist analysis of women's gendered experiences, including her own, in urban settings. She highlights how geography and culture jointly affect the "maps of danger" associated with women's fear of being subjected to violence by men. In Kern's words, a "geographic logic" asserts itself because "we [women] have very little control over the presence of men in our environments, and can't function in a state of constant fright, we displace some of our fear onto spaces: city streets, alleyways, subway platforms, darkened sidewalks."[37] Thus women "figure out which *places* to avoid, rather than which people."[38] She adds that the "personal mental maps of safety and fear" are "externalized onto the urban environment, into parks and laneways and parking garages."[39] Women's perceptions of these places and level of fear can change quickly in response to new events and circumstances. Compared to men, women are more fearful of violence in urban areas, as well as in the world more generally, but many men are also concerned about male-perpetrated violence in the urban environment and inner city.

In addition to our connections to the towns, cities, and trailer parks that give us our opportunities to experience everyday living in a reasonably well-delineated place, some of us also see ourselves as having an affinity for a more abstract region of the country. Until I moved to Florida after living my first three decades in Pennsylvania and Ohio, I had never really thought of myself as a Northerner, but now I do despite my living in a Southern state for an equivalent amount of time. The further I travel away from the university setting to the small rural towns outside of Gainesville, the more I think of my Northern roots and life perspective.

This imagined reality has become a more prominent aspect to my sense of place over time. In the United States, we've seen politicized regionalism intensify in recent years as politicians, news journalists, and media pundits repeatedly stoke the flames of division by referring to culture wars between blue and red states, urban and rural areas, and big coastal cities and smaller interior ones. We can grasp the essence of those divisions and their connection to place by contemplating Danny Zimny-Schmitt's recent story about traveling to all 3,143 counties in the United States, highlighting his progress on a map delineating every county.[40] A geographer and self-proclaimed "political nerd," Zimny-Schmitt embarked on this extraordinary journey during the COVID-19 pandemic to "read" and experience the landscapes of America. He was partly inspired by the hobbyist group the Extra Miler Club,[41] whose members seek to visit every county in the United States while sometimes also pursuing other travel goals (visiting every national park, driving on every interstate highway). Zimny-Schmitt was also looking for answers to help explain how we had become such a politically polarized nation.

Throughout his travels Zimny-Schmitt experienced countless settings populated with all types of people. As expected, these settings were embedded in diverse places steeped in distinct regional characteristics. Much of his extensive traveling took him through rural country and "small-town America," providing him with plenty of time and imagery for reflection. Notably, for him, seeing place markings like a state highway sign proclaiming "Life – Gun – Trump" or a framed quotation in a coffee shop, "All I need today is a little bit of coffee and a whole lot of Jesus," were reminders that the pervasive "Christian soul of America could not be ignored," especially in certain regions of the country. His recounting of his road trip illustrates the dramatic effect of ideology and symbolism on the mix of people, places, and belonging. To his credit, Zimny-Schmitt notes that, "With every thousand miles I drove, I found myself inclined to try to understand why these places were so different and less inclined to cast sweeping moral judgments." In other words, experiencing more diverse places and people with an open mind can inspire us to better understand others' place-based life perspectives and appreciate our shared humanity.

Part of the social tension Zimny-Schmitt felt traveling through different regions of the country is rooted in our contentious history. For many, many years we've wrestled with the fallout from the Civil War discourse that continues to differentiate Northern and Southern states by contrasting their signature lifestyles, beliefs, and rituals. We vary considerably in how frequently and fervently we use these regional place markers to define who we are, how we situate ourselves in everyday social exchanges, or when we participate in activist or entertainment events. The heated debates about removing symbols of the Confederacy, most notably the Confederate flag and war monuments, have showcased how many Southerners continue to embrace their regional identities and the values that the South historically represented. Likewise, as I'll explore in Chapter 4, Civil War reenactments showcase how rituals can symbolically highlight the significance of this sort of regional identity.

One additional layer of complexity can be added to the notion of a regional place having its own unique features. We can explore the long-standing web of relations that connects regional traits, rural life, and poverty. In their 2023 book, *The Injustice of Place: Uncovering the Legacy of Poverty in America*, three renowned scholars of poverty, Kathryn Edin, H. Luke Shaefer, and Timothy Nelson, collaborate on a remarkably revealing study of rural poverty in Appalachia, the Cotton and Tobacco Belts of the Deep South, and South Texas. Their analysis reveals the powerful mix of economic, historical, political, and racial forces that cemented the contemporary style of entrenched poverty that plagues the small rural communities in these regions of the country. Examining the particulars of the systemic inequalities that have defined these areas for centuries is beyond the scope of our discussion. However, we can enhance our understanding of the significance of place by reflecting on their summary based on their observational field work, in-depth interviews, and quantitative analyses:

> Each of the communities we examined for this book suffer not only from a legacy of grossly underfunded and often racially segregated schools, violence, and a collapse of the local social infrastructure but also from weak and often corrupt local government. In this way, America's internal colonies are similar to former colonies established by foreign nations around the world.[42]

Today, those who orchestrate the corruption and social division these researchers revealed are not inventing something new; rather, these patterns are rooted in the exploitative social systems that can be traced to the colonial period. Over time, these social patterns have reinforced stark pockets of inequalities that produce selective perceptions of ideational we-ness. Consequently, these divisions not only perpetuate in-group and out-group dynamics that solidify the disparate everyday realities of the haves and the have-nots, they also harden the objective and perceived realities of the places where persons from different social classes live.

An intriguing step beyond a regional place identity involves the connections we feel toward the cultural markers and geographical borders that define our nation. In the past decade, the rise in nationalism around the world, including the populist trends associated with the MAGA (Make America Great Again) movement in the United States, has been notable. This sort of ideology has weaponized feelings of we-ness to stigmatize immigrants and others who do not fit a certain demographic profile. MAGA enthusiasts' sense of we-ness is emboldened by their propensity to identify a common "enemy" that they believe threatens their feelings of entitlement, land claims, and insular definition of country.[43]

Russia's unprovoked war with Ukraine forcefully and dramatically illustrates the potential consequences of fervent nationalism. This war also reveals that place matters because social life happens –

both the good and the bad – in place. In war, and in more peaceful times, our physically embodied experiences occur in place and shape how we see ourselves, live our lives, interact with our communities, and assert our claims over places meaningful to us.

Beginning in late February 2022, and as I write these words in the summer of 2024, graphic videos, photos, and firsthand accounts of the massive destruction of Ukrainian homes, apartment buildings, schools, hospitals, pharmacies, community centers, churches, and more have dominated media coverage. Just days before the war, Ukrainians and others living there had pursued the rituals and routines of their daily lives. They had done so in the built environments that were now under attack; the ones that comprised their beloved communities. Now, those buildings, and the social worlds that breathed life into them, have been quickly and indiscriminately demolished before their very eyes. The world was shocked as it witnessed the transformation of millions of survivors into refugees seemingly overnight. Innocent Ukrainians, overwhelmed by death, personal hardship, and physical destruction were displaced from their homes, communities, and country. Yet, remarkably, their hearts were filled with a spirit of we-ness rooted in their inspirational love for country and community. Millions of brave and angry civilians, young and old, all genders, rich and poor, collectively employed creative and sometimes lethal ways to resist. They did so because the meaning of place for them framed their core sense of identity and community. To punctuate this pattern of loyalty, thousands of Ukrainians returned from foreign lands to fight for their native country.

The global audience of Putin's war, especially the Western world, scrutinized the contrasting human energies that generated extreme brutality and courage – dual expressions both ingrained in place-based identities. Putin and many of his followers wanted to reclaim some version of the old Soviet Union while most Ukrainians longed for their separate, national identity. Most onlookers grew to see how much place, and the perceptions of it, can make a difference in people's lives and is involved in the geopolitical calculations that determine the fate of entire populations. In a resounding display of solidarity with Ukraine, the Western world rallied in support of the Ukrainian people's right to defend their national borders and all the unique places that make it home to forty-three million people.

The outpouring of goodwill and resources was partly triggered by the world's respect for President Volodymyr Zelenskyy's leadership and the Ukrainians' unflinching will to fight and die for their land and freedom. Outsiders marveled at the passionate military and civilian response from people of all backgrounds. The Ukrainians' stand for freedom sent an unwavering message to the world that place matters and that its vitality is rooted in our ideational we-ness and deep dyadic bonds with family, friends, neighbors, and fellow soldiers.

Public Space

Local politicians, urban planners, architects, and business leaders are among the many community stakeholders who are ideally positioned to alter the physical and social landscapes of their communities. Of interest to us are their decisions to allocate, fund, and design what experts in urban development and community planning call "public space." Placemaking strategies to modify public space include both standard and incremental changes to a location as well as more transformative or "specialized" initiatives that are much larger in scale.[44] In Chapter 7, I'll elaborate on the objectives of different placemaking strategies that target communities. For now, let me emphasize why it is important to classify public spaces as a distinct type of place that is relevant to the promotion of group belonging and we-ness.

Public space can be defined broadly as all physical sites that are accessible to the public. Some are open (streets, parks, courtyards, beaches, public squares) and others are enclosed (museums, libraries, ethnic heritage sites). Today, community leaders and others who benefit from public space owe much to the innovative writing and research of twentieth-century trailblazers like Jane Jacobs and William H. Whyte. Jacobs, a journalist, published *The Death and Life of Great American Cities* in 1961 to challenge city planners to rethink the urban crises they were igniting due to misguided planning principles. Meanwhile, Whyte's impressive *Street Life Project*, which came later in the 1970s and 1980s, heightened our sensitivity to the many features of public spaces that affect pedestrian behavior and social life in cities. For more than sixteen years, the sociologist Whyte and his research team walked New York City's streets taking notes and pictures as well as talking to people. His observations and interviews captured what people thought, felt, and how they navigated their physical surroundings. As he concludes, "If there's a lesson in streetwatching it is that people do like basics – and as environments go, a street that is open to the sky and filled with people and life is a splendid place to be."[45] He advocated for public spaces to be designed in a grassroots fashion. We need to know how people want to use spaces and how they use them. Most importantly, Whyte wanted city planners to create dynamic physical settings that encourage people to engage with their physical and social environments. Doing so, he believed, would enhance our personal well-being and civic engagement.

Thus, community leaders can make value-based decisions about local land use and architectural design consistent with a style of placemaking that encourages a vibrant social life. Quality places reflect stakeholders' motivations to create and sustain places that offer people the best options to enhance their well-being and develop a healthy sense of we-ness. These local decisions can supplement the macro and historical initiatives created at the federal and state level, for example, the securing of land for parks and monuments in the 1800s and 1900s.

When public space is developed in the spirit of Whyte's call for action, people will be inspired to spend time in certain places and even enjoy their journey to get there. As the Project for Public Spaces' practical guide for placemaking asserts, to be successful, "cities need destinations."[46] And not just any destination will do. Cities "need destinations that give an identity and image to their communities, and that help attract new residents, businesses, and investment. But they also need strong community destinations that attract people." Moreover, these destinations need to have multiple places directly linked to them at that location. Creating places that encourage strangers as well as friends and family to interact is vital. Here again we see evidence of the perspective that promotes the critical connection between people, places, and a sense of belonging. These destinations can reinforce ideational forms of we-ness, celebrate deep dyadic we-ness, and create pleasant opportunities for people to experience spontaneous we-ness. Places like Bryant Park in New York City, The Bean in Chicago's Millennium Park, Boston's adult playground on D Street, and Los Angeles's Mojo Robot in San Pedro are several examples of placemaking projects that have enhanced the level and type of interaction in American cities.[47]

Sites for Exchanging Goods and Services

As expected, one consequence of living in a highly industrialized country where capitalism dominates is that many of the places that occupy our time and energy involve financial exchanges for goods and services. To varying degrees, we spend time at commercial and retail sites buying a variety of products, we have our vehicles serviced, we seek out therapy and bodywork, we pay for place-based entertainment associated with restaurants and in-person concerts, and much, much more. Sometimes we exchange goods and services in public space venues that have been created by city planners. For example, if we shop at a farmer's market or buy arts and crafts at a festival, the space for those events has often been produced by placemaking efforts to cultivate public space. Other exchange sites, however, are linked to private business ventures that try to create enticing places for people to visit.

One intriguing place that has received a fair amount of attention is the Black barbershop.[48] Much urban folklore is associated with this culturally rich and symbolically valued type of third place. Perceived as a safe haven, the barbershop enables Black boys and men to express themselves freely beyond the surveillance of white society. Those who visit can participate in rituals and routines that celebrate their ideational we-ness as "brothers." They establish dyadic forms of we-ness with each other and the barbers whom they often see as trusted friends, mentors, or wise men of the street. Sometimes they even benefit from experiencing a form of spontaneous we-ness with strangers to whom they relate because of their similar experience that is a byproduct of their shared race and gender.

Older folks, irrespective of race or gender, who reminisce nostalgically about a bygone era recall their exchanges with owners of local family businesses that catered to their needs. Over the years, they've created fond memories of the intimate exchanges they had with small business owners whom they came to see as part of their informal, extended family. Many cherish the idea of going to a place where the people who wait on patrons are their friends and neighbors. These types of establishments often resemble third places, and TV show producers have cashed in on the power of this image. Think of the iconic television shows in the last half century: *Happy Days* (1974–84), which showcased a 1950s Wisconsin-based Arnold's/Al's drive-in diner; the sitcom *Cheers* (1982–93), which was largely set in a neighborhood Boston bar of the same name; the New York coffee shop in *Seinfeld* (1989–98) where the main cast of characters were often found engaged in comedic repartee; and the six Gen X friends who at times navigated their romantic and career issues at a local coffe shop in *Friends* (1994–2004). These shows, with many scenes set in a business venue, portrayed characters celebrating their interpersonal bonds as they hung out in places that they deemed to be special. Plenty of other TV shows highlight the good-natured bantering, friction, and bonding between coworkers that is largely confined to a designated setting like an office, hospital, police precinct, and the like (the US version of *The Office*, 2005–13; *Grey's Anatomy*, 2005–present; *Suits*, 2011–19; and *Brooklyn 99*, 2013–21).

Even our homes can provide opportunities for monetary exchanges that are linked to a sense of we-ness. This is especially true for those who own their homes and have developed a sense of we-ness with others who either live in the house or visit and with whom they have business or service transactions. While homeowning can enhance our opportunities for building wealth, place attachment, and sense of we-ness, the home is also a potentially intriguing place for economic exchanges such as home repairs, remodeling, and landscaping that raise questions about place-based sentiments. If we consider the insider and outsider perspectives to place, we can imagine how a homeowner and the professional they hire to work on their property could collaborate to accomplish a place-based goal. Some "old-school" professionals – those who glow with integrity and take much pride in their work – bring a unique spirit to their understanding of another person's place and property. They carry themselves differently than the workers who are merely out for a paycheck.

It has been my good fortune to have hired a few individuals who could be described as fitting this "old-school" mold. I feel that they respected my property in a way that convinced me to trust them to share my commitment to my place. These professionals respect my place attachment by expressing a willingness to honor and enhance my vision. In these instances, my vision becomes their vision. But, in some instances, our brainstorming leads to a jointly constructed vision about my property. For them, taking pride in their work has meant that they need to collaborate with me to achieve a shared appreciation of the goals for improving my home. As such, they're willing to go the extra mile to make things "right." While I retain my exclusive ownership of my place, the project is perceived to be ours, and our shared goal provides us with at least a temporary sense of we-ness.

Institutions

Few people go through life without encountering meaningful place-based experiences that are tied to one, or typically more than one, of the following institutional environments: education, health care, religion, government, military, and criminal justice in the form of courts and prisons. The places associated with these social environments develop a distinct image based on the various properties outlined in the previous chapter. Most often, social structural and institutional features distinguish similar places from one another. The groups and organizations that comprise these institutions vary in how they're structured. Some promote a top-down business model, whereas others advance a more collaborative, horizontal approach that emphasizes self-management patterns akin to what organizational consultant Frédéric Laloux labels "teal organizations."[49] Whatever the model, individuals with different responsibilities and levels of authority coordinate these places and determine how they operate. How we fit into this structured set of relationships will often affect our sense of place and feelings of attachment.

When we participate in these institutional settings, we sometimes have little or no choice in which places we'll attend. This is especially true for individuals who end up in the prison system. The forced choice associated with being sent to prison often has negative and long-lasting consequences for inmates. These circumstances are particularly heartbreaking for people who end up in prison for crimes they never committed. In 2021, *PBS NewsHour* profiled one such man, Ricky Kidd, who was wrongfully convicted of two murders and spent twenty-three years in the Missouri prison system.[50] Released in his mid-forties, Kidd has seemingly made remarkable progress in rebuilding his life. Within a span of two years since being released, he married, moved into a house, became a father, and started a business in which he advocates for prison reform. Yet, the prison structure and memories are etched into his embodied life in disconcerting ways. Though now free to live in his own house, he describes how he constantly struggles with anxiety and "horrible nightmares." In post-prison life, he is constantly challenged to manage his frustrations with having decades of freedom snatched from him while also adjusting to a new life on the outside. Those circumstances have led him to undertake an unusual type of placemaking. Kidd created a replica of his spartan prison cell in a small basement storm shelter in his house that he visits almost every morning. He's stocked the room with the exact items he had in prison including a cot, handcuffs, toilet, basket of mail, and his prison uniform and ID – 528343. Kidd, a diabetic, also attributes his precarious health condition, including his emergency triple-bypass heart surgery since being released, to subpar prison health care, unhealthy prison food, and the stress he experienced while being wrongfully imprisoned. Prison, as a place, has profoundly affected Kidd's life, whether inside or outside of its repressive walls.

Kidd is just one of millions of individuals who have been influenced by their time behind bars. Those who served prison time during the COVID-19 pandemic faced especially troubling times. The pandemic created numerous logistical headaches for prison administrators, forcing them to experiment with temporary placemaking strategies. They struggled to mitigate the spread of the highly contagious disease in facilities where prisoners and staff go about their daily activities in restricted, overcrowded conditions.

In the mid-1970s, long before COVID-19 wreaked havoc, overcrowding in the prison system emerged as a problem when the number of incarcerated prisoners began to rise dramatically, reaching its peak of 2.3 million in 2008.[51] Between 1980 and 2000, hundreds of prisons were hastily built in the United States to accommodate the five-fold increase in the prison population.[52] It was during this accelerated mass incarceration period that stakeholders in the "prison industrial complex" (politicians, prison administrators, builders, and manufacturers of prison products and materials) undertook placemaking efforts that fundamentally altered how prisons are structurally built and organized.

In his 2005 book, *The Warehouse Prison: Disposal of the New Dangerous Class*, John Irwin, a criminologist and expert on the American prison system, issued a sharp critique of what are commonly referred to as "warehouse" prisons. Irwin sketches a historical account of how prisons evolved in the United States, culminating in the "warehouse" and "supermax" prisons that were initially built in the early 1980s. He notes that "security, efficiency, and economy dominated the planning and construction of most new prisons."[53] Those in charge issued revised correctional policies and procedures that were reinforced by a new prison model that "incorporates housing units, known variably as 'cell blocks,' 'wings,' and 'buildings,' that hold about 200 prisoners."[54]

The new prisons, typically located in remote, rural areas, are designed to manage large numbers of prisoners effectively. The system seeks to achieve this objective "through its technologically sophisticated architectural design and an extensive, restrictive, and relatively rigidly enforced set of formal rules and procedures."[55] The routines that are established in places like Solano, a California prison Irwin observed firsthand, limit prisoners' chances for self-development related to their life skills and attitudes. Prisoners have fewer options to initiate groups or clubs on their own that are based on their common interests with other prisoners. Consequently, inside the warehouse prison system, prisoners are limited in their ability to develop forms of dyadic or ideational we-ness that could emerge as part of an organically formed group. In addition, prison administrators, intent on reducing violence in recent decades, have instituted routinized daily schedules that shuttle prisoners from place to place doing mundane tasks, and force prisoners to spend more time in solitary confinement.[56]

In addition to prison time, many forced choices are made for us by others. When we're kids or elderly, family members often make them for us. For example, parents decide if and where their children will go for religious services, schooling, and health care visits. Likewise, much older children coordinate nursing home care for their aging parents. Although the effects associated with spending time in these places are typically not as debilitating as spending time in prison, and may even prove to be beneficial to us, these places can still have long-lasting consequences for those who experience them directly.

Many times, however, we make conscious decisions about the kind of place we want to experience. Take for example a couple who is expecting a child that jointly decides they want to pursue a home birth rather than the more traditional hospital delivery. Imagine, too, partners who see things differently and are forced to make a compromised choice that only one of them truly likes.

Choice, or lack thereof, was at the center of how people struggled to manage their affairs related to place in the COVID-19 era. During the peak of the pandemic, place issues became especially pressing and disruptive in the health care and education sectors. Health care professionals were forced to redefine their work areas and navigate them in novel, more detached ways. Virtual visits using telehealth services rose sharply in some areas for COVID-19 and non-COVID-19 patients alike.[57]

Health care professionals, for good reason, need to be concerned about picking up infections in their work environment, but COVID-19 compelled them to be super vigilant. With staff dressed in protective gear resembling hazmat suits, hospital wings filled with COVID patients projected an even more chilling image than that of the typical hospital ward. Unfortunately, many health care workers experienced considerable anxiety because they did not have adequate access to personal protective equipment (PPE) and were forced to compromise their safety standards during the emergency circumstances.[58] The hands-on, nurturing style of caregiving done well was now transformed into a more distant version of care that was provided by persons cloaked in cold-looking, sterile outfits. If they were lucky, patients and staff saw each other's eyes but not much more. Hospital rooms and hallways were filled with uncertainty, caution, and fear. Everyone looked suspicious and was suspicious. Even coworkers were inclined to see each other in a new light as they worried that members of their staff could be a viral threat to them.

In addition, patients were largely left to struggle on their own because family and friends were excluded from comforting their loved ones in person. Even patients on their deathbeds were isolated from family and friends, often dying alone. Regrettably, those who were pregnant were sometimes forced to go through labor and delivery without even their partner present. Exhausted and burned-out staff made Herculean efforts to console patients, but these places that housed pandemic sickness and death took their toll on everyone involved. At the same time, they inspired us to expand our perception of hospitals and, most importantly, the people who worked there. In the early days of the pandemic, the public gained new respect for health care professionals because of the dire personal risks they were taking to provide loving, essential care for the sick. As a result, the symbolic meanings people associated with this place were shifting so that many outsiders saw persons working on the hospital front lines as heroes holding down the fort in a battle against an invisible virus. The nonphysician insiders, on the other hand, assumed that once the COVID crisis passed, their temporary hero status would disappear, and they would become invisible to the public again.[59]

Like health care settings, schools and classrooms were transformed into places outfitted with new mitigation materials, computer technologies, routines, protocols, and anxieties.[60] With masked teachers and students physically distancing, classrooms seemed less intimate and more spacious. The new arrangements reminded everyone that the emerging discourse applied to schools and classrooms was incorporating another deadly fear that went beyond the image of the notorious school shooter. Parents, me included, had to make difficult decisions about whether they should send their children to school given these new perceptions of this place. To accommodate my son during parts of his seventh- and eighth-grade school years, I converted my home study into our shared educational space. Transforming this place meant that I was no longer just a scholar in "my" study, but a dad who monitored his son's educational activities in a more place-based fashion in "our" study. That arrangement, as countless parents can attest, generated plenty of moments of shared tension as we managed our respective views of our shared power to define this dynamic place. For millions like me, homeplace became the new face for schooling. The properties of school as a place reappeared in the remote learning environments that emerged in homes. They also comingled with and altered the preexisting rituals and routines that had defined home settings and the social life therein.

For many families not as fortunate as my own, "home" schooling was either impossible or a monumental challenge because the homeplace for many children was a tent, shelter, motel, or other dwelling with limited or no internet access and numerous distractions. Imagine being a fifth grader trying to manage virtual classes for an entire school day, week, and month while you're crammed into a small, dimly lit, cluttered, and noisy motel room with a parent(s) and multiple siblings – including a rambunctious toddler. While undoubtedly difficult, this situation, sadly, doesn't even capture the most challenging circumstances many children faced as they tried to transition to remote learning with limited computer tech and significant place-based obstacles.

Throughout the pandemic, we were constantly adapting to the contingencies that surfaced in the many places that make up our institutional lives. Each change illustrated how we are embodied beings entrenched in place. The pandemic showed us that we could no longer take for granted how seemingly insignificant features of place matter to us individually and affect us as members of groups that enable us to feel a sense of belonging. We also witnessed anew how the stark inequalities in our social class system drastically affected families' placemaking capacities to compensate for declining institutional resources.

Key Landmarks and Ceremonial Settings

In the United States and around the world, there are countless places that the public celebrates as landmarks, including geological landscapes and sites that incorporate elements of a built environment. As of February 2022, the United States has officially identified 129 national landmarks commemorating such diverse places as the Booker T. Washington farm, Grand Canyon, Statue of Liberty, Navajo dwellings, and George Washington's birthplace. Some of the national monuments are intended to preserve our sense of history and love for our country.

Numerous monuments are dedicated to groups of people who have been subjected to genocide, slavery, and persecution. For example, twenty-seven are associated with Native Americans and nine focus on African-American history. In 2016, President Obama also added the Stonewall Inn to this list of national monuments. This famous gay bar in New York City symbolizes the 1969 uprising that occurred on the site when police violently clashed with members of the LGBTQ+ community.[61] This place represents a truth spot and is generally viewed as the turning point in the protracted fight for what evolved into the LGBTQ+ rights movement.

A plethora of physical sites, museums, statues, and memorials that do not carry the federal "national monument" designation also grab the public's attention. In many instances, they nudge us to think of how we are connected to others in the present as well as to the historical legacy that unites one generation to the next. They are designed to use the power of place to generate collective memories, inspiring our sense of we-ness and collective identities in many instances.[62] These places can also stir our affinity with all of humanity and perhaps the biosphere too.

One place that carries this deep, abstract meaning for me is the Holocaust Memorial Museum in Washington, DC. In November of 1997, I skipped out of an academic conference in DC early one afternoon to visit this museum with a professional colleague and dear friend, Steve Gavazzi. Since neither of us had ever visited, we both underestimated the effect this excursion would have on us. We had already spent hours together during the morning and previous day, engaged in good-natured bantering with a bit of beer drinking the night before. On this afternoon, our upbeat mood carried us all the way by taxi to the museum. But that mood came to a screeching halt once we stepped inside and began to witness and experience the exhibits. We were quickly and similarly ensnared by our despondent, reflective state of mind.

Most significant to me was walking through a fabricated German town of the late 1930s or early 1940s that portrayed Jewish civic life under the oppressive Nazi regime. The sights, sounds, and feel of the city streets were steeped in realism, enough to bring goose bumps to my arms and anxiety to my heart. Another display highlighted the stolen personal belongings of Jewish people whom the Nazis had imprisoned and killed. Tattered shoes, dirty combs, household keys, rusty necklaces, worn-out toothbrushes, nameless wallets, and much more were piled in a heap – symbols of lives cut short by a deadly sea of prejudice and hatred. A third exhibit played first-person recordings of concentration camp survivors sharing their heart-wrenching stories while Steve and I sat mesmerized on benches in a solemn room. I was left to wonder about the places and personalities that embodied the experiences of millions of Jewish people and others who were persecuted during World War II.

Each of these exhibits, and others like them, took me to a "place" and era that seemed distant, yet personally relevant. It mattered to me, in part, because my father was a former US Army sergeant who fought in the Battle of the Bulge and guarded Nazi prisoners during the Nuremberg Trials. The museum became a unique place for me because it reinforced my sense of we-ness with my father. It also resurrected a son's pride in his father's willingness, like that of so many others of his generation, to accept the daunting challenge of confronting Hitler and the Nazis in this pivotal war. Although my humble father was a man of few words, he had shared enough for me to realize that he had been on the ground in places that held incredible historical weight. And although we had no Jewish heritage, my father's parents immigrated to America from Italy in the early 1900s. My grandfather had preceded my father in battle, fighting against Germany as an American soldier and interpreter in World War I. In addition, my distant relatives on my mother's side had emigrated from Germany to America. Thus, I felt that my family tree had engaged with the places that were implicated in this infamous war.

While this museum had solidified my family's connection to this distant place of war and tragedy, it also deepened my friendship with Steve. Later that night, and on other occasions since, we talked about the dramatic effect being together in the museum that day had on us. Steve's training as a professional therapist added value to his account of how moved he was by what we had experienced that afternoon. For him, the museum visit was not only a reminder of the cruelty that humans could inflict on one another, but also a renewed appreciation for the hopefulness that can exist in even the darkest of times. Our place-based adventure unexpectedly forged another enduring layer of complexity to our dyadic we-ness. Prior to that afternoon, we had simply been fun-loving Italian social scientists with overlapping substantive interests who happened to be rabid Pittsburgh Steelers fans. Being together in that remarkable place enabled us to appreciate more fully our shared humanity and mutual concern for social justice issues. As a memorial, this place of remembrance and honor effectively let us feel the human forces of hatred and resiliency that permeated a distinct place and time. The effects of place mattered to us then and now.

Memorials and other landmarks of remembrance can enhance our sense of community, but they can also stir controversy and conflict as noted earlier. Places that perpetuate mixed messages can inspire deep-seated forces of we-ness that pull some people together while pushing others apart. Landmarks, because of their emotional significance for many, can be the place-based catalyst for healthy public debate and social change. We've seen this over the past several years as competing groups wage battle over what to do with Confederate monuments and symbols that represent cultural ideals and historical events – a topic I'll explore further in Chapter 6.

Leisure Spots

Many of the places we enjoy the most are those that allow us to hang out and unwind or participate in hobbies and casual activities. Although our preferred leisure spots often vary depending on our mood and social circumstances, we can typically identify places that bring us the most joy. The number and variety of leisure spots is seemingly endless. A leisure-oriented place might be our living room as we watch TV and eat ice cream, or a neighborhood nature park that offers beautiful trails for meditative walks, or a local bar that sponsors a karaoke happy hour that brings out our silly side, or a raucous entertainment venue that represents a celebratory destiny at the end of a long road trip. While much of our leisure time is spent in the comfort of the dwellings where we live, I focus primarily on places that are accessible to others and require us to leave the dwellings where we sleep. Our ability to contribute to placemaking activities will vary considerably depending on the place and is typically less at those sites away from our homes.

Although some places are generically seen as leisure spots that enhance our joy, no place can inherently be defined that way. In other words, a place that one person finds to be an ideal leisure spot may be unappealing and even scary to someone else. Seen through the eyes of youth, a basketball court in the "hood," including the people who play there, may be a big draw for the Black kids who live nearby. However, that same court can intimidate rural white kids because they may have limited experience with places in the inner city and Black boys and young men. In addition, even though many people enjoy doing leisure activities in solitude, most are also drawn to places and occasions that enable them to share leisure time with friends, family, and even strangers.

One significant place-based issue related to leisure highlights our ability to experience it on our terms, whether that be in or out of our homes. Some are fortunate enough to have the discretionary income and social flexibility to pursue their leisure activities where they want, when they want, and with whomever they choose. Most of us with more limited means and less flexibility, however, must make calculated decisions about where and how we can engage in a leisure activity. Thus, we are forced to compromise when we are precluded from experiencing our ideal places or a specific type of place.

Accessing a preferred leisure experience is particularly challenging for persons with a physical disability. However, the Americans with Disabilities Act (ADA) signed in 1990 and amended in 2008 (effective January 1, 2009) has significantly improved the public accommodations for persons with disabilities.[63] Irrespective of whether a person has a disability, having access to our desired leisure sites can enhance our well-being, especially when we have control over the setting and circumstances. If we have access to our preferred places, then our attachment to those places is likely to grow as well.

The physical conditions of a place can go a long way in deciding whether we see it as a desirable leisure site. If we're considering outdoor activities, then climate conditions obviously can make a difference in how we perceive our options. Pleasant weather probably produces better opportunities for individuals to build their sense of we-ness through face-to-face encounters undisturbed by inclement conditions. People are more likely to meet up for a daily walk when the temperature is moderate rather than frigidly cold or steaming hot. Yet, if we're dealing with harsher weather, friends may forge a deeper appreciation for each other's support and company.

Beyond the physical, we can examine the mental dimensions of a leisure-oriented place. What public discourses and ideologies related to place affect our behavior when we pursue a leisure activity? Do we believe gender should affect one's opportunities to pursue the leisure activities of their choice? In other words, when we approach an outdoor basketball court, do we see it as a "man's" place or simply a place where anyone who likes basketball can play? Private workout gyms represent a type of place that has been dramatically transformed in recent decades. I've belonged to the same co-ed gym for roughly thirty-six years. Although in smaller numbers than men, women regularly lift weights in the various sections of this massive facility. This was a much less common practice at similar gyms fifty years ago. Men then were much more possessive of the gym environment than they have been in recent years. For their part, women were also less willing to assert their right to be in places that men had claimed for themselves. Today, men and women are more likely to be gym partners in these places than ever before. Nevertheless, there are still gendered places within the larger facility. For instance, with some exceptions, men typically dominate the basketball court while women are the primary users of the aerobics room. On the court and in the aerobics room, it is the gendered activity that drives the pattern of usage and sense of we-ness, not the features of the places themselves. A basketball game fosters competition whereas an aerobic or step class creates more of a choreographed style of group bonding. In addition, gyms have emerged that cater exclusively to women. These gyms create a place and ambience that is devoid of any direct male social effect. However, the imagined male gaze may still indirectly creep into some women's self-perceptions as they contemplate what they're doing at the gym.

Are we more likely to apply a competitive or carefree philosophy to sports? Do we see a tennis court as a site for us to prove our abilities or simply a place to have fun while exercising? Let's look at the competitive ethic more closely. Adopting a mentality that encourages competition in all contexts can make it difficult to play sports with a friend, partner, or family member who is far less inclined to do the same. Instead of augmenting our sense of we-ness through a shared activity, we may both get frustrated during our joint "leisure" time. Thus, understanding whether our approach to leisure meshes well with how our companion thinks about leisure can influence how we define specific places when we're together.

If we are a parent, do we feel that leisure for our young kids should be largely risk free? If not, are we open to having our children play at community-sponsored "adventure playgrounds" that resemble junkyards? These novel places encourage kids to be creative and take risks while providing them with hand tools and building materials with which to craft their own haphazard play structures.[64] In this free-flowing setting, kids have the chance to forge feelings of we-ness with playmates as they cooperatively engage with creative building projects. While adventure playgrounds are championed by many, most notably kids, they also raise concerns among some parents and community leaders due to safety issues. Thus, various stakeholders shape the placemaking environment that defines adventure playgrounds.

Another way we can take a critical look at leisure spots is by considering community stakeholders' response to the intersection of social justice issues and place. Many stakeholders have an opportunity to play a significant role in developing the built environment that supports leisure and sports activities. Places for leisure come in many forms that are either dependent on tax dollars or rely on private initiatives. These include paved paths for walking, running, and biking; off-road biking areas; playgrounds and parks; museums and theaters; bowling alleys and pool halls; recreation centers and private gyms; athletic fields and community pools; dance and art studios; and much more. We can even expand our vision of such place-based sites for leisure by including designated bike lanes since some people use these for more than transportation purposes. Together, these places provide people with a range of options to participate in leisure activities either alone or with others. However, we must realize that some people have more privileged access to certain places for leisure. Much of that privilege is associated with the kinds of financial resources people have, but individuals can also experience privilege or disadvantage because of their physical attributes, including disabilities.

Because of this, we must be attentive to how, where, and why places are constructed. Government and business leaders are directly involved in placemaking when they initiate the building and maintenance of recreational, educational, and artistic opportunities that are leisure-related for residents and visitors. The other path involves grassroots activism. Motivated citizens sometimes mobilize to propose enhancements to the built environment for leisure activities that are designed to promote the common good in their communities. As I explore more fully in Chapter 6, it is not uncommon for community groups to have different ideas about the infrastructure for leisure. The disagreements often address what should be built, where it should be located, and who should be the target group of potential users.

Transport Vehicles and Hubs

Most people in the United States spend a significant portion of their time, often daily, in some type of motorized vehicle designed to move them from one place to another. Much of the time, they're not alone. Cars, motorcycles, buses, trucks, trains (subway and rail), trolleys, boats, airplanes, and helicopters are the most frequently used machines today that allow us to share time and physical space with others during our travels. Unfortunately, sustaining interpersonal exchanges during travel is becoming more challenging as people become increasingly absorbed by their phones and social media.

These vehicles play an important role in our place-based experience because they allow us to experience multiple places throughout the day and during the course of our lives. Some of the vehicles are special because within a short period of time, they permit us to experience places that differ in terms of geological landscape, climate, and culture. Places defined by different physical conditions and symbolism can provide us with distinct opportunities to bond with our travel companions as well as strangers we meet along the way and at our destinations. One of the defining aspects of our contemporary time is that people with financial means take for granted how easily they can access such radically different places in a short time span.

We can also creatively think of these transportation vehicles as being their own kind of place. The properties outlined earlier help to differentiate how we perceive and experience them. For example, a car offers a romantic couple or a parent and their child much more privacy than a bus, train, or airplane packed full of people. I've interviewed fathers who welcomed the opportunity to drive their children to school or on athletic trips because they felt it afforded them a chance to have meaningful conversations if the kids were not distracted by their electronic devices. So, too, having our own plane, boat, or luxury car that enables privacy is filtered through the symbolic meanings of wealth and power that we attach to such items. We think very differently about the person on the private jet or in the limousine than the person riding the subway or taking an Uber or taxi.

Even leisure travel on large commercial cruise lines like Carnival offers us the chance to experience a kind of place-based social status that is connected to our mode of travel and play. Telling someone you're going on a cruise signals that you have the financial means to seek adventure on a touring ship. The cruise ship also functions as a mobile entertainment community, providing people the chance to bond with friends, family, and even strangers. Agreeing to go on a cruise with someone is typically a good indicator that the pair has already formed some type of dyadic we-ness because they will be living in close quarters out at sea with no easy "off ramp." For those not in a relationship, a cruise can offer an exciting opportunity to pursue a more superficial style of we-ness that can emerge from hook-up culture. Bonding with others on a cruise through heavy drinking and hook-up sex is seen by some as similar to college life.[65] Even young kids and teenagers typically find opportunities to bond and create we-ness with peers on a cruise ship because the staff organize programs to bring them together for play and social activities.

Those who work on cruise ships are also subjected to having their social life influenced by the properties of their floating workplace. The spicy romance discourses and symbolic meanings associated with cruise ship dating between employees create a uniquely mobile action setting with 24/7 possibilities. For employees on identical work schedules, the level of stability associated with cruise ship scheduling can create opportunities to spend enormous amounts of time together. As one experienced crew member observes, "in one week you might eat lunch with them three times, dinner four, drinks six times, go see a show, and have a formal evening at a fancy steak house. In between all that then go somewhere incredible – nothing like being able to go on dates in places like Bora Bora, Honolulu, Sydney, Puerto Vallarta, Bali, etc., to move the romance along."[66] But romantically involved employees must also negotiate their respective understandings of "we-ness" as they deal with the prospect of partners often leaving the ship to go home.

Vacationing or living at sea, away from city lights with brilliant star-studded skies above us, may cause us to wonder about places beyond our reach. Many of our earliest ancestors worshipped the sun by day and gazed at the stars come night. It is seemingly in our DNA to wonder about places beyond the confines of earth. Consistent with that observation, through time we have created temples and other sacred places for deities and assigned powerful meanings to distant stars, planets, and other celestial bodies. While the ancient Greeks believed that their gods resided on an earthly mountaintop, Mount Olympus, other cultures have imagined that their gods' "homes" are somewhere in the heavens or universe.

For centuries, science fiction writers like Isaac Asimov, Ray Bradbury, Gene Roddenberry, and many others have expanded our visions about these places beyond the earth. They tapped into our basic urges to fantasize about space travel and distant places through their books, TV shows, and movies. But it has not just been the artists of our time who have inspired us to think about places beyond our planet. In the early 1960s, President John F. Kennedy challenged Americans, scientists and engineers specifically, to land American astronauts on the moon by the end of the decade, and on July 20, 1969, we did. A few decades later, NASA launched the space shuttle era that brought new opportunities and discoveries as well as disappointments, including the devastating deaths of fourteen astronauts in the space shuttle disasters of 1986 and 2003.

Fortunately, the termination of that program did not end our fascination with these distant places. Instead, NASA shifted its business model and its resources to help create and partner with a competitive private space industry. In the summer of 2020, we saw Elon Musk's company SpaceX, using its Falcon 9 reusable rocket, transport two NASA astronauts to the International Space Station

(ISS). The following summer, Sir Richard Branson's *Virgin Galactic* and Jeff Bezos's *Blue Origin* took center stage by successfully launching the owners and several other notables to new heights in their supersonic suborbital rockets.[67]

The commercial spaceflight company Space Perspective is yet another futuristic business enterprise that will provide individuals the opportunity to experience place in a novel way far above the earth.[68] Sometime in the very near future, this company proposes to put space explorers into *Spaceship Neptune* for a six-hour journey to 100,000 feet. The space capsule will be guided on its ascent and descent by *SpaceBalloon,* which is the size of a football stadium. With room for eight passengers, bookings permit family and friends to sign up for an expensive adventure ($125,000 per individual), an experience that is likely to deepen their sense of we-ness. As of April 9, 2024, Space Perspective's co-founder Jane Poynter announced that 1,750 people have already booked their seats.[69]

These recent initiatives reveal that the seeds of private space tourism are taking root. Still, many commentators take issue with billionaires pursuing space travel when so many critical and life-threatening global issues remain unresolved.[70] It seems safe to imagine, however, that as we look to the relatively near future, the new age of private space travel is here to stay. In the short term, it will create fascinating opportunities for wealthy individuals to go to places that have only been accessible to a select cadre of astronauts. Eventually, future generations of the middle class are likely to travel together into space, to the moon, and beyond. When and precisely how this will occur is unknown, but it is reasonable to envision the individuals who engage in this private space travel bonding with each other in unique, meaningful ways. Just as sci-fi stories have predicted, some of these individuals will be living together in colonies on space stations, Mars, or some other habitable planet in the "Goldilocks zone." As we develop more sophisticated machines, we will become increasingly curious about places beyond earth, both those we are aware of and others that we have yet to discover.

Aside from our time in our transport machines, the time we spend in transportation hubs can affect us. Whether it be the airport, city bus or train station, or the neighborhood school bus stop, we rub elbows with our fellow travelers in these places. Before we became obsessed with cell phones, these sites offered participants more opportunities to meet new people or to interact with schoolmates. They continue to provide us with occasions to share either the joy of traveling for pleasure or the anguish of being forced to relocate to another place because of war, natural disaster, famine, or some other reason. The images of Ukrainians frantically trying to secure a spot on a bus or train to escape the horrors of war underscore the significance of this type of place. Moreover, disturbing reports of refugees being assisted or shunned based on their skin color by some who coordinated the out-migration reinforces the idea that a place, even one that is relatively temporary, can be meaningful for drastically different reasons.

Now imagine a more pleasant and exciting future where you or your descendants are together in a hub for space travelers preparing to step onto a spaceship. You are likely to be surrounded by family, friends, or strangers, just as you are when you spend time at an airport, train station, or bus terminal today. That will be a memorable place indeed.

Metaverse

As we ponder the future, we can also consider how the metaverse is destined to become another crucial and unique "place." Although Neal Stephenson coined the term "metaverse" in his 1992 dystopian novel, *Snow Crash*, it wasn't until the early 2020s that it began to enter the popular consciousness in a meaningful way.[71] Despite being ill-defined, the term and concept have been increasingly promoted by business leaders, government officials, marketing professionals, tech experts, and others.

So, what exactly is the metaverse? Mark Zuckerberg, the controversial CEO of Meta (formally Facebook), has succinctly, but vaguely, described the metaverse as an "embodied internet."[72] From this perspective, it is vital that we be able to tap into our physical senses more fully in various types of socially constructed virtual places, some of which we will design ourselves. Ultimately, the metaverse will also enable us to teleport virtually using more realistic hologram and avatar technologies that project "us" into virtual as well as real, physical places. According to Gene Park's 2021 *Washington Post* interview with Tim Sweeney, the founder and CEO of Epic Games, which developed the popular game *Fortnite*, Sweeney sees the metaverse as "an expansive, digitized communal space where users can mingle freely with brands and one another in ways that permit self-expression and spark joy."[73] More succinctly, in 2023, he says it is "an online social entertainment experience in a real-time 3D setting."[74]

The tech YouTuber Mrwhosetheboss (Arun Maini) posted a snappy video in November 2021 that summarizes the metaverse concept. There he uses a shorthand label to describe the metaverse as a "living shared everlasting virtual universe."[75] Marques Brownlee, another tech YouTuber, also provides an instructive overview of the metaverse and VR and AR technologies. He illustrates how individuals and companies can do next-level video conferencing (think immersive Zoom sessions) using VR technologies.[76] These technologies will foster more embodied types of experiences, eventually using live avatar photorealistic representations of individual users. The system will permit eye contact, disperse audio in ways that capture people's location in the room, and enable people to lean toward others and speak softly to them. All of these tech features and others will create options to interact with people in more realistic types of virtual places, presumably improving our chances to create and reinforce a sense of we-ness in those settings.

In contrast, Matthew Ball, a pioneering theorist and venture capitalist, provides a much more comprehensive and technical definition. Ball, in his 2022 book, *The Metaverse: And How It Will Revolutionize Everything*, defines the metaverse as being "experienced *synchronously* and *persistently* by an *effectively unlimited number of users* with an *individual sense of presence*, and with *continuity of data*, such as identity, history, entitlements, objects, communications, and payments."[77]

Obviously, Ball's detailed definition requires us to do some unpacking. For our purposes it makes sense to stress five points. First, the metaverse will not simply be a platform operated and controlled by a single company; rather, it entails the full range of interconnected opportunities in the 3D virtual world that will be facilitated by numerous big tech and smaller companies, some that have yet to be launched. Ball prefers to use the term metagalaxies for the more narrowly defined, company-based virtual reality programs. Second, the interoperable idea refers to users being readily able to take their assets or products (e.g., avatars, clothes, cars) from one site to another. This feature is a major technological challenge that will require widespread cooperation to create standard protocols for producing and distributing content. Third, the experiences in the metaverse are based on digitally created sensory images that depict a virtual world that unfolds in real time for multiple people. Fourth, the system allows an indefinite number of users to participate simultaneously in a virtual setting and engage in joint social activities. Fifth, users can express their individual sense of self which affords them the right to claim objects and places as their own. They will also have the right and capacity to exchange and sell their "things" and take them when they move between virtual sites.

Writing in the tech publication *The Verge* in 2021, Adi Robertson and Jay Peters suggest that the most recent "hype cycle" about the metaverse is a reflection of the significant advances in "graphics technology and internet connectivity."[78] These advances will enable the metaverse to provide users new and more satisfying opportunities. Thus, hardware and software developments associated with VR and AR will move us closer to what Zuckerberg labels a technologically enhanced "presence." That presence will allow us to feel as though we're interacting virtually with people and places more directly, rather than "watching them through a window."[79] It will also give us more sophisticated tools to create realistic avatars and holograms that let us either express ourselves authentically, or experiment with performative acts, cloaked in knowingly disingenuous, questionable, or unpopular personal attributes that hide our authentic sense of self. Eventually, the new generation of virtual reality tools will allow us to alter our gender, race, ethnicity, and body attributes in a realistic manner.

Notably, Zuckerberg is sufficiently enamored by the prospects of the metaverse that he rebranded his company as Meta in 2021, having already made it one of the most metaverse-focused companies in the world. His personal and financial commitment to having his company contribute to making the metaverse a reality increases the likelihood that the metaverse will shape the way we think and feel about places in the future. Epic Games has also positioned itself as a frontrunner in helping to build the metaverse. Sweeney, like

Zuckerberg, has been thinking about and planning for the metaverse for years. Sima Sistani, who was a senior executive at Epic and co-founder of Houseparty, an app bought by Epic in 2019 that was a face-to-face synchronous social network that fostered empathy in online communication, asserts that people will fundamentally alter how they've been interacting on the internet once they grow accustomed to the metaverse. Put simply, Epic believes users will be less focused on "sharing" and more concerned with "participating" with others across a diverse set of services. In Sweeney's words, the metaverse will be a "much more enjoyable and personal and empathetic medium than today's social networks."[80]

Philip Rosedale, founder of Linden Lab, was responsible for creating the acclaimed virtual world *Second Life* (*SL*) in 2003,[81] and is another important voice in the metaverse community. He is cautiously hopeful that the metaverse will eventually transition from being an inspirational dream to being real; however, he hedges his optimism by asserting that "most adults are not yet comfortable engaging with new people, or engaging socially, in a multi-player context online."[82] Many assume that this concern will fade as younger generations of tech-natives replace older, less tech-savvy people.

Ball provides a thorough historical and futuristic account of the roles specific companies have already played and are likely to play in getting us to the edge of a metaverse world and beyond. Companies have built and continue to enhance the hardware and software technologies that are vital to cultivating the business environment needed to develop this complex system. Many intersecting social, business, and technological forces must be coordinated to make an enterprise featuring virtual reality an objective reality, one that will eventually transform our lives in profound ways. As Ball explains, the metaverse is being incrementally developed because advances in the thriving computer gaming industry incentivize developers to create new products. These products and services are essentially part of a fragmented effort in digital placemaking that can potentially enhance and expand opportunities for virtual and augmented realities. In Ball's words, the emergence of the metaverse will mean that

> an ever-growing share of our lives, labor, leisure, time, wealth, happiness, and relationships will be spent inside virtual worlds, rather than

just extended or aided through digital devices and software. It will be a parallel plane of existence for millions, if not billions, of people, that sits atop our digital and physical economies, and unites both.[83]

Astute observers continue to offer diverse predictions about the nature, timing, and value of the metaverse. Yet, it's reasonable to conclude that more people will find themselves in the next five to twenty years regularly creating and navigating new types of virtual places and interacting with friends, family, colleagues, and strangers in these virtually constructed social environments. This future includes the types of hybrid experiences that Zuckerberg talks about where embodied hologram images of people will interact in real time, with real people, for work, socializing, and play.

This scenario is likely because more recent generations of teenagers and young adults have grown up in a world where they have been immersed in online and virtual worlds. Thus, they are more comfortable with what the metaverse will offer and they will position themselves to be the developers and users who play a significant role in shaping its development.[84] As a wide range of VR and AR technologies are refined and computing power is enhanced, individuals are likely to feel more impressed with their virtual reality experiences and see them as progressively more authentic.[85] As businesses of all types, and the education and health sectors get more invested in promoting their goods and services in novel ways, the links between virtual and real life will expand and deepen.

Consequently, individuals will develop stronger place attachments to the virtual places they frequent and sometimes build. The strength of our attachments to virtual places will be, in part, influenced by the interpersonal ties that individuals forge who share time together in the virtual sites that are relevant to all five social domains of our lives. For many users, their attachments will be stronger because they were involved, sometimes collaboratively, in creating the places that are meaningful to them. In addition, individuals immersed in the metaverse's virtual realities will encounter new experiences as they engage in special rituals, manage life transitions, and negotiate claims related to digitally rendered places.

In *Reality+: Virtual Worlds and the Problems of Philosophy*, philosopher David Chalmers challenges us with myriad provocative questions about how we perceive and experience our virtual worlds. He also encourages us to think about how we are likely to experience ourselves in virtual places when technologies inevitably make our virtual worlds more and more realistic and pervasive. Part of his thesis is that "Virtual worlds are not illusions or fictions, or at least they need not be. What happens in VR really happens. The objects we interact with in VR are real."[86] This premise assumes, then, that the places where our experiences happen in VR are real, too. This thinking mirrors the sociological wisdom of the Thomas theorem first articulated in the early twentieth century by the renowned sociologists W.I. Thomas and Dorthy Swaine Thomas: "If men [people] define situations as real, they are real in their consequences."[87] In other words, if we perceive and treat these virtual places as real, then they will affect us personally and can also indirectly have consequences for others. Our experiences in these virtual places can bring us joy, sorrow, laughter, fear, confidence, insecurity, and a whole lot more. Like many other tech experts, Chalmers predicts that,

> In the coming decades, virtual worlds will move far beyond games to become part of our everyday lives. Actions in virtual worlds will potentially be as meaningful as actions in the physical world. Crimes such as theft and assault in virtual worlds will affect real human beings and will be real crimes. To fully recognize this, we will need to treat virtual realities as genuine realities.[88]

This orientation to the metaverse underscores the fact that we will confront and reframe intriguing placemaking issues in our digitally constructed world that are comparable to the ones that define our experiences in the physical world. For example, just as physical places are gendered in our everyday lives, men are much more likely than women to participate in virtual spaces, and when women do, they are more likely to be harassed and bullied.[89] Likewise, persons who belong to other marginalized groups are likely to deal with bias and discrimination in the metaverse. Thus, making virtual places more welcoming and safer for everyone must be a priority for those who build and manage them.

Just as public discourses shape how people experience places in the real world, various ideologies and discourses about power, identity, autonomy, and community (or we-ness) will influence the trajectory of the metaverse. How, and the extent to which, we allow our experiences in the metaverse to compete with or complement how we experience our conventional, place-based, embodied lives will be revealed in due time. We may find that our fanciful ability to alter our embodied appearance to others in the metaverse will create a ripple or blended effect in how we see ourselves in the virtual world as well as in our everyday life. For instance, the person who has a physical or mental disability, but who presents themselves without one in a virtual place, may gain confidence in the places that require them to be physically present in real life. Alternatively, if we have negative experiences with virtual places, we may carry those sentiments into our everyday, organic worlds.

Granted, we may potentially find that our access to the metaverse is personally rewarding, but it's also possible that our immersion in this parallel reality will diminish our sensitivity to the circumstances and challenges of everyday life, for us and others less fortunate. As can happen with addiction, we can lose sight of our family, work, and community responsibilities when our virtual experiences dominate our lives. We can even develop a distorted view of contemporary social problems if we embrace an idyllic perception of "reality" that is based on our simulated experiences that do not reflect real life.

In addition, we need to be wary of how the metaverse will extend and deepen the kinds of negative experiences people are likely to have with digital technologies. In particular, we should be alarmed by the emerging research that appears to show how excessive social media exposure is producing negative mental health effects, such as depression, anxiety, ADHD and more, especially for youth.[90] One can assume that similar types of mental health patterns will materialize as we spend more of our time engaged with the metaverse. Thus, the metaverse, like most transformative technologies, is likely to generate a host of good and bad outcomes.

Although I've highlighted a diverse set of generic places, they each represent a common thread to our existence because they afford us opportunities to become more aware of our surroundings and often build a sense of we-ness. Cultivating our place consciousness typically requires a degree of mindfulness about how aspects of a place influence the way we see ourselves and experience the people in those settings. Different places can foster our unique attachments to them while enhancing our connections to the people with whom we interact. Our place attachments, rooted in our hearts and minds, are based on our memories of what has occurred in an action setting and our expectations of what is likely to happen there.

As noted earlier, although we hold memories in our separate minds, many are directly and indirectly shaped by social processes involving the collective memories we forge. Our collective memories are often the place-based thoughts that inspire us as group members and define our identities. The memories implicating specific place attachments to nature, homes, public spaces, communities, and more are affected by our life circumstances and social interactions. The type and intensity of many of those place attachments shift over time, leaving us to see ourselves in new ways. In addition, whether our place attachments are aligned with how others think and feel will alter how we think about and practice placemaking.

Chapters 1 and 2 demonstrate that we can enhance our understanding of our place-based memories and the bonds we experience with others by situating them inside a larger context, one that considers how place properties and different types of places affect us. Model 1 summarizes the basics of place that I describe in Part 1 of this book, including the ten place properties that influence how we experience ten generic types of places. The model also foreshadows what I turn to next in Part 2 by depicting the four interrelated *CART* processes of claims, attachments, rituals, and transitions as being at the core of our place-based experiences that we can attend to more closely as we develop a heightened place consciousness. Some properties and places will be more relevant to how we experience the *CART* processes, depending on our specific life course and social circumstances. Lastly, our expressions of deep dyadic, ideational, and spontaneous we-ness are tied to our place-based experiences. Ultimately, our interconnected experiences with place and we-ness influence our placemaking activity.

Model 1: CART social processes affecting place consciousness

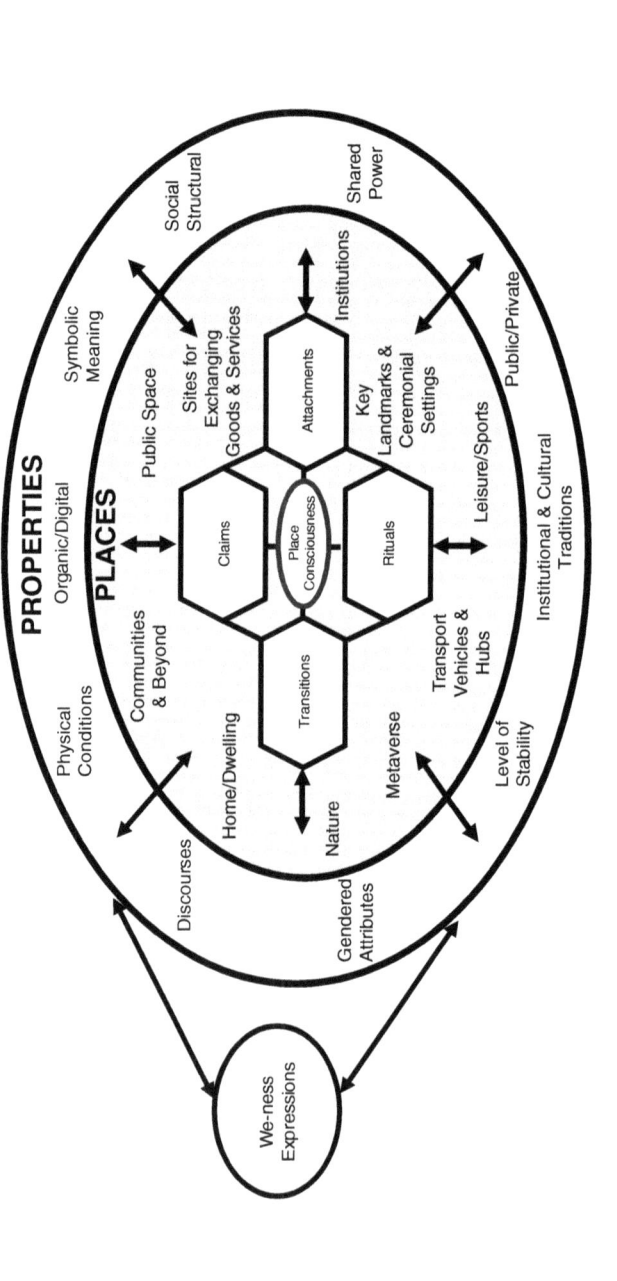

PART 2

Key Place Processes (*CART*)

We experience and make sense of the multilayered place landscape while engaged in a series of dynamic social processes. In Part 2 we highlight how our ability to negotiate place processes successfully builds on the basic insights we've developed concerning place properties and types of places. Our next step on this journey is to ask: What core social processes define our opportunities to experience and shape the places that matter to us? More specifically, how are the interrelated *CART* processes involving claims, attachments, rituals, and transitions vital to how we experience and understand a place? We must also consider how our calculated involvement in these critical processes can enhance efforts to promote personal empowerment, civic engagement, and social and environmental justice. Ultimately, these processes are implicated in our efforts to work with others to engage in ethical, constructive placemaking.

3
Attachments

Photo 5: Tile mural created in 2023 by the artist Harley Munger and located at Beachfront Park, Crescent City, California. It represents *Kamome*, the lost Japanese boat that was found in Crescent City and that inspired a sister-city arrangement between the residents of Rikuzentakata, Japan, and Crescent City. An identical mural was gifted to the people of Rikuzentakata. (Photo courtesy of Bill Steven)

On April 7, 2013, a small, empty boat, covered in barnacles and seaweed, drifted ashore in Crescent City in Northern California. The discovery of the boat, named *Kamome*, triggered a series of inspirational events that forged bonds between the peoples of two fishing communities, despite their living thousands of miles apart.

Kamome belonged to a Japanese high school, Takata High, located in the small coastal town of Rikuzentakata. The boat had been propelled on its two-year ocean journey by a massive tsunami that leveled the town on March 11, 2011, killing more than 1,700 people. Civic-minded students at Del Norte High School in Crescent City volunteered to restore the boat that summer and were able to return it to its Japanese owners in September of that year. The altruistic gesture prompted an unexpected invitation for the American students to visit their Japanese counterparts. Since then, regular student exchanges between the two high schools have taken place, culminating in the establishment of a sister-school arrangement. Over the years, each city has also sent delegations of government and business leaders to promote this productive cultural exchange. These visits have led to a series of unique ventures. For example, a local company in Crescent City, SeaQuake Brewing, launched a new beer named Kamone Ale. Representatives from both cities helped design the label, which includes place-based iconography that displays an image of the "miracle" pine tree in Rikuzentakata, the only one that miraculously survived the tsunami out of a forest of roughly seventy thousand trees. The label also includes an image of the signature California redwoods. As the cities' partnership expanded, residents' pride and attachment to their respective cities grew, as did their emerging cross-cultural sense of we-ness. In 2016, they formalized their relationship by establishing a Sister Cities International Partnership.

Ironically, Crescent City had also experienced a horrific tsunami in 1964. Eleven people were killed, and twenty-three million dollars of damage was inflicted when a seventy-five-foot wall of water slammed the town.[1] That tragedy is commemorated by various memorials including a bronze fountain sculpture and a painted mural prominently displayed on the local Del Norte Office Supply building. Residents of these American and Japanese small towns rallied in similar fashion to affirm their attachment to their communities and land. Thus, it was fortuitous that *Kamome* ended up in Crescent City, but it was a coordinated and generous community response that returned it home.

The *Kamome* story, which was showcased by NBC documentary coverage during the 2020 Olympics, reveals once again that disasters can bring out the best in people. The continuing chain of events confirms that our attachments to places and people are powerful forces that can move the human spirit. Many make the most of their opportunity to become more mindful, show empathy, engage in altruism, and rise to the occasion of demonstrating leadership when a disaster strikes.[2]

Memories and Expectations

The American and Japanese citizens who formed attachments to their respective coastal cities, and a fondness for their sister city, have done so through the memories and expectations they've experienced over time. They have accomplished this through their interactions with their fellow citizens and exchanges with their new international friends. A key lesson from these events is that the significance of place depends on social processes, and the people who fill them with life, memories, and emotions.

Sociologist Melinda Milligan provides a useful framework that highlights key aspects of how we relate to our built environment.[3] She proposes that place-based social interaction is the foundation for the attachments we develop to specific places. Part of our emotional connection to a place stems from the past interactions we had in that context – our memories. These memories can encompass positive as well as negative experiences. But if a place is to become meaningful enough for us to forge a strong attachment to it, our experiences must be sufficiently consequential to produce lasting memories.

Places can produce lasting memories in two general ways. First, we can encounter dramatic events that heighten our senses and push us to interact with others in a celebratory setting or crisis. These moments are often relatively compressed in time. For example, most of the five million diehard Chicago Cubs fans who spent their afternoon at Grant Park in downtown Chicago on November 4, 2016, for the World Series celebration that was 108 years in the making had fond memories of that place and experience etched in their minds. In decidedly different and ominous settings, the firsthand witnesses of George Floyd's murder and the soldiers who stormed the Normandy beaches were left with disturbing and everlasting memories that were generated in a relatively short timeframe.

Fortunately, a place-based experience restricted to a small sliver of time can also capture uplifting life thrills, many of which symbolize personal moments that we associate with our life's "bucket list." Years ago, I had a meaningful experience flying a four-seater Cessna plane. One of my friends at the time owned a landscaping company and had invited me to join him for the day on a consultation in Miami. He planned to rent a plane to fly the roughly 330 miles to his client's property. I had flown with him once before, but on that occasion, I was seated in the back, unable to observe how he operated the plane. On my second adventure, I sat next to him and on the initial leg of the trip I paid close attention to his every move as he managed the controls.

On the way back, I eased back into my "co-pilot" seat and began to relax. But this time, about halfway back home, Jim turned to me and casually asked, "Do you want to fly?" The question caught me off guard; my heart rate accelerated immediately. "Really? Hey, sure," I quickly replied. The next half an hour was probably the most focused I've ever been in my life. I was channeling every speck of my conscious energy to execute Jim's basic instructions. The plane had suddenly become a profoundly meaningful place to me. The airspace, with its largely blue skies and scattered wispy clouds became my aerial playground. Now, I had the ability to fly around, over, under, or through the clouds. I now had control over how I navigated the space that I had redefined as part of my new aerial leisure spot.

An alternative to these immediate and dramatic experiences that generate deep memories about place involves the accumulation of our numerous, ordinary memories over an extended timeframe. For many of us, this rendering of place is often reflected in our experiences with our childhood homes, communities, schools, and regular leisure spots. Our everyday interaction with family and neighborhood friends can culminate into a lasting sentiment, an enduring attachment to those places we associate with our upbringing.

Place-based life is more than our immersion in a pool of memories. We can, for instance, create a quasi-place attachment to a place that we've never experienced in person. As children, we may long to attend the university that our parent or older sibling attended even though we've never set foot on the campus. Or we might develop a strong affinity and sense of attachment to our ancestral homeland without having been there. Even though this broad interpretation of place attachment is based on narratives and understandings that are not connected to our own physical presence in a place, the stories related to this place can generate powerful impressions that affect how we think, feel, and act. Historically, as well as in a contemporary context, millions of immigrants have imagined their own style of place attachment to America. Those feelings prompted countless immigrants to venture here at great risk to themselves and their families. In previous centuries, people's daydreams about places on the western frontier grew into a psychologically projected type of place attachment that was built on other people's memories and stories. Thus, while our place attachment is typically grounded in our own direct experiences and memories with a place, we can be affected indirectly by others' experiences and stories.

Additionally, as we go about our daily affairs, we have opportunities to anticipate potential interactions that a place might produce for us. We tend to assign more intense meanings to a place if we expect that important experiences are likely to occur there in the future. The properties described in Chapter 1 can play a significant role in shaping what we expect will happen in a place. So, too, our past experiences in a place or similar places will contribute to our expectations. We build these perceptions over time and typically revise them as we encounter fresh experiences that provide us with new knowledge and sensations. In turn, our experiences can alter our level of attachment to a place and our connections with the people who interact with us there. In many ways, the quality and nature of our interactions will affect the extent to which we form a meaningful attachment to a place. Typically, when we have stronger place attachments that are reinforced by a solid sense of we-ness, we will be more motivated to invest in active placemaking.

The Person-Process-Place Model

Focusing on our memories and expectations reminds us that we need to consider the social psychological processes that make place attachments possible. If we wish to understand our place-based lives, paying attention to just the people and places is not enough. What also matters are the processes that instill life into a place. This is the message environmental psychologists Leila Scannell and Robert Gifford have conveyed. Their person-process-place (PPP) framework deepens our understanding of place attachment by highlighting the three interrelated dimensions that make our attachments to place possible.[4]

First, as a person, each of us develops our place attachments because we either have individual or group-based experiences in particular settings. We sometimes center our personal connections and memories about a place on the unique, individual experiences that resonate with us. For example, our attachments to our childhood home or a summer camp we attended for years are based on the personal bonds we've established in those settings. We make these connections because of how we experience significant moments in our life within a specific place. These moments may represent turning points in life that enable us to overcome a debilitating fear, find a soul mate, prove ourselves to others, or create another type of memorable experience. The bonds we forge to a specific place often reflect the cumulative effects of navigating meaningful rituals and routines in that place for months, years, or even decades.

We also develop attachments that stem from being part of a collective effort, one that emphasizes our desire to experience a sense of group belonging. Many group situations enable people to express thoughts and feelings about a place that preserve aspects of their culture and reinforce their sense of we-ness or collective identity. We see ourselves as part of something larger and recognize that our commitments to this collective identity shape how we experience a place. Consequently, the way we value a place can signal our appreciation for how it enables us to deepen our sense of we-ness and enhance our quality of life.

In short, we forge attachments to a place because of individual reasons, or we establish connections to a place because we embrace the kind of ideational we-ness and group identity that this book profiles. Sometimes we form our place attachments through our actions on both the individual and group level. This is the case for countless Ukrainians who know firsthand the joy of living in and then fighting for the communities that they grew to see as warm, inviting, and tightly knit. Additionally, the trauma associated with surviving this type of war zone can inspire a person to deepen their collective national identity, as Ukrainians have, and to take personal risks to honor that identity.

Second, according to the PPP framework, the social psychological processes that solidify our connections to place have an overlapping set of affective, cognitive, and behavioral elements associated with them.[5] In most instances, if we've developed an attachment to a place it is grounded in positive feelings. We feel satisfied and empowered by our pleasurable experiences that result in fond, lasting memories.

But, as noted earlier, this is not always the case. Bad feelings can mentally trap us in a cycle of dark memories about our time and unpleasant experiences in a place. Ukrainians who were forced to leave their homes and communities because of Russia's invasion will often have mixed feelings that keep them connected to their homes, neighborhoods, and homeland.[6] While many of their original feelings prior to the war reflect warm emotions, they are also likely to associate their more recent anxiety, sadness, and anger with the brutal tragedies they've endured in the same places. When displaced persons from Ukraine or elsewhere witness the built environments that represent their local places being demolished by war or disaster, it can leave lasting scars and muddle their attachments to a place. Those mixed feelings may be most disturbing when individuals grapple with the consequences of an unprovoked invasion that upends the rhythms of their lives and destroys their cherished places, slaughtering thousands of civilians in the process. Who can forget the horrific televised images documenting the deadly war crimes the Russian occupying forces committed in the small town of Bucha, Ukraine, near the capital city of Kyiv. As the Ukrainian refugees move on to new cities and countries, typically constrained by their limited financial resources and cultural barriers, they are forced to be creative and frugal in their efforts to engage in a temporary form of placemaking.

In addition to our feelings, we consider thoughts that reinforce our attachment to a place. As we engage with a place over time, we accumulate a series of memories, beliefs, knowledge, and symbolic meanings that help us to visualize and relive our experiences in it. When our lives unfold in a place, we expand our knowledge of it while developing our experiential sense of the self that it fosters. Our thoughts include how we come to assign meaning to a place and our perceptions about what it does for us. Over time, we splice together random and intentional thoughts that allow us to render an understanding of a place from our perspective. Those who see beyond their own blinders will also consider how others think about the same place. In the process, they will potentially expand their understanding of the place that matters to them.

As a boy, I was affected by the rituals and routines that defined my small, working-class town. These activities reinforced the town's rugged blue-collar ethos, enthusiasm for sports, and neighborly spirit. The town, which seemed big to me at the time, was physically defined by its extensive hills and valleys that accommodated numerous rundown factories that ranged from functional to dilapidated to completely abandoned. It also featured a Black population segregated in low-income housing on the west side. Early on, I learned to anticipate seasonal rhythms that brought a Memorial Day parade, a summertime local pool opening, Friday night high school football, and downtown Christmas lights. My carefree daily rhythms were filled with recreational sports, neighborhood play with friends, and friendly greetings from adults on porches, in yards, and in the streets. As I aged into my middle and later teen years, I began to see in a new way the practical effects of a declining rust belt economy. And once I left for college and returned for short visits over subsequent years and decades, I increasingly recognized the deeper meaning of some people's sentimental choice to stay in the area to be near family and their fear of moving beyond the familiar. I also saw in a new light how the luster of a cohesive small-town mentality and industrial base, which had once cultivated my hardworking personality, had now dimmed, offering youth and others fewer opportunities and support. The town seemed much smaller to me now, both in size and perspective. I clearly recognized the racial segregation and poverty that had only faintly registered with me in my youth, and realized how it was a real and symbolic byproduct of our society's racist past.

A place motivates and enables people to express themselves, so their relationship to a place evolves from their actions. As I show in more detail in Chapter 4, the rituals and routines of everyday life are critical to the way we deepen our sentiments about a place. Despite their importance, we often take these actions for granted; they become second nature to us. In their varied form, they include the basic things we do in a place to achieve our goals. For example, having lunch with our partner at a diner once a week or meeting a young mentee at their school every Tuesday afternoon to review math can contribute to our developing attachments to a place. In addition, our place-work can affect how we sustain our place attachments. The more sweat equity we put into designing, building, and maintaining a home, the more likely it is that we will grow attached to it.

Third, the PPP framework proposes that those who highlight the place dimension associated with place attachment often describe it as either emphasizing physical or social features. Our attachments to a place can sometimes be dependent on its unique physical features that provide us with resources or opportunities to express ourselves in ways important to us. A place can be meaningful to us because of its abundance of natural resources that allow us to live off the land, or its overwhelming beauty that calms our spirit, or its topographical characteristics that create options for our physical adventures. Most scholars of place, however, emphasize how our attachments to a place are based on the social ties that we build during our engagement with it. Soldiers who invest time and energy forging relationships with comrades on a military base in an unstable foreign country are likely to develop feelings of attachment to the base. In large part, their attachments hinge on their ties with those who serve alongside them, especially if they are executing risky missions together. The significance of this pattern was vividly displayed in the summer of 2021 during the United States' withdrawal from Afghanistan. American soldiers described their passionate commitments to the Afghans who assisted them in military operations over the course of two decades. In doing so, Americans linked their place attachments to Afghanistan as a country, and the work they did in a war zone, to the relationships they forged with their Afghan counterparts.

Motivating Forces

In *Chasing We-ness* I outlined ten motives that inspire us to develop a sense of we-ness with others. Similarly, I now turn our attention to what specifically motivates individuals to create and express their attachments to specific places, either as individuals or as part of a group. Typically, we can assume that we grow attached to places because doing so serves a purpose; it is functional for how we experience life.[7] Although there are various ways to categorize these motives, I rely heavily on Scannell and Giffords's thinking by emphasizing five distinct categories (belonging, identity, achieving goals, life course continuity, and survival/moral dignity). I also describe how these overlapping motives relate to how we pursue and maintain a sense of we-ness. At the outset, I focus primarily on how and why we grow attached to places that are relatively fixed objects. Yet, an interdisciplinary team lead by social psychologist Andrés Di Masso convincingly argues that "place attachment literature would benefit from greater focus on the specific interrelationships between the fixed and the mobile in people's actual experience of place."[8] I agree, so I deepen our approach to place attachment in Chapter 5 by highlighting a more dynamic approach. There I emphasize that when we undergo different types of transitions, it is useful to explore how various types of mobility affect the way we navigate place and develop attachments on our own and with others.

My purpose in this section is to explore the basic forces that drive us to feel connected to specific places. Having a better sense of what draws our attention to a place, and why it seeps into our bones and consciousness, is vital. This knowledge can help us to engage in more effective placemaking that enhances our personal well-being while nurturing a deeper sense of community for those around us.

Belonging

Previously, I highlighted how our social ties reinforce the idea that place matters to us. Many of our attachments to place reveal our penchant to be connected to something larger than ourselves, whether that group is a family, community, nation, or something else. By definition, a motive for place attachment that emphasizes a sense of belonging implies that a person can feel connected to others because of their place-based experiences. Our interpersonal ties to others mutually reinforce our attachments to the places that make these relations possible.

The relative timing of when we develop our attachments to a place, compared to when we establish a sense of group belonging, unfolds in numerous ways. Sometimes our place attachments and sentiments of we-ness emerge simultaneously, each gaining traction at roughly the same pace while mutually reinforcing each other. For example, sorority sisters are likely to deepen their attachments to the sorority house they live in while they're establishing and expanding both their dyadic and ideational forms of we-ness with their "sisters." The path by which these connections produce a reciprocal effect varies depending on the unique conditions that define any one sorority sister's life circumstances and exposure to different sorority regulations. For example, a chapter's housing policy, a type of place property, can affect the opportunities available to a new member to live on site.

Imagine the sorority sister who lives away from her chapter's house during her first year of membership. During this time, she might feel more connected to the philosophy of the sorority and individual sisters, while feeling less connected to the physical house as a place even though she may visit it regularly. However, once the young woman begins to live in the house, she may quickly form attachments to features of the house itself. Meanwhile, the young woman who lives in the chapter's house from the onset may simultaneously learn to feel attached to the physical house while embracing the sorority philosophy. Yet, eventually, this same person could become increasingly disenchanted with living in the house. She may even question her commitment to the ideational we-ness associated with the sorority life she initially embraced. Ultimately, any attachment and sense of bonding a person has to a place and the people associated with it is subject to change over time.

Identity and Self-Perceptions

Who we are and strive to be can be affected by place properties and the nature of our relationships with the people with whom we share experiences in various places. As alluded to earlier, our place-based identities are either individually focused, group-based, or a mixture of the two. Certain places enable us to anchor and express our individually oriented identities. These could include persons committed to being health-conscious, naturalists, adrenaline junkies, and the like. However, the places I highlight are those that enhance our group-based or ideologically driven identities.

Our motivation to be involved with the types of places that enhance our collective identities will also encourage us to seek out and participate in these places. Others who are associated with a place can function as influencers and direct or accompany us to a certain place. People sometimes recruit others to visit and eventually engage in activities that occur in specific places like a church, a school, a volunteer organization, or a business. When we're "recruited" to spend time in a place, we often already have a relationship with the recruiter. In this situation, we often build on that interpersonal we-ness while also developing our attachment to the place or places that enable us to cultivate our sense of we-ness and collective identity. Other times we take the initiative to seek out appealing places based on our values and interests.

When this occurs, we typically understand that both the places and the people associated with them matter to us. Many of those who stormed the Capitol on January 6, 2021, did so because they were eager to mobilize their collective identity as Trump supporters who, in their minds, valued the Capitol as a place to protest and assert their grievances as diehard Americans. While many of these Trump supporters had long-standing relationships and a sense of deep dyadic we-ness as mutual friends and family, others had met during the preceding months and years at Trump's political rallies or via online forums associated with groups like QAnon, Oath Keepers, and the Proud Boys. Some were connected primarily by their ideational we-ness; others also forged dyadic bonds face-to-face when they answered Trump's call to attend the DC rally and then march to the Capitol.

In recent decades, the internet has allowed us to search for those potentially meaningful real-world places more readily on our own. Thus, in addition to our real-world experiences, the age of the internet and social media presents us with intriguing opportunities to express our identities virtually. Most impressively, the evolving metaverse is quickly emerging as an alternative reality that offers new ways of thinking about and experiencing place that have implications for our identities and how we respond to others. Many have concluded that the metaverse can empower or compromise how we express our humanity. As noted earlier, the nascent metaverse will increasingly allow us to experiment with different identities that can enhance a fabricated form of self-confidence. This type of self-worth will be grounded in a socially constructed virtual reality that incrementally approximates the real world. Ever-improving VR technologies will allow us to explore the benefits and shortcomings of a virtual teleportation system. Using our life-like avatar, this system will situate us in virtual places where we will experience firsthand an embodied reality as part of an increasingly complex, simulated setting. These computer-enhanced places, complete with progressively more convincing real-life copies of our embodied selves, will allow us to actualize our individual and group-based virtual identities. Our fantasies will become ever more place-based in virtual worlds that we can modify.

In the virtual world and real life, we will have opportunities to work with others to create places anew so that we can express our identities alongside other like-minded people. We will engage in placemaking in virtual reality with the intent of creating places consistent with how we see ourselves and want others to perceive us. Placemaking in virtual places will empower us to overcome what we believe to be our identity flaws. Although we typically undertake this activity to enhance our own sense of self and life experience, our incentive to sustain the ambience and resources that are associated with a certain place can be augmented by our desire to preserve it for our friends, children, and other descendants. In the real world, the adult members of an extended family of hunters may devote themselves to remodeling the privately owned hunting lodge that has been in the family for generations. They can easily imagine how their children and grandchildren will enjoy this place-based family legacy. Whether individuals may someday express a similar kind of commitment to pass along something in the virtual world is an open and intriguing question.

Achieving Goals

An important aspect to how we think about ourselves involves our desires to achieve different types of goals, many of which may be informal and not well articulated. These can range from the desire to experience the pleasure of participating in an activity in an appealing leisure spot to achieving an advanced degree in an institutional setting such as a prestigious university. In these and countless other situations, we often associate a place with providing us the opportunity and resources to accomplish something meaningful to us. Some commentators refer to this condition as place dependence.[9] We often grow attached to a place that is linked to a goal we share and pursue collectively with family, friends, colleagues, and even strangers. Other times we may develop an attachment to a place because it serves our individual interests. Whatever the case, we recognize on some level that the place offers us the chance to express ourselves in ways that enhance our physical, emotional, psychological, or spiritual well-being.

Thus, the goal-based motive for establishing place attachment tends to be at least loosely related to our perceptions about our identity; basically, how we perceive ourselves and how we want to experience life. Similar to how we seek to bridge the gap between our identity and the identities of others, we often try to collaborate with people to pursue shared goals. We can come to appreciate these shared goals organically or we can strategically search for people who want to participate with us to achieve some group-oriented goal. A collective goal could be to get our neighbors to help us renovate a nearby untended field to provide the neighborhood kids and families a place to play, exercise, and have picnics. If achieved, this collective goal could bring families together and benefit many of those who live in the area. The volunteers who renovate the field and then use it may develop a sense of we-ness and a form of place attachment that reflects their involvement in the project.

Place attachments based on people achieving a goal that occurs in a place they enjoy can lead to the place having restorative value. When this place becomes a preferred site for people to hang out and meet others, it "improves self-regulatory processes by providing a secure, comfortable environment conducive to self-reflection, problem-solving, and stress relief."[10] Although the neighbors cleaning up the field would probably not envision their goal as one steeped in the language of restorative value, their efforts can still lead to a powerful place attachment. We see this type of place attachment happening with the increasing numbers of people who are participating in community gardens. As of 2018, there were over twenty-nine thousand community gardens in city parks in the one hundred largest US cities, a 46 percent increase since 2012.[11] Spokane, Washington, holds the honor of having the most community gardens (4.8) per one thousand residents in the United States as of 2022.[12] These sites bring people together to develop social relationships while growing their own food. This activity leads to healthier outcomes for the gardeners while also increasing surrounding property values.

Life Course Continuity

As mindful creatures, we have the capacity to do the mental gymnastics required to think about the past, present, and future. Appreciating our place-based roots can help us map out where we've been, where we are, and where we want to go. Our attachments to specific places give us the opportunity to connect the dots of the pattern that gives continuity to our life story. Thus, we are motivated to attach ourselves to the places that have played a significant role in shaping who we are and, presumably, who we will be in the future. Here, we can consider the idea of place identity, which refers to "such feelings about specific physical settings and symbolic connections to place that define who we are."[13] The values, beliefs, and attitudes that define who we are can be linked to attributes of place. For example, being raised in a harsh rural or inner-city environment can instill in us an appreciation for resiliency and a penchant for risk taking.

Researchers have proposed that our approach to place is shaped by processes associated with child development. Although young children are not inclined to process place meanings consciously, as adults might, they can manipulate images of place in their minds.[14] In fact, children may unknowingly experience developmental processes that help them to be more sensitive to the qualities of a place. Children's attitudes toward place tend to be oriented so that the "physical environment is valued for what you can do in it, rather than in and of itself or for social meanings."[15] One takeaway from research focusing on developmental processes and place attachment is that the mechanisms by which we experience our attachments to place vary considerably across the life course. In addition, place attachments created during childhood can lay the foundation for how the places are perceived by the same individuals once they enter adulthood.

Survival, Safety, and Moral Dignity

The most compelling motive for place attachment involves our basic survival needs – both physical and mental. Yet, many of us have the luxury of not having to worry about satisfying our basic needs to eat, drink, sleep, and to be psychologically at peace. The famous psychologist Abraham Maslov popularized the notion in the mid-twentieth century that we need to fulfill our physiological needs before we worry much about satisfying our higher order psychological needs.[16] However, sociologists David Snow and Leon

Anderson have more recently argued in their book, *Down on Their Luck: A Study of Homeless Street People*, that sustaining our sense of moral worth and dignity is a parallel critical need.[17] In other words, we wrestle in some ways to satisfy our physical and psychological needs simultaneously.

Irrespective of how we want to define our basic needs, our place attachments can be driven by our desire to feel a sense of security. Consequently, those places that we believe help us to feel more secure will assume a special spot in our hearts. Whether it is a makeshift bomb shelter that protects Ukrainians from Russian missiles, a friend's home that is opened to protect an abused spouse, or a secluded corner of an underground subway terminal that serves as someone's temporary shelter, we are motivated to perceive all sorts of places as providing us comfort when we're confronting difficult circumstances. Some of the places we form attachments to will bring us together with others who are dealing with similar problems, such as support groups for addicts or cancer survivors. In other instances, an office or room will connect us regularly to a person who provides us with one-on-one guidance or therapy.

Just as we are motivated in different ways to establish place attachments, our tendency to sustain these attachments will often be reinforced over time by our involvement in various rituals and routines. Sometimes these activities will already be embedded into the social and cultural landscapes we navigate. Other times, we will help to create rituals and routines that bring people together in certain places that are meaningful to us already, or the place where we begin to pursue these activities will begin to matter to us as we grow our social ties. Thus, by personally cultivating the skill of building meaningful rituals in various types of places, we can strengthen our placemaking capacity to forge healthy place attachments for ourselves and others.

4
Rituals

Photo 6: Aerial photograph capturing the Hajj – the annual Muslim pilgrimage to the Kaaba in Mecca, Saudi Arabia – in 2018. (iStock photos/prmustafa)

At the end of every Hijri year (in the Islamic lunar calendar), more than two million Muslims from nearly two hundred countries embark on the Hajj, a major religious pilgrimage. It takes them to Mecca, a city with a rich history and the most sacred place for followers of Islam. Situated in the western mountains of Saudi Arabia, Mecca is where Muslims travel to seek redemption. The religious significance of this place is tied to the events associated with the biblical figure Abraham, and later the prophet Muhammad, that occurred here long ago.

The focal point in Mecca is the massive Islamic Grand Mosque that covers more than eighty-eight acres, and the Kaaba within it – a fifty-foot-high stone building with golden doors and an unadorned interior room. A black stone, a gift from Abraham, is embedded in the lower corner of the Kaaba and is a sacred object that many seek to touch or at least see. The object is so revered that Saudi Arabian officials sponsored a virtual reality initiative in 2021 that allows Muslims to "touch" the stone remotely.[1] Increasingly, and in various ways, modern technology is redefining the options for Muslims to experience the places in and around Mecca that define the Hajj. Although these creative options provide Muslims who are less affluent or have a disability a viable opportunity to feel connected to sacred places, they presumably cannot replicate the experiential force that draws millions of Muslims to these sites. A virtual experience is unable to duplicate how being physically involved in the arduous journey can refresh one's soul.

One of the most famous and visually impressive place-based rituals in the world involves the massive crowd of pilgrims circumambulating the Kaaba seven times during Hajj. Pilgrims who participate in the ten-day Hajj are also involved in other memorable, large-scale, place-based rituals. For example, on the first day, pilgrims journey east of Mecca to a small city, Mina, where they rest for the night before traveling the next day to Arafat, situated eight miles farther east.

In a remarkable display of placemaking that supports the Hajj, the Saudi government created the City of Tents in Mina.[2] Today, this complex includes more than 100,000 air-conditioned, interconnected tents that can accommodate roughly 2.6 million people!

The most recent iteration of the City of Tents includes the provision of high-quality, fire-resistant tents. This plan was developed to respond to the deadly fires that occurred over the years when Hajj occupants were still housed in regular tents. The current complex offers a safer and more hospitable environment with communal areas, security fences, signposted corridors, and conveniences like kitchens, toilets, and electrical outlets. Each year, after the Hajj is completed, the temporary City of Tents is dismantled, and the materials are easily stored. These structural improvements in accommodations, though appealing for many, have ironically lessened the physical and psychological struggles that were intended to replicate the trials and tribulations endured by both the sacred religious figures and the earlier pilgrims. Although austere attire minimizes how social class is visually displayed, those with money can still pay for transportation and other amenities that make the experience less arduous. Even though there have been concerted attempts to make the pilgrimage less dangerous over the years, there has always been a concern that a person who goes on a quest to Mecca might not return alive.

Pilgrims engage in several other highly symbolic and place-based rituals. They do a fast walk back and forth seven times between two nearby hilltops (Safa and Marwa) to simulate Abraham's wife Hagar's desperate search for water for herself and her son. Later, pilgrims travel to the Mount of Mercy to participate in the "standing at Arafat," a ritual that requires members of the crowd to turn inwards to seek personal forgiveness at the place thought to be where Muhammad gave his last sermon. One of the culminating events, "Stoning of the Devil," includes packed crowds of pilgrims throwing seven stones at three different stone pillars to reenact Abraham throwing stones at the Devil to repel its temptation. Pilgrims continue to participate in these rituals despite knowing that people in the past have been crushed by the surging crowds. In 2015, for example, 2,400 pilgrims tragically died in Mina during the early morning when overwhelming crowd flows got entangled and compressed resulting in many people falling and being trampled. Pilgrims must increasingly worry about the extreme heat as well. More than 1,300 pilgrims died in 2024 because of scorching daily temperatures that ranged from 117 to 120 degrees Fahrenheit![3] Unfortunately, the raging climate crisis will generate deadly physical conditions that will mar the Hajj indefinitely. The Hajj is clearly a risky place-based ritual with potentially profound consequences for participants' sense of we-ness and physical well-being. Presumably for some, the virtual option's promise of safety compensates for its experiential shortcomings.

Although most public attention related to the Hajj is directed toward the participants, thousands of residents in and around Mecca work tirelessly throughout the year to prepare this sacred place for the annual arrival of the masses. Merchants have their own routines to follow as they methodically prepare to service and sell goods in the market to an international clientele numbering in the millions. Thus, many locals of Mecca are attached to this place for both its religious and commercial significance.

The natural landscape and built environment, each steeped in religious symbolism, provide Mecca and the surrounding areas with their unique meaning. More specifically, the rugged terrain, intense heat, market-style businesses, and symbolic sites are some of the critical aspects of place that reinforce the cultural and social activities associated with the Hajj. They add a performative dimension to the various types of places that make the Hajj possible. In other words, the distinct places associated with the Hajj enable individuals to experience the transformative power of place while on their spiritual journey. In addition, a Muslim's pilgrimage to Mecca is enhanced by the ideational and dyadic bonds of we-ness they experience throughout their quest. Many make the trek on their own, but others share the experience with family and friends.

In 2020 and 2021, fear of COVID-19 forced authorities to restrict the Hajj to only one thousand and sixty thousand authorized Arabian participants, respectively. In addition, the Hajj ministry dropped the "Guardian Rule" so that women can now take part in the Hajj without being accompanied by a male relative so long as they go in a group. Moving forward, this new arrangement should provide numerous women the opportunity to expand their sense of dyadic and ideational we-ness simultaneously.

Praying, chanting, walking, sleeping, and eating side by side with so many like-minded Muslims accentuates the intensity of a person's individual quest. That quest is largely realized in places of nature, tent dwellings, public spaces, sites for exchanging goods and services, ceremonial settings, and sometimes transport vehicles. Such places create opportunities to produce unforgettable memories that deepen, and often fundamentally alter, pilgrims' self-perceptions and life perspectives. For many, the final moments of the Hajj elicit feelings of accomplishment, a renewal of a religious identity, and a reaffirmed sense of commitment to a principled way of life. But many are left feeling momentarily sad, too. They must cope with the possibility that they may never return to this special place. They realize that they are unlikely to relive the intense, ecstatic energy of the crowded rituals that bring together two million fellow Muslims to nurture a sense of brotherhood and sisterhood – a type of ideational we-ness that is cultivated in an extraordinary place.

What Is a Ritual

Ritual, like place, is a commonly used word in everyday talk, yet social scientists remind us that there are plenty of nuances and much to debate about how to define it. When studying rituals, anthropologists, sociologists, religious scholars, and others assess different ways to categorize the diverse types of rituals, the purposes they play in our lives, and consider how we assign meaning to them. For our purposes, we can loosely think of rituals as social activities that are symbolically charged and provide a structure to how the members of a group or community of people regularly engage with one another. Typically, we assume there is some type of periodicity associated with a ritual. In other words, there's an assumption that the activity will occur at various points over time and that the timing is somewhat predictable. However, there can be considerable variability in how often specific people participate, ranging from only once to all the time.

While scholars interpret the concept of ritual differently, most would agree with anthropologist Roy Rappaport's characterization of ritual as "humanity's basic social act."[4] Thus, just as we should realize that place matters in our daily lives, ritual matters too. Not only does ritual matter, but it, like place, is ubiquitous. The sociologist Robert Bellah adds,

> although some forms of ritual have become less evident, or retreated from the public sphere, it is also true that even in contemporary society we remain surrounded by ritual in a myriad of forms. It might even be argued that ritual is to be found everywhere that humans live together if we look in the right place, although where those places are may be very different from one society to the next.[5]

Before turning our full attention to ritual, let's momentarily digress to differentiate ritual from its close cousin, routine. The typical person probably doesn't distinguish between the two, leading many to use these terms interchangeably, but social scientists and folks in the fields of personal coaching and self-help consulting tend to accentuate the distinction. They identify the difference in terms of the attitude behind the behavior.[6] Compared to routines, rituals are more meaningful, symbolic practices. They tend to be grounded in a strong sense of purpose and are more likely to be connected to something bigger than a specific practice, whereas routines are the more basic, less significant activities that we regularly perform. We often have routines out of practical necessity or an obligation to achieve something to make it through the day. Although routines can help us navigate our everyday lives, we're less psychologically and emotionally invested in them. Rituals, on the other hand, are more likely to shape who we are by providing us a sense of purpose beyond any given day.

When defined broadly, one similarity between rituals and routines is that we can perform each of these by ourselves. We can read a religious text and pray alone in the comfort of our own bedroom, or we can do multiple sets of push-ups and sit-ups every morning by ourselves before eating breakfast. Depending on who is interpreting these events, some would say that each of these examples illustrates either a ritual or routine. For us, the similarity in this instance is not relevant because personal rituals and routines done solo are not central to my objectives for this book. I primarily target the practices that involve, at minimum, one other person. I make this distinction because I focus on how rituals are relevant to the connection between place and our desire to achieve a sense of group belonging. That said, we must not overlook the fact that accomplishing our individual daily routines efficiently can give us more time to participate in rituals with others in consequential places. Under the right circumstances, a routine done alone or with others may evolve into a cherished ritual weighted with symbolism that we share with others.

Placing Rituals

Muslims, and persons of every other faith, can participate in rituals to express their devotion. When people of faith engage in rituals, they do so as members of a thought community. They share a sense of group belonging because they hold comparable views. Similarly, people can take part in rituals when navigating the other four social domains that I delineated in the Introduction (primary groups, community and community groups, sports and leisure, and work). Those rituals will be situated in the various types of places I've outlined previously.

Like everything we do in life, rituals always occur in a place, and many of these places are quite meaningful to us. Let's drill down, then, to explore the intersections that join ritual and place. How do rituals bolster our attachment to specific places? And how do the properties of a place cultivate our ability to get involved in place-based social practices or rituals that enable us to experience a sense of group belonging in the various social domains?

Some places, like the sites located in the region of Mecca pertaining to the Hajj, are religious landmarks. The short- and long-term value of sacred places like these is enhanced by the collective energy that is generated to preserve the memories that reinforce our attachment to a place. Participants' collective consciousness is heightened in places of this sort, even if the place and practices change in appearance or form over time. That consciousness, in turn, can promote creative placemaking initiatives that alter attributes of those places, like the initial inclusion of thousands of tents in Mina for the Hajj, and their replacement with upgraded, fire-resistant tents. While these sacred places are fascinating and consequential, most of us are more involved with basic rituals that occur in mundane, yet significant places.

Over a century ago, the famous French sociologist Émile Durkheim's classic book *The Elementary Forms of Religious Life* cemented his standing as one of the earliest and most thoughtful theorists on rituals, especially those connected to religion.[7] He helped pave the way for scholars and the public at large to look more closely at religious rituals. For Durkheim, and many others, rituals were a critical social form because they represented a pathway for people to express a collective consciousness. He believed that when people gathered to engage with each other in ritual activities they were filled with emotion. The rituals became sites that inspired a form of "collective effervescence" that offered participants the opportunity to internalize the remarkable sentiment that was being created by the whole group. Many of us have at least watched portrayals of this type of social energy in documentary footage of prayer or meditative rituals associated with mainstream religions and cults. Two notable examples include the dramatic piercing and related rituals associated with the Hindu festival of Thaipusam and the intense firewalking rituals on the island of Mauritius.[8] Some of us have also personally witnessed this type of energy up close while taking part in a faith-based ritual.

One contemporary anthropologist and cognitive scientist, Dimitris Xygalatas, has made it his life's work to integrate ethnographic methodologies with biometric sensing technologies to study the phenomenology and the physiology related to extreme rituals around the world. In *Ritual: How Seemingly Senseless Acts Make Life Worth Living*, Xygalatas creatively explores how people express themselves and bond in a wide range of fascinating rituals that are typically tied to special places.[9] Although Xygalatas devotes most of his analysis to understanding the cultural, social, interpersonal, and biophysical dimensions to these rituals, his detailed descriptions also reveal the impact of a place and its many properties (especially symbolic meanings) on people's experiences. Focusing on what anthropologist Harvey Whitehouse refers to as imagistic collective rituals – those exceptional rituals that provoke transformational experiences that are both private and communal – Xygalatas empirically demonstrates that such rituals can trigger both an intense personal experience and the collective effervescence that Durkheim theorized about.

Durkheim is also well known for extending his thinking beyond the sacred realm to comment on how rituals are connected to the evolution from less complex societies where people were largely self-sufficient to more complex societies that include greater specialization and division of labor. Rituals and other forms of cooperation become much more critical in sustaining these complex social arrangements that are based on people's diverse values, interests, and skills. Thus, in the modern world it is essential to design places that effectively bring people with varied interests and abilities together to form a productive sense of we-ness, one that enhances everyday social life by fostering practical outcomes.

In the past several decades, the sociologist Randall Collins extended Durkheim's work by developing a framework to understand what he labels "interactional ritual chains" – the countless microlevel activities that give meaning to our lives.[10] From Collins's vantage point, rituals are pervasive in everyday life. While they include religious activities, they encompass much more.

Like Durkheim, Collins points out that those who voluntarily get involved and stay involved with rituals do so because they enjoy the "emotional energy" they reap from the symbolic exchanges. Collins focuses on the interpersonal exchanges and cultural capital we contribute and develop from our involvement in these interaction rituals. For example, we can have general knowledge about specific ways of thinking, feeling, and doing that set us apart from others: Do we know how to work on cars, make pottery, invest in the stock market, play sports, cook gourmet meals, or navigate the street drug scene? Having specialized knowledge and skills enables us to discern if others are compatible with our social orbits, preferences, and capacities. This knowledge allows us to leverage our insider's standpoint to communicate with those who share similar attributes.

On a personal level, we often develop unique memories with others that allow us to acknowledge our shared history of social times – both good and bad – and have an intimate view of those shared experiences. Inside jokes, gestures, and shared evocative storytelling of special times enable us to feel a sense of affinity with others with whom we share a personal history.

Although Collins doesn't explicitly incorporate the concept of place into his scheme of interaction rituals, he highlights elements that can inform our efforts to link interaction rituals with place. In his model, the four elements that give a social act a ritual quality include the co-presence of two or more persons, a common focus of attention or mutual awareness of what is taking place, a common emotional tone or mood, and some sort of membership symbol to convey a shared reality or group belonging (e.g., physical objects, similar characteristics, mutually understood gestures, shared values and ideas).

None of these elements reference place per se, yet the last three features are connected to the place properties outlined in Chapter 1. Place properties, particularly physical conditions, symbolic meanings, and discourses appear to be front and center in the minds of those who are socially active with others in a place. For example, imagine a highly motivated group of friends who regularly seek out adventure at leisure spots by embracing the physical and psychological challenges that are fostered by ocean waves, river rapids, mountain peaks and valleys, and cave routes. Sometimes these adventures are not done in a strictly "together but alone" mode, rather the execution of the challenge may require individuals to display teamwork skills to navigate the rapids in a raft or climb a mountain while leveraging the mutual benefits of sharing equipment, food, and cautionary feedback in real time. Alternatively, think of rituals that take the form of marches and protests that create opportunities for people to express their political sentiments together at key landmarks or ceremonial settings in the form of government buildings. Protests and rallies are likely to be focused on a common cause, generate a shared mood, and display visible symbols in terms of attire, gestures, signage, and slogans that unite the participants in a meaningful place. Trump's infamously scripted MAGA rallies, replete with all the symbolic materials and activities, vividly illustrate these points.

Robert Bellah summarizes how group members engaged in interaction rituals connect "through their shared experience, feel a sense of membership, however fleeting, with a sense of boundary between those sharing the experience and all those outside it; they feel some sense of moral obligation to each other, which is symbolized by whatever they focused on during the interaction."[11] These encounters generate the emotional energy that connects people. One of the key consequences of this energy rests in its capacity to sustain and deepen rituals. Thus, it is vital to understand how place properties enhance or constrain the ritual processes and emotional energy that sustains a sense of group belonging in the various social domains.

Primary Groups

We share many of the interaction rituals that mean the most to us with our family and close friends in the comfort of our home or other hospitable dwellings. Some of the rituals that help us build a sense of we-ness with people in our close circle are based on sharing meals and celebrating special moments together. I have fond childhood memories of large summer family reunions with fifteen aunts and uncles, sixteen cousins, my parents, and an older sister at my maternal grandma's farmhouse in the small borough of New Bethlehem, Pennsylvania. We had picnic-style feasts that included corn on the cob, potatoes, and vegetables harvested from grandma's farm.

My grandma's expansive farm stood in stark contrast to my family's small brick home located in a densely packed working-class neighborhood. Her farm had a large wooden barn stocked with hay bales and a long rope swing with a launching point in the loft in addition to an attached garage that housed a tractor and lots of impressive tools. The property also included a pond with fish, a pigsty home to five pigs, a rowdy chicken coop, a small building that enclosed a water well with a communal tin drinking cup, a functioning wooden outhouse, acres of fields with or without crops depending on the growing season, a huge yard, and an old two-story farmhouse that had a spacious food pantry, mysterious attic, and a dingy cellar. The bedrooms and pantry each had their own unique, musty smells that were closely tied to memories in my brain, even long after my grandmother died and the house was sold. During my childhood and long thereafter, those smells instantly triggered sentimental memories that attached me to the farm and the activities that took place there, including having my older cousins mentor me about navigating life on a farm.

Grandma's farm was the kind of place that features numerous special objects that provide opportunities for those present to forge and reinforce interpersonal bonds and secure long-lasting memories. When objects like these are part of a place, they can promote bonds and a sense of we-ness that are imbued with expressions of risk-taking, curiosity, mentoring, and nurturance. Our identities are often connected to our physical surroundings and the tangible objects that matter to us. Sociologist Christena Nippert-Eng refers to these objects as "territories of the self." Referring to our embodied sense of self, she asserts: "We embed it in and associate it with a particular environment and its contents, including the people and objects appearing there."[12] Thus, the people, objects, and the way people relate to the items help to define how a place takes on meaning for those who experience it.

To illustrate, I'll share another anecdote from my personal vault. In my mid- and late twenties, after the rituals at grandma's farm were a thing of the past, I formed a new attachment to a friend's picturesque cabin retreat in Hocking Hills in southern Ohio. The setting drew a large array of gregarious friends, mostly in their twenties and thirties, who lived in Columbus. Ironically, we also called this idyllic place "the farm." Nestled in a high section of a thick, tree-covered rolling mountainside, the farm included a one-story, two-bedroom log cabin, grassy areas on all sides, a swimmable pond with a large floating wooden platform covered in green outdoor carpet in the middle that accommodated diving and sunbathing, and a handmade volleyball court in the grass. It also had a designated winding path that took people a hundred yards into the woods to a makeshift outhouse area tucked into a patch of surrounding trees. On various weekends, weather permitting, fifteen to twenty-five people could be playing by day and tent camping at night. Although our time spent together was largely spontaneous, we had unscripted rituals that allowed us to bond via cookouts, potluck picnics, skinny dipping for some, bonfires, volleyball games, frisbee throwing, hiking, stargazing, and much more. The secluded, tranquil, and festive site fostered opportunities to nourish existing friendships and to build fresh ones when the main crew invited wide-eyed newcomers. The farm, a place immersed in nature, was a special site for play, exploration, reflection, and communal bonding. Even though we had no clever nickname to identify ourselves as a cohesive group, we implicitly understood who the core and periphery members were in the farm crew.

David Purnell, the communications professor we met in Chapter 1 who shared his reflections on creating a sense of we-ness during his homeless stints, also illustrates the value of house- or property-based rituals that rely on food sharing to build community. For seventeen years beginning in 1999, after being homeless, Purnell lived in the Seminole Heights neighborhood, roughly three miles south of downtown Tampa, Florida. As he describes in his book, *Building Communities through Food: Strengthening Communication, Families, and Social Capital*, what was initially an impromptu dinner with five neighbors hosted at his house evolved quickly within three months to a weekly neighborhood dinner hosting twenty-five to thirty-five people.[13] After eighteen months, several other families gradually agreed to host some of these dinners. Throughout Purnell's description of the community building that occurred at these dinners, he emphasizes how features of the various houses – the intimate places that made this ritual possible – fostered a warm and inviting ambience. He highlights the practical assets like "large spacious indoor areas, including a dining room with a large table, [and] a separate kitchen" that could accommodate all the attendees. That these weekly dinners persisted unabated for at least nineteen years speaks volumes about how informal rituals connected to specific places can help create a sense of community. The mix of having designated and comfortable meeting sites, food, and a communal spirit can generate both an attachment to place and a sense of we-ness.

Before people make and share food with others as part of a bonding ritual, they must frequent places to buy at least some of the ingredients and cooking supplies. Even the folks who live on a working farm will travel to buy certain food items. Thus, place becomes significant in this domain because the places where people live influence their options for food shopping, an activity which can become a ritual for some people. People living in lower-income sections of major cities are typically located in a "food apartheid." Until recently "food desert" had been the commonly used term, but food activists assert that this term misrepresents the root causes of a community not having access to healthy food.[14] In these places, people have limited access to food, especially high-quality, affordable food that includes fresh fruits and vegetables. Having limited access to a supermarket forces community residents to pick up more expensive food at poorly stocked convenience stores or eat at fast food restaurants. Similarly, those living in distinctly rural areas have their own set of accessibility problems with food. Only about a quarter of rural food stores carry foods consistent with the USDA's Dietary Guidelines for America.[15] For many rural residents, the scarcity of nearby stores along with unreliable forms of transportation mean that they must manage their time and plan their food shopping more carefully than persons who have convenient food shopping opportunities.

While food apartheids are most common in low-income communities, they define the community as being a certain type of place wherever they occur. The hardships that inner-city and rural populations face while living in food apartheids can affect whether and how they incorporate ritual practices into their food shopping. How do some rural families create rituals out of the once-a-week mini road trips they take to grocery shop? How does the shared car-time and shopping-time translate into a stronger sense of we-ness or create disruptive tensions? Unlike those who have suffered living in food apartheids, I've had the good fortune of living within roughly a mile of large supermarkets for many years. That proximity has enabled me to develop family shopping rituals that have included my youngest son. While our ritual has evolved over the years as a result of him becoming more independent and eager to negotiate food purchases, we have the flexibility to integrate several quick visits to the store every week. These trips give us a chance to coordinate our joint shopping activity in a safe, familiar place with staff who often recognize us as a shopping team.

While I've leveraged a couple of "farms" and grocery stores to create bonding rituals with family and friends, and Purnell had his own neighborhood house parties to cultivate a sense of community, others grow attached to their own special places where they experience meaningful rituals and develop a sense of we-ness in their primary groups. For example, think of the small fishing boat, athletic facility, garage crammed with a band's musical equipment, hunting lodge, recreation center in an assisted living facility, or some other place where family and friends experience the informal rhythms of life produced by rituals. Profiling additional places is beyond the scope of what I hope to achieve here, but we should appreciate the breadth of places that we can use to develop this ritual sentiment with those who matter most to us. As we enhance our place consciousness, we can learn to dissect how specific properties associated with these key places alter how we see and express ourselves while relating to others.

Community and Community Groups

While Purnell's unique story bridges the primary group and community domains, other rituals may reveal themselves more clearly as being part of public places and spaces, such as schools, Boys & Girls Clubs, recreational and fitness facilities, daycare centers, local third places, neighborhood parks, community centers, and plazas. For example, school officials in nearly five thousand schools across the United States offer students the opportunity to maintain a school garden. First introduced in the early 1800s in Europe, flower, vegetable, and fruit gardens represent a valuable experiential learning tool for youth.[16] While school gardens are designed primarily to teach students about school-related subjects including health, nutrition, and environmental science, a school gardening program can also provide students with fun rituals throughout the school year. When students plant, nurture, and harvest their garden they learn to problem solve cooperatively. Students can also enjoy rituals that involve eating the food they've grown. Ideally, the rituals that emerge from school gardening, like those associated with community gardens, will help students appreciate being part of something bigger than themselves. These experiences can help students to learn how to be effective leaders and to work collaboratively with their classmates. Nurturing a garden, and claiming it as one's own, can enhance students' place consciousness and attachment. It can also inspire them to incorporate a garden into their own home and alter their sense of place both at school and where they live.

Community groups often work cooperatively on projects that sponsor public rituals. Those rituals are designed to bring people together and serve as a public relations initiative to build the community's identity. Many of these events overlap with the leisure domain described below in that they include fun activities, such as concerts, athletic races, parades, and more. Some communities invest large sums of money to build convention sites, athletic facilities, auditoriums, and other venues to entice locals and outsiders to bring their business to the area.

Numerous community groups seek to help individuals in need by creating place-based opportunities that include activities resembling rituals of social support. The Junior League of Miami, for example, has for many years sponsored the Inn Transition program with North and South facilities that assists women, many of whom are mothers who have been victims of domestic violence.[17] This women's volunteer organization coordinates a public-private partnership with Miami-Dade County to provide women and their children with transitional housing and support services. The South facility includes a fifty-six-unit, gated complex with two-, three-, and four-bedroom apartments, a community center, children's library, and a playground, all of which are conveniently located across from a public elementary school. Throughout the year, Junior League members sponsor various life-skills workshops and enrichment activities for the women, while offering regular childcare, entertainment, and counseling options for the children. The program's centralized physical design and interactive management plan inspire participants to establish a sense of we-ness among themselves and with the volunteers. The women directly benefit from sharing their joint struggles in close proximity as they navigate the stressful process of getting their lives back on track. So, too, the Junior League volunteers have enriched their bonds with one another as they have invested their time and resources into launching, expanding, and maintaining this place-based social service initiative.

Thought Communities

Faith communities regularly provide followers with place-based rituals that enable them to feel a greater sense of ideational we-ness with other members. While the previous discussion about Islam, Mecca, and the Hajj highlights one of the most elaborate rituals of its kind, there are more ordinary examples that faith communities integrate into their daily or weekly schedules. Religious rituals, which bring people together to participate in prayer ceremonies in places that can be adorned in symbolic representations of the history, key figures, and dogma of a particular faith, are seamlessly integrated into faith-based services. For example, Catholics are encouraged to light prayer candles in memory of loved ones in a special section of the church usually located off to the side of the main altar. This gesture is designed to signal a person's solidarity with the remembered person who may either be deceased or experiencing a significant life challenge.

In recent decades, discussions about the value of rituals and group belonging in the faith community have increasingly focused on the rise of megachurches. Defined as Protestant churches with regular attendance of two thousand or more during the pre-pandemic period, the number of these churches in the United States has increased in recent decades. In 2020, there were roughly 1,750 such churches; they have also become larger and significantly more multiracial since 2000.[18] Only 21 percent of megachurches in 2000 had a 20 percent or greater presence of persons of color, whereas by 2020, 58 percent of these churches were multiracial.[19] This trend has been generated by strategic decisions the leaders of these large churches have made to make their places of worship more inclusive and welcoming to new members. Thus, these megachurches are attempting to expand how participants perceive and experience their sense of we-ness as part of a religious thought community.

One team of religious scholars points out that megachurches are successful in recruiting and maintaining members for a couple notable reasons.[20] They argue that these churches are particularly good at creating an environment where the kinds of emotionally charged interaction rituals that Randall Collins theorized about can thrive. The leaders of megachurches have committed themselves to a style of placemaking that creates a physical, social, and spiritual environment that generates feelings of collective effervescence.

While the specific tactics vary, the rituals practiced in these churches are generally consistent with the main themes of Collins's model. For example, megachurches tend to discourage any type of formal dress code and they avoid traditional liturgies. Thus, while they in some ways initially downplay the group membership symbols that Collins touts as being critical to establishing ritual chains, megachurches reinforce that symbolic sense of shared experience once people are enthusiastically involved with church services and begin to participate in other church-related small group activities beyond the worship services.[21] Service rituals also incorporate contemporary music into worship time as part of the service, display words on large screens to help participants get involved even if they don't know the words, and use cameras to project images of in-house worshippers onto a screen that everyone can see. The goal is to create an inviting place that amplifies a large-scale group mood that is energetic, inclusive, and authentic. Yet, the ritual-based energy that helps to create a powerful collective experience is ultimately used to inspire participants to look inward when the pastor extends an "altar call" to invite congregants to come to the front of the church and "accept Jesus as their personal Lord and Savior."[22] This segment of the service melds the important "me-oriented" religious sensation for those who respond to the altar call with the "we" experience that includes other participants' heightened sense of togetherness as they watch. Focus group interviews with megachurch participants reveal that their feelings of belonging within the church are fostered by their sense of place consciousness – members are aware of and embrace their church's creative efforts to grab and keep their attention by stimulating their emotions.

Megachurches benefit from the uplifting energy large numbers of people can produce when gathered in a place that accentuates the entertainment and emotional features of a religious service. These churches can also use the technologies that facilitate online worship to create a virtual place that is inviting and provides participants a sense of belonging. During the COVID-19 pandemic, calls for online worship were intensified with many churches attempting to adapt their in-person rituals to an online platform. However, while a Pew Research Center report in August 2020 found that many people responded to the pandemic by spending more time engaged with an online religious service, it also found that most people indicated that they planned to go back to in-person services after the pandemic was over.[23] Even though online participation patterns may decline, millions of people will still be involved with an online church experience.[24] The enthusiasm for online churches is echoed by one online pastor, James Emery White, who encourages other like-minded pastors to "plant" their own church online.[25] White emphasizes the appeal of creating an engaging "digital campus" where you are greeted by staff and pastors that in many ways mirror what it's like to attend a church service in person. Nonetheless, the digital, remote church format limits the opportunity to create the group-based emotional energy that flourishes in the typical megachurch physical environment. Whether futuristic VR and AR programs might eventually provide congregants a more engaging experience without them being fully present in the physical context is an intriguing and open question.

Although religious connections to places and rituals can be quite powerful, many of us rely on rituals to express other types of strong personal sentiments. We demonstrate our life philosophies, identities, and commitment to social and environmental justice issues through rituals that accentuate a place's meaning. One type of ritual that has received a considerable amount of attention over the years is Civil War reenactments.[26] These rituals, staged primarily but not exclusively in Southern states, are some of the more theatrical representations of how sentiments of regional attachment – a form of identity construction – involve a participant's desire to achieve a sense of group belonging. Every year, thousands of people don Union and Confederate uniforms and equipment to participate in realistic enactments that showcase the power of visual history.[27] Conducted in vast fields that are often the same or similar to those where real Civil War battles were brutally waged, these rituals reinforce participants' and observers' sense of a regional collective identity. They can also represent intergenerational rituals that include adults passing on cultural knowledge to their children. Some contemporary father and son pairs participate together just as family members really did during the Civil War. While these rituals can be viewed as opportunities to express connections to a thought community, for some, they also represent a form of leisure. In either case, they remind participants and onlookers alike that place, and the social life that occurs within its borders, can be influenced by and also contribute to history in profound ways.

Some of the rituals that bring people together do so by commemorating events that we associate with distinct places, such as the annual reading of the nearly three thousand names that acknowledge those who died from the 9/11 terrorist attacks in New York City and Pennsylvania. The ceremonial events that occur at the 9/11 Memorial and Museum in New York City and the Garden of Reflection 9-11 Memorial in Pennsylvania, both imbued with place-based symbolism, are essentially rituals for celebrating the collective consciousness that represents our national identity as Americans.

People who have strong ideological convictions are often energized if they have developed a sense of place attachment that is part of the collective consciousness of like-minded persons. People can align themselves with places they've experienced with others directly, or they can even feel connected when they are aware of a place's standing in a larger movement, despite it being far away. For instance, union members might embrace a union hall or a recreational site where union members regularly socialize, such as a local bar, bowling alley, or community hall. Those who are members of civic organizations like the American Legion, the Moose, Rotary Club, and other similar groups are likely to have a meeting hall that represents their special place, which is where members reinforce their sense of we-ness by participating in various formal and informal rituals.

Leisure and Sports

City leaders, such as mayors and key members of community-wide organizations, often have a voice in developing satisfying place-based rituals. These take the form of farmers' markets, concerts, festivals, parades, athletic competitions, and other public events. Communities that pride themselves on being a tourist magnet or hub for specific sporting and cultural activities tailor much of their public relations activity toward a supportive style of placemaking. They aim to convince the public that they've constructed appealing places and rituals that cater to people's entertainment and service preferences. Even the communities that do not project themselves as tourist destinations often promote place-based rituals to provide entertainment options for their residents and to promote community solidarity. Those who sponsor and coordinate public rituals can bring people together in ways that enhance their well-being and contribute to productive outcomes for the community.

The small rural town of Clarksdale, Mississippi, provides an instructive case study that highlights both a city's placemaking efforts to promote leisure and the community's mixed responses. In his incisive ethnography of this town, *I Don't Like the Blues: Race, Place, and the Backbeat of Black Life*, sociologist B. Brian Foster highlights how the interconnected forces of Black identity, racial politics, social class, and Southern rural culture shape the local response to the state's public relations campaign to raise the area's profile as a blues tourist attraction.[28] In the early 2000s, Mississippi's political and business leaders endorsed the Blues Commission that was tasked with promoting the message that the Delta was the "Land of the Blues." Since then, numerous influential stakeholders throughout the region have invested substantial resources into promoting blues-related festivals, clubs, media profiles, travelogues, tourism pamphlets, billboards, and more. Constructing and refurbishing the infrastructure to support this venture, and fine-tuning the promotional message, has been a top priority.

Clarksdale, which had been an active hub for blues music and culture for decades prior to the most recent campaign, continues to be at the center of the blues world in the Delta. Although the tourists and the locals directly involved in supporting the entertainment sector of the city have enthusiastically embraced the blues scene, Black residents in the area have largely ignored it. In many instances, they disdain it. Why?

Foster heard a similar despondent, collective refrain during the 2014 to 2019 period when he asked Black residents why they didn't participate in the city's blues scenes: "Clarksdale's blues scenes were for white folks. The music catered to white audiences. White people owned the venues. Many Black residents even saw the buildings and performance spaces, themselves, as white, places they could not go to without encountering some level of racial discomfort or unfair treatment."[29] Despite being linked by history and their racial heritage as the creators of the blues genre, contemporary Black people in Clarksdale are disconnected from the places and rituals that define their city's blues scene. Foster captures the practical consequences of these sentiments about blues places and culture in Clarksdale by highlighting a fascinating process he labels "place-unmaking." He reminds us that "Boycotting and withdrawing from certain types of public spaces and civic services have long been ways for Black folks to challenge unequal living conditions." Thus, instead of playing an active role in shaping the appearance, ambience, and meaning of the places that house the blues, Black residents indirectly leave their mark on the Clarksdale blues scene by not being part of it.

Foster shares how his participants framed their stories by suggesting that the "blues was something they had lived, something that belonged to them, something they took pride in. They told me the blues was a part of who they were." They understood that pain and suffering are the seeds of the blues movement. However, these same participants also made it clear that "We ain't that no mo." They do not want to be defined by the pain and suffering they believe to be the lived experience of poor rural Black people struggling to stay afloat in a turbulent sea of racism. Today, their sense of we-ness as rural Black Southerners living in Clarksdale is rooted in their rejection of the style and appearance of white blues that now permeates the places that make up the city's entertainment center.

Yet, place and community still matter to them. So, as Foster observes, they lean into their informal "placemaking practices" closer to home to cultivate their sense of we-ness: "Black Clarksdalians today make their front porches into the backrooms, hidden in plain sight, where friends and family share laughter and secrets."[30] These folks, alienated in some ways from portions of their segregated residential community, nurture their own intimate places and the informal rituals that bind them to those who matter. They do so while intentionally avoiding those "old and misused" places that were once part of the older generation's lives when the places existed in a different form.

In addition to the music scene, an important feature of many community environments, big and small, involves sports teams and their fan bases. In the world of both amateur and professional team sports, the intersection of place and ritual is most vividly on display in terms of the home-field or home-court advantage. For various reasons, almost all teams will have more success playing at home than away. One of the main advantages for the home team is that its players will have the luxury of being supported by their cheering fan base. The sense of we-ness that a home crowd generates during a game with home team players is etched in sports folklore. Some sports venues have achieved iconic status in players' and fans' eyes, and some venues are even recognized by the more general population of sports fans (e.g., Wrigley Field, Yankee Stadium, Fenway Park, Madison Square Garden, Boston Garden, Lambeau Field, Wembley Stadium).

Irrespective of the specific facility, home team players commonly use the phrase "not in our house" to convey their conviction that they will not allow a visiting team to come to their facility and beat them. This linguistic turn of phrase conveys a type of place attachment that is common among players and fans alike. Using terms like "house" and "home" in the sports world reflects our broader inclination to define ourselves symbolically through our attachment to the places and people that matter to us. Just as family members are more likely to feel relaxed and comfortable in their own home, so, too, athletes savor the comfort of their familiar physical surroundings that include their supportive fans. Some teams embellish pregame, in-game, and postgame rituals that are designed to unite players with fans, deepening their ideational we-ness in the process. For example, when Green Bay Packers football players leap into the stands after scoring a touchdown at Lambeau Field, the celebration between the player and the small group of fans who have physical contact with the player in the end zone is vicariously shared by all Packers fans and players either in attendance or watching on a screen. This, and similar rituals, intensifies the collective consciousness that unites the fan base and team. Similarly, the tailgating parties that precede many major college and professional games are another place-based ritual designed to generate the emotional energy and sense of group belonging that is ideal for a rabid sports fan base.

More modest rituals with athletic overtones are also shared with everyday folks during their weekly routines. Friends who regularly meet up every Sunday morning on the tennis court or at the local gym at 7:00 a.m. are using this ritual to not only stay fit but to honor their friendship. Some physically active parents and children create similar rituals that bring them together to ride bikes, play catch, run, or participate in some other form of exercise on a regular basis. Whether it is with friends or family, these rituals are often repeatedly performed in the same place. Consequently, the participants, especially if they are truly enjoying the experience, are likely to develop some level of place attachment and a sense of we-ness with those who join them.

Fitness centers, whether school-based or private businesses, can encourage participants to recognize working out as part of a larger social ritual. For example, fitness centers can promote various sessions (e.g., yoga, kickboxing, Zumba, Pilates, and group cycling) that encourage individuals to participate with workout buddies. Some of the more affluent centers also offer inviting spaces to hang out with friends or family after a session. Those spaces can include a deli, juice bar, and lounge areas to eat and relax. In addition, owners of fitness clubs can create the means for users to give feedback that is meant to modify the gym's rituals. When users feel they're invested in the facility and what happens there, they are more likely to make suggestions and see their participation as being part of a larger community of health-conscious people.

Work

The COVID-19 era taught us critical life lessons about how social (physical) distancing restrictions can curtail the way we navigate taken-for-granted places where emotionally laden rituals are typically performed. During the pandemic, health care facilities were one such place. Medical staff in many instances were forced to alter their standard care practices and place themselves and their patients at risk by reusing PPE or not using the highest quality gear available. Without directly referring to rituals, one distraught nurse reported how she had to alter her style of nursing during the COVID-19 period:

> I am a hugger. I hug my patients if they let me when they are suffering. I hold their hands. I never let my patients die alone if I can help it. But during this time, I could not offer comfort the way I know how. I couldn't sit with the patients as they were dying because someone else needed me. At the end of my shift, I get into my car and I weep. I weep because I feel like I am not doing enough.[31]

The COVID-19 protocols redefined the unit's practices – their rituals and routines. The new rules and norms limited this nurse, and countless others, from developing the fleeting sense of we-ness they might otherwise establish with desperate patients.

Confronted with an unprecedented crisis, hospital administrators and government staff were forced to repurpose various areas to accommodate the surge of COVID-19 patients and the deceased. Converting surgical and general recovery rooms into COVID-19 wards and restricting how lunchrooms and other meeting spaces were used became a common practice in many hospitals across the country and world.[32] Hospital settings became even bleaker when testing and triage areas were established outside the hospital building. Refrigerated trucks were sometimes parked in service areas to accommodate the overflow of corpses. In some places, temporary field hospitals were quickly constructed to compensate for hospitals' inability to expand their services fast enough because of limitations in space and personnel. These physical modifications compelled health care professionals to adapt by creating new procedures and rituals to manage the crisis.

In the health care and elder care worlds, we grew accustomed, sometimes begrudgingly, to thinking about alternatives to what had become common practices. We initiated more exchanges using telehealth technologies, allowing us to remain at home, and we were more likely to entertain the idea of keeping elderly people from residing in assisted living facilities. This meant reimagining what health care workers could do to help family caregivers monitor the care of their elderly loved ones in their homes.

The COVID pandemic accelerated the use of telehealth. For some providers, this gave them more latitude in how they constructed and linked their professional image to a specific type of medical office and examination room. In the future, face-to-face examinations and consultations will continue, but health care providers will communicate with their patients in various other ways.

Additionally, COVID taught many of us who work, whether it be in the health care field or elsewhere, that we could experiment with alternative ways to work after being forced away from our familiar rituals and routines by COVID policies and practices. Personally, I was forced to learn quickly how to manage online classes and to hold productive Zoom meetings with my research assistants. I, along with millions of others, looked for ways to adjust to unfamiliar situations that made me feel at times out of place and isolated. It may be less than ideal to have a birthday celebration for a beloved colleague via Zoom or to have a drive-through student graduation "ceremony" rather than gathering in person, but lasting memories can still be forged in a shared virtual space or improvisational ritual. In fact, we may encode more lasting memories when the circumstances surrounding a ritual are distinct or bizarre.

Whereas COVID-19 prompted many health care facilities to redefine their worksites as being more dangerous places, many other occupations have routinely had to consider placemaking initiatives in the form of safety protocols to address hazardous work environments. Extraction mining (e.g., coal, oil, gas) and wildland firefighting, to name but two, are among the many professions that are associated with risky worksites.[33] Historically, one of the key features of these places is the gendered atmosphere that perpetuates stereotypical masculine behavior. The masculine workplace philosophy has rewarded stereotypical displays of masculinity including independence, intimidation, and risk-taking while discouraging help-seeking behavior. In recent years, in addition to implementing newer technologies to promote safety, some leaders in these occupations have supported procedures and placed-based rituals to enhance workers' solidarity and respect for safety issues. The more sensible safety practices encourage workers to hold each other accountable to make wise decisions and to avoid unnecessary, foolish risks. Fortunately, some progress has been made to alter the work culture of these places so that workers (men in particular) relate to one another in a more collaborative way with safety concerns foremost on their minds. Practices that support the common good are gradually being introduced by management to help improve risky worksites.[34] While altering the work culture and implementing safety protocols at a worksite may fall outside what is typically viewed as forms of placemaking, these activities represent some of the most consequential ways managers and business owners can make places more appealing. Unfortunately, not everyone can take for granted that they can go to work and return home unharmed.

Rites of Passage

One of the more intriguing and widely researched class of rituals includes the various rites of passage that enable individuals to transition from one identity to another. Religious rites of passage are perhaps the best known, but many others fall outside the sacred realm. Like those with religious implications, the secular ones are often connected, at least superficially, to specific places. Before exploring how transitions are relevant to place, let's extend our discussion of rituals by considering the relevance of rites of passage to place-based transitions.

More than a century ago, the French scholar Arnold van Gennep advanced ritual theory in his classic work, *The Rites of Passage*, by naming the concept and outlining his insights about the basic structure of key life transitions, such as birth, puberty, marriage, parenthood, old age, and death.[35] With a focus primarily on nonindustrialized, homogeneous societies, van Gennep sought to highlight how rituals structure the life transitions individuals experience over the course of their lives. He describes three phases of rites of passage that also affect how people negotiate their evolving lives in more complex societies. The first, *separation*, captures how we symbolically shift away from an identity we had previously embraced. This shift involves a loss or sense of moving on from whatever familiar position we held before. In doing so, we transition into a state of *liminality* in which we are faced with a degree of uncertainty. We recognize that there has been some type of disruption in the typical way we've been ordering our life. Although many adjust well to this identity shift, some perceive the change as a crisis. Finally, when we arrive at the *incorporation* phase, we have moved on emotionally, psychologically, and socially, and now see ourselves differently. We are immersed in a new way of life.

Ultimately, many modern-day rites of passage in the everyday realm emphasize the social dimensions that bind individuals to one another in a select group such as a gang, fraternity or sorority, sports team, work crew, secret society, and the like. Some of these rites of passage resemble hazing practices that test a person's commitment to a group's ideology or mission and its members. They are designed to promote loyalty and solidarity.

Other rites are less like hazing and more akin to a developmental agenda to empower individuals to make healthy choices that will enable them to appreciate their heritage and potential so they can live more productive lives. Some rites of passage are designed to "graduate" a person from a lesser to a more mature version of themselves. Broadly defined, some of these initiation rites create a pathway from adolescence to adulthood, or in a gendered world, from girlhood to womanhood and boyhood to manhood. One common version of this developmental type of ritual includes adolescent rites of passage that happen in diverse settings, such as the community, agency, church, therapy, school, and family. Initiatives, including the Afrocentric rites of passage that are largely coordinated through a church, school, or community organization in urban areas, represent efforts to enhance child and adolescent development with an emphasis on cultural heritage.[36] While the age of a participant helps to mark eligibility, cultural attributes are relevant as well.

Whether they take the hazing or supportive form, the activities that define the process for a rite of passage sometimes, but not necessarily, occur in a place that has special meaning to the group. For instance, street gangs notoriously claim a geographical territory as their turf, one that they are expected to control and defend against rival gangs. Many gangs also have an initiation ritual that serves as a rite of passage into the group. Some gangs require a potential recruit to earn their status as a gang member by performing an aggressive act against others outside the gang's turf, often in a place associated with a rival gang. Other rites of passage can happen on the gang's own turf. While gangs use different phrases comparable to "jumped in" to mark the hazing ritual, the basic parameters of the event are essentially the same: a recruit voluntarily submits themself to a vicious beatdown from gang members. Acceptance into the gang is contingent on being able to survive the beating without fighting back or showing weakness. Once accepted, the new gang member is likely to express a more authentic appreciation for and loyalty to the places that the gang claims as their own. In addition, the separation and incorporation phases of the rite of passage will alter how a gang recruit perceives the places that matter to them and why.

Rites of passage have consequences for new gang members and prompt us to ask various questions. Does joining a local gang provide the neophyte a stronger sense that they will be able to protect their family and home? Are they less likely to see their home and family as a refuge? Do they embrace a gang's special places and rituals once they've been incorporated into the everyday mix of gang life?

A very different style of developmental ritual is illustrated by the "firewalk" rite of passage supported by a small public high school in California. The school has forged productive partnerships with different community agencies and seeks to develop bilingual health professionals to diversify health care institutions. Education researcher Marnie Curry offers an intriguing ethnographic case study of the firewalk that highlights the significance of place. She shows how the staff and students at this predominantly Latinx-populated school, with a high proportion of teachers of color, have cultivated a school environment that fosters "authentic cariño" (heartfelt care). This style of caring promotes a "vision of caring grounded in Latinx cultural values" while emphasizing "familial care, intellectual care, and critical care."[37] This approach has been institutionalized in the school and encourages teachers to express a holistic interest in students comparable to parental care. Students are also urged to develop productive "habits of the mind" in an environment that teaches them to appreciate how their experience is connected to social justice issues involving ethnicity, social class, and gender.

At its core, the firewalk occurs in a classroom setting where students sit in a circle with a teacher-facilitator for roughly thirty-minute sessions. Although this ritual is named after the classic firewalking ritual that requires participants to walk barefoot over hot stones to test their resolve and courage, the high school version does not include this physical element. Instead, firewalkers take turns being on the "hot seat," fielding a series of pointed questions from their peers and teachers about their experiences related to their life habits and aspirations. Firewalkers are expected to be vulnerable, authentic, self-reflective, and decisive about their life habits and future career and civic goals. Students are required to go through this rite of passage as sophomores and then again as seniors. The senior firewalk is more intense and personal with the firewalker seated on a chair in the middle of a tight and closed circle. When the questioning portion of each session is completed, the facilitator asks the witnesses to stand if they believe the firewalker has been "real." Firewalkers' ability to proceed to their junior year and to graduate requires that all witnesses in the two sessions grant them these privileges. When the positive feedback is not unanimous, firewalkers must confront the observers' objections and articulate an acceptable response to resolve the outstanding concerns.

Aspects of place, the larger social and physical conditions, contribute in a meaningful way to how the firewalk ritual is framed. The physical decor throughout the campus accentuates the school's multiethnic and progressive social philosophy. Vibrant murals with culturally symbolic elements decorate the stairwells. Some murals display words of wisdom, such as "I choose to live by choice, not by chance." Classroom doors have painted images of prominent social activists (Gandhi, Cesar Chavez, Rosa Parks) and the inside of classrooms are adorned with students' inspirational work, Mexican flags, political posters, and "habit charts" that highlight key life practices. Thus, students are immersed in a physical environment that celebrates cultural diversity, empowerment, and social activism. The cultural discourse and institutional norms that permeate the school situate students in a learning environment that acknowledges how their positions and circumstances in the larger social landscape can affect their personal growth and opportunities. Students are also inspired by their physical surroundings to embrace their human agency and ability to chart their own future course. In addition, organizers of the firewalk take sophomores on a four-day camping trip with tents into Yosemite Park three days prior to the ritual. In that natural setting, students participate in a series of rituals, including a seven-mile mountain hike, that encourage interpersonal trust and community building. Students deepen their sense of dyadic and ideational we-ness in this natural setting, which increases their comfort with being held accountable and holding others accountable during and beyond the firewalk ritual.

In the modern world, we are increasingly aware that there are a multitude of choices we can make that will lead us down different life paths. We need to further appreciate how the place that grounds our activities can fundamentally influence the resources at our disposal and the life aspirations we adopt. Whether we're experiencing a basic ritual or a rite of passage, the places where they occur contribute to the transformation of our identities and ways of relating to others. Those of us who are responsible for helping people effectively navigate rites of passage should be mindful of and take a leading role in managing the relevant place properties that implicate how we can help others make successful transitions.

Social Solidarity

In addition to helping individuals process personal and group changes, rituals are valuable because they can enrich a social group's solidarity. Bellah astutely observes that "Only ritual pulls us out of our egoistic pursuit of our own interests and creates the possibility of a social world."[38] Rituals provide the practical means by which we come together to recognize our shared understandings, purpose, and options to spend time together. They're also valuable because they enhance our sense of dyadic and ideational we-ness with fellow participants. Years ago, I used to show a documentary to my classes about a street gang in Oakland, California, in which the members practiced a ritual of visiting deceased gang members' grave sites. There they took turns standing near the tombstone and pouring beer onto the ground as they shared spoken tributes for the former gang member. That cemetery, a symbolic place for these gang members, gave them a site to perform rituals that reinforced their sense of group belonging and shared histories of grief.

Every ritual occurs in some type of place; thus, efforts to promote solidarity through ritual are, by definition, place-based. Opportunities to engage in rituals that help build a sense of we-ness or solidarity exist in each of the five social domains and all ten of the places described above. In some places we will have more freedom to construct our own rituals. In others, we are beholden to stakeholders who create the infrastructure and norms that make it possible for us to relate to others in a way that enhances our sense of group belonging and social solidarity. Even in settings where the structure is created for us, such as sites that facilitate conflict resolution, we may still be able to work alongside others to promote placemaking activities that serve our interests. But places vary considerably in how much autonomy we have in shaping the circumstances that will ultimately affect us for better or worse.

When a place breeds opportunities for people with different social backgrounds, values, and skill sets to step outside their everyday silos and routines, people may realize that they have more in common than they imagined and can actually get along. Such a place can be a game changer if it invites people to step forward to communicate and bond with each other in places that matter to them. However, it can also stir anxieties and generate heated confrontations between people and groups who share opposing worldviews.

One such place to bring diverse people together is Carnival. This festive ritual has a long, rich history and is practiced in many countries where the Catholic Church is well established. The celebrations occur right before Ash Wednesday, the first day of Lent. In the United States, the main celebration associated with Carnival occurs in New Orleans on the last day before Lent, better known as "Fat Tuesday" or Mardi Gras.

Internationally and historically, Carnival is an exceptional ritual that has taken on many forms. Some scholars depict it as reinforcing social solidarity by creating a liminal space for temporary social transformation. Renowned author Rebecca Solnit, writing in *A Paradise Built in Hell: The Extraordinary Communities That Arise in Disaster*, likens Carnival to revolution, suggesting that it is "an overthrow of the established order under which we are alienated from each other, too shy to act, divided along familiar lines. Those lines vanish and we merge exuberantly. Carnival is a hectic, short-lived, raucous version of utopia, one that matters because it is widely available."[39] This ritual of merrymaking and performative art temporarily turns the social order on its head by encouraging participants to invert the prevailing statuses and roles that segment persons into their privileged and disadvantaged positions based on characteristics like social class, race, gender, and sexual orientation. For a brief period, individuals are liberated from the prevailing hierarchy. But Solnit also reminds us that there is much debate about "whether carnival is truly subversive or the way an unjust society lets off pressure that allows the status quo to stand."[40]

In the United States, the distant and recent history of Mardi Gras is tainted with racist overtones that limit its ability to build an inclusive community. Writing for the *Tulane Hullabaloo*, Avery Anderson recounts Mardi Gras's history, showing how various white krewes over the years have perpetuated racist tropes while creating a somewhat segregated celebration.[41] Krewes are groups that help to organize activities for a Carnival celebration. Between the mid-1800s and the mid-1900s, Mardi Gras, by celebrating white supremacy, was in part a "public forum" to challenge the Reconstruction philosophy and race-related initiatives.[42]

In 1957, a group of wealthy businessmen formed the Mistick Krewe of Comus and reorganized the Mardi Gras celebration into a format that featured a parade of floats sponsored by different krewes and catered to the wealthy factions of the city. Several decades later in 1991, Dorothy Mae Taylor, the first Black woman to serve on the New Orleans City Council, expressed her concern with the bigoted practices that were affecting Mardi Gras. She proposed an ordinance that was designed to prevent krewes from practicing membership discrimination based on race, gender, and religion. A significantly watered-down version of the ordinance with no legal penalties and no mention of gender passed the following year without Taylor's support. In recent years, krewes of Black people, women, and other marginalized groups have emerged, but the ritual continues to be tainted with the legacy of white, Southern, male privilege. For example, within the past several years, krewes continue to distribute racist memorabilia and floats have made fun of Dreamers (undocumented immigrants who identify as American and entered the United States as children) and the former NFL quarterback Colin Kaepernick, who protested police brutality. Despite these shortcomings, Mardi Gras does create festive opportunities for people to establish more limited forms of group belonging.

New Orleans, with its complex history dating back to the early 1700s of integrating a variety of European, Indigenous, African, Antillean, Latin American, and Asian people, has produced a unique local ethnicity. One folklore scholar referred to this process as "creolization," a "synthesis of the various cultures in the unique New Orleans melting pot as they interacted one by one with the original French, Franco-American or Afro-French population."[43] From this remarkable mixing of cultures the Creole language, New Orleans cuisine, and traditional jazz music were born. The Mardi Gras festivities emerged from this larger creolized place and its multifaceted cultural heritage. As a result, New Orleans is a distinct place with its own special identity. The city is even home to a nonprofit, Grounds Krewe, that epitomizes the progressive segment of this culturally diverse place. This krewe promotes waste prevention, recycling, and sustainable products at New Orleans's special events – including Mardi Gras.[44] It specializes in trying to make throws (items that people on floats toss to parade-goers) at Mardi Gras environmentally friendly.

The place properties associated with the Mardi Gras ritual are best viewed as being part of the leisure and sports worlds, as well as the community domain. However, similar properties associated with rituals encourage people to bond in every social domain. Unfortunately, though, just as facets of a place can bring people together, they can also create divisions and push them apart. If the norms and symbolic meanings attributed to a place promote a reputation that is appealing to white nationalists, it will discourage most people from feeling at ease. Thus, a place can foster solidarity on a narrow stage yet disrupt it on a wider one and vice versa. Rituals can solidify the collective consciousness of embedded groups (e.g., krewes), which in turn ignites the tensions between disparate groups, a topic we'll explore in Chapter 5.

Efforts to design healthy places and rituals should always scrutinize how particular subsets of people will be affected. Many attempts to promote social solidarity leave certain groups feeling left out or disadvantaged. Solidarity for some can mean isolation for others.

On an individual basis, our personal desires to improve our lives often result in us navigating rituals, like those associated with pledging a fraternity or sorority or being an active member of a book or hunting club. When we manage these rituals effectively, we often create opportunities to experience new places. In these new settings, we can deepen our relationships with people we already know or meet strangers who we will eventually bring into our personal circle. The circumstances that result from participating in successful rituals might take the form of expanding our involvement with a romantic partner in a new residence, growing our interpersonal ties with a set of coworkers at a new worksite, or hanging out with friends who expose us to a new leisure spot. Whatever the case may be, our experiences with ceremonial and everyday rituals connect us to people in specific places and separate us from others. Occasionally, our separation from others reflects both a physical and social separation; other times we may be physically present with members of an "out-group" in the same space, but socially distant because we have aligned ourselves with a group that disparages them. These sorts of arrangements occur frequently in school settings and prisons where cliques or gangs take hold and group members claim a place as theirs, while trying to ostracize or banish others.

Only the most nationalistic rituals such as reciting the Pledge of Allegiance, singing the National Anthem, or celebrating the Fourth of July holiday are likely to bring people together on a grand scale at social events in public places. And even then, the ritual is designed to differentiate Americans from everyone else in places that typically matter to us.

The absence of rituals that promote social solidarity in a community can be fatal, especially in times of social disorganization that occur during environmental disasters and military conflicts. For example, recall my description of the senseless loss of life that occurred in the 1995 Chicago summer heat wave mentioned in Chapter 1. Hundreds of people died because people were isolated from members of the community and left without support. Solnit captures the life-giving value of healthy, everyday rituals by noting, "If a disaster intensifies the conditions of everyday life, then the pleasures of everyday affection and connection become a safety net or survival equipment when things fall apart."[45]

5
Transitions

Photo 7: Volunteers with Aguilas del Desierto (Eagles of the Desert) during one of its regular organized searches to rescue or recover migrants along the United States–Mexico border. Southern Arizona, March 2020. (Photo courtesy of Henri Migala)

"We all come to the United States with that same hope, for better opportunities, a better life. And, well, my brother came trying to look for his American Dream." But the brother Ely Ortiz speaks of, Rigoberto, never had the chance to experience that dream, despite walking on American soil for at least seven straight days. Rigoberto and his cousin tragically died in 2009 while trying to cross the unforgiving Arizona desert after crossing the Mexican border. Severely dehydrated and exhausted, they were able to reach Ely by phone after the coyote, or smuggler, who led them across the border abandoned them in the middle of the desert on a large US Air Force bombing range. Ely, who had immigrated in the 1980s to the United States from Mexico and was living in San Diego with his family, immediately drove to the immigration checkpoint in Arizona seeking help. Unable to secure assistance from the officials there, he tried the Mexican consulate but was turned away. Despite his diligent efforts, Ely was left without an immediate solution; he was unable to search for his family members during the narrow window when he potentially could have saved them.

Five months later, after overcoming long odds to gain permission to search for his brother's and cousin's remains, Ely remarkably found their decomposing bodies in the desert. Though traumatic, the discovery provided Ely and his family a sense of closure. Finding the bodies was a turning point for Ely; it revealed his life purpose. In 2012, Ely founded the nonprofit Aguilas del Desierto (Eagles of the Desert). From the outset, its place-based mission has been to help distraught families find the remains of migrants who do not make it out of the desert alive and to rescue others who are stranded there. Ely and his dedicated army of volunteers do coordinated searches twice a month from Friday to Sunday, covering ten to fifteen miles per day. Over the years, they've responded to more than six thousand calls for help. In 2020 alone, Aguilas helped save ninety-four lives and recovered the remains of ninety-seven people.[1]

Most recently, Ely has expanded Aguilas's mission to spread awareness about the dangers of crossing the border on foot. Volunteers target migrant shelters in Mexico, Guatemala, and Honduras and deliver a message that accurately conveys the excruciating demands of a desert crossing. It involves upwards of twelve days of hiking over rugged terrain in unbearable heat with temperatures well over one hundred degrees Fahrenheit and requires one to two gallons of water per person, per day. A twelve-day supply of having just one gallon daily equates to roughly a one-hundred-pound burden at the outset that migrants need to carry themselves. Migrants must also worry about cartels, snakes, and exposure to the elements. Unfortunately, many migrants are ill-informed and often intentionally misled about the difficulties of engineering a successful trek across the border. Many expect that it will take only a few hours or at most a few days to cross the Mexican border and arrive at a safe destination in the United States. Misinformation and disinformation about the physical conditions of the journey produce horrific consequences. One report indicates that since 1998, 7,805 people have died trying to cross the United States–Mexico border, and thousands of others are still missing.[2]

For over a decade, Ely has struggled with his personal vision of America and the Arizona desert. He describes himself as having survivor guilt that emanates from him having the good fortune of making it to the United States, whereas his family did not. He also relives a brotherly sense of we-ness when he makes his numerous trips to the desert: "Every time we're out there carrying out a search, I feel that he's out there walking with us, especially in the area where I know he took his final steps. When we're there, I feel him watching over us."[3] Working with his nonprofit, Ely's time searching in the desert also creates opportunities for him to reinforce his dyadic and ideational bonds with other volunteers, some of whom share the experience of having lost loved ones to the perilous desert. When remains are located, Ely is well-positioned to empathize with family members' grief.

The ideals and visions that motivate migrants like Rigoberto and his cousin to embark on such a high-stakes journey are not new. For centuries, millions around the world have seen America as a special place steeped in hope and opportunity, worthy of the risks associated with migration. Thus, the physical conditions, symbolic meanings, and cultural traditions associated with America as a place contribute to how people frame their anticipated and actual place-based transitions from one country to another.

The migration flow at our southern border illustrates how a place is defined by both its physicality and perceptions of it. To appreciate the meaning that is assigned to a place, like an origin or destination country involved in migration or the Arizona desert, we must differentiate it from other places. For Rigoberto and millions of others like him who are willing to embark on a major life transition, America is perceived to be significantly different from their native lands. The parents who flee their homelands to protect their children from gang recruitment or retribution tend to see America as a place that will offer them refuge from such horrors. The migrants who recognize that the quality of life is higher in America are more apt to take risks to pursue better economic opportunities. Using a comparative lens, then, migrants are more likely to see the challenge of crossing the dangerous desert as less ominous than trying to survive in their home country.

Context

Migration along the southern border of the United States is one of the more politicized issues involving place. It reflects how critical life transitions are often connected to the realities of place. Not surprisingly, an obvious image that comes to mind when people think about place and transitions is the residential move. Almost all Americans will at some point experience what it's like to pack up one's belongings and move from one residence to another, with some resettling many, many times. Ironically, while modern technologies have led us to become a mobile society in many ways, residential mobility patterns have declined considerably in recent decades. In the mid-1980s, for example, almost 18 percent of Americans moved every year, but that figure dipped to roughly 10 percent in 2019.[4] In the 1980s about 15 percent of people moved locally and 3.3 percent were involved in interstate migration. By 2019, those figures dropped to roughly 8 and 1.5 percent, respectively, with the decline being most pronounced for those who are the most mobile (young adults and renters).

Of those aged eighteen to twenty-four, 25 percent moved, but only 6 percent of persons aged sixty-five and older moved during the 2017–18 period. The gap between renters and homeowners was roughly the same. In addition, people from low-income backgrounds move more often than those with higher incomes. US Census Bureau Current Population Survey data charting moves between 2018 and 2019 show that most occur over relatively short distances: 65 percent move within the same county, 17 percent between counties but in the same state, 14 percent between states, and 4 percent from abroad. Overall, the main reasons people cite for moving include a need for new or better housing (40 percent), family-related concerns including a change in marital status (27 percent), and job-related circumstances (21 percent). This distribution of where and why we move suggests that while most of us will adjust to new houses and neighborhoods, we can still frequently maintain our attachments to local sites, such as gyms, churches, workplaces, or parks that remain accessible to us.

In addition to residential moves that include efforts to escape poverty and violence, academics have studied a wide range of other "mobilities," such as urban gentrification; tourism; displacement of refugees because of war, disaster, and disease; and human smuggling. In each of these scenarios, place properties and people's perceptions of place influence how individuals navigate specific life transitions and experience place attachments, displacement, rituals, and conflicts. Scholars' extensive work on mobilities informs my broader focus on the meanings and consequences of a wide range of place-based transitions, especially those that directly involve other people, and some that do not include migration.

Andrés Di Masso and his colleagues, drawing on an environmental psychological perspective, offer a novel and nuanced way to understand mobility and place attachments by proposing that we focus on the interplay between what they call "fixities" and "flows."[5] In their model, place potentially includes a mix of spatially stable and bounded features associated with it, as well as the more fluid qualities of place that accentuate elements of movement. We can move our physical bodies from place to place, but we can also do imaginative, virtual, and communicative "travel" using various technologies that can be interpreted as forms of place-based transitions. Di Masso's team reinforces the field's recent trend of dismissing a narrow and rigid "sedentarist approach to social relations." They challenge this perspective that privileges rootedness and views too much mobility as inherently problematic. Instead, their more dynamic conceptual approach resonates with the modern social landscape because it acknowledges that we have become more accustomed to living in a mobile world in which aspects of our environments – places, people, and our relation to each – are constantly in flux. Our modern world requires us to be more aware of and adept at dealing with different types of transitions that affect our sense of we-ness and well-being. Many of these transitions require us to manage how we navigate different types of places and the movement between them.

Even though a range of mobilities are relevant to my thinking, I use the term "transitions" to signal that my observations extend beyond commenting on our physical movements within or between places. In doing so, I more fully capture both our corporeal movements as well as our perceptions about place that influence our identities, physical movements, and placemaking efforts. Thus, I dissect eight overlapping transitional themes to explore the fluid aspects of place, including our many expressions of physical mobility. The transitional themes I outline are not meant to be exhaustive; however, they deepen our appreciation for how sense of place, place attachment, displacement, identity, rituals, conflict, and interpersonal belonging are key forces in our lives. As alluded to before, these themes are also relevant to how we consider transitions involving rituals and rites of passage.

Although largely beyond the scope of the materials in subsequent sections, Arnold van Gennep's early twentieth-century insights about nonindustrialized peoples' intriguing rites of passage are instructive as we explore transitions and place. From his anthropological perspective, practices that accompany rites of passage are connected to our physical movement from one place to another and what he labels the "territorial passage."[6] He suggests that people often encounter a symbolically meaningful type of "neutral zone" when they move between places – entering one and exiting another. The areas that people leave and enter can include countries, physical regions, significant buildings, homes, and rooms. In addition, the anthropological record documents that when people transition from one social category to another, there is often a corresponding shift in the places where they are expected to spend their time as well as those that are discouraged or forbidden. In our modern world, we also gain or lose access – at least in the form that enables us to feel accepted and comfortable – to places over the course of our lives. These patterns follow from van Gennep's observation that "spatial separation of distinct groups is an aspect of social organization."[7]

Scaling Interpretations

Social life includes notable life transitions that alter the way we see ourselves and respond to others. They unfold as we engage individually and collectively with the social world in various places. Some transitions are major and singular in form, while others occur as part of a web of overlapping experiences. Some significant transitions are publicly marked via social rituals like graduations, weddings, and funerals, while others happen more organically away from the public eye, such as when people fall in or out of love while interacting in certain places.

Our cognitive framing of place affects how we think about place-based transitions including mobilities and their relationship to deep dyadic and ideational forms of we-ness. Expressions of we-ness are often embedded in a larger frame of we-ness, such as a small team of four people working on a project inside a local company of one hundred employees, which in turn is part of a much larger national corporation. Viewing we-ness and place in this way allows us to broaden the context for thinking about place, because we can consider different scales or levels that are nested (domestic private property, neighborhood, city, county, state, region, country, continent, globe). Thus, when we discuss the fixities or flows associated with places and transitions, we must consider the context and levels for the different places that are implicated. Likewise, it is useful to discern whether features of a place are changing or if people are simply perceiving a place differently and responding accordingly.

To understand how place properties affect us during transitional moments, we must first understand the contours of different places and how they overlap. However, as noted earlier, identifying the borders that precisely define a place can be a tricky conceptual exercise. We can experience a place as bleeding into another or being enveloped by it. Think of how soldiers try to make sense of where places known for active combat converge with places of relative safety. Our standpoints also position us to perceive our place-based transitions with unique insights, biases, and expectations. It often matters whether we are experiencing a transition between places from the vantage point of a person who is a homeowner, apartment dweller, homeless person, city dweller, American citizen, domestic or international migrant, refugee, native born resident, or something else. Moreover, our life experiences as a person of color, single parent, sex worker, young or elderly person, as well as other statuses, can shape how we relate to transitions linked to places.

We can apply a narrow or wide-angle view of the place-based changes we experience, both as a unique individual and as a member of a group. We might, for instance, move from one house and neighborhood to a different dwelling and neighborhood but remain in the same town or urban area. When we use the city as our primary reference point, our transition or mobility can be viewed narrowly as an internal move that occurs within the city. The transition can still affect the rituals we engage in, our sense of we-ness in different social domains, and our well-being. The move might result in us making a significantly longer or shorter commute to work, and the need to send our children to a different school that may be of higher, equal, or lower quality. We might feel as though we've secured a living arrangement that allows us to feel safer in our new neighborhood and improve the appearance of our social class standing. We might even be able to sustain our romantic partnership more easily because our residential move positions us geographically closer. Alternatively, our residential move might lead us to perceive ourselves as living in a more dangerous place that also lowers our social class. It could even sabotage our romantic relationship. Still, despite any of these outcomes, if we use a wider lens, it could reveal that we've retained our core regional identity and have sustained our allegiances to the local professional and collegiate sports teams. Thus, we could continue to see ourselves as a "Southerner" or "East Coast person." Likewise, we might still view ourselves as being someone who identifies with the city in which we live. If we feel our move has led to some undesirable consequences, taking this broader perspective can help us to minimize the disruption to our overall sense of self and we-ness.

Journey Time

While recognizing that typical mobility patterns were altered during the primary COVID-19 years, and compared to the declining trend in residential moves, we are part of an increasingly mobile society in our everyday life activities, both physically and virtually. This is especially true for the temporary forms of mobility that involve leaving our homes to go to work, shop, play, and socialize. Still, the increased use of modern technologies has facilitated a shift toward accomplishing things online that were once done in person, such as shopping, conference calls, health care visits, business exchanges, and more. Consequently, the nature of mobilities is evolving and creating new opportunities for how we live and think about the places that matter to us. Looking forward, computer tech experts assume that the metaverse will fundamentally alter how some people conceive of their identities and respond to place, leisure, and work.

Thus, it makes sense to pay attention to how, why, and with what effect we continue to physically go from place to place. Our place consciousness and sense of well-being partly hinge on how we feel about our travels from one place to another. The experience of physically getting to a different place can create calm, excitement, tension, fear, as well as other emotions not only for us but for our travel companions. Anyone who has survived being stuck in a car during rush hour traffic will appreciate how an otherwise appealing vehicle can transform itself into a stifling prison on wheels.

We can think of a vehicle as being a separate, unique place. Typically, it serves a distinct purpose during our transition from our point of origin to a destination site. The most common transportation paths begin at our homes, then incorporate time at work, school, shopping, or a leisure spot, before we eventually return home. We also make plenty of trips directly to secondary places other than our homes. A subset of people is constantly transitioning between places because of family and job responsibilities. Whether it is a parent "chauffeur" for three very busy and tightly scheduled kids, long-haul truck driver, Uber or taxi driver, or home care nurse, many people spend a great deal of time driving as they transition from one place to another. Many of us experiment with rudimentary placemaking strategies to manage our car-time. We sign up for SiriusXM radio; have books, magazines, or podcasts available; place a laptop on the front seat; position a cell on the dashboard; store accessible snacks; and stockpile business, casual, and workout clothes to accommodate potential transitions in our daily schedule. Those of us who are in their vehicles a lot often feel like we're living out of them, which underscores the value of putting thought into effective placemaking.

Typically, we each develop our own attitudes about using different vehicles to get from place to place. Although we hold general sentiments about this sort of travel, our mood may also depend on when, where, and for what purpose we're making a trip. Our travel companions can also influence us in different ways. Obviously, some people do not have the financial means to use vehicles for their travels. In addition, not using a motorized vehicle is an option that many adopt, preferring to walk or bike. Being outside of an enclosed vehicle, they have opportunities to experience more intimately the places and the people they share time with along the way.

We must not forget, too, that for many homeless people certain vehicles – whether they are functional or not – serve as a shelter and temporary home. Even subway cars can take on this alternative function as we witnessed when Russia invaded Ukraine and displaced millions of families. Thus, dire circumstances can prompt people to redefine how a vehicle matters to them.

For some travelers, riding on a packed, dirty subway car may be a stressful way to start the day. Others will be invigorated by the excitement of being surrounded by a kaleidoscope of humanity on a subway car. In some ways, it may even have a calming effect. Same place, same people, but very different reactions to the physical and social surroundings. Similar kinds of place-based "moments" can also affect the same subway riders as they journey away from work or school and back to their homes. When they arrive home, they may find themselves transitioning from, say, chaos to tranquility or from exhilaration to boredom.

Irrespective of the mood that a transition from one place to another produces, it can be influenced by the conditions associated with the mobile place and the travelers' perceptions. The mood might also be influenced by whether the traveler is making the journey exclusively alone or with only strangers, versus with one or more known and trusted companions.

In the United States and elsewhere, negative impressions of the subway system depress people's willingness to use it, especially because many Americans are worried about being a crime victim in this setting. Unfortunately, the public's exaggerated fear of subway crime is affected by how they consume high-profile media reports. David Graham, writing in *The Atlantic* immediately after the infamous New York City subway shooting incident in April 2022 that left twenty-three people injured (including ten who were shot), profiles the operational challenges the subway system has faced over recent decades.[8] Graham reminds us that the fear of subway crime has a long history. In the 1980s "subways were viewed as dangerous and seedy hellscapes." In response, previous New York City leaders improved the public's perception of the transit system by initiating a massive subway cleanup that included, among other things, removing graffiti, mopping urine from floors, and removing homeless people. But over time significant safety concerns resurfaced. Ridership declined dramatically too because of fears of COVID-19. Graham succinctly lays out the current catch-22 scenario:

> In absolute terms, the number of crimes in the subway is still very low – but perception of crime is more important to the public, and an elevated perception of crime risks sending the New York City system and other transit systems into a death spiral, where fear of crime begets low ridership, which in turn begets more crime.

Recall the Thomas sociological theorem that when we perceive things as real, our perceptions foster real consequences.[9]

We can also consider, in contrast to the autonomy that driving offers, how people feel about not having any say in determining scheduling, routing, or the decision-making that takes place once passengers board a subway car, bus, or plane. Although automobile drivers, especially those in metropolitan areas, will confront traffic jams and various delays during peak driving hours, they typically have the option to take alternative routes or time their travel according to predictable traffic patterns and their own schedule. Even though drivers are likely to feel frustrated and helpless when they're stuck in a traffic jam, they enjoy having more autonomy and control than persons who use public transportation.

The individualistic ethos that has branded us historically as American pioneers, has also dampened our enthusiasm for investing in mass transit systems that many perceive as a threat to our autonomy. Yet, while Americans are far less likely than persons from other parts of the world to use mass transit, one 2017 study still showed that 16.1 percent of the United States population reported using transit services within the past month.[10] It also revealed that buses and rail services attract different types of people. Black people are more likely to use buses while white people and Asians are more apt to get around via the subway and light rail services. The racial profile of users also reflects the income profile of users, with lower-income individuals being more likely to use the bus and persons from higher-income backgrounds using rail. These differences in the demographic backgrounds of transit users mean that the place profile represented by each form of transit can be defined by both the physical attributes of the equipment and the backgrounds of those who use it.

Whether it is a trip to work, school, leisure event, family visit, road trip, or something else, if we're physically able, we're likely to find ourselves regularly making different types of trips between places. The transport vehicles and transportation hubs that are part of our everyday trips can alter our sensitivity to place, mood, sense of we-ness, and more. Certain trips, especially carpooling and long road trips with family or friends, are steeped in a ritual quality that leaves a lasting impression. Such trips can draw us closer to our companions because of our intimate exchanges. For example, I have fond memories of being fourteen years old when my older sister, Paula, and her husband of four months, Bob, unexpectedly invited me to join them on a two-week cross-country adventure for their summer "honeymoon." The three of us traveled by car from western Pennsylvania to an Air Force base in Grand Forks, North Dakota, to visit our uncle and his family. While I already had a solid relationship with my sister, the trip created unique opportunities for me to develop my little brother–big brother bond with Bob. He gave me several chances to make my driving debut on isolated roads on the base by putting me behind the wheel of my sister's 1970 Plymouth Duster. I also recall being elated when Bob allowed me to steer from the passenger seat for countless miles on the open North Dakota interstate with my sister sleeping in the backseat. Although Bob has forgotten these moments, I have clearly not. These fleeting yet decisive rituals led me to deepen my emerging sense of we-ness as a teenager with my then twenty-one-year-old brother-in-law.

Vehicular trips, unfortunately, can also create anxiety and tension that drives a wedge between people. Having a heated argument in a spatially restrictive car can easily inflame any bitterness people may feel for one another. How we manage the emotional energy and logistics of being in proximity, with limited options to part ways on the journey, is often consequential, for better or worse. Depending on the circumstances, we may experience a mix of emotional reactions to our companions on any given day. Our interactions can foster both deep dyadic and ideational we-ness or strip us of any chance to embrace a meaningful affinity with our fellow travelers.

Hollywood has cashed in on the intrigue of companion travel by promoting diverse storylines that explore the theme of place in motion. These movies center the diverse forms of action and dialogue in a range of vehicles including station wagons, vans, RVs, buses, cars, planes, boats, and spacecraft. Movies like *Smokey and the Bandit* (1977), *National Lampoon's Vacation* (1983), *Planes, Trains and Automobiles* (1987), *Rain Man* (1988), *Thelma & Louise* (1991), *Speed* (1994), *Apollo 13* (1995), *Titanic* (1997), *Pirates of the Caribbean* (2003), *Little Miss Sunshine* (2006), *Poseidon* (2006), *Snakes on a Plane* (2006), *Logan* (2017), and *Jungle Cruise* (2021), as well as many others, showcase how transport vehicles provide a backdrop and momentum for different social exchanges as people travel by road, in the air, or on the water. Although movie producers vary in how prominently they connect the vehicle to the plot in these sorts of movies, attributes of the vehicle – including whether it is a site for a crisis – often play a key role in setting the stage for the dramatic or comedic effect.

Transport vehicles can also take on significant meaning in times of war. We saw how the large navy ships, and ultimately the smaller Higgins boats that delivered Allied soldiers to the beaches of Normandy, played a crucial role in how soldiers mentally and physically transitioned from a place of relative safety to one of heightened anticipatory fear and seasickness, and ultimately to the deadly battlefield on the beach. Similarly, we can consider how other soldiers in planes, tanks, and other armored vehicles deal with the theater of war. How do they manage the transitions from base camps or relatively safe places to places where injury and death are acute possibilities? During these transitions, soldiers are exposed to grave risks and their camaraderie is tested.

Additionally, transport vehicles feature prominently in rescuing civilians from war zones and natural disasters. In recent years, we've witnessed harrowing videos showing soldiers and aid workers maneuvering planes and buses to get civilians out of harm's way in Afghanistan and Ukraine. Likewise, from 1975, we have equally dramatic and oft-seen footage of a twelve-hour operation that involved troops frantically evacuating American personnel and South Vietnamese civilians by helicopter from the American embassy compound during the fall of Saigon at the end of the Vietnam War.[11] Together, these images of rescue missions illustrate how our sense of place is shaped by how place attributes are combined with transitional themes that underscore place attachment, displacement, and conflict. These images also symbolize the complex international role the United States has played as a superpower that is often entangled in the politics of foreign places.

New or Familiar

Every place that has ever mattered to us is one that we had to experience for the first time, even if we can't recall that initial encounter. On many occasions, especially as we become more self-aware in our youth and young adult years, we'll recognize when we're on the verge of entering a place that we've never experienced before. Depending on our mood and the context, our ignorance of the place can generate varied emotions that are either debilitating, uplifting, or mixed.

When, why, and how do we conclude that a place is familiar to us and no longer new? A clear-cut response is open to interpretation and not always possible. Thus, we should think of our familiarity with a place as existing on a continuum. On one end are those people who have a great deal of exposure to and knowledge of a place and the other end represents those who have absolutely none. Admittedly, we can have some intimate exposure to a place yet still feel that things about it are strange or foreign to us. Defining the threshold at which we characterize a place as no longer new but rather something that is familiar is an open question. Much depends on the size and complexity of the place in question and how we think about it.

To illustrate how the newness of a place can be consequential let's consider one of my earliest memories: my first day of class in the first grade at Sacred Heart School. I was seated in the second row near the door as the bell rang to start the school day. My teacher, Sister Ursula, was standing at the front of the class and began to welcome us to the next chapter in our young lives. She was friendly and energetic. Only a minute or so passed before the entire class could hear the faint screams of a high-pitched, young voice in the hallway. Despite the door being closed, we turned our heads and locked our eyes in that direction. Within seconds the voice grew more intense and louder; eventually, the words were audible: "I don't want to go, let me go! Let me go!" Then the door swung open, and they appeared: one short nun and one smaller, unruly girl – Nannette. Sister Isabella, clad in her official black habit, was the school's principal. Exasperation was stamped on her face. Her hand was firmly latched onto the young girl's tiny arm. The girl was outfitted in a red plaid skirt and vest, the official uniform for girls at this private Catholic school. She was kicking and flailing her body, doing her best to escape the nun's grasp. But she was no match for the stern-looking principal who hung on tightly. In short order, the principal gently moved the girl into a seat directly in front of me. By this time, she had settled down a bit, presumably because she realized her new classmates were watching.

Quite the first impression. "Why was this girl acting so crazy?" I thought to myself. I was shocked and puzzled. Ten minutes earlier, despite my mother's initial pleas to the contrary, I had insisted that she just drop me off in front of the school because I wanted to walk in by myself. My mom relented and I was on my way to first grade. My older sister had been going to this school for seven years and now it was my turn. I wanted to explore and see what it looked like inside. And although I wasn't too happy about being forced to wear a white shirt, red clip-on tie, and uncomfortable dress shoes, I was looking forward to being in the mysterious big brick building that I had seen for several years when my parents took me to the adjacent church on Sundays. I knew it would be filled with lots of rooms, kids, and a cafeteria. Fortunately, even though Nannette was less eager than I was to be a part of this new place, she walked into class the next day without a peep. She quickly adjusted to school and revealed herself to be self-confident and assertive. We became good friends within weeks.

Why did Nannette and I have such drastically different experiences that first day? I don't know for sure. She had two older sisters who attended the school, and one was in the same grade as my sister. So, like me, she presumably had people in her life whom she trusted and who were comfortable at the school. Perhaps her sisters didn't like the school and indoctrinated her with their disdain, but that is unlikely. Nannette was more outgoing, self-assured, and adventuresome than I was, so it presumably wasn't her shyness that triggered her reaction. What I do know is that we each entered this new place armed with distinctly different orientations to our youthful adventure.

The underlying lesson to be gleaned from this childhood episode is that the same place, whether it is a new or familiar one, can mean very different things to individual people. Tara Westover, the person referenced in the Introduction who was homeschooled by her strict Mormon parents in rural Idaho, provides us with a comparative glimpse of what a college classroom lecture feels like to someone who has never set foot in a formal classroom prior to enrolling at Brigham Young University. In her very first session of a class about art in Western civilization, Westover learned immediately that this university classroom was a completely different setting than sitting with her mother for a makeshift homeschooling lesson. After seeing other students raise their hands to ask a question, she took the plunge to ask the professor one of her own. She started to read a passage from the course textbook and then paused, saying, "I don't know this word," and then asked, "What does it mean?" The ensuing classroom mood, as she describes it, was punctuated by complete silence and stares. Then the professor, with "lips tightened," responded, "Thanks for *that*," before returning to his lecture. As she sat in silence looking at her shoes, she was overwhelmed because she perceived her classmates were thinking that she was a "freak." She writes, "Of course I *was* a freak, and I knew it, but I didn't understand how *they* knew it." A fellow student who was sitting next to her, and who had chatted warmly with her before class began, turned to Westover at the end of class and said, "You shouldn't make fun of that. It's not a joke." The word in question was "Holocaust." Westover immediately went to the computer lab to learn why her question had precipitated such a reaction. In this novel (for her) classroom setting, unlike in her homeschooling environment, Westover needed to navigate not only her ignorance, but the fact that strangers were poised to judge whether she belonged at *their* school and in *their* class.[12]

Westover vividly demonstrates that while objective realities matter, so do our subjective interpretations. Fortunately, while it is not always possible to identify the underlying reasons for why people assign different meanings to the same place, some credible explanations often surface if we know where and how to look.

As emphasized in Chapter 2, memories and expectations are relevant to understanding how we express attachment to a place. They also affect our various place-based transitions. Our ability to adjust to a specific place and make a smooth transition can be enhanced if we've been there before and developed at least a superficial familiarity with the circumstances and the rituals that define it. But being familiar with a place – having memories of it – is not a recipe that always delivers a wonderful experiential outcome. Familiarity can breed anger, disgust, fear, and resentment. We see this with abusive homes and debilitating workplaces. Some unfortunate people are intimately familiar with these circumstances and understandably despise the place where these bad things happen.

Granted, a victim in an abusive family is likely to see their house and homelife as growing more threatening over time, but they might also develop coping strategies anchored in place that help them to survive the trauma. They might, for example, take refuge in certain rooms of the house that they do not directly associate with the abuse. Or, they may spend as much time as possible at a friend's home that takes on special meaning for them because it is a safe space. From the victim's perspective, the abuse could be viewed as a regular occurrence or seen as rare and sporadic. Although the victim's perception of the frequency of the abuse can affect the person's well-being and coping, once the abuse begins it is likely to become a familiar feature of the homeplace. Thus, our memories of a place, good or bad, influence what we expect will happen there and prime us to react in predictable ways.

We can profile a more wholesome scenario by considering the schoolteacher who retains the same classroom for numerous years and "grows into it" as they get more accustomed to their position. Ideally, year after year the teacher develops a stronger sense of their professional identity. They can also enhance their sense of we-ness with their colleagues and become more familiar with the school and their classroom specifically. Teachers often have a great deal of freedom to organize and decorate their classrooms. Consequently, they can design a place that reflects their personality and their teaching philosophy. The inspired first-time teacher with their own classroom can adapt over time by transitioning their classroom space into a special place they share with their students. At some point in a teacher's occupation of a classroom, they will no longer see their room as new to them.

A forty-one-year-old seventh grade science teacher, Brandon, once shared his place-oriented philosophy with me as I sat in his museum-like classroom interviewing him about his involvement with young students:

> My classroom is a lot different than a teacher's classroom … I have bones and skeletons and furs and rocks from every place I have been around the earth. And kids, when they come in, they're like, "Wow," and I'm like, "Touch it," and they're like, "We can touch things?" And they can take things home, if they want to … like, that chunk of rock or something, all they have to do is sign it out. And they're like, "Why do you let us do that?" I said, "So my logic is why not let you check it out and when you're done with it at home, you'll bring [it] back at the end of the year or whenever you're done." And that's what happens … I try to do the mysterious thing, because right away kids come in and they're all wondering so I've already activated their curiosity about science.

For the first eleven years of his life, Brandon's deep love of the land was cultivated by his Native American grandfather who helped raise him on a South Dakota reservation. Now, as an enthusiastic science teacher, Brandon is poised to express his appreciation for nature and culture by creating a classroom setting that is a place for curiosity. By allowing kids to take objects from his classroom he is encouraging students to extend his classroom ambience into their own intimate places at home.

The power of this sharing resonated with me when Brandon told me about one of his former students who initiated a surprise phone call to him. As part of the backstory for his exchange with this student, Brandon first describes an end-of-school-year ritual he does with his students that involves him modifying a story his grandfather used to tell him. The story was about two "Indian braves" who travel across the plains and are stricken with sadness as they bear witness to all the destruction that white people have brought to the tribes. When they pray for guidance, the Buffalo Woman spirit appears to them. She tells them that they can help their people if they accumulate as many pebbles as they can by the time the sun comes up the next day. Viewing the spirit's instructions as nonsensical, the boys largely disregard them, but they still manage to pick up a handful of stones. When they empty their backpacks later that night, they see that the stones have turned to gold. When the Buffalo Woman reappears, she tells the boys that they can now help their people a little, but they could have done much more if they had listened well and followed directions.

At the end of the school year, Brandon piggybacks onto his grandfather's tale by clarifying his teaching philosophy to his students, reminding them that he's continuously shared bits of knowledge throughout the year. For my benefit, he reenacts his storytelling to the kids:

> I put "pebbles" out in front of them and I told them, "I'm not gonna tell you to pick them up." You know, "All year long, this is what I've done for you. I've put little 'pebbles' out in front of you and some of you have picked them up. Some of you just brush them on the floor. Some of you just ignore them." And I said, "It is my hope that one of these days, when you reach into your pocket, you find gold."

Afterwards he allows each student to take and keep a pebble from his stash as a memento.

With that as the elaborate backstory, Brandon shares the surprising conclusion of his story by describing the conversation he had with the former student who contacted him unexpectedly:

> He said, "You know I don't even know why I looked your number up. But I found your number in the school directory and I wanted to tell you that last night I was gonna kill myself." And I'm like, "Well … Why didn't you?" And he said, "Because I looked up on my shelf and I saw that stupid rock you gave me." And I said, "'ell, good! You have a piece of gold." And, it's things like that … Why do I keep doing and decorating the room the way I do? Because I think that it makes a difference.

This potentially suicidal boy had the good fortune of having a piece of Brandon's classroom with him when he needed it most. Apparently, the stone reminded the boy that someone cared about him and had made the effort to support him earlier in his young life. While we can't take an entire place with us when we leave it, we often take mementos as reminders of how a place, and the people we interacted with there, have made a difference in our lives. Sharing ourselves with others and anchoring those connections to aspects of a place can produce powerful effects.

Another type of place scenario that addresses familiarity issues occurs when we engage with a novel place, but one that resembles somewhere we've been before or have firm preconceptions about. In this case, we're likely to have expectations about place features and the social life and rituals that occur there. Depending on the conditions, our anticipation can be filled with joy, fear, or indifference about what is likely to happen. A person raised in rural America is likely to feel at ease going to events staged in a rural area, even those far from where they live. Persons with a country lifestyle, for instance, are likely to feel comfortable at a rural county fair that features 4-H exhibits, deep-pit barbecuing, and country music whether it occurs in Alabama, Missouri, Texas, or West Virginia. But a person with deep urban roots who is biased against rural festivals, because they supposedly cater to "rednecks," is likely to feel apprehensive about going to one in real life. Getting people to view new places, as well as familiar ones, with fresh eyes is often challenging, especially in the age of the internet and social media. For better or worse, these technologies prime us by exposing us to countless images and descriptions of places we've never been to in real life.

Sometimes we'll navigate the practical realities of being simultaneously immersed in familiar places that are similar but distinct from one another. Transitioning back and forth between these two places can be stressful and disorienting. For example, children whose divorced parents live in separate residences are often tasked with moving between homes. Formal and informal custody arrangements tend to create conditions that lead to kids spending different amounts of time in each of their parents' separate places. Opportunities to experience different rituals and forms of we-ness with others living in each residence can shape children's place attachment. For instance, in one setting a child might be an only child and receive a great deal of attention while being wrapped up in a stepsibling arrangement in the other home. Learning to make the necessary adjustments might be most difficult early on but it can be an ongoing challenge for years. Having multiple and perhaps overlapping networks that create feelings of we-ness can complicate how a child perceives and acts in a place. In addition, parents can have different amenities and house rules that influence children's willingness to spend time in one home versus the other. For example, one house could be preferred because it has a pool, larger yard, basketball hoop, more private bedrooms and bathrooms, more reliable internet connection, and convenient access to a fun community center.

Many college students, whether their parents are living together or not, also navigate different places simultaneously. Those students who live away from their childhood home during most of the school year but retain their bedroom and other house privileges at their parents' home must manage their transitions between their school place and home on special weekends, holidays, and summer break. Some parents are eager to rearrange their homes when a child "leaves" the nest. A college student may have to deal with a younger sibling taking over their room, or perhaps their room has been repurposed into a workout room, study, grandma's bedroom, or something else.

People often struggle if their transition involves getting accustomed to a place for which they have little or no preparation. Such an unfamiliar place, like a new state or country, prison, dormitory/fraternity/sorority, or workplace setting, may require us to be more attentive to our personal identity as we navigate a new set of expectations. Becoming familiar with and possibly attached to a new place will force us to put into perspective the previous experiences we had with different places, people, and rituals.

Imagine too, occasions when we are exposed to a new place and never return, yet our experience fundamentally changes how we see ourselves and others. We become intimately in touch with the place, but it occurs as part of a one-time exposure rather than over many different moments that are interrupted by life routines in other places. Religious pilgrimages and adventures to iconic natural and built environments typically occur this way and can have a profound effect. My previously mentioned visit with a friend to the Holocaust Museum in Washington, DC, is a perfect example. When we visit these types of places, we often accumulate information about the place beforehand and develop expectations that prepare us to experience it in certain ways. In addition, when we initially visit a celebrated place like this with others it can strengthen our deep dyadic and ideational forms of we-ness as well. Sharing the experience broadens our opportunities to craft our memories and reconstruct them later.

We can contrast these situations with how individuals experience prison. Every prisoner has had to deal with that first day and night behind bars when their life dramatically changes. Prisoners are confronted with the physical realities of being confined with limited opportunities to move from place to place. Those of us with no firsthand experience in the prison system have likely seen riveting movie depictions of what it can be like to be behind bars. In addition to whatever preconceptions they have, new prisoners quickly learn experientially about the intimidating norms and rituals that define social life in prison. Prison rituals and routines affect how individuals perceive not only their fellow prisoners and guards, they also contribute to how prisoners experience the key places that mark prison life (cell, shower, cafeteria, recreation yard, infirmary, and library).

As noted earlier, when a person visits a new place, they typically have preconceived notions and expectations about what it will be like. Many people who end up in prison personally know someone who has served time, so they've heard stories about life on the inside. In addition, according to Bureau of Justice Statistics data from thirty-four states, an astounding 62 percent of those in state prisons are rearrested within three years of release, and 71 percent within five years.[13] Thus, a huge proportion of the prison population learns what it's like to transition back to prison after unsuccessfully trying to readjust to civilian life. The communities where many ex-cons return are defined by poverty, limited job opportunities, few social supports, and high crime rates. Although prisoners do not always return to the same prison from where they were released, they will reenter the prison system equipped with their understanding of the key places in prisons that they acquired from their previous incarceration(s).

Although returning to prison represents one of the more well-known examples of an individual going back to a consequential place, the readjustment process generally is relevant to how people deal with other places as well. Think of the high school or college dropout who returns to school, the soldier who is honorably discharged but reenlists, the person who leaves their childhood hometown for many years and then returns to live and work, or the person who leaves an office job but is rehired a few years later. Each of these reentry transitions affords the person a unique opportunity to come back to a place where they can reflect on the personal memories and life expectations they've generated in recent years. As they navigate their new situation, they can also integrate their recent life experiences with the knowledge they generated from being in this setting before.

From a placemaking perspective, the extent to which a person sees a place as new or familiar can affect the place-related decisions they make as they transition between places. Even in those situations, like a prison or detention center, where a person has little opportunity to be a placemaker, their level of familiarity with the place may influence whatever input they have in altering it.

Alone or Together

When we experience a transition associated with a place, we do it individually or with others by our side. In this book, I emphasize how our experiences in place are related to circumstances that cause us to express, reinforce, or diminish our sense of we-ness and group belonging. Consequently, I highlight how we collectively navigate certain place-based transitions. If we are closely involved with others during the transition process, it can intensify our experience while deepening the memories of how any changes associated with a place affect us and others – either positively or negatively. Although I concentrate on our joint endeavors in place, much can and does happen to us when we experience a place by ourselves. Those solo moments are relevant to what this book covers if they ultimately influence our involvement in group activities situated in a place.

One of the most obvious group transitions is the one experienced by families who undertake a residential move. Moving together as a family produces a range of issues that are not a problem for the individual who moves alone. Family members might have different perceptions about the value of the move and competing expectations of how it should take place. One spouse may like their new neighborhood, city, state, and workplace while the other feels alienated in all four of these types of places. To make matters worse, one child may push to stay in their current school because they want to continue to play on their sports teams and graduate with their friends while their sibling is eager to move because they detest being at their school. The latter child fears walking the school hallways, using the bathroom, sitting in classrooms, and eating in the cafeteria. At school, they live in a perpetual state of crisis because they are relentlessly bullied, so much so that the places themselves are symbolic and painful reminders of their maligned status. Understandably, then, the sibling who wants to stay is attached to their school and the athletic facilities associated with it, whereas the bullied child is not attached whatsoever to the school that they find threatening. Such tension between family members, or others who are undergoing a transition together, can arise when people "voluntarily" leave one place for another or when they are involuntarily displaced because of war, disease, or disaster.

Military families often face their own unique set of challenges related to moving. Couples with ties to the military, with or without children, must navigate stressful situations if they are forced to make repeated moves over time with little or no say in the destination or timing of those moves.[14] The move for military couples can be especially difficult when it involves a reassignment to an unfamiliar culture abroad. Stress is likely to be heightened for the person who is an unenlisted "trailing" partner because their daily rituals and routines will be most affected. The trailing partner is expected to adjust to life as a military spouse/partner who resides on a base or in a nearby community. That person frequently struggles to sustain their preferred trajectory with respect to their educational and work preferences, especially if the move is outside the country.[15] Although the increasing availability of online educational programs, remote employment opportunities, and modern tech that enhances communication with friends and family has provided some relief, the experience of feeling displaced can still be profound.

Obviously, our chances of experiencing interpersonal conflict are much greater if we move with others. Yet, conflict can still emerge between the people moving and those who stay in place, especially if those who stayed had an option to leave. Bitter feelings between those who leave versus stay might distort perceptions of the places implicated in the disagreement such as a house, apartment, neighborhood, or city. A place that once gave rise to pleasant memories might now be a stark reminder of an unsettling set of circumstances that resulted in people living in different locations. As a result, the meanings a person attaches to the same place are much less optimistic than before. However, a joint move can also provide us with opportunities to receive social support from those going through the process with us.

Instead of narrowly focusing on one family's move, imagine a company of sixty to two hundred soldiers who are deployed overseas together. This massive mobilization includes a complex matrix of individual and group-related transitions anchored to the perceptions and practices involving place. Obviously, members of this company will be influenced according to whether they're being assigned to a military base during peacetime or if they are being inserted into an active war zone. Whether soldiers are leaving behind a romantic partner and children can also affect their perspective on their deployment. The familiarity theme, though relevant to both peacetime and wartime deployments, is likely to be crucial in the wartime situation, and intimately connected to what sharing a transition with others entails. Soldiers' preconceptions of their destinations will influence how they deal with their circumstances and talk about their expectations, fears, and uncertainties. It will also matter how many, if any, of the leaders or fellow soldiers in the company have experienced the exact destination or a similar place. If a strong sense of we-ness and trust have been established, then the experienced soldiers are likely to play a significant role in shaping how newcomers anticipate their combat deployment and operation as soldiers in the field of battle – a new, foreboding place.

Another feature of our collective experience with a place includes how we manage our placemaking activities with others. Although I address this practice more fully in the final chapter, let me distinguish between two broad types of collaborative placemaking. One type involves individuals working together to either forge a new place or fundamentally change a preexisting place. For example, this might be the difference between co-owners of a health club building a new facility from the ground up versus planning a major renovation of a standing structure and club. In both cases, the participants are working together to create a new place consistent with their joint vision. Granted, some people may represent a more dominant voice in this exchange, but at least two people are contributing their ideas and trying to make a difference. In the worlds of politics and business, people could band together to designate a particular undeveloped area or unused building as a commemorative site that might include a museum, statues, or ceremonial rituals. Again, they are collaboratively trying to build something new and different.

A second type of placemaking is designed to challenge and alter the meaning of a particular place. Here the effort is to undo an image that is no longer appealing. Sometimes people also want to develop a distinctly new message about the place that goes beyond merely disregarding the previous meaning. Politically minded people are well known for challenging how a place is currently being used or has been used. Their objective is to redefine the place. This occurs frequently in places that have been associated with some sort of social injustice, especially with regard to race and gender issues. Recent politicized attempts to remove Confederate monuments and other similar symbols from public places are designed to solidify how the public should view such images and to see in a new light the physical landscapes where they've been featured.[16]

Unlike the placemaking efforts just noted, collective efforts can also emerge that resemble what has been labeled either "placekeeping" or "placeguarding" initiatives.[17] Here some individuals and groups try to resist a proposed change to a place by joining forces to preserve public symbols in the form of monuments and other artifacts. Others collaborate to maintain a neighborhood's ambience and image while resisting what are perceived to be unwelcomed gentrification efforts by outside experts and stakeholders. For example, numerous groups have been formed in cities like Milwaukee, Wisconsin; Portland, Maine; Detroit, Michigan; and Brooklyn, New York, to challenge various funded community arts projects that are seen as ignoring local voices about community development. In other instances, groups can leverage their sense of we-ness and assert their claims to control access to their local natural resources. Such was the case when Indigenous descendants of the Lakota, and their allies, initiated a remarkable protest in 2016 of the construction of the Dakota Access Pipeline (DAPL) in Standing Rock, North Dakota, to protect their drinking water and sacred grounds.[18] Successful placekeeping initiatives often emerge because stakeholders already have a strong sense of we-ness, but these initiatives can also intensify people's sense of affinity with one another as they rally to protect places they cherish.

Temporary vs. Permanent

As with familiarity, our attempt to define a place in terms of its degree of permanency is not a straightforward matter. Much is in the eye of whomever is connected to the place.

Some places can be eliminated and repurposed so that they immediately take on new meaning. This happens all the time in the world of construction when buildings are leveled and new ones are raised to replace them. However, it typically is not just one physical building being replaced by another; the purpose of the building often changes, too. What once was a dilapidated and unoccupied house with an occasional squatter, a site that represented an eyesore to nearby residents, might now reemerge as a renovated neighborhood café or art gallery. If successful, the café could transition into having the reputation and functionality of being a trendy third place for the locals. Within a couple of years, locals may perceive the café as a permanent fixture of the neighborhood. But what happens when business declines or the owner decides to sell the property and the new owner converts it into a mobile phone retail store? And what role, if any, do local social activists play in trying to prevent outsiders from buying and transforming properties that will alter the neighborhood infrastructure and culture?

Another way to think about a place's permanency is to consider it from the perspective of the people who interact with others in that place at a specific point in time. Imagine that a person who is only in town for the weekend happens to visit the place and ends up making friends with three locals who regularly frequent this place together. The solo visitor's possible place attachment is likely to be quite different than it is for their three new friends. For the out-of-town visitor, this place represents a temporary spot in their ongoing life experience, even though they may carry fond memories with them when they return home. The three friends, on the other hand, see this place similarly to how the characters on the classic sitcom *Seinfeld* from the 1990s viewed the coffee shop where they regularly hung out and bantered.

This element is significant because we are likely to approach our transitions differently if we believe a place is only temporarily going to be a part of our life rather than indefinitely. Presumably, we will feel more comfortable allowing ourselves to grow attached to a place when we see it as being more permanent. Our logic: Why get attached to a place if we know we're not going to be involved with it for very long? Presumably, then, we'll be more likely to commit time, energy, and money to placemaking activities if we anticipate that we're going to be involved with a place long-term.

Digitally Mediated Performance

Another feature of place with transitional overtones is revealed in Germaine Halegoua's work that dissects how digital media can be used to accentuate "place as performative process." This perspective invites us to see our encounters with and attachments to place as a dynamic part of our socially constructed reality. In recent decades with the introduction of new digital technologies, the intersection between people and place has fundamentally changed and continues to evolve in fascinating and sometimes controversial ways. Many are far less supportive than Halegoua is with our obsession with using digital media in various places. In historical terms, we can emphasize transitions by noting how our contemporary experiences with place are now more frequently mediated in diverse ways by digital technologies. In addition, we can also highlight how transitional aspects of social life are mediated by digital technologies in a more immediate, moment-to-moment context when we are immersed in a place.

As mentioned in Chapter 2, Halegoua examines "how and why place is made and what types of places are socially and technologically produced through our imaginations of and engagement with digital media."[19] By viewing place as process and performance, we can further appreciate how digital technologies afford us opportunities to present ourselves in certain ways while we are anchored to both specific and generic places. These technologies also alter how we navigate interpersonal exchanges relative to place.

Every day, especially in urban areas, "people consciously employ and actively seek out digital media (such as mobile phones, wireless and fiber-optic networks, ubiquitous computing and navigation technologies, and location-based social media) in order to create and negotiate a new sense of place."[20] When we engage in routine practices that involve digital technologies, we create unique occasions to embed ourselves in a place while simultaneously building a sense of place. We also develop and use digital practices that allow us to share those places with others (Facebook, Instagram, Snapchat, or TikTok postings), whether they are with us in person, or situated elsewhere as they respond vicariously to our performance. A performative approach is relevant in at least two critical ways to how our digital life links our individual and collective identities to places that matter to us. It has implications for how we use digital technologies to transition from one distinct place to another (e.g., home and a sports venue) and it affects how we make sense of the same place over time (e.g., a neighborhood prior to and after gentrification). The person who is a dedicated alum of a sports-crazed university may lean into their collective alum identity as they use social media to chronicle their cross-country trip to attend their university's championship game. Likewise, a person who sees themself as a longtime neighborhood activist may use social media to post an impassioned visual portrait of how the physical streetscape and social ecology of their community is being fundamentally uprooted because outside commercial developers are being driven by their self-serving business values.

Life Course View

Some transitional experiences related to place involve individuals changing their perceptions of a place over time as they mature and accumulate new experiences. As mentioned previously, my view of my hometown changed once I transitioned from being a naïve boy to an independent man who had experienced different places around the world. My training as a social scientist further altered the way I interpreted my hometown's social and economic landscape. While this sort of shift in perspective is not automatic as people age, people frequently change how they see their hometown and other childhood places as they mature and accumulate worldly experience. This might be particularly true for someone raised in a small and isolated community. Moreover, the nature and intensity of a person's place attachment can shift considerably as they refine their worldviews.

We adopt new standpoints and modify others as we move through the life course. We modify our standpoints, in part, because we engage with the world via bodies that are subject to change as we transition into puberty, adulthood, and our later years of life. In addition, we can experience physical changes that reflect our improving or declining health. For example, compared to a person with a physical disability, an able-bodied person is apt to be more oblivious to some of the practical aspects of navigating situations in a specific place or moving from one place to another. But now imagine how this able-bodied person sees places in a different light once they acquire a disability and can no longer take accessibility issues for granted.

Shifts in standpoints are also relevant to how we experience place when we adopt new roles and have fresh experiences with different facets of life. Our new experiences as legal adults, spouses, parents, members of a political party, workers, persons who identify as nonbinary, and much more inform our approach to the various places that matter to us. The local gay bar that we once saw as repulsive when we were a homophobic nineteen-year-old can take on new meaning if we redirect our life path to become a progressive pro-feminist person who is an ally of the LGBTQ+ community. Consider, too, how a woman who lives in an environmentally compromised area near a chemical plant all her life learns to harbor new fears and anger about this place as a mother of young children, sentiments that she did not possess when she was an uninformed young girl.

Places continually change in subtle and sometimes dramatic ways. Thus, when we consider how transitions along the life course alter individuals' perceptions, we must acknowledge that real, often observable, physical changes to places are also occurring simultaneously. Thus, studying people's place-based transitions involves understanding the mix of subjective and objective forces that affect how people see and respond to social life in the different places that matter to them. We see this clearly when considering the able-bodied young person who lives in a cold, isolated rural area with no access to a health and fitness center. Although he's challenged to find convenient ways to incorporate rigorous exercise into his life, he is committed to keeping himself healthy and fit. He cobbles together a program that includes running outside in frigid temperatures, hiking, and lifting free weights in his house. After this young man experiences a car accident and finds himself permanently using a wheelchair, his exercise options are much more limited in his local community. Consequently, his perceptions of both the place where he lives and his body change. If we insert an uplifting twist to the story, a local entrepreneur decides to renovate a large building and convert it into an impressive fitness center. In addition, the young man's older brother agrees to move and come live with him. Now the young man has a new facility that allows him to sustain his fitness despite his disability and he has his brother as a workout buddy and support person. These new developments can alter how this young man views the meaningful places in his life.

Claiming

Our sense of how permanent a place is in our lives is sometimes related to whether we feel we have some type of claim or formal ownership over it. We can claim a place informally in our hearts and minds, or we can establish our tie to it with legal documentation. When we orient ourselves toward a place from a position of having deep thoughts, memories, and feelings about it, we are often willing to make sacrifices to preserve and enhance it. Imagine the professional athlete who informally claims their entire hometown or a Boys & Girls Club in it as "theirs." They do so not because they in any way legally own these places; rather, they express these claims because they realize those places paved the way for their successful upbringing. Their sense of loyalty and obligation compels them to give back to the community and a key organization that provided a safe place and mentorship for them to become a productive, civically engaged adult.

The legal route, on the other hand, is much more formal and enables us to lay claim to houses and properties, business facilities, cars, boats, and other place-based entities that we can acquire or have been gifted to us. Our legal connection to a place gives us the power to make critical decisions regarding it. Thus, the distinction between a heartfelt and legal form of claiming can have important implications when others legally contest our own claims. Yet, these distinctions may be largely irrelevant in those instances where specific people assert both heartfelt and legal claims to a place and others do not challenge them.

Although we often feel attached to the places we claim, this is not always the case. Place attachments and expressions of claiming often overlap, but they are distinct concepts. In other words, we can claim a place – even a home or property – but not feel emotionally attached to it in any meaningful way. People often go through the motions of living in a home they legally own but neither like nor are motivated to maintain. Thus, a primary distinction between claiming a place and being attached to it is that we can be attached to a place without having any meaningful control over what happens to it, or we can assert a lot of control over a place without being attached to it.

Place attachment usually infers a positive sentiment that is based on memories, expectations, beliefs, knowledge, and symbolic meanings that foster our affinity for a place, including a bond with the social life that we associate with it. In addition, we will be hesitant to release our hold on such a place. We may develop attachments to places that lead us to experience some negative feelings, but even these places can generate other, more enjoyable feelings as well.

Claiming a place tends to have three elements associated with it. First, it prompts us to feel that we have a vested interest in voicing our expectations about a place's future development. Sometimes, it may even lead us to feel we have a sense of entitlement and should have a say in decisions associated with it. Second, in addition to the informal or formal rights we might have regarding a place, we also recognize that we have responsibilities as to what we do with or in a specific place. These responsibilities generally prompt us to think about ways we can protect the place from declining and enhance its chances to thrive. Third, we will often act on that sense of responsibility by investing our time, energy, and resources into sustaining or improving the quality of the place.

How are the claims we make in relation to a place connected to the way we experience transitions? How do we negotiate with others what our standing is relative to place? These processes come alive when a person or group of people move into a home that is occupied by others and possibly owned by someone else as well. This arrangement commonly occurs among stepfamilies when someone moves into a house where members of the other side of the stepfamily have been living. It tends to be most striking when the move is for an indefinite or extended amount of time. The process involves choreographing the family dance that includes persons with distinct family identities and transforming it into a smooth flowing arrangement of activity in and outside the home.[21] Those involved must reconcile how to find comfort in sharing space and redefining the entire place/house, as well as certain smaller places/rooms, as "ours." This process is intimately tied to the circumstances of people forging a sense of we-ness that incorporates how they individually and mutually perceive the places where they engage in their daily activities, such as eating, sleeping, relaxing, studying, working, doing chores, and more.

In addition to our home connections, the process of growing attached to a place and claiming it can occur with gyms, schools, churches, neighborhoods, cafés, parks, and other facilities or areas of nature that are a part of our lives. When individuals are committed to a place, they often suggest ways to improve it, resembling a type of placemaking that promotes transitional moments for the place. Owners of a place can consider changes by asking motivated participants to make suggestions, big and small, for improving and expanding how the place caters to their needs. Participants responsible for managing a place as well as those who use it can work collaboratively to realize their respective visions. My own fitness center provides members opportunities to submit suggestions into a drop box to improve various assets in the gym. Staff members follow up with a phone call and occasionally implement suggestions.

Because place involves both process and structure, our attachments to a place will result in us being affected by the transitional elements relevant to it. When a place that matters to us changes, our life is likely to be affected in various ways as well. In addition, the type of claims we express toward a place will affect how we perceive and deal with any transitions that alter a place's profile and our activities therein.

6

Claims, Control, and Decision-Making

Photo 8: Azovstal Plant, Mariupol, Ukraine, after the Russian invasion and devastating bombing in 2022. (Photographer: Pavel Klimov; Reuters release)

Shortly after Russia unleashed its relentless bombing campaign on Mariupol, Ukraine, in the spring of 2022, roughly one thousand desperate civilians – mostly women, children, and elderly persons – fled to the Azovstal steel plant to seek refuge.[1] Some stayed there for nearly three months. By early April, thousands of dedicated soldiers from the controversial Azov Regiment (formerly the Azov Battalion) also retreated to the site. Founded in 2014 as a volunteer paramilitary militia to fight pro-Russian forces in the Donbas War, this regiment was later integrated into the Ukrainian military and vowed to do everything possible to protect the city and its civilians. Since its inception, however, this fighting force has drawn scrutiny because some members have openly embraced far-right and neo-Nazi ideologies.

The Azovstal industrial complex, which became operational in 1933, is one of the largest steel facilities in Europe and is located near the coast of the Sea of Azov, across the river from the downtown area. Covering four square miles, it has numerous large furnaces, warehouses, and railroads. More than ten thousand people were employed there before Russia's invasion. In a bygone era, the renowned plant was at the center of the Soviet Union's efforts to build railroads and ships before it was privatized in 1990 when Ukraine gained its independence. But during Putin's war, production stopped. Instead, civilians and soldiers sought safety in the massive underground maze of bunkers and tunnels within this facility that was designed to serve as a bomb shelter. The Soviets, who planned and executed the facility's rebuilding in the 1940s after the Nazis destroyed much of it, began by constructing the bomb shelter and then building the new steel mill on top. In 2022, ironically, the dark and dingy subterranean place became a makeshift, life-saving shelter for many Ukrainians who were confronted by a lethal Russian invasion. The factory had been similarly used during the Nazi invasion of the Soviet Union in World War II and the bunkers protected people during the pro-Russian separatist attack of Ukraine in 2014.

In the most recent war, Russia's overwhelming bombardment quickly turned the beautiful coastal city into a grim landscape of rubble while also severely damaging the expansive factory. Russian soldiers had surrounded the complex by early March and cut off food, water, and medical supplies from those who were sheltering so they were forced to fend for themselves. Eventually, essential supplies were depleted, leaving the civilians and soldiers in a hopeless situation. They were isolated with no reasonable chance of prolonging their stay or being rescued by outsiders. Unfortunately, the initial allure of a bomb shelter rapidly morphed into the fear of a death trap. A mother, describing the situation that existed in April, captures the dire circumstances of life in the shelter by reflecting on how children coped: "We had papers and pens, and the children would draw fruits and food, because they were hungry. Sometimes they would play games like 'Going to the Supermarket,' so they could pretend to buy food, or they'd be chefs at a café. Their games became connected to the food they didn't have."[2] In an interview with NPR in early May, a naval border guard inside the plant described the situation as "catastrophic." In his words, "It's getting worse every day. We can't do anything about it because we're trapped. No one can bring us any kind of aid. We're trying to help civilians with food and medicine. We will not leave them hungry and fighting for survival, but we can only share what we have."[3]

In the first half of May, the remaining civilians in the shelter were evacuated. After three months of fierce fighting, the siege came to an end on May 20 when more than 2,400 Ukrainian fighters surrendered on orders from the Ukrainian high command. Throughout the sheltering period, the steel plant held incredible symbolic value for Ukrainians and Russians alike, especially in the eyes of Presidents Zelenskyy and Putin, although the meanings differed dramatically. While the Ukrainian forces continued to fight and protect the sheltering population, the steel plant was characterized inside of Ukraine and to the Western world as a remarkable site of resistance. It was a place that reminded all those with an ounce of empathy that Ukrainians were a proud and courageous people, unwilling to surrender their land and way of life to an invading, barbaric army. That the plant was, in appearance and ambience, a rugged place where manual laborers had recently done the difficult and dirty work of forging steel punctuated the heroic storyline that featured brave soldiers and civilians living and fighting side by side in harsh, restricted conditions. Holding steadfast day after day to their rightful claim to the plant and city, the soldiers and civilians sent a resolute message to Putin and his forces that Ukrainians harbored a steely national identity and deep-seated sense of we-ness. They were not Russians, nor did they want to be usurped or ruled by the Russian state. Moreover, Ukrainians, including most notably

President Zelenskyy and his military leaders, recognized that the standoff at Azovstal prevented a significant number of Russian forces from being redeployed to fight elsewhere. Thus, the resistance at the plant was saving lives throughout the country while preventing Putin from asserting a face-saving victory in the critical port city of Mariupol. The steel plant had become a remarkable public and symbolic place, gaining worldwide recognition.

Regrettably, Mariupol and the Azovstal steel plant were ultimately claimed by Putin and his generals.[4] Those who had physically been inside the city and plant had already established their impressions of Mariupol and the factory prior to the invasion, and then again after the bombing began. Those impressions no doubt evolved in complex ways during the siege. Looking forward, Ukrainians may someday truly liberate the city and steel plant from Russian control. If they succeed, they are likely to establish memorials to remind Ukrainians and the world of both the atrocities and heroism that occurred in these revered places that trigger somber memories, but also images of kind, caring, and selfless acts. The factory will become a national and international landmark celebrating the value of fighting for democracy while reinforcing Ukrainians' patriotism and sense of honor.

Alternatively, Russia could continue to occupy this land and factory indefinitely while fabricating a narrative that celebrates a false liberation theme – the notion that Russia's operational mission was to "de-nazify Ukraine." In this scenario, Russia would likely rebuild the steel mill once again and fashion an accompanying public relations message that asserts how the factory is allowing Russians to recapture the glory of the Soviet industrial era. Only time will tell what type of placemaking emerges in the years ahead. It is clear now that both Mariupol and Azovstal will remain significant places, perceived in various ways depending on whether an insider or outsider perspective is used to assign the meanings.

The Claiming Process

By studying Russia's invasion of Ukraine and the social responses it generated, we can learn invaluable lessons about power, courage, humanity, empathy, altruism, leadership, gratitude, group belonging, and much more. To do so, we must dissect the multilayered narratives that define this critical moment in world history, either in real time or with the benefit of hindsight. Most importantly for what we explore in this book, the war-related events in Ukraine provide concrete examples of how different aspects of place matter for an individual and a group. Whether it is the attachment to a place, the rituals that bring a place to life and give it meaning, the transitions whereby individuals move between and within places, or the contested struggles as well as collaborative efforts to define, claim, and shape a place, there is much to consider when assessing what happens in a place.

Although the political and real-life stakes of what occurred in Ukraine in 2022–4 are quite serious, some conflicts related to place have far more limited, perhaps even trivial, consequences. As noted in the previous chapter, the claiming process that shapes our orientation toward place permeates the social landscape; it touches all five of the social domains I discussed as well as all ten of the types of places I've outlined. When we seek to assert control over aspects of a place that is of interest to others, it highlights the potential tensions we can experience as individuals or as members of a group involved in place-based activities. A key feature of our placemaking experience includes both our "rightful" and contested claims to shape decisions that affect both how a place is defined and what activities occur therein. In moments of decision-making involving places and placemaking activities, we see how social forces influence our options to assert control and resolve potential conflicts. Those decision-making processes will vary according to whether they are driven by coercive tactics, intense negotiations that culminate in a resolution that is less than ideal for at least one party, or built on amicable, cooperative exchanges.

As we navigate places that matter to us, we sometimes encounter tensions that have significant ethical, legal, and political implications that manifest themselves on various levels of the social landscape. Our desire to be in control, combined with the basic assumptions associated with scarcity and private property, provides the foundation for how many Americans orient themselves toward a place. Many of our daily decisions, and some of our most stressful conflicts with others, involve place-based matters. Consequently, we often find ourselves in a position where we need to reconcile our place-based interests because they clash with what other individuals and groups want and expect.

Depending on the circumstances, our desires to claim and control aspects of social and physical landscapes affect how we individually, or as part of a group, relate to a place that matters to us. Although conflict and friction do not play a prominent role in every place where people make decisions, they are palpable features that taint our experience with many places or lurk as real possibilities in others. Our conflictual experiences are often reinforced by others with whom we share a group identity and who have a stake in how a place is defined, altered, or used. Similarly, our camaraderie often reflects how we collectively manage a shared affinity for aspects of a place that limit others' unfettered inclusion.

In some cases, the disagreements and confrontations between opposing sides may extend beyond one specific place and implicate various places that share something in common. For example, human rights activists have protested for almost twenty years against the fast-food chain Wendy's for not joining the Fair Food Program that is designed to protect farm workers' rights. While activists discourage people from frequenting any of the more than 6,500 Wendy's restaurants in twenty-nine countries, members of this social justice group also target the places that are at the root of the problem. They highlight the "subhuman conditions" associated with the work camps and fields where impoverished farm workers grow, harvest, and package tomatoes.[5] Thus, the message from this dual focus on restaurants and farms is that the unacceptable work practices that happen on tomato farms should also affect how consumers perceive the restaurants that utilize their products. The activists' place-based confrontation with Wendy's management calls for a boycott of the restaurants and a new set of practices for the tomato farms.

Features of the Claiming Context

We can develop a deeper appreciation for how the claiming process is intimately tied to cultural and social contexts if we highlight several themes, including a few that resemble those introduced in our discussion of place-based transitions. As with the other categorizing schemes I've used throughout this book, I do not suggest that this scheme is exhaustive. However, it highlights critical distinctions that influence how we assert and manage claims about places.

Individual or Group

As noted earlier, we develop place attachments in various ways that include our individual actions as well as our investments in larger groups. Many times, we assert our individual claims about place by engaging with only a small number of people, including one-on-one exchanges. When we make claims on our own behalf, our personal standing and resources will be especially important. In legal settings, we may be assisted by an attorney who brings to bear their personal expertise and the resources of their firm. But often when we personally negotiate informal claims, what matters most is our human and social capital as well as our experience with a place. Do we have the financial and educational resources to make our claims in a convincing way? Do we know people who might assist us behind the scenes to gather useful information or share their personal experience with a similar scenario? Have we accumulated knowledge about a place because of our long-standing history with it? In addition to these valued resources, our personality attributes may also play a pivotal role. Generally, we are more likely to get our way and have our claims honored if we are assertive and outspoken. If, on the other hand, we tend to be a passive person, we are less likely to make our demands known or to assert our place-based rights.

When we are associated with a group, we might actively help others advocate for the group's claim, or we might permit the leadership of our group to take charge while hoping for the best. In contrast, we might demonstrate our own leadership and empathy skills by taking on the responsibility of inspiring others to develop a collaborative approach to placemaking. We can try to establish partnerships with other groups that will strengthen the likelihood that our claims will be respected.

All groups, by definition, include individuals. However, groups vary considerably in how their members are connected, make decisions, and think about a particular place. There may be nested groups within the larger one that support different approaches. Sometimes, a group may not have a clear, unified stance on their placemaking ideals and activities. In those instances, the group's ability to bring about change will be hampered. One segment of a group may be willing to provide access to a place to members of an outside group whereas a different subset of members may advocate for exclusive control of who can stake a claim to a place. Thus, the ability to build and manage a sense of we-ness will influence how effective groups are in asserting their claims on places.

Physical and Social Scope

Closely linked at times to the question of whether we are engaged with a place as an individual or as part of a group is the scope of the place in question. Throughout this book I've provided numerous examples to illustrate the wide range of places that matter to people. Some are relatively small and intimate like our homes, whereas others represent massive places that are marked by formal political boundaries, such as those pertaining to nation-states. Situated in between are places like our public parks, communities, and corporate buildings that we claim while implicitly or explicitly negotiating our claims with others. These examples convey both the varying physical and social scope of specific places. The physical conditions of a place, including architectural design features, can influence how we express our claims and efforts to control it. At times those physical aspects will affect us individually, but they can also affect our collective response. Although we focus much of our personal energy on places that are relatively small in scope, we sometimes assert individual claims with respect to larger scale places like schools, churches, and regional areas. As a member of a group that is making place-based claims, we are more inclined to have a vested interest in places that are larger in scope. Nonetheless, some of our small group alliances with family members, close friends, or work associates can help us to deal with individually oriented place concerns. For example, we might persuade a family member to leave the house to check into a drug rehab facility or encourage a workmate to take better care of our shared workspace.

In our everyday lives, we are most likely to navigate place issues with our family, close friends, and sometimes workmates. Seemingly trivial issues – like what radio stations get to be saved and played while sharing time with passengers in a car – can emerge as a place-based consideration. Although still relevant at times, the advent of smart phones has lessened the frictions over radio stations that once infiltrated the car zone. Now kids and adults have more viable options to be plugged into their own audio space while sharing time in the same place. When this occurs, the place that once operated as an engaging, interactive site is transformed into what sociologist Sherry Turkle coined the "alone together" arrangement. A scenario such as spending time together in the car is diminished by the less socially invigorating exchanges that people have when they discard quality conversation.[6] With mixed results, contemporary audio and visual technologies enhance our ability to create private space within shared places.

Efforts to assert claims in relation to public places and national territories often demand that individuals and groups devote time to coordinating their interests and developing partnerships and alliances to achieve specific placemaking goals. Such efforts sometimes require groups to compromise or change their mindset. With the increased attention on mass shootings, many school officials and other stakeholders have coordinated their efforts and pushed to increase visible symbols of deterrence, such as school resource officers (SROs), metal detectors, and surveillance equipment. Many conservative-leaning politicians have called for a larger law enforcement presence on school campuses, with some wanting to encourage teachers to carry guns. Those who embrace this NRA-oriented approach usually want to "harden" schools.

Other interested parties voice opposition, citing the lack of solid evidence that these practices are effective while questioning the inappropriate ties between school safety advocacy groups and security industry organizations.[7] Those less enthusiastic about increasing the police presence in schools fear it will alter the atmosphere of these learning environments. Some even want to limit their involvement. For example, those in charge of the Chicago school system dramatically decreased the number of officers working in their schools by one third between 2020 and 2022, and those who are present have a reduced role.[8] The rationale for this policy shift is that having police on campus was increasing the number of arrests and suspensions, especially among Black and Latinx youth. The change in outlook places a premium on encouraging teachers and staff to express empathy and to reach out to students proactively before trouble escalates that would require disciplinary action. Initial reports are promising with preliminary data showing that Chicago high schools were significantly less likely to call police on their students in the first semester of the 2021–2 school year. On a national level, a 2014 school climate survey of middle and high school students found that students perceived outside surveillance cameras more favorably than inside ones. Inside cameras tended to lower students' perceptions of "safety, equity, and support."[9] A report from the Center for American Progress also calls for greater investment in evidence-based initiatives like violence prevention programs, teacher training, and peer mediation.[10]

Unfortunately, placemaking debates instigated by school safety concerns are becoming increasingly more complex and heated. Regrettably, we have now entered an era marked by a six-year-old boy who snuck a loaded 9mm gun into his elementary school in Virginia, which was equipped with metal detectors, then shot his twenty-five-year-old teacher in the hand and chest.[11] Fortunately, the schoolteacher survived, but this once unimaginable story reinforces the public's fading memory of an era when schools were perceived to be places free from onsite shootings and killings.

In recent years, large-scale initiatives to alter how we manage places have been significantly influenced by the creative use of social media. Contemporary media platforms enable people to articulate more readily their place-based claims and to mobilize like-minded people to support concerted efforts to define a place in an alternative way. Redefining a place may require that specific decisions are made and implemented. Social media clearly encouraged individuals to come to the area that was eventually labeled George Floyd Square during the most active protests. But social media can also be used in destructive ways to broaden the reach of groups committed to terrorizing people. Gangs operating in Haiti have effectively used platforms such as TikTok, Instagram, YouTube, WhatsApp, and X (formerly Twitter) to assert their claims to control what happens in their communities. The gangs use social media to recruit members, threaten rival gangs, and instill fear in the general population and politicians by showcasing their violent acts or promoting their many kidnappings – 225 in the first three months of 2022, a 60 percent increase compared to the same time the previous year. In today's information age, those who control and manipulate social media platforms can have a disproportionate effect on how places are perceived, defined, and used.

Degree of Permanency

Just as we discovered while exploring place transitions, our approach to negotiating place claims is likely to be affected by how permanent a place feels to us. Do we perceive that a particular place-based decision will likely only affect us for a brief period of time? Or do we recognize that our experiences and decisions involving a place will have long-term impacts for us, and perhaps others as well?

Time, from a physics perspective, has objective, measurable attributes, but our sense of everyday time is culturally and socially constructed. How we experience a place is filtered through a lens that we've developed as a person immersed in culture. That cultural landscape provides us with an understanding of the rhythms of time and events that unfold in various places. Our personal familiarity with time in relation to a place is shaped by the types of exchanges we have with others who also have a vested interest in that place. Sharing time with others while navigating a place, whether as companions, collaborators, or competitors, can alter our sense of whether our engagement with a place feels more temporary or permanent. Similarly, our sense of how time relates to place can be affected by whether our experience feels like intimate companionship or superficial association.

For example, a fifteen-year-old foster child who has been shuffled between seven different foster homes during the past twelve years is less likely to have developed an attachment to any of their "homes" compared to the foster child who was adopted at age three and has lived with the same family, in the same house, for the past twelve years. The more mobile child will have endured a long litany of place-based circumstances and a series of transient relationships with various foster parents and other kids living in the different houses. This child probably had less input in shaping the places where they lived, increasingly seeing each successive place as one where they didn't belong. Their unfortunate life circumstances gave them little basis to claim the places that sheltered them. With this as their backstory, they likely would have seen any new placement as an unstable waystation during a turbulent childhood spent trapped in the foster-care system. On the other hand, the foster child who had the good fortune of living the past twelve years in the same house with the same family is more likely to feel a sense of permanency. As a result, they are more likely to feel as though they have established a sense of we-ness with their foster family and have a voice in household placemaking.

Mobile migrant, business, and military families represent another important subset of individuals who must grapple with unpredictable, transient life journeys that displace them often. When forced to leave temporary refugee camps, neighborhoods, and schools on a regular basis, such families have less opportunity to establish their roots in any one community. With the understanding that any uprooting or reassignment will lead to more goodbyes as well as challenges to learn the rhythms of a new place and culture, people develop coping mechanisms to make peace with their changing circumstances and hope for the best.

The sense of temporal stability or instability is also reflected in how larger groups of people perceive the places that matter to them and express a commitment to be involved in securing or altering features of these places to enhance their well-being. Those most involved in community and regional environmental groups often have long-standing ties to an area and feel invested in their placemaking activities. Their community ties often compel them to be supportive of each other and to enlist the help of other citizens to control the use of sensitive lands. Moreover, our national identities often bolster our sense of cultural legacy and desire to be involved in placemaking activities that reinforce our preferred images of how a place like our country should look and operate.

The complex interplay between community spirit and environmental activities has been dramatically displayed in Louisiana for decades. These complexities reveal how people can have mixed feelings about how committed they are to embracing a place as a permanent, desirable force in their lives. Ironically, many people living in communities along the eighty-mile stretch of land adjacent to the Mississippi River between Baton Rouge and New Orleans, called by some the "petrochemical corridor," and derogatively referred to by others as "Cancer Alley," or more recently "Death Alley," have strong attachments to their communities even though these areas are marred by extremely high pollution levels generated by resource extraction and chemical industries in the area. However, some residents, like Dean Millet, a commissioner for St. James Parish, Louisiana, have hesitantly spoken out in favor of more environmental regulations and selective permitting for new plants.

In March of 2019, Commissioner Millet, a longtime resident of the area, shared his place-based views of the community during a commission meeting, voicing his opposition to a permitting request submitted by Wanhua, a Chinese-owned chemical plant. He initially began his emotional remarks to the audience by revealing that several months earlier, he had felt guilty when he went home after voting in favor of a permit for a plastic manufacturing plant. That lingering sentiment inspired him to expand on his personal reflections:

> I'm talking from my heart right now. I got a family. I got children. I got grandchildren, I'm one of the few that can say, I [am] proud to say I have my kids within five miles of me. I have four kids. All of them

came home because they love St. James Parrish. But so many of my friends are gone. Yes, they worked in St. James Parrish, but no, they wanted to stay in St. James Parrish, [but] they moved to some other parish. Yes, we've got great jobs, they've got great jobs ... the environmental impact they're putting on their families, that's what all these people are scared of.[12]

Millet contextualized his comments by mentioning that he and another commissioner had worked in the chemical industries, so they knew what went on back when they were working – hinting at the industries' environmentally dangerous practices. But he is also well aware of how these petrochemical plants generate valuable economic opportunities for locals.

Unfortunately, Louisiana residents living in or near Death Alley have felt trapped by the difficult calculation that juxtaposes the everyday tangible benefits of economic prosperity with the more elusive, and often less immediate, health risks associated with the petrochemical plants. Sociologist Arlie Hochschild's perceptive ethnographic study *Strangers in Their Own Land: Anger and Mourning on the American Right* reveals the tensions people living in this area experience directly and indirectly because of the tradeoffs they have made for decades between jobs and health.[13] Large portions of the population, as well as governmental leaders, have ignored or downplayed the stark environmental effects of the petrochemical companies and continue to do so because these companies help them pay their bills and financially support their communities. Many of these companies, like Dow, Shell Global, and Sasol, also seek to establish a sense of goodwill within the community by providing financial support to community organizations and projects as well as national organizations that have a presence in Louisiana. For example, Dow contributes to the Audubon Nature Institute and Shell supports the National Fish and Wildlife Foundation. These gifts are designed to establish a sense of we-ness and bridging social capital that connects the company to the community. Historically, the government's response, both at the state and federal levels, has favored economic development over environmental protection. Two decades ago, the inspector general of the Environmental Protection Agency (EPA) concluded that Louisiana's poor record on environmental regulation is in large part due to "a culture in which the state agency is expected to protect industry."[14] Thus, concealing the physical and psychological consequences associated with these polluting industries is made easier when companies are perceived to be adding economic value to the community.

The lack of effective government oversight has provoked some residents to speak out and take more decisive action. For example, those associated with the Coalition Against Death Alley (CADA), founded in 2019, challenge the status quo by protesting the degradation of their environment from the more than two hundred petrochemical companies in the area. The activists involved with this coalition confront government agencies about not doing enough to regulate the existing plants' polluting practices. They also work to mobilize communities to stop new petrochemical plants from being built. CADA's explicit mission is to "pressure industrial giants and governments to stop the ongoing poisoning of majority-black communities in Louisiana's 'Cancer Alley.'" In their words, they've taken up this fight because "The production and wastes from these state-supported industries are life threatening, emitting hundreds of known cancer-causing chemicals that are also known to cause birth defects, cardiovascular complications, autoimmune disorders and respiratory diseases."[15] They portray what they are confronting as an "ongoing silent genocide." Although the language may sound hyperbolic to some, this tone vividly reflects the sad reality on the ground for others. Indeed, one 2015 EPA health assessment for residents living near a Denka plant in St. John the Baptist Parish that releases chloroprene and other chemicals found that they had a lifetime cancer risk that was eight hundred times above the national average. If not a protracted genocide, then at least a deliberate disregard for human life in the name of profit. While Denka has made significant upgrades to its plant to reduce the emission of chemicals, they are still above the recommended levels.

Moving forward, CADA's effectiveness will be partly contingent on how well this group can capitalize on the passion of its long-time residents who are eager to strengthen their sense of we-ness as Louisiana people. Many of these people value family and want their children and grandchildren to be healthy and safe, free of the constant worries of what breathing polluted air and drinking contaminated water can do to the human body.

The industrial and social mix in the petrochemical corridor has pitted subsets of residents against one another as they struggle to prioritize either their economic standing or their physical well-being. Many individuals who have established a sense of we-ness with people (including family members) working in the petrochemical field or in conservative-leaning segments of the community have not taken kindly to those who have aligned themselves with environmental values and political causes that could impede economic development in the area. Thus, different subsets of Louisianians who each love their regional and local cultures have been entangled in a major confrontation over their placemaking values and efforts.

Type and Degree of Confrontation

Several scenarios capture how we try to claim and control our surroundings – the places that structure and provide meaning to our lives. The most confrontational scenarios receive more attention here because they are often relevant to social inequities and influence our personal and social well-being the most. The shorthand labels I'll use to identify the place-based claiming scenarios are contested, unstable resolution, and mutual negotiation.

Contested

Contested scenarios produce some of the most heated and consequential exchanges between interested parties. In these situations, individuals or groups have well-defined views about how their rights and responsibilities are related to a particular place. The participants typically understand what is at stake and are prepared to voice their claims regarding a specific place. On the one hand, interested parties may be actively involved in sustaining or expanding their "rightful" claim and control over a place. They may be compelled to defend against others' encroachment into what they identify as their place and the opportunities therein. On the other hand, individuals and groups exist on the outside looking in and to a varying degree intend to assert their power to redefine a place. That desire, in the volatile overlapping worlds of national politics and the military, is exhibited when leaders and the countries they command try to conquer other sovereign nations. On a grand scale, the war in Ukraine fits the description of a contested scenario, with the Ukrainians fighting valiantly to hold their country together while protecting it from an invading nation. On a smaller scale, the battle for control over the Azovstal steel plant also represents a contested scenario.

While scenarios of this type unfortunately involve political and violent elements at times, physical violence is not always a part of what takes place. The Wendy's boycott movement described earlier is one such case of a nonviolent contested scenario. Another volatile example of this situation includes instances in which diverse stakeholders, some local and others from outside the community, get embroiled in a major dispute about how a community should rebuild after being devastated by a major natural disaster. We saw this vividly in the aftermath of Hurricane Katrina in September 2005 when in the subsequent weeks, months, and years, residents, city officials, community groups, developers, politicians, and others found themselves calling for alternative recovery strategies to rebuild New Orleans. In his 2013 book, *Coming Home to New Orleans: Neighborhood Rebuilding after Katrina*, Karl Seidman, an economic development expert and senior lecturer at MIT's Department of Urban Studies and Planning, provides an excellent close-up, detailed, and technical account of the multi-layered and contentious rebuilding process in this iconic city.

Seidman bases his observations of New Orleans's complex and disjointed rebuilding trajectory, in part, on his in-depth case studies of six different neighborhoods, two of which were heavily flooded. In broad terms, Seidman frames the challenging dilemmas of effectively creating a reconstructive placemaking strategy by noting that:

> While lives and families can be restarted in many locations, a city and its culture are necessarily tied to a place. Rebuilding a city requires reconstructing the physical place. For New Orleans, a city whose unique life and culture are entwined in landscape, architecture, and

history centered around its neighborhoods, rebuilding meant not only attending to the massive physical task but restoring the city's cultural and social life to those neighborhoods.[16]

In New Orleans, the main rebuilding strategies varied based on concerns related to the timing of reconstruction and substantive visions of what rebuilding would entail. Simply put, much of the debate revolved around whether the city should seek to rebuild quickly in ways that would largely replicate what the city was before, or rather address long-term environmental concerns related to climate change and the legacy of racism, poverty, inadequate affordable housing, poor schooling, and dysfunctional politics in the area. These and other concerns, including whether some neighborhoods should be reduced significantly or even eliminated, prompted many stakeholders to feel as though their interests were not being taken seriously enough.

Seidman also emphasizes the value and effectiveness of grassroots initiatives. In the case of New Orleans, as well as other local efforts to rebuild cities affected by disasters, he is most concerned with how well neighborhood members develop shared goals for rebuilding and mobilizing local and external resources to realize their plans. Two neighborhoods in New Orleans showed how important it is to treat "repopulation as a communitywide commitment and project," with one affirming this approach by marketing "Broadmoor Lives" lawn signs and banners in the first winter after the disaster.[17] This message assumes that people from the neighborhood have a robust place-based identity that is reinforced by the interconnectivity of individual households. It reminds people that prior to the disaster, a sense of community permeated the area, one that presumably is more resilient than the buildings and properties destroyed or damaged by Katrina. The grassroots organizers that coordinated neighborhood rebuilding plans were confident that the hurricane and floodwaters would not erase the community we-ness that defined the place that residents called home, even if they had been temporarily displaced. They were also prepared to confront other stakeholders outside the neighborhood whenever they tried to express a claim on the land that did not adequately represent the views of those who currently lived there or had been displaced by Katrina.

New Orleans has a unique cultural legacy of Creole urbanism and a precarious history of land management tied to water threats dating back to its founding in 1718 by the French. But the chaos and tensions that emerged post-Katrina are circumstances other cities also experience with recovery planning after a disaster. Reflecting on this general point, one interdisciplinary team that studied New Orleans after Katrina observes that:

> cities and regions seeking to reconstruct after a disaster seem to simultaneously pursue goals to rapidly recover the familiar and aspire to reconstruct in safer, better, and sometimes more equitable ways. Conflict arises between groups or institutions and even individuals pursuing these different goals because they cannot be given equal attention in time, resources, and values. In addition, in accomplishing one goal, another may be less achievable.[18]

Now, two decades post-Katrina, many of those who remained, as well as those who were permanently displaced or had childhood links to New Orleans, feel as though their previous claims on their home and neighborhood have never been adequately respected. Frustration for some stemmed from their belief that the federally created Road Home Program, designed to distribute monies based on pre-storm home values or the costs of repairs, did not treat people living in Black neighborhoods as well as it did those living in white or mixed neighborhoods.[19] As a result, some returning and former Black residents were forced to tolerate an unpredictable situation because they were powerless to have their claims fully recognized.

A pandemic, like a natural disaster, can also create friction as individuals and groups confront each other over their respective rights to make place-based decisions. Imagine, for example, how different stakeholders were involved in heated battles about what should be done in schools to protect students, teachers, and staff from contracting COVID-19. Who should have a voice in deciding school-related policies? Many parents demanded that their voices be heard and respected. Whereas some parents wanted strict guidelines enforced for masks, vaccines, contact tracing, and social (physical) distancing, others were adamantly opposed to some or all of these measures. Similarly, students, teachers, school officials, and politicians in different jurisdictions around the country expressed wide-ranging preferences. What everyone had in common, however, was that they all felt they had legitimate, emotionally laden claims about a place – schools – so the disagreements were often quite heated. News reports of rowdy school board meetings underscore the vitriol generated by this place-based issue highlighting the human need for control.

In many instances, what transpires in these contested scenarios includes a transition into an understanding whereby one side asserts a more decisive role. When this happens, decisions about place will more clearly favor one person or group at another's expense. As a result, the unequal balance of power and influence alters various participants' orientation toward a place; the inequity can produce reactions ranging from mild annoyance to seething anger laced with images of vengeance. Finding enough common ground to diffuse and resolve the situation with as little conflict and pain as possible is challenging, especially if those involved are wedded to rigid, principled beliefs.

Unstable Resolution

When a person or group has successfully asserted their interests, a place is likely to take on new meaning that has practical consequences for all involved. Individuals and groups may be left with different levels of access to a place. Restrictions on certain activities may be enforced or activities may be eliminated entirely according to how the place dispute was resolved. Sometimes the resolution will be grounded in a legal decision that privileges a person or group while limiting others' options. In divorce decrees, one party may be assigned the family home and any additional properties, leaving the other party with no legal rights for those places despite their financial and possibly sentimental value. When a place-based conflict is resolved in this manner, it will likely lead to either disappointment, resentment, or even hostility. Yet, those who have experienced this kind of setback may simply concede and not fight the outcome and ruling; instead, they learn to adapt to the new conditions and restrictions. However, other aggrieved persons and groups may take exception to this ruling and challenge it – sometimes resorting to violence.

American history is replete with major contested scenarios that ultimately morphed into post-conflict arrangements in which the involved parties grappled with some type of unstable place-based resolution. One of the more consequential examples is the Mexican–American War of 1846–8 that was precipitated by the United States annexing the Republic of Texas in 1845 and the two countries' inability to agree on whether the southern border of Texas ended at the Nueces River (Mexican claim) or the Rio Grande (United States claim).[20] When the war officially ended with the signing of the Treaty of Guadalupe Hidalgo, the United States had appropriated, through physical force and monetary means, roughly 525,000 square miles of what had been Mexican territory.[21] The territory that was once part of Mexico now makes up all or part of what eventually was redefined as Arizona, California, Colorado, Nevada, New Mexico, Texas, Utah, and Wyoming. Most Americans are ignorant of these details, but the war should be remembered for generating Americans' new place consciousness about the acquired land. Personal and collective awareness has evolved over the many years since the war ended, enabling Americans to mentally fold the territory – now southwestern states – into a more expansive place-based national identity. With the passage of time, this region, with its Spanish influences in architecture, cuisine, and customs, came to be understood as an authentic part of the United States. Thus, even though many people are unaware of its politicized origins, we now recognize this territory as the southwestern region of the United States. The settlers who lived there after the war came to see themselves as Americans. But for the tens of thousands of Mexican citizens who were living on land claimed by the United States in 1848 (and those affected by the United States' purchase of land from Mexico in 1854 that is now southern Arizona and New Mexico), life was often difficult because they were stigmatized, lacked practical protections, and often lost their land.[22] As with most antagonistic resolutions that involve a place, some participants are more likely than others to endure harsh inequities.

Before, during, and after the United States claimed these southwestern lands as its own, the government was executing an even larger land grab and genocide across the country. Our government, formed by European immigrants and their descendants, exterminated and forcefully removed millions of Indigenous people from their homelands.[23] In the process, the United States used brute force and financial leverage to appropriate Indigenous homelands, making this territory federal property. Much of the land was later bought, given to, or sold by individual Americans and institutions. For example, the 1862 Homestead Act, signed by President Abraham Lincoln, used some of this appropriated land to provide farmland parcels to settlers if they agreed to live on the land for five years.[24]

Initially, the contested scenarios being replicated throughout North America were fiercely and violently disputed affairs between the white settlers aided by their government and Indigenous tribal nations. However, as the nineteenth century wore on, Indigenous peoples were unable to withstand the newcomers' expanding desires for land and thirst for gold. Tribal leaders – with a few exceptions like the fabled Lakota chief Sitting Bull who refused to sign any treaties – increasingly realized that they would need to sacrifice their land if they wanted to save their people. For centuries, efforts to redefine Indigenous peoples' territories were tied to appallingly unfair treaties. Between 1777 and 1868, 368 treaties were negotiated and signed by US representatives and tribal leaders. Regrettably, many were broken and the inequitable reservation system that emerged in piecemeal fashion irrevocably damaged Native cultures. Millions of Indigenous people were either killed or removed from the places that had symbolically and practically grounded their lives and those of their ancestors. They were then forced to learn new ways of living. The ability to sustain their collective identity and sense of we-ness became increasingly difficult as they were confronted with colonizers' unflinching commitment to strip them of their cultural heritage, language, customs, and identity.[25]

Today, despite the large number of active treaties and the 326 reservations that can be found across twenty-five states, the average American knows very little about these treaties or the standing of the roughly 5.2 million Indigenous people who live on or off a reservation.[26] The late senator Daniel K. Inouye of Hawaii described our ignorance about treaties by saying:

> I would venture to guess that to the extent they have had occasion to think about them, most Americans think of treaties as ancient relics of the past that have long since been forgotten and which certainly have no relevance to modern society … Too few Americans know that the Indian nations ceded millions of acres of lands to the United States, or that … the promises and commitments made by the United States were typically made in perpetuity. History has recorded, however, that our great nation did not keep its word to the Indian nations, and our preeminent challenge today … is to assure the integrity of our treaty commitments and to bring an end to the era of broken promises.[27]

Unfortunately, many Americans are unaware that the US government violated the 1863 Treaty of Ruby Valley with the Western Shoshone Nation that deals with twenty-six million acres of Native land in Nevada. Once twenty-first-century federal bureaucrats discovered that the land was more valuable than it was thought to be when the treaty was signed, they started to confiscate the territory and treat it as "public land." It's been used extensively for military purposes (especially nuclear testing) and private gold mining operations with no direct profit sharing with tribal members. In addition, these forms of land use have produced damaging environmental effects in the region.

Sisters Mary and Carrie Dann were two of the more publicly visible members of the Western Shoshone Nation who strenuously fought to retain their ancestral lands. They received media coverage for protesting the US Bureau of Land Management's demand that they pay grazing fees for the cattle they raised on their ranch located on tribal land.[28] Although the Western Shoshone as a nation filed formal suits in previous decades to protect its legal title to the land that had been taken from it, those efforts were unsuccessful.

In 2004, President George W. Bush signed a bill that distributed monies to about six thousand tribal members, monies that the US government had set aside for this land.[29] Considerable legal and political controversy surrounded the final process by which some spokespersons for the Western Shoshone Nation accepted financial compensation. For many years, this Native tribe was largely united in refusing to accept any remuneration for land members did not wish to sell, but over time some Indigenous voices were reluctantly "willing" to settle this long-standing dispute.[30] The sense of we-ness that had once united tribal members had been splintered in some ways by generations of suffering that resulted from white encroachment and the dispossession of Native lands. Refusing to accept the compensation was increasingly perceived to be a less viable option for desperate tribal members.

Historian and activist Rebecca Solnit, writing in *Storming the Gates of Paradise: Landscapes for Politics*, extends our view of the continuing struggles that Indigenous peoples face when it comes to managing the displays and activities at historical monuments commemorating Native culture, including sacred burial and other spiritual sites. Solnit explores how persons linked to European and Native cultures have clashed over the representation of historical figures, events, and rituals involving places like the Little Bighorn Battlefield National Monument in Montana, Devils Tower National Monument in Wyoming, Rainbow Bridge in Utah, and many more. Emphasizing the sacred places without physical statutes, Solnit reasons that:

> some of the friction arises because many contested sites are federal land; another problem is that natural sites are not visibly tied to specific cultural practices, as is the case with, say, churches. An interpretation dependent upon oral tradition is less distinct than one embodied in architecture and sculpture – it changes how people look rather than what people see.[31]

Thus, Solnit's observation reminds us that a place, whether adorned with physical structures built by human hands or not, is always socially constructed in some form or fashion.

The mainstream Americanized orientation to place is influenced by our cultural traditions. Western representations of place as experienced through visual imagery, compared to the oral traditions of non-Western cultures, may be more meaningful to some observers.

Irrespective of how the different parties have perceived these monuments and sacred sites, the intensity and immediacy of the protests and lawsuits that define these confrontations between worldviews often fade. The contested scenarios have shifted into a less confrontational resolution phase even though the disagreements may never be fully resolved in the minds of some. Thus, although this new resolution phase may be unstable, it lacks the intense confrontational energy that marks the contested scenario previously outlined.

While the Mexican–American War and the US treaties with tribal nations are two of the most consequential examples, our social landscape is littered with places that accentuate an arrangement that has followed a major contested situation. We can find these in our homes, communities, businesses, and other organizations. Many of us enter places without a full understanding of their place-based history. The claims on a place could be ones that were built on the struggles of others who came before us. For example, the accomplishments of the civil rights and labor movements are often threaded into our current taken-for-granted experiences with various places. Whatever the circumstances and the origin of a place-based dispute, if we are associated with a place as individuals or as members of a group, we will likely be affected by how the situation was resolved.

Mutual Negotiation

A third type of place scenario relevant to confrontation is a situation in which conflict is avoided. This scenario would not include significant claims that are being actively and overtly contested in any meaningful way. Likewise, the third scenario would not involve circumstances that once accompanied a contested confrontation. Rather it would represent a less confrontational arrangement where some level of resolution is achieved.

In these situations that are mutually negotiated, conflict is typically avoided because the participants establish an equitable standing regarding the place(s) to which they are both connected. While conflict and confrontation are possible, they are avoided. Adverse scenarios are often averted because participants are not looking to exploit others and they are willing, in principle, to cooperate to achieve mutual consent about matters related to a place that generates shared interest. Romantic partners who have similar commitments to and investments in their home, business partners who own a facility and respect each other's property rights and obligations, or neighbors collaborating on a community development project represent just a handful of the arrangements in which people often have a clear understanding of their shared claims to specific places.

However, a mutually negotiated arrangement can potentially fall apart. If so, this scenario can start to resemble a situation in which people and groups have contrasting visions of what they want to experience and what they're willing to tolerate. Two friendly middle-class families may decide to purchase a vacation home together and amicably split their time there. At the outset, they recognize they have an equal stake in the decision-making relevant to the upkeep and use of this place. But imagine that one of the participants in this friendly interfamily arrangement experiences a sudden career change that results in a much more flexible lifestyle. Consequently, they could ask the other family in their real estate partnership to alter the original arrangement. They might try to buy them out, propose renovations to convert the shared place so that it will accommodate their desire to work remotely, or reduce the time the other family spends in the jointly owned home. If the other family feels comfortable with the suggested modification, the families can continue to enjoy their adapted claims to the vacation property. However, the other family may not be comfortable with altering the arrangement and the families could find themselves at an impasse that leads them into a contested scenario. As we all probably know from personal experience, people can and often do change their posture toward places and end up creating friction with others who feel pressured and imposed upon.

In addition to the agreements individuals make with family and friends, representatives from much larger groups, organizations, and even nations can forge a mutual understanding of their respective shared claims to a place. One intriguing multicountry scenario that illustrates this possibility involves the former US naval air station in Bermuda that was once called Kindley Field. The base, built in 1941–3 in response to the horrific events that were defining

Europe prior to America's formal involvement in World War II, was operated by the US Air Force until 1970. It was then returned to the Bermudian government and now operates as an international airport. One of my research assistant's grandfathers, a retired US senior medical officer in the navy who served for several years on the *USS Nimitz* stationed in Bermuda, describes the relations between the British and American officers, their families, and the native Bermudians as "very positive." According to this officer, Americans were not treated as foreigners; people were friendly with each other, and strong friendships emerged between the native Bermudians and the military personnel and their families. To facilitate this shared appreciation for place and culture, officers' children living on the base were required to attend a "host nation's" class. There, on this relatively small island, they learned about the culture and customs of the host nation, enabling families to develop a shared cuisine, style of dress, and more blended culture. While Bermuda was a self-governing British territory during Kindley's operational years, and remains so today, the diverse collection of people who lived in Bermuda and the officials who negotiated the US military presence there were comfortable with their shared claims related to this place. These sentiments evolved, in part, because those associated with the island were allied in their forceful opposition to Nazism and were aware of the larger geopolitical, military concerns that brought them together. As time passed, Bermuda and the base became a type of expanded community and transport hub with institutional features as well. The equitable power sharing that occurred on the island helped to foster an extended sense of we-ness among the various groups that maintained a presence there.

Time Varying Forces

Social change is endemic to society. It should be no surprise, then, that a scenario once defined by active conflict that shifts to an unstable state of resolution can be fundamentally altered by the changing conditions of the times or new circumstances that directly affect the participants invested in a place. Thus, either personal or large-scale changes can transform how people and groups orient themselves toward places. Depending on the circumstances, the transformation can prompt the interested stakeholders to become more or less cooperative.

Shifts in Discourse

An underlying state of conflict, tension, and recognition of injustice with regard to places can reemerge with more force when a scenario is recast in a new light by social movement activities, new data, a dramatic event, or some other trigger. For example, in the past few decades, the public discourse in the United States about Indigenous peoples and other disadvantaged racial and ethnic groups has shifted, notwithstanding intense conservative backlash that challenges this evolving discourse. Activists and scholars have vigorously interrogated how the Morrill Act of 1862, sponsored by Vermont representative Justin Smith Morrill, was responsible for redistributing public lands to states and territories for the purpose of helping to finance struggling colleges around the nation.[32] The public land in question had been dispossessed from tribal nations either through seizure, unratified treaty, or ratified treaty – although many were fraught with fraud or executed via coercive tactics. The Act, signed into law by President Lincoln, covered at least 79,461 parcels of land totaling 10.7 million acres, with much of it located in twenty-four western states. States were promised between 90,000 and 990,000 acres based on their proportional congressional representation.[33]

Recently, historian Robert Lee and journalist Tristan Ahtone, writing for the nonprofit media outlet *High Country News*, painstakingly collected and integrated the disturbing details of how land transfers were coerced from Indigenous peoples to support white colonialism by salvaging our institutions of higher education during economically challenging times. The authors of the "Land Grab Universities" report were awarded the prestigious George Polk Award for Education Reporting in 2020. The authors, assisted by an innovative team of other research and media professionals, also created an interactive public use database at landgrabu.org. This database provides access to the primary data linking land transfers from nearly 250 Indigenous tribal nations to fifty-two universities that profited at the time of the grants and in some cases continue to profit.[34] As Lee and Ahtone note, "Land-grant universities were built not just *on* Indigenous land, but *with* Indigenous land."[35] Many universities were given land far from their home state and permitted to profit from these grants as they saw fit. When adjusted for inflation, the grants were valued at about a half billion dollars.

The idea of the land-grant university was founded on the belief that individuals, primarily white men, needed educational options to enhance their knowledge and skill sets related to agricultural and applied science.[36] As Ohio State professors Stephen Gavazzi and E. Gordon Gee note in their book, *Land-Grant Universities for the Future*, this new category of colleges and universities was designed to elevate the masses of working-class people, notably teenagers and young adults.[37] In the early years, administrators and instructors at land-grant institutions were expected to embrace the noble mission of promoting the public good, especially in their local communities and states. It was also hoped that attendees at these schools would develop a kind of ideational we-ness as first-generation college students committed to improving their lot in life.

Being curious, I explored Lee and Ahtone's user-friendly database to check out the flow and impact of the land transfers they documented, both from a university and state perspective. I'll take the liberty of sharing a quick snapshot of several things I found personally meaningful; I encourage readers to do their own search to learn about the places and tribal nations that matter most to them. The University of Florida (UF), where I've spent most of my professional career, received 90,226 acres, raised $79,968 from the land transfers, and did so at a profit ratio of 44:1. The land parcels were transferred from 121 different tribal nations, all outside the state of Florida. In many instances, tribal nations received no financial compensation. For instance, 5,605 acres were taken from the Wil-lay Nation without compensation from an unratified treaty seizure. My PhD institution, The Ohio State University (OSU), benefited even more. OSU received 614,165 acres, raised $340,818, and at a profit ratio of 10:1. Like UF, every parcel of land OSU acquired came from outside the university's home state, with land transferred from 108 tribal nations. Finally, while the tribal nations from Ohio did not have any of their lands transferred to the land-grant initiative, eight parcels that collectively amounted to 960 acres were transferred from tribal nations in Florida to universities outside the state. While significant, this pales in comparison to the 16,524 parcels grabbed from California that totaled 1.7 million acres, raised $3.7 million, and were distributed to thirty-two land-grant universities.

My practical exercise, using concrete data that document financial accountability streams, intensified my reaction to the short- and long-term consequences of the enormous and shameful wealth transfer from tribal nations to largely white settlers and their ancestors. It added a spark of specificity to the general message that is conveyed by broader narratives and media representations of the history of white colonialism in America. The database, and the authors' descriptive snapshots of it, reminded me of the data and storytelling that economics expert Richard Rothstein provides in his remarkable book, *The Color of Law: The Forgotten History of How Our Government Segregated America*.[38] In a similarly meticulous manner, Rothstein lays out the policy backstory of how the legislative actions that built and continue to reinforce wealth inequities between persons of color and white people are both insidious and systemic. In short, wealth transfers between advantaged and disadvantaged populations have been deeply rooted in our racist laws, traditions, and practices that are place-based. Sharon Stein, a white settler scholar from the University of British Columbia, captures the big picture succinctly: "There would be no higher education as we know it in the United States without the original and ongoing colonization of Indigenous peoples and lands, just like there would be no United States."[39] A bold but accurate assessment of our history.

Whether we consider the land transfers that were used to fund land-grant universities or other lands that were seized and applied for different purposes, each of the many tribes that had land seized by the United States government, or were by law restricted in how they could use the land, has its own unique place-based story. However, while the places differed in size, topography, access to natural resources, and the cultural expressions and symbolic meanings associated with them, one unifying theme defines Indigenous peoples' relationship to the land historically. Prior to learning about the white settlers' approach to private property, the Indigenous peoples had no conception of owning the land they lived on or the animals that surrounded them. They saw themselves, and continue to see themselves, as being in harmony with the natural world. In addition, they perceived themselves to be stewards of the plants, trees, mountains, rivers, animals, and everything else that surrounds them in the integrated, ecological system made available to them by a creator. From the white settlers' perspective, white people had either "discovered" or "won" the land; either way it was their *private* land.[40] Thus, Indigenous peoples' fundamental conception of place contrasts sharply with the Western worldview. This example underscores a critical reality associated with property that distinguishes a place as either private or public: the matter can be contested by different stakeholders.

It was the white settlers' perspective toward land ownership, and to tribal peoples' collective identity generally, that led to the passage of the 1887 Dawes Act, otherwise known as the General Allotment Act.[41] Named after its sponsor, Senator Henry L. Dawes of Massachusetts, this Act was yet another blow to Indigenous peoples' efforts to cultivate their relationships in the places that mattered to them. The policy was designed to promote the concept of private land ownership while fracturing tribal nations' social structures and collectivist orientation toward reservation land, which had been held in common by tribal members.[42] The basic idea was to distribute individual land allotments of 160 acres to the male heads of households and encourage them to become farmers. The large portions of remaining land were dispossessed and became federal land that was sold or given away to white homesteaders. In addition to the cultural damage inflicted, the policy typically failed to help individual tribal families whose newly "acquired" land was typically ill-suited for farming. They often did not have the appropriate tools or finances to support farming, and many were also not interested in adopting this way of life.

At the turn of the twentieth century, President Theodore Roosevelt voiced his views of this Act by professing,

> In my judgment the time has arrived when we should definitely make up our minds to recognize the Indian as an individual and not as a member of a tribe. The General Allotment Act is a mighty pulverizing engine to break up the tribal mass. It acts directly upon the family and the individual.

While Roosevelt's language and tone is patriarchal in this and the larger statement that defends the Dawes Act, he also asserts that "The Indian should be treated as an individual – like the white man."[43] But this latter statement should not be interpreted as a gesture of goodwill toward promoting equality. Roosevelt was no friend of the Indigenous peoples and did not believe they should have the same rights as white people. What he and other politicians wanted was a convenient way to get rid of the tribes so that they could end the treaties and gain access to the land the Indigenous peoples occupied.

This brief account offers only a glimpse of the complex circumstances associated with transitioning from an active contested phase to a less conflictual resolution scenario. The contested and resolution scenarios have been and continue to be associated with the overlapping experiences of Native peoples, government stakeholders, and the non-native population. The Dawes Act underscores how the government and white settlers stripped Indigenous peoples of their most basic place-based opportunities to nurture forms of ideational and deep dyadic we-ness. Beyond illustrating how Native peoples' place attachment needs have been disregarded for centuries, I extend this critical example in the next chapter by discussing how a growing network of activists, scholars, and university leaders are employing *MEAL* life skills to acknowledge and pragmatically address, through reparative efforts, the long-term implications of land-based wealth transfers that adversely affected Indigenous peoples. These activities illustrate the types of time varying cultural forces that can alter how individuals and groups engage in placemaking.

Our opportunities to control access to places and contribute to placemaking activities can change over time as we individually or as a group gain or lose power, authority, and influence. Over time, persons of color, women, LGBTQ+ persons, those living with a disability, and other marginalized groups have gained more opportunities to stake a claim in various places and assert their newfound leverage. For example, since the late 1970s, women have increasingly gained more power in asserting their claims in sports landscapes and leisure spots more generally. Young women in high school and college have gained more opportunities to define sports fields and arenas as places that should accommodate their needs and respect their accomplishments. Professional female athletes have slowly received more recognition in the sports landscapes that matter to them. For example, the media frenzy in 2023–4 over Caitlin Clark, the former collegiate women's basketball star at Iowa and now professional player with the Indiana Fever, has generated an extensive and controversial debate in the sports world and mainstream news alike. Much of the gendered and racialized debate focuses on the so-called Caitlin Clark Effect, referring to her economic impact on the sport, including advance ticket sales, sold out arenas, spikes in TV viewership, and advertising deals.[44] In venues hosting sporting events, crowd size and the level of enthusiasm go a long way in defining the symbolic meaning of a place and a crowd's manifestation of ideational we-ness. In addition to female athletes' ascendancy in the public eye, women reporters have more access to professional men's sports locker-rooms and are earning more chances to be "talking heads" and analysts in sports media settings, including for men's collegiate and professional sports.

Considering our ever-changing cultural climate, individuals and groups invested in the LGBTQ+ community have their own set of issues with placemaking implications. In recent decades, national polls document that public opinion is growing more supportive of LGBTQ+ issues.[45] Social policies and practices, including the 2015 Supreme Court's decision in *Obergefell v. Hodges* that permits gay marriage, have gradually followed suit. Despite these advances, in the relatively recent past, far-right Republican lawmakers and the activist Supreme Court are threatening that progress.[46] These conservative efforts will continue to jeopardize place-based landscapes for LGBTQ+ people. The actions may have their most pernicious effect on young people who are psychologically and emotionally the most vulnerable and subject to intense bullying. In particular, numerous bills have been introduced recently that restrict transgender youths' rights in school settings including sports venues, bathrooms, and health facilities.[47] The conservative discourses and initiatives, including the 2022 "Parental Rights in Education" law (opponents call it "Don't Say Gay") that restricts teachers' ability to mention topics related to sexual orientation or gender identity in Florida schools, make these critical places symbolically and pragmatically uninviting and less safe for our youth who do not identify as cisgender heterosexuals.[48] Moreover, the conservative legislative and judicial trends can harm persons irrespective of their age who define themselves in ways that depart from traditional gender and sexual identities.[49]

Just as discourses can change over time, groups can develop new ways of thinking and feeling about certain places. Thus, another way to think about time and place is to realize that a particular place may become relevant to different groups in different ways with the passage of time. For example, long before white European settlers ever set foot on North American soil, Indigenous tribes were waging violent battles with each other over the land they occupied. While some of those battles continued even after white settlers arrived, the more consequential contested struggles were between Native tribes and white settlers and the United States government. In more recent years, additional types of confrontations have arisen that include corporate entities, especially those in the extraction industries (oil, coal, ore, natural gas), that are seeking to control lands that have meaning to various tribal nations and are sometimes owned by the federal government. This example illustrates that the groups interested in making claims over certain places can change over time and may even form unlikely alliances to combat third party attempts to assert their place-based claims.

Leveraging Assets

In many scenarios that involve a real or possible confrontation about place claims, one of the persons or groups involved has an advantage in having their claims respected and executed. While leverage tactics can be used in all the scenarios previously outlined, they are most common in the contested and resolution settings. In each instance, the participant with greater leverage has more control than others and can use that advantage to dictate the terms of how a place or places can be accessed and used. In addition, the moral standing of the person or group with more leverage does not always have to be high. In fact, those with more leverage are often perceived to be ruthless in how they treat and control others while pursuing their own interests in specific places.

Leverage is grounded in one or more of the three standard expressions of power: coercive, utilitarian, and normative.[50] In settings where coercive techniques are readily used, those without power will have limited opportunities to assert or negotiate their claims about place issues. For example, outside of rioting, prisoners have little recourse to shape the layout or rules associated with places inside the prison that affect their daily existence. Even rioting may not bring about the desired effect from prison management. Meanwhile, those who find themselves in arrangements where the more advantaged person or group relies on monetary or values-oriented ways to entice others to comply will also have more opportunities to negotiate a bigger role in deciding place-related matters. Salaried employees may be granted the right to decorate their offices as they see fit. They may even have a chance to select their preferred office space. Similarly, various corporate divisions may be given considerable leeway in how they arrange entire office floors. Administrators can make decisions about increasing worker privacy or increasing opportunities for coworkers to interact with each other formally and informally in various places.

Those with a distinct advantage in controlling aspects of place often have experience with encouraging, manipulating, or coercing others to behave in certain ways. They are typically positioned to convey the image that they are willing, if necessary, to use their assets to achieve the desired results. Although extreme forms of coercion are sometimes necessary to get others to comply, milder forms of encouragement may be all that is needed to convince people to respect place claims. However, just because an individual or group may have the ability to exert their leverage does not mean that they will. Some powerful individuals and groups respect and accommodate the place-based desires and needs of those who have a vested interest in a place but have less leverage.

The parent-child relationship is a scenario that frequently produces conflict and tension. We understand that while the balance of power is typically tilted toward the parent having significantly more leverage, most parents' relationships with their children are not commonly labeled as being actively contested over place-related matters. Most contested matters are likely to be resolved relatively quickly despite some lingering disputes. Exceptions will occur though, like the eighteen-year-old who repeatedly challenges his parents to allow his girlfriend to sleep over.

As a parent, when we learn that our child has significantly misbehaved, we may feel that we are morally obligated to do our best to teach them right from wrong. One tactic available to us is to restrict their access to a car and to the places they would visit if they had the freedom to drive there. We are also likely to believe that we have the right to restrict our teenager's use of their car even though there's an understanding that the car is "theirs." In this instance, we are making the moral claim as a parent that we have the right to control our child's access to certain objects and places. Our child may vehemently disagree and contend that we do not and should not have the right to restrict their placed-based options in this way. In this instance, the conflict is more about how we are managing access to a place rather than how we want to arrange a place. Today, as parents, we also have the practical advantage of using apps to monitor the location of our kids, which provides us even more leverage to assert authority over where they travel to and hang out. But we can also assert our place-based claims about their bedrooms, the house, or car more generally by restricting their ability to bring certain people or items, like drugs, alcohol, and guns, into those places.

A unique instance of how a parent can manipulate place as a punishment is the parent who doesn't allow their minor child to return home after being placed in a juvenile detention center because of a domestic violence incident. One intake officer at such a facility, and coincidently a research assistant of mine, offers an insider's view of the tensions that sometimes arise in the placement process. While doing detention risk assessments, she's encountered parents who request that their kid be retained in the facility despite her officially evaluating the youth as being eligible for discharge, and the parent reporting no fear of being victimized or injured. The parent's reasoning is that they want their child to "learn a lesson" or to get help. Sometimes a parent even refuses alternative placements for their child, such as a relative's home or a domestic violence respite shelter. If there are no available options for an alternative placement, or the parent refuses the service, the child is likely to end up in a secure detention center where they will be surrounded by other youth who have committed serious crimes. In addition, they will be displaced from their school, friends, and family. Unfortunately, exposure to detention is often associated with negative physical and mental outcomes for youth.[51] Here again, we see that a person's exposure to or displacement from significant places – the action settings that give meaning to our lives – can have profound personal consequences.

Leverage can also affect the ways we determine who has the right to make decisions about what happens in a place or what features it includes. A principal may tell their students that rigid policies will be relaxed or practical school amenities will be added if the students achieve specific goals linked to their grades, standardized test performance, good behavior, or volunteering. Failure to meet these goals may result in less desirable outcomes for students. The "power-over" type of control can influence how leverage is used to monitor access to a place, or the opportunities to control characteristics of it. What begins as wholesome encouragement or persuasion may deteriorate into a more negative form of coercion. In rare instances, those in charge of controlling aspects of place might also shift away from using coercive techniques and adopt more supportive strategies to inspire the behavior they want to see.

Just as individuals and groups can gain leverage, they can lose it too. Take for instance the elderly person who has been able-bodied and mentally sharp throughout their adult life. They've lived independently in homes in which they asserted their legitimate claims to control what took place on their property. But with time, as happens to many of us, they become less capable of physically navigating the places that matter to them, and they may also lose the cognitive ability to make the decisions necessary to live independently. When this happens, it can be a traumatic experience for those who are losing the ability to do placemaking for themselves as well as for the family members who often need to step in to make those decisions. My older sister and her husband often faced those practical decisions when my parents, who lived nearby, were unable to drive safely and could no longer handle living on their own. Informing my father and then my mother that they should relinquish their car keys and their right to travel independently from place to place was a necessary, but difficult, step for my sister to take. Likewise, when my father's vascular dementia eventually put too much pressure on my elderly mother to care for him, herself, and their house, my mother eventually realized it was best that she and my father sell their home and move into an assisted living facility. In doing so, my parents no longer could assert the same type of control over their living environment compared to when they lived together in their own home.

A common pattern that restricts our place-based leverage results from our declining mental and physical abilities as we age, but plenty of people also lose their place-related freedoms when they deal with an addiction, a major health crisis unrelated to aging, or a serious financial problem. Compared to a sober and financially stable adult, a person who has serious drug or financial problems, which often go hand in hand, is less apt to keep themselves in good standing with their homeplace. In other words, they are more likely to be limited in making homeplace decisions, get evicted from their apartment, default on their home loan and relinquish their house, and experience homelessness.

For the parent who is forced to deal with their teenager or young adult child who has a drug problem, they will be less likely to leave their child home alone or to give them the keys to the car. The parent's trust, or the lack thereof, is a critical element to the parent-child relationship and without it the parent is apt to minimize the child's freedom to make place-based choices. Irrespective of age, when individuals lose control of themselves because of a substance abuse problem, they often lose their leverage to engage in activities that affect their relationship to place.

The place claims made by parents and kids, in addition to the countless others who deal with life away from family relations, are integral to the most volatile and politicized decisions associated with how people navigate their relationships with place. But the other three *CART* processes involving attachments, rituals, and transitions are also critical to the mix of activities that shape how we make sense of the places that matter to us. They inject our claims with passion and purpose while affecting our personal well-being. They impact how we try to change a place or stabilize our preferences about it via our placemaking efforts. One fascinating insight about the *CART* processes is that they constantly leave their mark on us as we formally and informally deal with place properties in assorted settings and engage in various types of placemaking. When we look at our participation in making personal and group decisions that focus on place, we find that our diverse experiences across the five social domains overlap. They are consequential to us personally and to the larger social landscape. That broader social context that is anchored to diverse places generates opportunities for us to experience a sense of we-ness.

PART 3

Constructive Placemaking

We can personally and collaboratively do placemaking in diverse ways that fundamentally improve social conditions and our well-being. In the everyday world, we should therefore explore practical opportunities to leverage our sense of we-ness while promoting ethical, constructive placemaking in our primary groups, communities and community groups, thought communities, leisure and sports settings, and at work. In this final section, I ask: How can we apply the breadth and depth of our understanding of the basics of place and the *CART* processes related to claims, attachments, rituals, and transitions to promote life-enhancing forms of placemaking in these key social domains? In addition, how can we cultivate *MEAL* life skills (mindfulness, empathy, altruism, and leadership) to strengthen our collaborative efforts to engage in productive placemaking? Fortunately, understanding the breadth and depth of the place landscape can improve our efforts to foster personal empowerment, civic engagement, and social and environmental justice.

7

Cultivating Place Consciousness to Enrich Society

Photo 9: Damanhur, federation of spiritual communities, northern Italy; annual photo of the Spiritual *Popolo* in the Open Temple. More on https://damanhur.org/. (Photo courtesy of Damanhur)

For centuries, people throughout the world have tried to cultivate communal arrangements in special places to create an ideal society – utopia. Presumably, an imagined utopian world could be realized in various forms depending on the members' ideals and motivations. Typically, a utopian state assumes that those involved want to achieve uplifting bonds with each other and with the place they mutually define as home or the center of their community. Whatever its specific form, a utopia, for most people, includes a safe physical environment, one that enriches both personal and communal life. A utopian social world is also supposed to provide a supportive environment for individuals and groups to experience healthy life transitions and lifestyles. Unfortunately, most attempts to create long-lasting communal societies based on utopian ideals have eventually failed to live up to the hype.[1]

But for the past nearly fifty years, a fascinating utopian-like place – the Federation of Damanhur – has flourished in a secluded slice of the Piedmont Alps in northern Italy.[2] In recent decades, Damanhur has increasingly become a vibrant federation of spiritual communities with roughly six hundred participants living on site (with hundreds of others living elsewhere) and its own constitution. People of diverse ages and backgrounds live in multiple-family dwellings that incorporate communal and private spaces. In addition to having its own culture, art, music, currency, businesses, children's schools, an open university, and numerous ongoing research groups, Damanhur has been recognized by the United Nations as a model for a sustainable eco-community.[3]

Over a fifteen-year span beginning in August 1978, the excavation work that was born from this social experiment proceeded unabated away from public scrutiny as the initial cathedral-like structures of Damanhur were secretly built inside a mountainside. It remains one of the most intriguing and enduring social arrangements of its kind. The physical rally point for Damanhur is a unique, place-based subterranean complex of distinctive interconnected Temple rooms encompassing thousands of square yards and miles of corridors adorned with varied forms of magnificent, colorful artwork.[4] Referred to as the Temples of Humankind, these structures are located between 100 and 262 feet underground. In the early years before the site's public disclosure, roughly 150 followers ultimately dedicated themselves to doing laborious, artistic placemaking, although much of the work in the first several years was completed by a smaller group of 15 to 20.[5] With no special engineering skills or heavy equipment, the Damanhurians miraculously used only hand tools and their bare hands to excavate an expansive, five-layered set of tunnels and structures. They were led by Oberto Airaudi (or Falco Tarassaco, which translates to Falcon Dandelion – based on the group's naming convention of choosing an animal first name and plant surname) and were emboldened by a spiritually imbued sense of ideational we-ness and many dyadic expressions of we-ness.

When Italian authorities finally discovered the project in fall 1992, the officials initially threatened to dynamite the site if the location of the temples wasn't revealed. Remarkably, though, once Tarassaco gave the state prosecutor a personal tour, the official emerged and expressed his heartfelt conviction to protect the Damanhurians' creation. The eco-friendly, artsy project eventually gained the Italian government's legal approval in 1996 and was opened to the public. Today, it receives guests from all over the world and has established a network of ties to other groups emulating the Damanhurian philosophy.

A key feature of Damanhurians' worldview is their belief that the earth is a sentient creature and that they have tapped into the powerful legacy of Egypt and Atlantis.[6] They expect and embrace change while envisioning their community as an active research laboratory for the future. In Tarassaco's words, Damanhur

> was born to bring together the dreams of many people, to create something new, something never imagined before, something that this time could actually become a reality. We need reality today, therefore it is necessary that dreams come true so that they can allow us to carry on dreaming. Damanhurian philosophy is based on action, to do, to act, to believe in what you are doing, to give meaning to things.[7]

Similarly, effective placemaking involves imagining and doing, shaping places to enhance the individual and social experience.

After extensive study, reflection, and international travel, Tarassaco intentionally located the project at precisely the point where four synchronic lines or energy streams intersect. These lines, which are thought to be part of a global system, are the foundation to the Damanhurian philosophy of knowledge and are believed to be "energy rivers" that connect all life forms and the earth to the cosmos and divine powers.[8] Damanhurians believe too that these lines transmit various forms of information and are time traveling portals. Although skeptics challenge many of the Damanhurians' beliefs as foolish and fanciful while questioning their cult-like orientation and the secrecy behind some of their practices, I choose not to judge the authenticity or soundness of their philosophy and practices.[9] Rather, my purpose in profiling this community is to reveal that a small group of people fortified with conviction, a collective consciousness and sense of we-ness, and a willingness to embrace a dynamic existence can create amazing places that are environmentally friendly and foster personal growth, social harmony, creativity, and social justice.

With artistic flair and proficiency, Damanhurians have for nearly fifty years accentuated the symbolic and physical properties of place. Writing for *What Is Enlightenment* magazine in 2007, Ross Robertson eloquently describes what he saw during his multiple-day tour of Damanhur where he was able to speak with Tarassaco, six years prior to the philosopher's untimely death. According to Ross, the Damanhurians have "codified and immortalized their entire esoteric scheme into sacred architecture, in the form of a gigantic chain of underground temples that looks like it came straight out of the pages of Tolkien."[10] Their majestic Temples of Humankind signal Damanhurians' place consciousness and their dedication to nurturing the connection between human life and divine forces as well as the humanistic ties that connect healthy "me" and "we" forms. Ross conveys his passionate admiration for the symbiotic relationship Damanhurians have with place by highlighting what they and others before them have worked so hard to create:

> Inside the Temples of Humankind, it was abundantly clear how proud the Damanhurians were of their rich collective history, because it had been recorded *everywhere*. The walls were like history books adorned with paintings of many of the same people I met while I was there … These walls bore cosmic histories also, panoramic visions of the birth and evolution of the universe and allegorical scenes of war between good and evil in the hearts of men. There were mosaics and statues of the gods and goddesses of Greece and Rome, Sumer and

Babylon, Hindu and Zulu, Axtec and Algonquin. And of course, the omnipresent motifs of Egypt and Atlantis – shifting sands and swimming dolphins, warriors and dragons, scarabs and hieroglyphs, Osiris, Anubis, and the falcons of Horus. These artists' marvels were not just mythological but technological as well. They had eight-meter-wide domed ceilings of stained glass, backlit by neon. They had secret doors like those in the pyramids of the pharaohs, except these were *motorized*. Secret motorized drawbridges dropped from walls and hidden motorized stairs dropped from the floor at the touch of unseen remote controls. They even had strange subtle-energy healing beds that looked like a cross between a CAT scan machine and the bench Dr. Frankenstein used to bring his monster to life.

Ross's depiction highlights the impressive nature of the Damanhurians' elaborate investment in what is, essentially, a form of placemaking, one that is spiritually inspired and artistically performed. Jeff Merrifield, a writer who visited Damanhur numerous times over many years, draws similar conclusions. Merrifield was inspired by his own observations of the physical grounds and social interactions as well as interviews with Tarassaco and many of the other participants who have played major roles in shaping the physical, artistic, and cultural surroundings.

The type of placemaking that has transformed Damanhur into a successful eco-community highlights the four *CART* processes of claims, attachments, rituals, and transitions. Once their excavation work was discovered by authorities, Tarassaco and his collaborators fought to claim this site as officially their own. While they were eager to continue their work and usage, they also agreed to shift their stance to permit outsiders to frequent the temples and larger community. The scenario, engulfed by a land ownership dispute, shifted from what seemed like an unstable resolution to a mutual agreement once the Damanhurians' claim was officially recognized. Today, they have ambassadors responsible for pursuing partnerships with groups and communities outside of their own and have increasingly created opportunities for people from around the world to visit and even experiment with the Damanhurian way of life.[11]

That the Damanhurians have been willing to invest so much time and hard work into developing this place underscores their level of attachment to it. It reflects their commitment to cultural and spiritual diversity as well as to artistic expressions that capture their beliefs about the interconnections between living creatures and divine forces. Over time they have developed a coded language and introduced rituals and rites of passage that they practice in the temples and larger Damanhur community. Many of these activities, including symbolic dances, are kept secret from those outside the federation. The place-based rituals enable followers to celebrate their shared commitment to enhancing their spiritual connection to each other and their surroundings, including the cosmos and divine forces more generally.[12] Because Damanhurians embrace personal and communal change as part of their life's journey, they use the temples and the facilities within Damanhur to experience and study various types of transformation, both individually and in their social groups. Place-based spiritual and social transitions, then, are fundamental processes that are woven into the fabric of Damanhur. Their teachings and practices are also consistent with the *MEAL* life skills because they encourage mindfulness, empathy, altruism, and collective leadership in how they organize their government, schools, businesses, leisure activities, community service, and most importantly, their spiritual journey.

Technically speaking, the Damanhurians have not followed the advice of Sarah Williams Goldhagen, the architecture and design critic, who called for builders to rely on seasoned designers with specialized training in *environmental aesthetics* and *experiential design*.[13] Nonetheless, despite the Damanhurians' lack of formal training in design and their practice of not explicitly identifying the ethical principles for creating good and enriching places, their style of placemaking has still decisively valued the *BASIN* principles of beneficence, autonomy, social justice, inclusive collaboration, and nonmaleficence. From the outset, their artistic and spiritual backgrounds have inspired the Damanhurians to recognize how a place's physical and spiritual elements can inspire individuals and a community.

Place Consciousness and Placemaking

Although the Damanhur story highlights the value of place consciousness and placemaking for a community of passionate, like-minded people, relatively few of us can relate to being so intensely invested in a group that is engaged in a massive placemaking project. This is especially true when comparing ourselves to the early Damanhurians who did the backbreaking work on the Temples for so many years. Still, most of us have experienced being around others in one or more of the five social domains (primary groups, community and community groups, thought communities, leisure/sport, and work) while we developed a shared sense of place, grew attached to a place, and informally got involved in some limited form of joint placemaking. We may have even formed a kind of shared place awareness with others as we jointly honed our appreciation for a place's special meaning to us. When we experience a sense of we-ness while navigating specific places, we typically are cognizant of our emotional state and the practical challenges we face at the time. We recognize that when we are in a certain place, we tend to feel either good or bad about our interactions with the people who are around us. We may also register a sense of feeling good or bad about ourselves. In an ideal setting, aspects of the place and the people with whom we interact will help us to express our authentic selves; we will feel relaxed and confident. Despite our basic awareness of our sense of we-ness and self that are place-based, we tend not to grasp the full complexity of the intersecting aspects of place that shape the quality of our experiences and our well-being. This blind spot is consistent with Goldhagen's thesis that we are too often oblivious to how place attributes influence our thoughts, feelings, and actions.

Similarly, we are often not fully aware of how our orientation toward a place or interconnected places is affected by our relevant mental map. Scholars in numerous fields, including geography, psychology, and history to name but a few, have integrated this concept into their studies of cognitive processing and the mental ordering of ideas.[14] While the mental map is defined in various ways, the one most germane to this book focuses on how we organize our perceptions of our spatial surroundings. That mapping serves to situate us vis-à-vis the spatially oriented information we accumulate throughout our lives in all sorts of action settings. While each of us has a unique mental map for a specific setting, people who belong to a particular group can have comparable mental maps that are shaped by their exposure to cultural, social, political, and physiological forces. In other words, our subjective perceptions that comprise our mental map can be shaped by those who want us to "see" the world in a particular way. Whether we perceive a place as near or far, welcoming or unwelcoming, belonging to us or others, or easy or difficult to traverse can be influenced by things such as the media we've consumed, the people we've talked to, the cultural and political norms we've internalized, the desirable or unpleasant encounters we've had, and the cognitive and physiological attributes that govern the sharpness of our physical senses and mental processing abilities. In addition, those of us who have a detective-like eye for dissecting our physical and social surroundings will be better positioned to reconstruct an elaborate mental image of a place's various features.

Our capacity to engage in constructive placemaking is likely to be enhanced when we have a keen sense of how our personal mental maps work for places we wish to change. Thus, we should strive to develop a better understanding of the forces that affect how we perceive the spatial dimensions of certain places. This type of understanding is especially needed for the politically motivated stakeholders who have competing images about national territorial borders that fuel serious conflicts and produce territorial identities.[15] However, being more fully aware in this way can also help those in less significant, more everyday sorts of contexts. In short, mental maps are vital to how we develop attachments and claims for diverse places. We should ask: Why is it that we perceive the spatial characteristics of a place as we do? What are the major differences in the mental maps guiding individuals and groups? Why do we have an accurate or muddled mental map of a specific place or the route from one place to another? How and why has our mental map changed over time?

In some instances, we may be challenged to redesign our mental map as we deepen our place consciousness and pursue placemaking from a more knowledgeable and ethical vantage point. Presumably, when we are more attentive to the properties that define a place that matters to us and the impressions we develop about it, ourselves, and others by relating to the place, we are more apt to forge a detailed mental map that captures its key qualities. Professionals in various fields embrace this viewpoint, devoting themselves to finding ways to study and improve people's ability to create useful mental maps, some related to places.[16]

Having read Parts 1 and 2, I trust that you can see more clearly how our sense of group belonging and identity are connected to the places that matter to us. Developing a fuller appreciation of the social forces, circumstances, and properties that affect our reactions to a place can also allow us to deepen our sense of identity and commitment to the group settings that nurture our personal development and healthy social relations. When we understand the full gamut of place-based conditions, processes, and structures that either constrain or enhance our well-being, we can be more decisive and play a pivotal role in placemaking activities, especially in collaboration with others. In addition, although discussions about placemaking are typically associated with the professionals who formally do community development and urban design, I expand this concept to account for how professionals and nonprofessionals alike, in all sorts of settings, can shape the places that matter to them.

I use Model 2 as a visual representation of the larger context that frames my thinking about the varied ways we can engage in constructive placemaking activities. More specifically, I discuss placemaking examples relevant to the five social domains. These broad domains incorporate the basics of place discussed in Part 1, most notably, the ten generic places and ten place properties. It is here in the social domains including specific places like homes, communities, institutions, the metaverse, and others that the interrelated *CART* processes involving claims, attachments, rituals, and transitions also occur. As we've learned, the consequential *CART* processes influence how we perceive and navigate places. These processes are particularly relevant whenever we try to alter places to make them more beneficial to us and others. Being more sensitive to how the *CART* processes are part of a web of forces that influence our experiences with places should sharpen our understanding of how our activities

Model 2: Ethical placemaking in five social domains involving CART processes

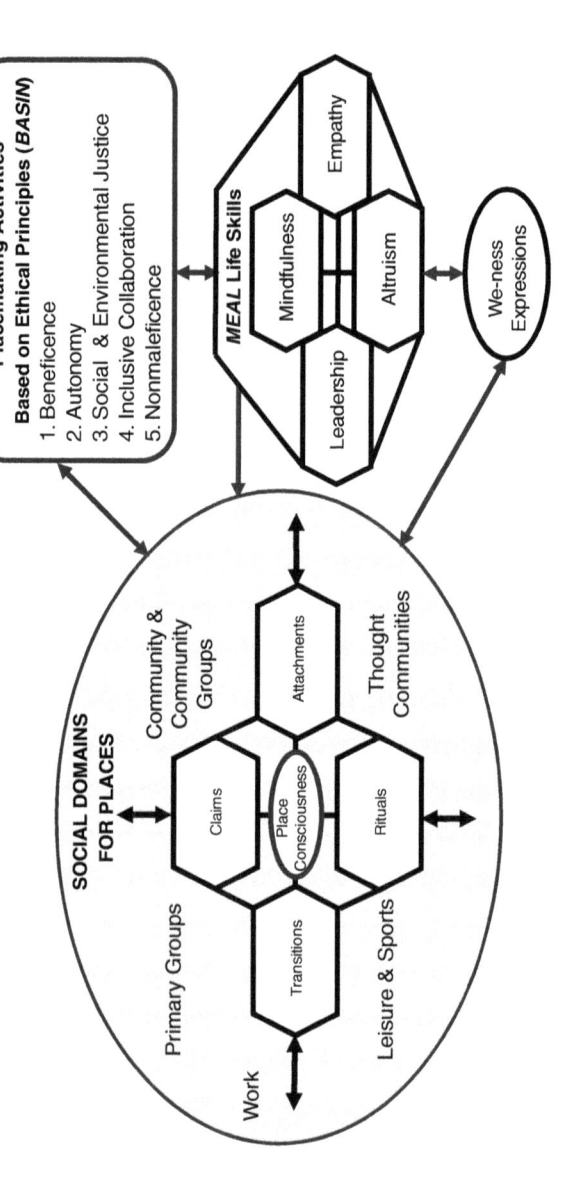

in a place can affect us personally while also altering features of the place itself. As noted in Chapter 2, our heightened sensitivity to those place processes will enrich our personal place consciousness and also contribute to a collective place consciousness.

I discuss how our placemaking should ideally be guided by the *BASIN* pool of ethical principles (beneficence, autonomy, social and environmental justice, inclusive collaboration, and nonmaleficence). When applied responsibly, these principles will shape our expectations and decision-making in ways that enhance our well-being and the greater social good. In addition, the *MEAL* life skills involving mindfulness, empathy, altruism, and leadership can give us the means to engage effectively with the places and people that matter to us. Throughout, we've emphasized that the *CART* processes provide the backdrop to cultivating *MEAL* life skills, and these skills, in turn, provide individuals with human, social, and cultural capital that enable them to enhance their place consciousness and placemaking capacities. In many instances, our potential to effect constructive placemaking that is ethically sound and seeks to promote social and environmental justice depends on what others think and do with respect to specific places. Our placemaking efforts are likely to be enhanced if we can cultivate a collective place consciousness and sense of purpose with others who are invested in promoting the same places. The sense of we-ness we forge through our place-based rituals and routines is a vital part of the placemaking process.

Levels and Types

If we want to devise strategies to improve our experiences with places, we need to appreciate the scale of the places in question and how places relate to one another. Just as we can establish a sense of we-ness that differs depending on the size of the group we join, so too we can grow attached to places of varying reach or scope. From the relatively narrow ties we establish with family members to the larger set of ties we develop with like-minded environmental activists to our even broader sense of affinity with fellow citizens of planet earth, we have the capability to find meaning in life by focusing on groups of different sizes. Similarly, we can grow attached to places that are narrowly defined like our homes, more expansive places that include our schools or cities, and much larger places that are, for example, represented by our native or adopted country and the entire planet. In many instances, the scope of a group that we have developed a sense of we-ness with corresponds to the scope of the place that matters to us, but not always. For instance, we might be attached to New York City largely because that is where we've moved to spend time with our romantic partner yet have no substantial bond with New Yorkers per se, or any of the community groups and activists who are devoted to improving the city. In general, though, the depth and breadth of our attachment to a place will be enhanced when we establish a sense of we-ness with a group or groups that coincide with the scope of the place that matters to us.

In Chapter 2, I identified a selective set of ten different types of places as part of a basic scheme to capture the wide range of consequential places that affect our lives. They included nature, homes or everyday dwellings, communities, public space, sites for exchanging goods and services, institutions, key landmarks and ceremonial settings, leisure spots, transport vehicles and hubs, and the metaverse. These places, and our relationship to them, can change over time. The more we can deepen our place consciousness, the better equipped we will be to foster healthy relationships with the places that affect us now and in the future.

If we are to understand and navigate place, we must recognize that some places are embedded or nested in other places and some can be used for multiple purposes either on a regular basis or intermittently. In fact, some places can be used for multiple purposes simultaneously. Think of how large parking lots are turned into sites where health professionals administer tests for viruses and distribute vaccines. Community auditoriums can house disparate events like music concerts, arts and crafts fairs, and gun shows. Vans can be both a transport vehicle and a home. Likewise, a more conventional multiuse vehicle, the RV, is prominently depicted as being part of American folklore. As a distinct, mobile place, the RV often facilitates the creation of long-lasting, place-based memories.

As we search for insights that will help us enrich the many places that matter to us via different styles of placemaking, it's practical to frame our observations by organizing them according to the five social domains described previously. Focusing on these domains encourages us to accentuate how our experiences with developing a sense of we-ness and group belonging overlap with our approach to placemaking in different types of action settings that often implicate social and environmental justice concerns.

Insights for Social Domain Placemaking

Primary Groups

Money matters in the world of placemaking on every level. People with more money have extra clout in realizing their place-based desires. Thus, our ability to engage in personal forms of placemaking that affect how we experience our homes, immediate neighborhoods, and transport vehicles that we personally claim is dependent on the resources we have at our disposal, as well as our imagination and freedom to make choices. The poorer we are, the less equipped we are to make significant changes to the places that matter to us or to simply leave one place for a more appealing one. Having ample finances often enhances our options to make decisions about place.

Poor people, irrespective of their racial or ethnic background, are more likely than those with financial means to feel residentially trapped, unable to move by choice to a better home and neighborhood. Even the poor who have a place to call home are more restricted in the types of modifications they can make to it. Furniture, accessories, paint, cleaning supplies, plants, electronic security systems, and other items may be beyond their budget. The homeless grapple with even more daunting obstacles to placemaking.

Today, the racial disparities in placemaking abilities witnessed in primary groups are historically rooted in the far-reaching legacy of unjust policies, practices, and patterns related to housing discrimination and urban/suburban development. Collectively, the disparities that emerged contribute to the negative images that the public has of specific communities and the quality of community-based placemaking that I address in the next section.

The glaring and persistent wealth gap between white families and families of color has meant that white parents and grandparents have been, and continue to be, better positioned to pass on inherited wealth to younger generations within their families. This is especially noteworthy because homeownership is such an important intergenerational instrument to facilitate wealth accumulation. The insidious history of racial discrimination in the housing industry has produced stark inequalities that have persisted throughout the twenty-first century. According to an analysis by economists for the National Association of Realtors, 72.1 percent of white Americans own their own home. In contrast, only 61.7 percent of Asian Americans, 51.1 percent of Hispanic Americans, and 43.4 percent of Black Americans are homeowners. Between 2010 and 2020, the rates for homeownership among these four categories declined only for Black people.[17]

Richard Rothstein, the economic policy expert, provides an incisive and scathing account of how white officials in government, banking, and building construction sectors systematically and unfairly conspired for centuries to limit housing options for persons of color.[18] These official policies and practices (e.g., redlining), many of which were unconstitutional, continue to have a lasting effect in the early decades of the twenty-first century by reinforcing racial disparities in various areas of life affecting well-being.

The pernicious long-term effects of previous housing and development policies are clearly reflected in personal and family wealth, in addition to being the root cause of the perpetuation of impoverished, segregated neighborhoods where persons of color disproportionately live. Rothstein identifies various progressive strategies to address the ill effects of the bigoted policies and practices that perpetuate racial inequalities. However, he also forcefully asserts that "until we arouse in Americans an understanding of how we created a system of unconstitutional, state-sponsored, *de jure* segregation, and a sense of outrage about it, neither remedies nor reparations will be on the public agenda."[19]

Regrettably, this is the kind of ugly American history that many conservative politicians vehemently fight to purge from our collective memory and understanding of systemic racism. Today, emboldened by misguided legislative initiatives that politicize our educational system and truth telling, these politicians aim to grossly distort the racially tainted story of placemaking in America. Such initiatives have the effect of preventing contemporary youth from being exposed to significant historical examples of race-oriented placemaking. For example, too few know about the placemaking that preceded and followed the horrific carnage instigated by a violent mob of white locals that resulted in the killing of three hundred Black people, along with the total destruction of thirty-five city blocks of the Greenwood District, known as Black Wall Street, in Tulsa, Oklahoma, in 1921.[20] Unfortunately, the public good is not served when millions of Americans are deprived of learning about the development, destruction, and then rebuilding of this unique place in American history. This remarkable place illustrates how placemaking strategies can integrate primary groups with people active in other social domains.

For America's young people, opportunities to engage in domestic placemaking are dependent on their family's circumstances, including their parents' financial resources and philosophy about sharing them. We are all aware of the "rich kid" stereotype that portrays some young people as being spoiled by their parents (and sometimes other adult relatives) who gift them extravagant monetary goods. Several of these goods include what we've described as types of places, most notably, a home and car. Some middle- and upper-class parents can also provide their children with access to places that kids from less affluent backgrounds could not afford or could only frequent if they benefited from institutional financial sponsorships. These places could include access to expensive leisure spots, high-end retail stores, elite colleges, ceremonial sites, and public spaces and nature venues that require expensive travel. Within these settings, "rich kids" can express their identities by flaunting their participation in and control over certain places. For example, inviting friends to ride in their expensive car or to spend time together partying at their decked-out house are crude placemaking tactics that enable a select subset of young people to manage others' impressions of them. Kids can passively receive gifts, or they can ask their parents to purchase items that they can use for this style of placemaking and impression management.

Family circumstances, even when they are sometimes quite good, can dramatically shift because of conditions beyond family members' control. Thus, families often confront difficult life transitions that fundamentally alter their home-based options for placemaking. Each year millions of people around the world are either evicted from their homes, their homes are damaged or destroyed by a natural disaster, or they are forced to leave because of other dangerous or debilitating personal circumstances. According to the Eviction Lab housed at Princeton University, more than 1.3 million families were evicted or had their mortgages foreclosed between March 2020 and November 2022, just in the seven states and thirty-one cities it tracks.[21] In recent years, global warming patterns have increased the number and severity of natural disasters, resulting in more and more people being displaced from their homes.[22] While having one's home destroyed or severely damaged can be overwhelming for any family, it can be particularly devastating in the short and long term for those with limited financial resources who struggle to bounce back. The disadvantaged and uninsured in these situations are impeded from pursuing practical forms of effective placemaking. They cannot, for instance, buy a different home or repair their own.

Finally, many older adults who confront chronic physical and mental health challenges must make difficult decisions (or have them made for them) to relocate, often to an assisted living facility. Recently, many of the millions of seniors (healthy or not) who move each year and have the financial resources, hire certified "senior move managers" who typically are associated with the National Association of Senior Move Managers founded in 2002.[23] These professionals do much of the labor-intensive work of sorting through a lifetime accumulation of personal possessions to help seniors downsize and reestablish a furnished residence elsewhere.[24] Sometimes these professionals assume a collaborative placemaking role when they are charged with the symbolic task of redecorating a senior's new place in advance of a relocation. In these arrangements, professionals are entrusted to listen to the wishes of seniors and their family to create an appealing, personalized living environment during what is often a highly stressful time.

Although some moves and placemaking are planned, other types are not. Turning our attention to the significance of disasters on particular areas, we learn that one study found that migrants to a new location that had experienced a natural disaster within the previous two years were slightly less likely to become homeowners, and this pattern was more pronounced for those areas that had suffered more severe disasters.[25] Finally, compared to the years 2009 to 2021, more than twice as many people in 2022 were forced to flee their homes and land around the world because of conflicts, violence, and fear of persecution and human rights violations. And although the annual displacement number for 2023 was lower than in the peak year of 2022, it too was significantly higher than any previous year since 2009. This left more than 117.3 million people with severe challenges to participate in placemaking activities on their own behalf.[26]

Creative policy and programmatic initiatives that seek to address the needs of individuals and families who are struggling financially can provide more placemaking choices. Initiatives can indirectly help people's placemaking efforts in modest ways, thereby helping them enrich the places they call home. Although typically limited in scope, these initiatives can provide people with a sense of autonomy to shape their immediate living environments. For example, programs like Orlando's Coalition for the Homeless of Central Florida, founded in 1987, use various strategies to help homeless people transition to more stable housing.[27] The Bridge Housing offered by this group gives homeless persons opportunities to experience a temporary style of placemaking prior to their moving into an affordable unit. In their permanent place, the previously homeless can reestablish their appreciation for organizing and decorating their own space so they can derive personal meaning from it.

While having money often enhances our ability to do informal placemaking on our terms in an intimate place where we share life with our family and close friends, our placemaking opportunities are also affected by the gendered politics of place and the social relations that occur in that action setting. As the earlier example of parents and children illustrates, when we share living space with others, our placemaking options are affected by the relative power we have in the relationship. All things being equal, a person with more status and power is better positioned to make autonomous decisions about the places that matter to them, whether it be related to features of a house, cabin, yard, car, RV, boat, or some other intimate place.

For centuries, power dynamics have been woven into the patriarchal norms that dominate our heteronormative, domestic landscape. Historically, the home, colloquially referred to in traditional circles as a "man's castle," has been a place that symbolically accentuates the conventional gender order. In practical terms, men's dominant status in the larger society has enabled them to assert their privileged position when executing placemaking decisions about the home that involve significant expenditures.

Yet one historical consequence of the separation of family space and workspace generated by the industrial revolution has been that domestic space – the home – also came to be defined and claimed as a woman's territory. This framing affords "the woman of the house" the "freedom" in many instances to make decisions about interior decor and space management. These activities can loosely be perceived as a style of placemaking. For big purchases, the stereotypical, gendered challenge was for the twentieth-century woman to convince her husband or partner that he should pay for her placemaking requests. As depicted in the 1955 short film *A Word to the Wives*, the woman's persuasive tactics could lean heavily on getting her husband to imagine that his role as a provider, and by extension his manhood, were being judged.[28] The film, showcasing two married, middle-class white couples, illustrates how a wife can supposedly trick her husband into providing her and the family with a modern new kitchen with all the latest dazzling appliances. My students over the past several decades have interpreted this gendered scheme as obsolete in many respects. Nonetheless, the gendered expectations about how a home is managed as a place still ring true for a significant subset of adults. But as the proportion of heterosexually married and cohabiting women working outside the home has increased in recent decades, and as men increasingly show more interest in housing decor, many modern couples do home-based placemaking differently than earlier generations of couples. Now, women are increasingly likely to make as much or more money than their male partners, which provides them with greater leverage than earlier generations of women. At the same time, however, more contemporary men are less willing to abdicate all the interior decision-making to their female partners. Many men assume, for instance, that they'll play a more active role in placemaking decisions in the home; they want to be a more active participant beyond just paying for things. Thus, for many couples, negotiations unfold in different ways compared to their parents' and grandparents' generations.[29]

Finally, because more people today are living alone or with platonic companions in apartments, condos, and houses, they are navigating a different set of circumstances compared to what earlier generations confronted. The growing proportion of adults living alone, for example, only need to consult themselves when they contemplate how they might physically alter aspects of their homeplace. Consequently, people are spending less time, on average, engaged in joint placemaking activities with a romantic partner. In some ways this results in more autonomy and fewer hassles, but it also means that individuals are spending less time experiencing the joy of doing couple-based placemaking that can intensify a sense of we-ness.

Communities and Community Groups

Of the five social domains, the public is most aware of placemaking as it is executed by professionals working on community projects. These professionals – the architects, urban planners, and designers of the world – have focused primarily on what geographers have traditionally defined as "place-based" communities, which are differentiated from the more recently labeled "post-place communities," or what I refer to as thought communities.[30] The ongoing debate over the precise definition of community is largely beyond the scope of our purpose here, but it is noteworthy that social scientists have traditionally described communities as being associated with three elements: place, interest, and identity.[31] While I highlight place-based communities in this section, I also acknowledge that community leaders and consultants who encourage placemaking in cities and towns increasingly emphasize how individuals living in these environments engage in rituals and routines that lead them to identify with the place and express a sense of we-ness toward it. Sentiments about a community's culture matter because they can compel people to embrace a common cause to improve a place's amenities.

Decades ago, Daniel Kemmis, a former Montana legislator and small-town mayor, captured the complex interplay between politics, city culture, and civic engagement in his insightful book *The Good City and the Good Life: Renewing the Sense of Community*.[32] Drawing on his extensive firsthand experience working with diverse stakeholders involved in shaping urban, suburban, and rural environments, Kemmis shows how place matters to people and how those people, when they collectively take the reins, can engage in consequential forms of placemaking. Profiling Baltimore as one of numerous cities that have rallied professional stakeholders and the public to do effective placemaking, Kemmis describes how local citizens have

> succeeded in creating a number of strong, good places that sustain and nurture citizenship itself. It is precisely the healing of places – the creation of new structures of wholeness – and the remembrance of the stories of what it took to do this that gives citizens a place to stand, a place to look back in memory and forward in anticipation.[33]

While locals can strategically create enriching places that invite people to meet, socialize, and cultivate their mutual sense of we-ness, Kemmis accentuates the value of the process of sustaining a good place. When people successfully do placemaking while buying into working side by side with others to build a better place, they tend to reinforce their collaborative spirit of citizenship. That spirit, in addition to the places that were created anew or rejuvenated, will be enhanced when the principles of beneficence, autonomy, social and environmental justice, inclusive collaboration, and nonmaleficence are honored. In these moments, the post-place sense of community will be strengthened and will reinforce people's commitment to the physical places where they, as embodied social beings, think, feel, and interact.

An important feature of this process involves the willingness of participants to afford each other a sense of dignity while also respecting them. Richard Harwood, the founder and president of the Harwood Institute, and author of *Stepping Forward: A Positive, Practical Path to Transform Our Communities and Our Lives*, has devoted his professional career to consulting with diverse community groups and organizations to bring about deliberate, principled change. He helps them discover their purpose and nurture their "civic culture." In his words,

> In communities, civic culture matters. It's how community works; how trust and public will form; why and how people engage with one another; what enables change to grow, even accelerate; and how ready leaders, groups, and everyday people are to undertake change – and their appetite for it. People's sense of dignity is shaped by their community's civic culture.[34]

Cultivating Harwood's notion of civic culture depends on people's willingness to embrace the principle of inclusive collaboration. Honoring that principle enables diverse stakeholders to develop a broader sense of we-ness that extends beyond their narrower, potentially competing interests. Ultimately, the bonds stakeholders forge will be grounded in the experiential wisdom they derive from living embodied lives in places that carry special meaning to them, like many of the generic places outlined in Chapter 2.

Perhaps the biggest issue for those involved in placemaking in communities and civic groups is finding a way for all interested parties to establish a shared understanding of what a place should be like. Determining the shared understanding and then getting important stakeholders to rally behind the plan is an important first step in effective community placemaking. As Harwood suggests, it is critical to get citizens to identify what kind of community they want to live in. Building that shared understanding and collective sense of purpose is essential for mobilizing the resources needed to make productive changes. Ideally, any placemaking activities should be seen as rewarding by the largest and most diverse collection of affected people possible. Those working to enrich a place or action setting should be mindful of how their actions enhance or impede social justice.

One of the most contentious issues facing communities around the globe in recent years, especially urban areas, is gentrification. In the early 1960s, the British sociologist Ruth Glass first introduced the term to describe the process of middle-class gentry moving into working-class areas in London where they renovated dilapidated housing, ultimately resulting in most of the working-class residents leaving the area. Since then, the concept has been the focus of intense debates about how to define it and its ethical implications. It remains a muddled concept with no clearly agreed upon, precise definition. Moreover, it is often interpreted to have racialized connotations. The types of neighborhoods where gentrification is a possibility are typically central city areas that have been adversely affected by disinvestment and are occupied by low-income residents.[35] Philosopher Daniel Putnam succinctly notes that the one common thread to the gentrification process is that it involves an "influx of relatively affluent people to low-income neighborhoods,"[36] and greater financial investments and resources follow. In his view there are numerous normative questions associated with gentrification that implicate social justice issues. Most importantly, varied interpretations of the scope and meaning of displacement are central to such concerns.

Previously, in Chapter 1, I used the ongoing gentrification initiatives in Puerto Rico to illustrate how a place's degree of stability fluctuates in response to the claims different stakeholders assert over land and the built environment. This troubling scenario mirrors the sentiments journalist Peter Moskowitz shares in his book *How to Kill a City: Gentrification, Inequality, and the Fight for the Neighborhood*.[37] Focusing on New Orleans, Detroit, San Francisco, and New York City as case studies, Moskowitz chides local governments, developers, and "yuppies" for the damage being inflicted on American cities and the disadvantaged people who live there – or once did. From his vantage point, the process may be multifaceted and complex, but his take-home message is clear and simple: precious local culture is being lost and lifelong residents are being displaced by those with deep pockets.

The Puerto Rico experience mentioned earlier similarly encapsulates the gentrification forces that can wipe out local culture. That process is rebuked by many, including Spike Lee, the moviemaker and New York City resident. Lee pejoratively labels the type of gentrification processes that have transformed many city neighborhoods as the "Christopher Columbus Syndrome." In his widely circulated, blistering remarks during the Q & A session of a Black history event at Brooklyn's Pratt Institute in 2014, Lee passionately challenged those who saw gentrification as being a positive force in New York City:

> You can't discover this! We been here. You just can't come and bogart. There were brothers playing motherfuckin' African drums in Mount Morris Park for forty years and now they can't do it anymore because the new inhabitants said the drums are loud. My father's a great jazz musician. He bought a house in nineteen-motherfuckin'-sixty-eight, and the motherfuckin' people moved in last year and called the cops on my father. He's not – he doesn't even play electric bass! It's acoustic! We bought the motherfuckin' house in nineteen-sixty-motherfuckin'-eight and now you call the cops? In 2013? Get the fuck outta here!
>
> Nah. You can't do that. You can't just come in the neighborhood and start bogarting and say, like you're motherfuckin' Columbus and kill off the Native Americans. Or what they do in Brazil, what they did to the Indigenous people. You have to come with respect. There's a code. There's people.[38]

The essence of Lee's remarks is intimated in the less confrontational yet powerful observation by Stacey Sutton, an urban planning scholar, who argues that "gentrification is fundamentally a social justice problem."[39] In other words, economic inequality is the driving force that fuels the practice and decisions associated with gentrification. For Sutton, urban planning decisions, including those related to gentrification, ultimately come down to the basics of "what we value, who we value, and how we want to act upon that."

A less ominous and more nuanced interpretation of the effects of gentrification is offered by Lance Freeman, an urban planning professor from the University of Pennsylvania, who has a keen interest in building more equitable neighborhoods. One of his detailed studies uses national survey data that followed individuals from 1986 to 1999 and charted whether those living in urban areas remained in their neighborhoods or moved out of them.[40] He concludes that gentrification does not appear to play a decisive role in displacing former residents as is often purported. He argues that gentrification may limit low-income people, notably Black people, from entering a gentrified area, but the process tends not to push masses of low-income people out of their neighborhoods. He does find that those most likely to move into a gentrified neighborhood are more well-educated white people. Freeman maintains that the changes to a gentrified neighborhood are more dependent on characteristics of who moves into it, suggesting that "neighborhoods can gentrify without widespread displacement."[41]

In 2006, Freeman also qualitatively explored the gentrification issue in his controversial book *There Goes the 'Hood: Views of Gentrification from the Ground Up*.[42] His study of two largely Black inner-city neighborhoods in Manhattan and Brooklyn reveals that residents who remain in gentrified areas offer mixed reactions to how gentrification has affected their lives. Thus, Freeman encourages those interested in understanding gentrification to avoid jumping prematurely to conclusions about this vexing social process. Commenting on how the politicization of this issue has narrowed observers' views, he contends that "political combat does not lend itself to nuanced positions. Rather the protagonists must stake out a position and fight for it. In this way the characters in many of these stories appear one-dimensional, singularly focused on stopping gentrification or maximizing property values."[43] Freeman believes that gentrification generates considerable improvements in the form of better city services, safer and cleaner streets, better schools and grocery stores, and other amenities for the original residents while also producing real costs via higher rents, the disappearance of local culture, and the reshaping of local community norms.

Sutton further clarifies that there are both direct and indirect versions of displacement. Whereas some people are forced out or choose to leave gentrified areas, many others remain but are indirectly affected because members from their close social networks leave the neighborhood, or they feel isolated because the types of businesses that move into the area are ones they can't afford.[44] This perspective mirrors how geographer Mark Davidson views displacement as being far more than a spatial process that forces people to move. It involves the transformation of a place's culture that prompts people to reimagine their communal surroundings in ways that leave them feeling a sense of loss of place because of the middle-class habitus they inherit – the group culture of manners, attitudes, preferences, and morality that shapes how people think, feel, and act.[45] In other words, individuals can feel desolate without ever physically leaving a place.[46] Drawing conclusions from her own quantitative study of New York City between 1970 and 2010, Sutton concludes that "even middle-class Blacks and Latinos are increasingly unable to remain in gentrifying neighborhoods as processes of change extend across the city."[47] She warns that we need to consider how much gentrification "entrenches a racial pattern on a city's landscape, much like urban renewal and redlining."[48]

As the preceding discussion suggests, the debate rages on among academics and activists as to the nature and scope of displacement. Those in favor of gentrification point to how it enhances neighborhoods financially while strengthening the local economy. Developers and others who stand to benefit economically from gentrification often speak of "urban renewal," rather than using the ethically loaded term "gentrification." Meanwhile, critics emphasize how gentrification leads to the displacement of financially disadvantaged residents – typically persons of color – who can no longer afford to live in the neighborhood, often jeopardizing whatever sense of community previously existed there. These critics question why government agencies have previously neglected these disadvantaged areas, having done little to promote public goods and services before more affluent people moved in. Regardless of where one's opinion falls when assessing the relative merits and shortcomings associated with gentrification, the five ethical principles emphasizing beneficence, autonomy, social and environmental justice, inclusive collaboration, and nonmaleficence should ideally guide placemaking efforts in areas that are undergoing gentrification.

When we consider what gentrification does and how we can manage it fairly, we should appreciate the larger context within which it occurs. The immediate effects of gentrification are always felt locally, but most serious students of gentrification acknowledge that the complex forces that cause and shape it are national and international in scope. More specifically, the process of gentrification is contingent on countries with more advanced economies having transitioned to postindustrial economies. Various scholars have alternatively referred to this new economy as the "creative economy," "innovation economy," or the "knowledge economy."[49] Irrespective of what we call modern economies, the societies that thrive in these new economic worlds have transitioned from manufacturing goods to producing, exchanging, and implementing ideas. As a result, the types of middle-class jobs that were once readily available in previous generations are shrinking, while job growth is concentrated in the low-wage and high-wage ends of the job market. Consequently, the shifting composition of the built environments and work ecologies in urban areas fundamentally relates to gentrification.

Just as gentrification is tied to national and international patterns, this process is frequently connected to broader public investments in the city that can be loosely defined as communal forms of urban placemaking.[50] Many areas are gentrified because the public has invested in upgrading subways and other forms of mass transit, creating new charter and magnet schools, renovating parks and green space, and revitalizing waterfront districts by converting warehouses and factories into commercial attractions.[51] Government agencies, urban planners, developers, builders, mortgage lenders, real estate agents, and others with interests that align with these sorts of activities often find themselves cooperating to promote placemaking in specific areas. White middle-class women have frequently been identified as an important force in driving the gentrification process, whereas women of color often step up to challenge it.[52] Typically, the women of color are more likely to oppose gentrification because they are more apt to be concerned about their own or their neighbors' displacement and loss of community culture.

When city stakeholders apply the five ethical principles to place-making, community leaders and citizens will generate ideas that ultimately lead to affordable housing as part of what Sutton labels "revitalization" initiatives. These grassroots projects have the benefit of honoring the spirit of inclusive cooperation so that new design proposals will have been vetted and shaped by the everyday people who will be affected most directly by a changing neighborhood.

To illustrate, let's look at how the seeds for this type of revitalization effort were planted several years ago as part of an innovative project launched in Gainesville, Florida, where I have lived since 1988. Here a team of researchers with interests in race, social justice, urban planning, and architecture did a five-decade case study of neighborhood planning in Porters, a historically Black community of roughly five hundred residents located near the downtown.[53] The researchers' historical analysis was informed by their complementary pilot project, Neighborhoods As Community Assets, that spanned 2017–18.[54] That project was designed to develop a new practice, "Participatory Neighborhood Narrative (PNN)," that could be used as a form of "communication and capacity-building" to guide local planning.[55] As self-proclaimed "equity-minded planners," this team documented both the negatively toned, dominant narratives that were embedded over the years in various planning documents, newspaper articles, and other sources as well as the more recent "counternarratives" that were generated by Porters' residents, many of whom had intergenerational ties to the community. This inclusive process helped to replace the "forgotten neighborhood" narrative with one celebrating the image of "home."

The research team's efforts using the PNN practice are consistent with the ethic of inclusive collaboration because they encourage planners to allow local participants to tell their stories about their community, sharing their perceptions of it and attachment to it. Equity-minded planners are driven by the philosophy that they "can better partner with residents to understand and represent their counternarratives. Through this community dialectic, planners can dismantle their own presumptions, recognize residents' expertise regarding community needs and challenges, and better discern the ways in which racism persists, pervades policy-making, and impedes equity."⁵⁶ Planners who engage with community stakeholders in this fashion enhance their ability to be a valuable resource by partnering with residents while being guided by ethical placemaking principles. In doing so, they elevate the voices of residents who lack the decision-making influence and financial resources of politicians and wealthy developers. In the Porters narrative project, researchers were able to show contemporary planners a roughly fifty-year historical account of how "dominant narratives stigmatized the neighborhood and relegated its residents to second-class citizenship shaped by their race and street address. When used in planning politics, the stigma reinforced racism."⁵⁷ In Gainesville, the team illustrated the type of decisive role planners can play in the planning process when they inject a counternarrative that contributes to "dismantling long-enduring narratives and reinventing the relationship between planners and marginalized communities."⁵⁸

While the research team in Gainesville played a pivotal role in helping Porters' residents discover and express their activist, placemaking voices, community residents in other cities often mobilize themselves to advocate for their best interests. For example, a passionate group of mostly young women of color have recently asserted themselves by advocating for Miami's Little Haiti as part of an anti-gentrification movement. These women have challenged what they perceive to be culturally insensitive gentrification projects tied to the Magic City Innovation District. The projects have been championed by mostly men who promote a form of "cultural branding" designed to appeal to Miami's development and tourism industries. Marta Gierczyk, a professor and Miami-based activist, conducted an insightful ethnography of the complex and heated gendered politics associated with these women's neighborhood justice efforts.⁵⁹ She labels the women activists "killjoys" because the urban planning community casts them as "problematic and sensational" when they challenge the profit motives of those in power. From the women's perspectives, those in power push for a culture-driven style of gentrification of Little Haiti that distorts the local narrative and tries to co-opt a "heritage neighborhood" theme. The outsiders' message is that they need to take charge over managing the community's cultural assets lest they be squandered by the locals.

Yet, as Gierczyk documents, there is considerable variation in these women's visions for the community and their tactics for achieving their aims despite opposition from the oppressive, male-dominated urban planning network. Thus, this study discourages us from lumping gentrifiers and local residents into simplistic, homogeneous camps. Local activists in Miami and elsewhere can share a similar concern about being politically disenfranchised, and even have concerns about physical and cultural forms of displacement, but still have serious disputes amongst themselves about their objectives and strategies to achieve their desired goals. In short, the social dynamics of community placemaking can be volatile, challenging, and messy within and between key stakeholder groups. They are also increasingly likely to be influenced by women's legitimate demands to be at any table where urban planning and placemaking decisions are being made.

The politics of placemaking have recently been on display in a different yet powerful way for stakeholders involved with smart city development. According to Germaine Halegoua, these cities are "places where digital media is aggressively integrated as infrastructure, software, and hardware; information is regarded as a necessary resource for coordinating technologies and actions; and data is [sic] collected, analyzed, and shared in the service of city management and responsiveness."[60] Some of these places are referred to as "smart-from-the-start" cities while others are established cities, such as New York and Singapore, that committed to a retrofitting process incorporating state-of-the-art technologies.

As might be expected, the digital placemaking integral to the high-tech, smart cities designed from the start emphasizes a business-friendly environment. These cities are "framed as places of communality, 'joint venture,' partnership, and cohabitation around a common cause: profit, progress, and economic development."[61] A couple of the newly constructed cities include New Songdo, South Korea, and Masdar City, Abu Dhabi. The public relations message common to these places is one that accentuates an entrepreneurial sense of we-ness. Promotional materials that target lessees and residents, such as those related to Masdar City, also try to market a sense of neighborhood and community well-being. However, Halegoua contends that these efforts lack authenticity. She criticizes the top-down approach to placemaking that occurs in Masdar City as well as similar smart-from-the-start cities. The expert approach fuels significant tensions between those placemaking stakeholders who build and try to "sell" a place and those who move to the city. By not securing adequate input from potential and current residents, placemaking in smart cities represents a detached form of "re-placing" that fails to create genuine place attachment among residents. Pulling no punches, Halegoua claims that "planning rhetoric situates users as customers rather than as civic-minded actors to the point that people are not wholly envisioned as agents within the urban ecosystem but as sensing nodes and data points that interact with it."[62] She recommends that developers and designers reimagine the city as a "field of care" to facilitate that emotional connection people can have with a place.

The previous examples of community-oriented and expert-driven placemaking provide a brief glimpse of how the social dynamics of contemporary placemaking are intertwined with the politics of place. As is the case with the politics that define any aspect of life, our socially constructed personal standpoints alter how we interpret the symbols, values, and resources associated with a place. Whether we identify as a man, woman, or nonbinary person; someone who is of a particular racial or ethnic background; a working- or middle-class person; an individual with or without a disability; or someone with any number of embodied attributes that influence a person's place perspectives, we enter the placemaking landscape equipped with our own history and beliefs. Thus, because the way we navigate an action setting can be shaped by the politics of place, we should try to enrich our place experiences by applying different *MEAL* life skills when we interpret and navigate them. Cultivating mindfulness, empathy, and collaborative leadership skills can help us develop a fresh sense of place, while sharpening our understanding of what we and others situated in that place are feeling. There may even be circumstances that invite us to express altruism to those who frequent the place.

We regularly use our ability to empathize by imagining how others are feeling and experiencing a particular situation, one that often is connected to a place. In the future, innovative technologies will allow us to expand our empathic reach while refining the placemaking process. More specifically, placemaking will take on new forms when we eventually build, refine, and gain access to sophisticated technologies for experiencing immersive VR place-based environments. Ultimately, we will be able to use mixed-media and multi-sensory apps to enhance our appreciation for how we, as well as others, can experience different types of natural and built environments. Some of the natural places will be projections of what they could be like if left unprotected from environmental degradation. In addition, simulations of the built environment will sometimes be places in the design stage that are not yet real. Imagine a proposed community development or a major sports complex like the controversial Miami Freedom Park that is being promoted by David Beckham and Jorge Mas.[63] Other virtual sites can include real places that we have yet to visit.

One technically gifted Australian-based team of experts in computers and architectural design is developing and testing a VR prototype that is quite promising. Ideally, it will demonstrate that "immersive mixed-media and multi-sensory environments allow designers and audiences to express and experience intangible aspects of place that are extremely challenging to communicate using other means."[64] This team foresees that professionals in fields like design, architecture, and city planning will be able to present audiences with simulated experiences that will generate a constructive feedback loop for optimizing the placemaking of built environments. Using technology in this way to create "place illusion" for retrieving audience input honors the inclusive collaboration principle for placemaking.

Consistent with Ed Yong's emphasis on the diversity and richness of our sensory abilities, multi-sensory design technology appeals to our embodied way of experiencing place. While this team's prototype was initially designed to deliver information to our human senses involving visual, aural, and kinesthetic stimuli, the team hopes to refine their prototype by including olfactory and other stimuli. Having processed participants' feedback, they also realize that they need to incorporate simulations of social activity to bring places to life.

As we contemplate the principle of social justice, especially as it relates to environmental justice, VR technology portends appealing possibilities. For example, it could be used to provide an audience with a realistic sense of place via an authentic place-based simulation of a site that has been drastically transformed because of climate change. Environmental activists could show local populations an accurate and compelling representation of the consequences related to beach erosion by creating a virtual space for them to experience a projected place that has been altered by significantly rising sea levels. Although serious efforts to develop and use VR technology to inform urban and city planners' decisions remain in the early stages, the technology, when perfected, is likely to revolutionize the technical and interactive processes related to placemaking for those with access to it. As a type of affordance, this technology is likely to inspire the public and placemaking professionals to be more mindful of place, empathize with each other more effectively, and adopt more cooperative leadership styles. It could also be exciting to use, even if the imagery is depressing.

A less techy, yet enlightening, approach relevant to community placemaking is practiced by experts in art and sound who act as social activists. In this role, the specialists create rituals that support acoustic ecology. For example, beginning in 2016 several activists partnered to develop the Soundwalks in the Parks series and The 606 Soundscape Project in Chicago. These activities were designed to teach people how to listen more carefully to the soundscapes in their urban environments. People who engage in soundwalks take guided walking tours of their communities to enhance their "sonic awareness." Just as we see places, we hear them too. However, the sounds of a community are often experienced as background noise that does not fully register with us. Given a nudge, we can be inspired and trained to "hear" the local sounds while interpreting their meaning for our everyday life and well-being. This activity can deepen our sense of place and place consciousness.

Soundwalk practices can also engage communities by helping them generate experiential knowledge about how their social context is affected by the various sounds produced in their built and natural environments. Those who serve as sonic teaching artists assert that these practices can empower local residents from all backgrounds: "Once a community gains a sense of ownership of this knowledge, it can take more control in setting community goals and participating in decision making."[65] In short, soundwalks can promote more collaborative forms of placemaking if locals increase their knowledge about and emotional investment in the soundscapes that shape their communities.

Thought Communities

The earlier discussion about a relatively small city like Gainesville that is home to both a major university, and a long-standing neighborhood like Porters, illustrates the ways place-based communities can engender attachments and a sense of we-ness related to a place. A similar sense of we-ness can also be derived from attachments to larger, symbolically significant land masses.

An additional layer of the attachment process emerges when our commitments to physical places are influenced by the sentiments we express as part of a thought community. As we saw in the previous chapter, competing place-based claims can fuel outrage over the dispossession of Indigenous peoples' lands. This scenario reminds us that social activists aligned with thought communities are often energized by similar place-related disputes. In general, when people are compassionately engaged with human rights issues, their concerns are frequently linked to their feelings about how places are defined, used, and controlled.

Let's return to the controversial dispossession of Indigenous lands to elaborate this point. Recall our previous discussion of how the "Land Grab Universities" report for *High Country News* sparked outrage and concerted action.[66] Various like-minded individuals committed to social justice proposed that the public and universities initiate a series of atonement steps to acknowledge the pernicious harm and indignities that white Americans have perpetuated against Indigenous peoples for centuries. Stephen Gavazzi and John Low, professors associated with The Ohio State University system, have spearheaded the call for decisive actions to be taken on this front. In 2020, Gavazzi, Low, and other faculty and staff associated with The Ohio State University launched the racial justice project Stepping Out & Stepping Up (SOSU).[67] This project, in partnership with the First Nations Development Institute, a national economic justice organization, has pursued a twofold mission. First, it seeks to promote a shared and truthful understanding that reveals how land-grant universities exploited Indigenous peoples and dispossessed them of their land. Second, it intends to forge a variety of collaborative relationships at different levels of intensity that bring together land-grant universities and Indigenous communities. Ideally, these collaborative efforts will generate an action plan for specific reparative initiatives to assist the Indigenous peoples who have been dispossessed of their land. As social justice activists, the sponsors of the SOSU project suggest issuing formal land-acknowledgement statements, providing financial assistance for college students of Indigenous heritage, devising strategies to enhance partnerships between land-grant universities and tribally controlled colleges and universities, and asking tribal leaders to identify what can be done to address their peoples' hardships.[68] The project is essential because it shares information with tribal leaders about how the dispossession of their ancestral lands has been used to fund land-grant universities. Ironically, many of the tribal leaders were unaware of this connection prior to being interviewed by project staff. Given the complex and exploitative history that frames the competing claims to Native lands, this broad initiative invokes placemaking themes in unconventional ways, yet its purpose is consistent with the five ethical principles central to this book.

While many people thrive through expressing a form or sense of community that is connected to a physical town, city, region, nation, or tribal lands, people sometimes experience community separate from those types of places. People can develop forms of ideational we-ness that are connected to other meaningful and specific places in the built environment. Such places often sharpen people's sense of identity and purpose in life. They provide a site for individuals to confront social inequalities and prejudices that restrict their access to resources, opportunities, and acceptance. Thus, for some, a place may represent a haven that allows them to present their authentic

Chapter 7: Cultivating Place Consciousness to Enrich Society | 287

self in public. Sometimes the place may also serve as a rallying point, providing like-minded individuals the chance to mobilize for social action. Historically, Black churches and Jewish synagogues have played a pivotal role in deepening members' sense of we-ness and resolve to confront social injustices, especially during turbulent times. During the civil rights era, for example, Black churches were a critical agent of social change; more recently, they have supported protests generated by the Black Lives Matter movement. The Black barbershop, which was discussed in Chapter 2, represents a more casual place that provides a comfortable space for those who cherish their Black cultural heritage.

The LGBTQ+ community is yet another increasingly visible thought community with strong, intersecting ties with place. Not so long ago, members of the LGBTQ+ community were seldom favorably portrayed in popular movies, TV shows, and other media outlets. So too, public discourse did not center LGBTQ+ issues as a noteworthy and common story in our social narrative. Lastly, the internet and convenient hookup/dating apps did not exist. In this earlier era, the rampant stigma and limited tech resources meant that those who navigated some version of the LGBTQ+ social landscape struggled to find welcoming places to be with others who had similar gender and sexual identities. Faced with such repressive conditions, the underground gay bar scene gave individuals opportunities to meet and hang out with others who knowingly shared their desires and identities. Many people took their first decisive steps toward coming out by visiting a gay bar.

In an earlier time, these bars were stigmatized and typically not widely advertised because gays and lesbians were treated like outcasts. But today, similar bars are more visible; many are even enjoyed by allies to the LGBTQ+ community. Unfortunately, the recent backlash generated by far right religious and political ideologies has spawned a new wave of violent rhetoric targeting LGBTQ+ people. The horrific and deadly mass shootings at the Pulse club in Orlando in 2016 and Club Q in Colorado Springs in 2022 spotlight the hate that gay bars and their customers are subjected to from bigoted segments of the larger population. Ironically, although the United States and other western countries in recent decades have become more progressive and accepting of the LGBTQ+ community, queer places remain steeped in fear because of the elevated hateful anti-gay rhetoric. Consequently, these places still offer refuge, yet they signal potential danger as well.

Archivist Art Smith, in his remarkable project GayBarchives, captures the intense attachment many people have experienced toward gay bars since the early 1900s. Launched during the pandemic, the project documents the eclectic gay bars scattered throughout the country that provide members of the LGBTQ+ community with opportunities to develop a sense of community and find sanctuary.[69] As of June 2023, Smith had archived information on over 4,200 gay bars, mostly in the United States.[70] He has also compiled an impressive inventory of over 150 video interviews with individuals who have been intimately involved with owning, writing about, or frequenting gay bars since the 1960s. One of the entrepreneurs Smith interviews, David Fischer, owns several gay-oriented properties in St. Petersburg, including a gay bar. Fischer, who lived in Orlando at the time of the Pulse shooting and was deeply affected by it, describes how that experience and others have made him acutely aware of the dangers the LGBTQ+ community face when they venture into clubs like his. As a result, he has installed a high-tech security system to minimize the risks patrons face when they enter his bar.[71] In addition to wanting to produce unique and memorable design features in his club and other properties, safety is front and center to Fischer's placemaking efforts.

In a 2020 interview for the Campaign for Southern Equality, Smith criticizes the limited breadth of many gay history projects because they tend to only "focus on the people and the politics." He adds, "Too few even recognize the enormous contribution made to our community by the bars and the people who became 'family' because of them. They were our safe havens."[72] Smith's project reinforces the central message of this book, that place matters for people irrespective of their class, race, ethnicity, gender, sexual orientation, gender identity, or whatever other characteristics are used to define them. It also signals that the politics of place may be distinctly salient to those who feel ostracized from more mainstream places.

Chapter 7: Cultivating Place Consciousness to Enrich Society | 289

Writing in *Metropolis Magazine* on behalf of members of the LGBTQ+ community, journalist Leilah Stone contends that,

> as long as we exist, we will always need queer spaces. We will always need spaces that are fluid, malleable, and transformational … The way we inhabit our bodies changes how we inhabit the architecture surrounding us … If change is the only constant in life, well, we all stand to learn a little bit more about thinking and building queer.[73]

Some of the spaces Stone refers to include bars and clubs like the historically significant Stonewall Inn where the 1969 uprising occurred, but they also include other diverse places like New York City's Bluestockings, a radical, co-op bookstore located on the Lower East Side of Manhattan that caters to "all genders, cultures, expansive sexualities and identities."[74] As a place that supports an activist social agenda, Bluestockings is run by numerous worker-owners who engage in a style of placemaking that showcases the store as a relaxing, educational, and inclusive public place.

The scope of places around the world like Bluestockings that welcome queer people is creatively documented in *Queer Spaces: An Atlas of LGBTQIA+ Places and Stories*. This 2022 volume, edited by designer Adam Nathaniel Furman and architectural historian Joshua Mardell, compiles a contemporary collection of images and essays that illustrate the wide-ranging ways places can be built, managed, and displayed that enable individuals who are members of the LGBTQ+ thought community to navigate life effectively.[75] It is incumbent on all of us to support and protect these unique places – ones typically organized and frequented by members of the LGBTQ+ community.

But those who design, operate, and monitor more generic places for the public should also strive to create affirming places for persons who represent the full spectrum of races, religions, genders, sexualities, and embodied identities. Just like ethnographies have shown that city ecologies in places like Ithaca, New York, and Portland, Maine, for example, can affect how queer identities are expressed, policies and initiatives tied to other action settings involving businesses, schools, houses of worship, leisure sites, and more can enhance participants' chances to feel accepted while growing more attached as a result.[76]

Leisure and Sports

Typically, when we think of the diverse places associated with leisure and sports our thoughts drift to images of kids at play, people recreating with friends and family, or athletes of varying ages and abilities competing at a sports venue. Focused on these settings, most of us are less likely to wonder about placemaking efforts that implicate social justice issues. But we should. Fortunately, some leisure scholars do highlight the inequities of how parks and recreational amenities are distributed in different communities.

Leisure and sports scholars have generally explored how people navigate and form attachments to all sorts of recreational places that are home to different types of social exchanges. Researchers interested in place and space themes have studied disparate forms of leisure, including informal cycling group rides in rural and urban areas in England,[77] a famous skateboarding site called the Big O in Montreal,[78] an annual outdoor tenting festival in rural central Pennsylvania,[79] the Colwick Parkrun for recreational runners in Nottingham, England,[80] varied groups that hike the Appalachian Trail,[81] and so much more. One of the common threads distinguishing this genre of leisure research is that it underscores the value of understanding how our place attachments are mediated by the gratifying interactions we have with like-minded people in specific places. These types of studies also help us appreciate the leisure rituals that bind us together in places we find meaningful. While exercise-oriented leisure activities can benefit us physically, the social component of our leisure activities can also provide the social support we need to sustain our emotional and mental health.

Beyond the personal fun and rewards, we should recognize, too, that the social domain of leisure and sport is represented by places that demand critical reflection. Leisure and sporting activities often occur in places where ethical placemaking, or lack thereof, has important implications. Back in the Jim Crow days, for example, various racial policies and practices explicitly impeded Black people's and other racial minorities' access to recreational lands, facilities, and opportunities. In her provocative book *Caste: The Origins of Our Discontents*, Pulitzer Prize–winning journalist Isabel Wilkerson describes in excruciating detail how white people across the country, North and South, went to great lengths to restrict Black people's access to public pools because they believed they would be socially and physically contaminated by Black people.[82] Amazingly, the state supreme court even ruled in favor of the town of Newton, Kansas, which argued that Black people could never be granted access to the public pool it built in 1935, a ruling that excluded them from that pool for decades. The practical outcome of Newton's policy was far from unique; Black people were denied access to public pools in many towns throughout the United States.

Fortunately, the 1964 Civil Rights Act prevents operators of swimming pools and other recreational facilities from explicitly discriminating against persons of color when making decisions about who is permitted to use these community assets. Integrated public pools are now part of our taken-for-granted social landscape. Yet, a racial and social class gap persists as to who has easy access to recreational opportunities located in our natural and built environments. While Black people theoretically stand to benefit from legislation that forbids their exclusion from public pools, it is somewhat of a moot victory for Black people if there are so few accessible to them. As mentioned in Chapter 2, the national park system is also beleaguered by a racialized legacy of limiting the participation of persons of color that has perpetuated long-lasting consequences.

Ironically, prior to the civil rights era, Black people had a significant presence in coastal land ownership along Chesapeake Bay and the Atlantic and Gulf coasts. These Black people, as well as their families, friends, and customers, who lived largely segregated lives in these coastal areas, had easy access to the beach, water, small shops, and restaurants that offered convenient and relaxing leisure options for Black people. But in the 1960s and shortly thereafter, these Black landowners were quickly dispossessed of their land by a white-dominated economic force that Andrew Kahrl, an historian and African-American Studies professor, calls "coastal capitalism." The white representatives of this powerful force swept in quickly, buying and developing the land to support expensive homes, large hotels, and commercialized tourism. In his book *The Land Was Ours: How Black Beaches Became White Wealth in the Coastal South*, Kahrl leverages a series of case studies to reveal how this transformation altered coastal communities and pushed Black people away from culturally distinct communal places that had previously generated leisure activities for them. Kahrl, moved by a nostalgic reckoning, is sensitive to the social injustice that resulted when Black beach culture was erased because of coastal real estate development. He reminds us that "washed away in Americans' rush to the sea are the mom-and-pop restaurants, do-drop inns, nightclubs, and seaside amusement parks that sustained black social life, nourished cultural traditions, and gave rise to forms of black business activity and struggles for economic empowerment throughout much of the twentieth century."[83] Regrettably, the frenzied and unfettered commercialization of these pristine beach properties was not guided by the ethics of a principled, orchestrated type of placemaking. Rather this brand of coastal capitalism disregarded the nonmaleficence principle by upending Black coastal culture and precipitating environmental damage.

The lingering consequences of systemic racism produced by legalized segregation, discriminatory housing policies and practices, and fear of racial violence continue to reinforce inequalities in outdoor and recreational activities for communities of color. More generally, the concentration of poverty that disproportionately affects poor Black people, Indigenous peoples, and other persons of color has meant that they live in cities and municipalities where they have access to far fewer quality parks and recreation amenities compared to more affluent Americans. "Recreational apartheid" is the label Richard Kraus, the well-known recreation author, used to refer to the differential two-tiered system of publicly funded parks and recreation resources for affluent and poor communities.[84]

Public placemaking, including the distribution of the resources designed to promote people's leisure and sports experiences, is political. Biases can taint public officials' decisions about where new recreational facilities, parks, and creative green spaces are located.

But placemaking can also be an agent of social change that helps reverse the long-standing effects of racial inequities that are embedded in the spatial patterns of leisure resources that either foster or hinder physical, mental, and emotional health.

Access to places that promote safe walking, running, hiking, cycling, and other forms of exercise and recreation is associated with healthier life outcomes for participants. Thus, planning decisions can have dramatic effects if they create or deny recreational opportunities to persons of color and those who live in marginalized communities.[85] If community leaders, especially those involved in coordinating the efforts of parks and recreation departments, want to engage in consequential placemaking that produces life enhancing outcomes, they need to embrace the ethical principles linked to social and environmental justice, inclusive collaboration, and beneficence. In addition, when a place is equipped with leisure and sports facilities it gives those in the community greater autonomy to enrich their lives.

Writing in the *Journal of Park and Recreation Administration*, leisure scholar David Scott proposes six ideas to improve the delivery of leisure services to poor Americans. Although he does not explicitly foreground matters of place, his recommendations can inform how a diverse coalition of stakeholders can engage in placemaking that will produce healthier outcomes for low-income community residents. Scott initially suggests that leaders in the parks and recreation field develop strong allies both inside and outside the areas where poor people live, such as "federal, state, county, and local government agencies; youth serving organizations and faith-based groups; legal organizations; non-profit conservation groups; schools and universities; and corporations and businesses."[86] We can augment Scott's list by stressing the value of incorporating local residents. The principle of inclusive collaboration requires leaders to work closely with those who would be most affected by any initiative to expand and enhance leisure options.

Scott next underscores ways to improve poor people's access to the recreational resources that can improve their health. Building and locating the needed facilities in park-poor communities is likely to be most effective, but we must also do a better job of providing viable transportation options for poor people to get to whatever facilities are in the general vicinity.

Building new recreational resources for disadvantaged Americans has been on Robert Garcia's mind since at least 2000. That year, Garcia, a civil rights attorney in Los Angeles, got involved in a form of social justice–oriented placemaking when he dedicated himself to creating more green space and improving the rundown schools in LA's poorest neighborhoods. From the beginning, he recognized that he and other stakeholders needed to tackle two interrelated problems: "more parks in underserved communities, and the need to build and modernize public schools, including providing playing fields, pools and parks that could be used during school, after school, and by the community on weekends."[87] Garcia responded by launching The City Project, and within a few years he stabilized and expanded his work, teaming up with a successful LA nonprofit, Community Partners. This collaboration resulted in his team creating or preserving more than one thousand acres of park space in the county. Staff also helped facilitate a grassroots effort involving residents of South Central LA that prevented a power plant from being built on the site of Baldwin Hills Park – located in a Black community – and then they prevented a garbage dump from being placed near the park. Another major achievement was creating the Los Angeles State Historic Park in the Chinatown neighborhood. Most recently, The City Project has been working on restoring the Los Angeles River's fifty-two-mile ecosystem and creating a national park that will cover many areas, including low-income predominantly Asian and Latinx neighborhoods. These accomplishments highlight the project's emphasis on environmental and health justice. Finally, the project has helped to build about 130 new schools that include additional recreational opportunities, and it has spearheaded the renovation of hundreds more.

An initiative that builds and renovates new schools can complement Scott's objective to implement formative leisure experiences for young kids. For example, we need more educational programs to help kids become more knowledgeable about and value leisure and recreational activities. These programs can cultivate kids' interests in leisure activities while also helping them to develop the skills necessary to feel comfortable in leisure settings. Because these activities will, by necessity, occur in specific places, we should also strive to deepen youths' place consciousness, especially as it relates to experiencing outdoor and recreational activities. Enhancing kids' place consciousness will cause them to become more actively aware of how their physical environments afford them numerous chances to be active in leisure and sports.

Although many of us feel safe and comfortable in the places where we do leisure and sports, the same cannot be said for those who live in low-income neighborhoods. Unfortunately, the fear for one's safety is a significant impediment for many who might otherwise be open to getting more involved in these activities. A basic social justice objective, then, is to create safer streets so that more people will feel they are in control of their lives because they can safely get to the places that matter to them. The fears that permeate numerous low-income communities must be addressed if we are to undertake successful placemaking that honors residents' practical sense of autonomy – the freedom to travel to recreational sites and to also participate without fear once there.

Scott's final two suggestions are to develop a set of welcoming norms at the recreational sites that encourage low-income participants to feel comfortable without being stigmatized and to make visits to these places more affordable for those who are poor. Thus, building or renovating leisure and recreational places in or near low-income communities is a critical step in placemaking. However, we must also invoke our empathy skills to make these places inviting and accessible to the individuals who can benefit from them the most.

Another form of consequential placemaking related to leisure and sports, but one that does not explicitly focus on social or environmental justice concerns, involves the marketing category of "destination branding." Some marketing professionals make their living by promoting specific destinations to potential tourists. They do so by making promises to them about what kinds of enjoyable and memorable experiences they can expect to have if they visit. This sort of endeavor sometimes involves community development activities that mobilize local stakeholders and the broader public to provide feedback on the places they call home.

One team of marketing scholars astutely asserts that "A destination is both a geographical place and a metaphysical space determined by a network of meanings and values that are attached to it."[88] This layered interpretation combines an appreciation for the geographical insights that frame the physical features of a destination and a social science understanding of the unique cultural and social processes that distinguish the habitus found there. Continuing, the team notes that "Destinations are embedded in places. Consequently, destination branding should be guided by the theory of place and sense of place so as to benefit from and contribute to the place's natural, cultural, social, and economic wealth."[89] Done well, destination branding is built on a deep understanding of a place's identity and the "core attributes that define its character. These are very much related to its culture and core values."[90]

Working closely with residents living on the remote Chatham Islands in New Zealand, a community with a population of roughly six hundred people, the research team highlighted the value of gaining an intimate understanding of the residents' sense of place. This ethnographic project helped the team develop a destination branding model that focuses on four constructs: time, landscape, ancestry, and community – constructs that reportedly can be adapted to capture the sense of place for residents who live elsewhere. By tapping into these constructs, marketers can grasp more fully the "communal meanings" and sense of place that residents generate based on the way they see, feel, and practice their everyday social lives. The model reminds us that people, embedded in a specific place where they are influenced by historical, physical, and climatic forces, create shared meanings of what it's like to live there.

To their credit, this team provides another example of how different styles of placemaking can honor the principle of inclusive collaboration. But unlike many typical community development initiatives that seek to produce public goods, these branding specialists incorporate residents' everyday experiences and their sense of place into forms of messaging driven by a profit motive. More specifically, the main goal of branding specialists working in this setting is to enhance tourism that, in turn, will presumably benefit the islanders. Still, a branding destination strategy that helps residents identify and shape their narrative can be viewed as ethically sound. As the team suggests, it is vital to position residents' "voices at the heart of the branding strategy" because they rely on it being successful enough to boost the tourism they need: "Leaving residents aside in the branding process would lead to a lack of recognition, acceptance, and commitment by the local community affecting the quality of the tourism experience."[91] With that being said, the placemaking focuses on the needs of the community and tourists. In contrast, recall that those living in Miami's Little Haiti, Puerto Rico's coastal areas, and other gentrified communities often feel as though their voices are ignored by stakeholders who wish to capitalize on their land and culture.

In the world of branding destination initiatives, one setting where residents' voices are more regularly consulted includes the promotion of significant events that attract large numbers of participants. Over recent decades, city stakeholders have increasingly pursued a type of placemaking by proactively using big events, many of which focus on leisure or sports activities, to help a city thrive and develop a more distinct place identity. Marketing professionals like Greg Richards, professor of placemaking and events, stress that the successful promotion of events can enhance a city's economy, tourism, and reputation. Richards instructs that the

> more holistic approaches to placemaking that have emerged and which events have now become a part of, consist of three important elements: the physical city itself, the lived experience of place that is shared among the stakeholders or users of the city, and the symbolic imaginings of the city that are projected through city images and brands.[92]

Richards describes in detail how the professionals who are committed to making places more distinctive, and to promoting cultural tourism, are turning to the creative industries, such as architecture, design, art, music, literature, and culinary heritage. Showcasing creativity is often linked to the emerging field of creative tourism, which combines tourism and the creative economy. According to the Organisation for Economic Co-operation and Development, an intergovernmental organization representing thirty-eight member countries, this partnership has produced "knowledge-based creative activities that link producers, consumers and places by utilizing technology, talent or skill to generate meaningful intangible cultural products, creative content and experiences."[93]

The creative placemaking movement that targets tourism has inspired cities throughout the world to identify and develop local physical and cultural resources in a way that accentuates a place's distinct assets while appealing to tourists. It is defined as a process to "strategically shape the physical and social character of a neighborhood, town, tribe, city, or region around arts and cultural activities. Creative placemaking animates public and private spaces, rejuvenates structure and streetscapes, improves local business viability and public safety, and brings diverse people together to celebrate, inspire, and be inspired."[94] Although a project's strategy to engage tourists in the local culture and to even request feedback from them may be viewed as inclusive by some, others are apt to challenge it if they see the creative placemaking as reinforcing an elitist gentrification process. Thus, just as different people can see the same place in divergent ways, observers are also likely to support alternative forms of placemaking to shape it.

Another way to interpret the phrase "creative placemaking" in relation to leisure is to consider how online games like *Horizon Worlds*, *Minecraft*, *Second Life*, and many others afford users opportunities to build and experience a virtual world. These sites also give users the chance to forge and reinforce a sense of we-ness as they collaborate on these projects. *Second Life*, which I mentioned in Chapter 2 in relation to the metaverse, has a relatively small but loyal following. Users can create highly customized avatars, buy and sell land, create all sorts of landscapes and structures, engage in play and commerce, and socialize in various ways.[95]

Some of the placemaking that occurs in *SL* portends a futuristic vision of placemaking connected to place-based "virtual settlements." This type of settlement represents "a cyber-place that is symbolically delineated by topic of interest and within which a significant proportion of interrelated interactive group-CMS [computer mediated communication] occurs."[96] Researchers committed to "cyber-archaeology" have explored how users express themselves and interact as members of a virtual community in places like *SL*. For example, some scholars have focused on "heritage" sites that take the form of "museums, commemorative monuments, conserved buildings and artifacts and replicas of actual heritage sites."[97] This research considers how "virtual communities use heritage sites to create both a sense of belonging and a sense of 'place.'"[98] When users make the effort to preserve and blog about official heritage sites, they help to establish a narrative and image of the virtual community whose members have built and sustained a virtual place. The placemaking involved in creating, preserving, and marketing these virtual sites resembles the cultural processes found in the physical world, including protesting collectively in front of specific sites. However, users often visit *SL* heritage sites on their own rather than in groups, which is more frequently the case in the physical world. Moving forward, users are likely to engage in more collaborative placemaking as newer technologies facilitate the building of virtual sites that more closely mirror our everyday physical world.

Placemaking in virtual worlds can be either a solo or collaborative leisure activity. It can also be an experience that overlaps with how we participate in social domains related to primary groups, community groups, and work. Family members and friends sometimes collectively buy properties, build structures, and socialize with avatars while in virtual environments. In addition, instructors are experimenting with ways to use *Minecraft* as an educational tool to afford youth and young adults with opportunities to work together to design places as part of urban planning programs.[99] Some users in *SL* have even found ways to monetize their online activities for real money. Efforts such as these sometimes enhance a designer's and user's options for placemaking and collaboration.

At present, we can only speculate whether individuals will become more active in leisure-oriented placemaking in virtual places. But it seems safe to assume that online placemaking will play an increasingly significant role in various domains of people's lives in the coming years, providing them with unique opportunities to establish place attachments to virtual places.[100] The decisions people make as part of this type of placemaking will also influence their sense of well-being, in addition to having implications for whether they and others believe they're living a good life.

As with other communication platforms, constructing places in virtual worlds can potentially generate meaningful collective memories for the participants. So, too, similar to other media technologies, memories are likely to be disproportionately shaped by the contributors who are more privileged and powerful.[101] Thus, in the virtual world, some users, and the groups to which they belong, will be able to assert more control over different aspects of the placemaking process. Ideally, though, individuals who get involved in building or placemaking in these virtual worlds will be encouraged to embrace the ethical principle of inclusive collaboration.

Work

As we move deeper into the twenty-first century, our rapidly changing workplaces represent some of the more exciting and critical sites for formal and informal displays of placemaking. Professionals in fields related to design and architecture are ideally suited to help enrich the places where we work. Although these professionals typically refer to their contribution as a form of "design," they essentially do various sorts of placemaking. Professionals from other fields also advocate for and work to create more inviting, healthy, safe, and productive places by collaborating with each other within and across disciplines as well as with diverse clients.

The COVID-19 pandemic altered work routines for many of us temporarily, and in some cases permanently, but millions continue to spend half or more of their waking hours doing work in some type of built environment away from home. The buildings vary in size, configuration, technological sophistication, cleanliness, safety, natural accents, as well as other design features. Our workplaces include white-collar office facilities, blue-collar factories and warehouses, restaurants, small shops, and numerous other physical structures. Although these structures are similar because they all have walls, a floor, a roof, doors, furniture, and often windows, too, their diverse design characteristics produce different embodied experiences and action settings for those who work there. The symbolism and rituals that give meaning to the work-related activities that occur inside the structure also vary widely. Let's not overlook that work happens in other types of places, such as agricultural fields, that do not have typical physical structures associated with them. Critical decisions with placemaking implications are made in these action settings as well.

For over a century, researchers and consultants from numerous fields have explored how built environments for white-collar and blue-collar jobs affect our physical and emotional well-being, productivity, creativity, level of collaboration, and more. Although we may personally recognize many of these place effects, we are sometimes unaware of how elements of a building's structure and design influence us. When our place consciousness is more refined and active, we increase our chances of noticing these effects.

In *Cubed: A Secret History of the Workplace,* author and advocate for working people Nikil Saval constructs a fascinating social history of workplaces, primarily those that have housed knowledge workers since the mid-1800s.[102] While highlighting the evolving cultural landscape, Saval reveals how prominent designers and engineers introduced and promoted a range of workplace innovations that for a period of time shaped office space arrangements and the work-based social life that materialized. Frederick Winslow Taylor, a notable American mechanical engineer, was one of the earliest and most consequential advocates of new workplace designs and practices to maximize efficiencies in the late 1800s and early 1900s. Taylor, and especially his influential disciple William Henry Leffingwell, who in 1917 published a noteworthy book, *Scientific Office Management*, adamantly pushed to have the office space for white-collar workers mirror factories' regimented production lines.[103] Long rows of neatly arranged desks situated in large open areas were commonplace in white-collar office spaces in the first half of the twentieth century.

One of the insightful threads to Saval's historical analysis of workplaces is his description of the competing cultural images that emerged to define the different place-based physical realities and work culture of manual labor and office work. White-collar work came to be seen as having more prestige despite accusations that non-manual work was emasculating. In addition to the basic divide characterizing blue-collar and white-collar places, there was an important historical evolution of office design. The intimate spaces of the countinghouses common in the mid-1800s where a few clerks and the business owner worked side by side in the same small room gave way to distinctly different arrangements where numerous clerks were packed into large impersonal spaces while their managers were separated into their own private offices. Saval captures the unpleasant and rigid experience of the typical office clerk in this new factory-like setting:

> Men with stopwatches record the motions of his pencil, his filing habits, when and whether he goes to the bathroom, how long he lingers at the watercooler, how many minutes he wastes. The viscous silence of the old office is sliced through with the high-pitched metal clack of the typewriter, the adding machine, the sliding and slamming of file cabinets. He clocks in and out; shrill bells ring in his workday and push him out squinting into the early evening darkness, shoved and jostled by the black-coated thousands following him, out of his office, in an endless, dark stream.[104]

Saval's description reminds us that our sense of place is affected by all of our senses, including the soundscape that may often go unnoticed, especially once we grow accustomed to it.

Since those early days, we have experienced various movements that have produced additional changes in workplace settings. In the late 1950s, Quickborner, a German consulting firm, introduced the world to the concept of Bürolandschaft (or "office landscape"), which envisioned a more humane way to organize office space. Like Taylor's design, this model adopts an open floor plan, but it also encourages a more natural approach that incorporates plants and screens that appeal to individuals and work teams. The workspace physically arranges employees into groups based on their communication needs and their relations to colleagues. Managers are even integrated into the open plan and away from private offices. This post–World War II design philosophy includes principles consistent with a world that was aspiring to be more egalitarian, inclusive, and collaborative. The progressive design was a response to the rigid hierarchies that had previously ruled the workplace for decades.

In the 1960s, the inventor Robert Propst introduced the white-collar world to his "Action Office," a flexible furniture system designed to encourage a worker's physical and mental health, privacy, mobility, and flexibility in doing their work. Unlike the open plan, the Action Office and its successor Action Office II were designed to give workers more freedom in shaping their ideal workspace and to provide them a degree of privacy from peer and managerial surveillance. Propst's primary emphasis was on the individual rather than the work team per se. However, his ideas, much to his dismay, ultimately were adapted to create the rigid cubicle design that was more constraining than anything Propst had imagined. In time, the cubicle came to be satirized in pop culture; it symbolized the office worker's boredom, insecurity, and oppression. Saval describes the detrimental effects of the cubical as

> putting people close enough to each other to create serious social annoyances, but dividing them so that they didn't actually feel that they were working together. It had all the hazards of privacy and sociability but the benefits of neither. It got so bad that nobody wanted them taken away; even those three walls offered some kind of psychological home, a place one could call one's own.[105]

More broadly, the cubical design bolstered the patriarchal culture that perpetuated gendered inequities in the office workplace via lower pay, restricted opportunities, and sexual harassment. Eventually, and perhaps nudged on by a stew of social forces that emerged from women's physical propinquity in the workplace, women began to develop a loosely defined type of ideational we-ness. They experienced themselves as disadvantaged, white-collar female workers. The classic 1980 movie *9 to 5*, starring Lily Tomlin, Dolly Parton, and Jane Fonda as three clerical workers demanding and extracting better treatment, helped to reinforce this shared collective identity. It inspired women to be more supportive of one another as they challenged the gendered status quo of the office workplace. Much of this was done informally because the 1980s and subsequent decades brought a reduction in union membership and fewer worker-initiated collective efforts to improve the workplace.[106]

Beginning in the 1980s, we also saw an uptick in the number of dot-com and tech companies experimenting with flatter management hierarchies. Some of the bigger companies started to introduce a wide array of workplace amenities like gyms, daycare facilities, health clinics, restaurants, and more. Designers were challenged to create "hip" environments for the workplaces of the new economy, most notably the companies in Silicon Valley. The "office of the future" was expected to extend the open plan in new ways by fostering informal, creative collaboration and spontaneous interactions between workers from different ranks and specialties. Big tech companies like Apple, Google, and Facebook are several of the better known and most extravagant examples of contemporary campus-like worksites that support a futuristic work ecology. These workplaces provide employees with a more holistic experience by offering them diverse options to express and integrate their professional and personal identities while in a shared work environment. The sites are also designed to strengthen workers' sense of ideational we-ness and commitment to the company brand while creating conditions that can enhance dyadic and spontaneous forms of we-ness.[107]

Thus, a modified version of the 1950s German-origin Bürolandschaft approach remains relevant today in our digitally enhanced work world where flexibility and collaboration are increasingly vital. Gartner, the tech research and consulting firm, even referenced Bürolandschaft in its 2016 report, "Top 10 Emerging Technologies Driving the Digital Workplace,"[108] even though it is not what we typically think of as a technology. In today's rapidly evolving high-tech workplace, a key challenge is finding design arrangements that enable employees to work effectively with one another while seamlessly connecting onsite and during remote exchanges. As iterations of the digital workplace emerge, they will incorporate augmented and VR technologies into office workplaces in new ways, further expanding our perception of what workplaces represent and how we must learn to adapt to use them effectively. These technologies will create new ways for workers to develop and navigate all forms of we-ness.

Most recently, in 2022, Andy Lantz, creative director and partner at RIOS, an award-winning international and transdisciplinary design firm committed to social, environmental, and spatial justice, identified what he believed to be the five major trends affecting workplace settings. These trends capture key themes tied to future placemaking initiatives that target the workplace. Lantz highlights the need for workplace designers to consider the best ways to integrate new technology into the workplace to help people navigate between their work responsibilities at a worksite and in non-work places; "capture the voices" of employees to enhance "authenticity"; celebrate diverse workstyles to ensure workers are empowered to contribute irrespective of their work preferences; be sensitive to wellness concerns and help workers feel comfortable by including natural features like interior gardens and landscapes; and, most importantly, enable individuals to feel a sense of belonging and community at work.[109] The last trend is distinctly relevant to the concerns expressed throughout this book about using places to cultivate we-ness. So, while nurturing personal well-being is important, strategies that enhance communal well-being and teamwork, productively linking the "me" to the "we," are highly valued as well.

These trends emphasize strategies that maximize how workplace technologies can help workers cultivate their personal and professional well-being. In addition to technologies, we can consider the impact of architectural design. The International WELL Building Institute (IWBI), founded in 2013, has emerged as a major voice in drawing our attention to how the built environment that provides the foundation for our work activities influences our health and well-being, for better or worse. IWBI champions an evidenced-based approach that is designed to measure, certify, and monitor various building features that affect our health and well-being. Armed with the catchy slogan of supporting "people-first places," IWBI has developed a WELL rating equity measure to assess the quality of an organization's design. The approach focuses on seven areas including air, water, nourishment, light, fitness, comfort, and mind.[110] Leaders who strive to enhance key building attributes like these can improve employees' work experience.

Similar to the other four social domains previously discussed, there are professionals who specialize in designing and redesigning workplaces to make them more people-friendly and to promote creativity, cooperation, and physical/emotional well-ness. The Cornell University International Workplace Studies Program (IWSP), founded in 1989, is one of many organizations that has emerged in recent decades to study and consult on different workplace strategies.[111] IWSP and other organizations recognize workplaces as a sort of "complex ecosystem" embedded in a physical and social setting.

In general, contemporary design professionals who devote themselves to helping organizations improve the quality of their work areas are increasingly exploring options to include workers' feedback on shaping features of the work setting. Called either "participatory design" or "co-design," this strategy directly embraces the principles of autonomy and inclusive collaboration by seeking input from workers and encouraging them to feel as though they have a hand in structuring their work environment. Although few research studies have systematically explored the extent to which a participatory design is responsible for workers' improved well-being, preliminary and anecdotal evidence suggest that it matters. What we do know for sure is that design makes a difference; what's less clear is how much it matters to individuals that they work in a setting where they are empowered to shape features of the built environment that represents their workplace.

One type of placemaking that can benefit from a co-design strategy involves implementing workplace accommodations for persons with disabilities. Roughly 25 percent of American adults have some type of disability, and many of these individuals work outside the home or would be willing to do so if they were adequately accommodated.[112] One study finds that roughly one-third of non-working people with a disability who applied for vocational rehabilitation services and were living in Mississippi, New Jersey, or Ohio, reported that they would be more likely to be employed if they were provided with accommodations.[113] Nonworkers cited concerns about an inaccessible workplace or lack of transportation as major impediments. Thus, it is critical to make the workplace accessible and appealing to individuals irrespective of their physical, mental, or emotional status. This objective is consistent with various ethical principles, most notably beneficence, autonomy, social and environmental justice, and inclusive collaboration.

The United Nations frames the intersection of the workplace and disabilities as a social justice and human rights issue. According to the UN interpretation, the source of the problems people with disabilities encounter at work comes from outside the individuals themselves. In other words, the difficulties stem from institutional failures to address adequately the differences in ability that exist within the human population. While leaders in the field of disability studies label this approach the "social model" of disability, the United Nations Convention on the Rights of Persons with Disabilities of 2006 (CRPD), and some disabilities scholars like Theresia Degener, expand this view by supplementing it with a "human rights model" of disability.[114]

In the United States, the impetus to focus more forcefully on workplace issues was reinforced by the passing of the Americans with Disabilities Act (ADA) in 1990, a piece of legislation that honors the human rights philosophy. While there is considerable debate about how much progress has been made in making workplaces more accommodating for persons with disabilities over the past thirty-five years, numerous researchers and advocates have addressed the issue. For example, in an extensive 2017 review article published in *Disability and Rehabilitation*, the authors closely examined a subset of 117 articles published from 1990 to 2016 that focus on workplace accommodation issues involving persons with physical disabilities.[115] The authors identify twelve separate categories of workplace accommodations, lumping these into three broad groups, including accommodations that address physical barriers and enhance workplace and workstation accessibility, increase workplace flexibility and worker autonomy, and promote opportunities to include and integrate a person with a disability. To varying degrees, all the accommodations the authors delineate can have implications for the built environments and action settings associated with work. Of particular interest, though, are their observations about the "built environment." Practical kinds of accommodations can come in many forms, including "ramps, railings, and automatic doors, changes to floor surfaces, fitting doors with ramp handles as opposed to levers or knobs, implementing Braille signage, and equipping elevators with voice-activated controls."[116] Assistive technology devices will also need to be adapted to future workplaces. For example, it may be necessary to designate a separate office space for users to maximize this accommodation if the quality of voice recognition software is compromised by the noise generated by an open floor plan. Employers can also hire accommodation consultants to provide guidance on what types of architectural accommodations may be needed in a specific workplace.

Ultimately, the workplace accommodations that are introduced and the manner by which this happens, should be guided by an inclusive approach that cultivates coworkers' sense of ideational we-ness. Ethically grounded placemaking that discourages the marginalization of persons with disabilities is more likely to emerge when employers embrace the *MEAL* life skills, especially empathy and a style of leadership that accentuates a "power with" rather than a "power over" approach.

Most of the recent research on workplace design, which we can loosely frame as having placemaking implications, targets white-collar workplaces. But a loosely defined and life-enhancing form of placemaking also occurs in blue-collar industries. Manual laborers must navigate their physical surroundings that often include health risks, such as exposure to dangerous machinery and hazardous materials. While many of these places include standard factory and warehouse sites, others consist of a potential mix of built and natural environments like those involving oil rigs, fishing boats, mines, agricultural areas, and forests.

Blue-collar workers sometimes work in the same setting for years, but many manual laborers move from place to place because their job requires them to be mobile (hazardous waste cleanup crews) or their work opportunities are seasonal (agricultural pickers). Although we tend to think of white-collar workers as developing stronger attachments to the places where they work, blue-collar workers can also form strong attachments to workplaces, especially ones that include long tenures and shared risk-taking. For example, miners, especially men, have historically forged complicated types of attachments to the dangerous and harsh mines that provide them an opportunity to be traditional breadwinners. Doing risky work side by side with a familiar crew in a mine, on an oil rig, or at a construction site, can solidify workers' intense feelings about a place and their attachment to it. Repeatedly sharing blue-collar rituals and routines in an action setting can become part of the calculus by which workers perceive their workplace. Moreover, the friendships that emerge from sharing difficult and risky experiences in foreboding places can breed a sense of we-ness and deepen workers' attachment to the action setting.

While employers incrementally responded throughout the 1900s to union demands and were forced to display a bit more concern for blue-collar workers' safety, it was Richard Nixon's signing of the Occupational Safety and Health Act (OSHA) in 1970 that officially put employers on notice that they needed to step up and make worksites safer.[117] Overall, worksites associated with blue-collar work have become safer. Data from the US Bureau of Labor Statistics indicate that the incidence rates (per 100 full-time workers) of nonfatal occupational injuries and illnesses in private industry decreased steadily from 10.9 in 1972 to 2.8 in 2018.[118] Work-related fatalities have also decreased since 1992, although at least 30 percent of fatalities actually occur on the street or highway separate from a workplace situated inside a building.[119] While it is impossible to determine how much employers' contributions to enhancing worksite safety altered these statistics, it seems reasonable to assume that there's been some effect. Still, many employers are not as vigilant as they should be in monitoring workplaces as is documented by OSHA, which annually releases the ten most frequently cited standards.[120]

Fortunately, employers, managers, and employees committed to safety can turn to the National Institute for Occupational Safety and

Health (NIOSH), which offers a wealth of information, guidance, and evaluation materials to improve workplace safety. NIOSH's program mission is to help "employees, unions, and employers recognize and control health hazards in their workplace."[121] This organization, and others with similar objectives, underscore the point made in Chapter 4 that responsible initiatives are increasingly promoting safety protocols for blue-collar workplaces.

Some safety measures require employers to make decisions that alter or reinforce aspects of the physical landscape or built environment, including the equipment essential to the job. But safety measures also involve the social processes that help to create and reinforce a core company value that promotes a culture of safety. Thus, a critical goal for employers should be to get employees to develop a sense of we-ness as coworkers so they will be better positioned to hold each other accountable to follow safety protocols. Creating a company culture that normalizes and rewards peer-supported safety precautions is ideal. In addition, progressive placemaking initiatives should frame safety issues more broadly by improving the company culture so as to confront and ideally eliminate instances of sexual harassment and bullying.

One unconventional but vital workplace where employers need to become more mindful, empathic, and responsive to the needs of their workers is large scale agriculture. Most employers in this industry need to do more to see and treat their workers with the dignity and respect they deserve. This issue is most relevant to the expanding portions of the country that are being subjected to distinctly warmer climates. In the United States, foreign-born agricultural workers – who make up about 75 percent of the one million or more hired crop workers – are at particularly high risk because only about half are authorized to work in the country. Thus, the owners of the places where these marginalized workers pick fruits, nuts, and vegetables or engage in other farm-related tasks have little financial incentive to alter work conditions.

Research studies are mounting that document the adverse effects of heat events on the physical and mental well-being of field workers. According to a Centers for Disease Control report, crop workers are twenty times more likely to die from illnesses associated with heat stress than the civilian worker population.[122] One research team writing in the journal *Environmental Research Letters* paints a grim picture of the conditions affecting these workers' health status. They "may be subject to hazardous working conditions, harmful living conditions, non-livable wages, and unfair labor management, with power structures and other structural vulnerabilities preventing workers from exerting control over workplace safety and health practices." Thus, we can frame these workers' complex circumstances by noting that "Their elevated risk derives both from the nature of the work – outdoors and with high physical demands – and from compounding vulnerabilities such as poverty, migrant status, language barriers, and barriers to acceptable health care."[123]

Unfortunately, the climatic conditions these workers face are predicted to only get worse. Whereas the average picker today deals with twenty-one days per year in which the daily heat index exceeds workplace safety standards, estimates based on the impending effects of climate change project that the same worker will experience thirty-nine such days by 2050 and sixty-two unhealthy days in 2100.[124] Although it's beyond a company's ability to reduce the heat index directly, employers can implement various onsite strategies to help mitigate the unhealthy effects. They can, for example, supply more breathable clothing. Many field workers already wear protective clothing and personal protective equipment (PPE) to minimize their exposure to harmful chemical agents. If advances are not made to make PPE both breathable and protective, the workers will be forced to choose between subjecting themselves to intense heat or chemical exposure. Other adaptive measures that encourage more breaks, slower-paced work, or opportunities to spend break time in air-conditioned facilities may prove to be effective, but they can be costly or impractical, and some will also reduce overall productivity. However, if the employers in charge of these workplaces embrace the ethical principles laid out in this book, they will introduce interventions and educational practices that support a healthier balance between their profit motive and workers' rights and safety.[125] For example, they might consider positioning mobile air-conditioned trailers near field workers for use during their breaks. Ideally, employers will work collaboratively with the agricultural workers to find practical ways to alter these essential outdoor workplaces to make them less risky.

Whether we focus on workplace ideas related to Bürolandschaft, holistic approaches, "people-first places," participatory design, accommodations that enhance accessibility, or adaptations to workplaces that lack the stereotypical built environment, we can deepen our appreciation for the value of ethical placemaking initiatives. We can do so by attending to the *MEAL* life skills and *CART* processes. If stakeholders invested in enhancing workplace conditions heighten their place consciousness, they will be better equipped to understand how place processes related to claims, attachments, rituals, and transitions affect people's perceptions of and experiences in their workplace settings. Our placemaking efforts can be consequential when we empathetically address workplace characteristics and how they affect workers' experiences related to their well-being, identity, and productivity.

In sum, a keener place consciousness can help stakeholders frame an understanding of place across social domains and facilitate effective collaborations. Thus, how we express place consciousness can affect our capacity to contribute to ethical placemaking initiatives that benefit us personally and enrich the social landscape. Clearly, our well-being is connected to how we experience places, so we must cultivate every opportunity we can to improve their quality.

Epilogue: A Placemaking Roadmap for the Future

Photo 10: View of Earth (clouds above the African continent) as seen by the Apollo 17 crew traveling toward the moon, published March 2, 2021. (Unsplash/NASA)

One of my main objectives has been to present an expansive roadmap to illustrate how our embodied social existence is fundamentally place-based. This roadmap assumes that we cannot socially exist outside of place and that places are diverse, complex, and dynamic. The countless places on earth play an essential role in how we see ourselves and how we live. At the extremes, our perception of our blue marble earth can shape our collective biosphere consciousness, while our experiences with the smallest, most intimate places where we sleep, eat, and express our feelings for each other can mold our personal sense of self. The logical extension to this sort of thinking is that we must improve the places that serve as our action settings if we are to enhance our personal well-being and social conditions. To engage in fruitful placemaking in those places, we need to understand how they operate, why they matter to us, and how various stakeholders affect them. We must also commit to work by ourselves and with others to learn how to use our institutional and interpersonal resources to engage in constructive placemaking.

CART Processes

Our starting point for this journey is to appreciate the four basic *CART* social processes that accentuate place as an action setting. If we are to cultivate strategies to make the various places that are meaningful to us more appealing and life-enhancing, we need to consider the web of place claims, attachments, rituals, and transitions that influence how we socially assign meaning to places and navigate them.

Recall that we illustrated in the final chapter the challenge of navigating this web of place processes by profiling community development issues related to the Porters neighborhood in Gainesville. Researchers used the Participatory Neighborhood Narrative approach to help the residents counter the disparaging community narrative that had been constructed by local officials. In response, the residents produced a more appealing story highlighting their shared community spirit and sense of ideational we-ness. We can view the series of exchanges that led to this outcome as integral

Model 3: *CART* social processes

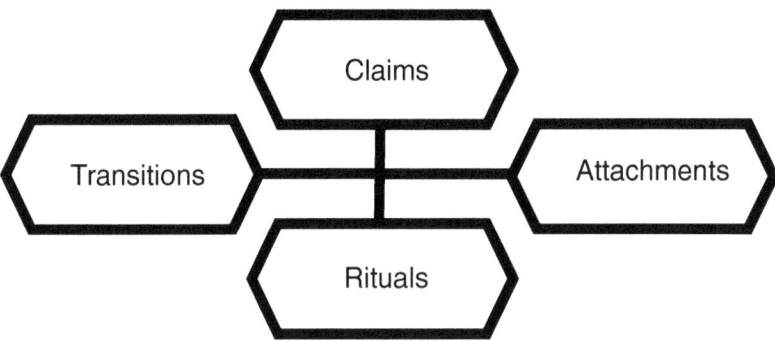

aspects of an ongoing claiming process involving diverse stakeholders. As the residents collaboratively reengaged with their community in new ways, they clarified their personal and group claims to their neighborhood while deepening their attachments to it. These efforts also strengthened an intergenerational community sentiment that older residents shared with neighborhood children in the form of a children's book. Additionally, the PNN approach fostered community rituals that heightened awareness of the consequential place transitions the community had previously encountered and would need to negotiate with city planners moving forward.

The PNN project reveals the value of ethically oriented planners securing local groups' input to design places they find appealing. Thus, much can be gained by providing local placemaking groups the opportunity to leverage their sense of we-ness to generate powerful collective memories. Such memories strengthen place attachments and remind people of their role in orchestrating positive transitional moments connected to place.

Social Domains

Throughout this book I've challenged us to deepen our place consciousness to enhance our own lives. In addition, I've stressed how we have promising options to participate in more collaborative forms of placemaking across all five social domains. Ultimately, making places better usually involves thoughtful and collaborative placemaking. Our efforts to build a sense of group belonging and we-ness with others is intimately connected to how we try to make places better. Other than the limited number of places that we have direct and total control over, by definition we must typically work with others to forge a cooperative form of placemaking:

- Primary groups
- Community and community groups
- Thought communities
- Leisure/sports
- Work

We can appreciate our options for collaborative placemaking more fully when we understand how our attachments to specific places are influenced by our experiences in the five social domains listed above. If we are to engage in thoughtful placemaking, we need to be attentive to the values, norms, and practical realities that guide our experiences in these social domains, especially how we experience a sense of we-ness in them. Thus, the quality of placemaking can often be enhanced when placemakers study how people perceive and navigate their life experiences in connection with these broad social domains and the related places that matter to them.

Types of Places

Placemaking has to occur somewhere; thus, we need to think beyond the generic *CART* processes and social domains. We must develop a multilayered and deep understanding of how the *CART* processes are relevant to the different types of places that are potentially implicated in our placemaking initiatives. The action settings highlighted throughout the book represent an eclectic, though by no means exhaustive, collection of places that bring us together in various social settings. These settings are connected to the previously noted social domains as well. I've encouraged us to imagine how we experience ten broadly defined places:

- Nature
- Communities and beyond
- Sites for exchanging goods and services
- Key landmarks and ceremonial settings
- Transport vehicles and hubs
- Home, dwelling, and everyday life
- Public space
- Institutions
- Leisure spots
- Metaverse

Apart from the metaverse, most of us can easily tap into our personal memories to reconstruct images of our experiences in each of these places. In many instances, these places also contribute to the types of collective memories we develop and share with others who have a vested interest in them. Building healthy placed-based collective memories can intensify our sense of ideational and deep dyadic we-ness. When we feel a sense of we-ness with whomever is present or implicated by a place, we typically find it easier to engage in effective placemaking with them. If, on the other hand, our exchanges involve persons we define as not being part of our in-group, it will be more challenging to engage in collaborative placemaking with them, though not impossible. Consequently, finding ways to bridge the divides between people is vital. If we cultivate healthy forms of we-ness between persons from seemingly disparate groups, we increase our chances of seeding constructive forms of placemaking that appeal to a wider subset of people. However, ties that reinforce group belonging can also motivate stakeholders who harbor conflicting claims about how a place should be managed. When this happens, enhanced forms of we-ness can solidify people's convictions about alternative placemaking objectives.

Place Properties

Our placemaking efforts are likely to be most effective if we have a nuanced understanding of the place of interest to us. This notion highlights the value of considering how the meaningful properties or attributes of a place define it and influence how people relate to it:

- Physical conditions
- Symbolic meaning
- Shared power
- Institutional and cultural traditions
- Gendered attributes
- Organic/digital
- Social structural
- Public/private
- Level of stability
- Discourses

The examples presented throughout the book illustrate that how we experience a place is rooted in the way we orient ourselves to the many properties that distinguish one place from another, and how we interpret our encounters with the people involved with each setting. Taking the time to process how various properties affect us can refine the way we construct and use mental maps to make sense of and navigate various places.[1] We must learn to identify and evaluate the forces that have shaped our mental maps, and the maps of those who share a similar cultural and social background.

Ethical Principles

As noted, effective placemaking must focus on the *CART* processes, social domains, types of places, and place properties relevant to a project. But placemaking also typically involves various stakeholders who have vested interests in the places that matter to them and opinions about the changes that are being considered. Accordingly, since placemaking involves change and change requires that value-laden decisions be made, ideal placemaking demands that placemakers attend to ethical concerns.

Constructive placemaking is often the byproduct of cooperative partners sharing a strong sense of we-ness. However, even without a robust sense of we-ness, individuals can still do worthwhile placemaking if they embrace the ideal that placemaking should be guided by the five ethical principles (*BASIN*) I've emphasized throughout:

- Beneficence
- Autonomy
- Social and environmental justice
- Inclusive collaboration
- Nonmaleficence

Placemaking that adheres to these principles can and should be incorporated into all five social domains – primary groups, community and community groups, thought communities, leisure and sport, and work. When we honor these principles, we set the stage to motivate people to invest their emotional, psychological, physical, and financial resources into making places more enriching. Overall, principled placemaking can advance our personal well-being, community development, and social and environmental justice.

MEAL Life Skills

We will be primed to adopt the five ethical principles and engage in effective placemaking if we also apply the *MEAL* life skills of mindfulness, empathy, altruism, and leadership. Using the *MEAL* approach compels us to take stock of our own perspective while listening to and incorporating others' experiences with a place into our decision-making. As I've discussed at length elsewhere, our attempts to pursue healthy expressions of we-ness require us to be mindful and purposive in our relations with others.[2] Ideally, we must adopt a deliberative approach to constructing a sense of "me," one that embraces a biosphere consciousness while appreciating an ecological perspective. It positions us to play a critical role in helping to cultivate a spirit of interdependence that leads to healthy displays of we-ness. Similarly, if we deepen our personal place consciousness – that self-awareness that allows us to accentuate how aspects of place in our everyday lives shape how we think, feel, and

Model 4: *MEAL* life skills

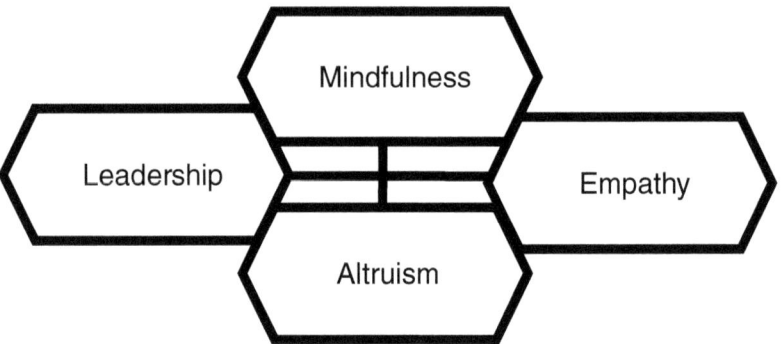

act – we will strengthen our ability to contribute to collective and effective forms of ethical placemaking. We are more apt to develop a mindful approach if we sharpen our sensitivity to our surroundings by acknowledging our personal umwelt – our individualized perceptual field that allows us to process the sights, sounds, smells, tastes, and tactile sensations that make up the places we navigate. In addition, our mindfulness is also deepened when we tap into how our embodied sense of self, or our proprioception, affects the way we process our action settings.

Embodied Self and the Built Environment

We can enhance our embodied experience of place by continuing to develop our understanding of how the architectural properties of our built environment affect us, individually and collectively. Research is mounting that clarifies how the architectural structures we build influence how we think, feel, and act.[3] As our knowledge grows, we increase our chances to design physical environments that enrich our spirits and enhance our lives. Now, we have the means to design action settings that improve our well-being and social life in the places where we engage in activities connected to family, community, religious and political activities, leisure, and work. Part of the challenge is to convince professionals in the building and urban planning fields that they need to deepen their own place consciousness while strengthening their commitment to design strategies that privilege people's sensory needs. The new architectural training should prioritize designing places that enhance people's opportunities to experience healthy forms of we-ness. Whenever possible, designers should stress an inclusive approach, one that secures feedback from those who are or will be directly affected by a built environment.

Part of the placemaking process focuses on the shapes of buildings, the arrangements of the built structures, and the material aspects of the built environment that influence how we process different types of sensory stimuli we encounter. The other feature involves how design can alter the circumstances by which we socially navigate various spaces and places. Do we, for example, have ample opportunities to have spontaneous, fruitful encounters in public and work settings? Are we in built work environments that maximize our desire and ability to collaborate? Unfortunately, the economic interests of builders are often in conflict with what would best serve people's sensory and social needs. In addition to designing structures that empower us, designers need to create environments where we casually greet each other in safe places and grow more comfortable with our surroundings.

Cultural Forces and the Self

Realizing how our physical sense of self is socially affected by cultural norms requires that we understand how cultural forces influence how we see ourselves and navigate different places. Because cultures are always evolving, our vision of what place represents is likely to change over time as well. The changes will be spurred on by a wide range of technological developments that challenge conventional wisdom about what constitutes a physically bounded, yet socially constructed place. As the virtual and augmented realities of the metaverse or Reality+ are incrementally refined in the future, we will incorporate these technologies into all domains of the social landscape. As a result, future generations will need to expand their understanding of placemaking to accommodate a broader interpretation of place that accounts for virtual worlds. Many of us will immerse ourselves in virtual places that we or others create. Our experiences there will be consequential for us and others. In addition, it is a good bet that more and more of us will spend an increasing proportion of the day immersed in these digitally constructed realities. Thus, we must push ourselves to better understand how we develop healthy and unhealthy attachments to virtual places while experiencing the other three processes (rituals, transitions, claims) in these contexts as well.

In addition to considering the virtual worlds that will increasingly touch our lives, we must also reflect on the wide array of current and emerging digital technologies that enable us to navigate places in the physical world. These technologies afford us ever-expanding chances to experience place as a performative process. All the properties of place outlined in this book, including the extent to which we experience transitional features of place as part of a digitally mediated performance, can shape how we express our personal and collective identities. In addition, the sentiments we embrace in action settings that are digitally mediated will have implications for the way we experience dyadic and ideational forms of we-ness. As our daily rhythms are permeated more and more with time spent managing communication technologies that connect people to each other and to places, we will need to understand how these technologies affect us personally and impact our communities. We must explore creative practices that harness these technologies to cultivate our personal well-being and contribute to the greater good.

The Future of Place and Placemaking

Looking forward, new technologies and other cultural developments will shape how we think, feel, and act in our action settings. Historically, advances in diverse technologies, especially those directly related to transportation, communication, and construction, have repeatedly altered our relationship to places. Some technologies enabled us to reach places not yet discovered, others gave us new ways to have embodied experiences with the places we did frequent, and some permitted us to create built environments that transformed how we spend time in all five social domains. Of particular interest is how future technologies will create new opportunities for us to process information about the places we wish to visit and those we experience physically firsthand or virtually. Just like the innovation of night vision goggles in the 1930s transformed how German soldiers experienced the nighttime battlefield,[4] the everyday person of the future may have the option of being armed with all sorts of external and physically implanted nanodevices that will enhance their limited human senses and umwelt. One national survey in 2016 found that 32 percent of Americans would want an implanted brain chip if it could significantly improve their ability to concentrate and process information.[5] That figure is likely to increase once the process is normalized by family, friends, neighbors, and colleagues sharing encouraging stories.

When we and our descendants are immersed in places in the near and distant future, we will be able to see, hear, feel, touch, and smell our surroundings differently than our ancestors. Moreover, those advanced technologies will also enable us to share place-based experiences differently with others. Those of us old enough to remember life prior to cell phones are uniquely positioned to evaluate how our placed-based lives have changed in the new cell era. We should also be able to imagine how social realities intertwined with place will continue to expand the human experience as we encounter new technologies.

But we should be leery not to be overly optimistic that our new-age, digitally mediated relationships with places will successfully open up exciting new vistas for us to explore ourselves and others in diverse settings without generating adverse effects as well. We must consider how these new ways to experience places may sometimes sabotage the interpersonal chemistry and "magic" of our embodied, shared humanity. Just as social media has been singled out for propagating negative mental health conditions, our emerging interpersonal experiences with places mediated by high tech modalities may produce unwelcome personal and interpersonal consequences, some of which may be unforeseen at this moment in time.

In addition, our relationship to places will evolve in response to both anticipated and unanticipated normative changes to the cultural landscape. For example, as a growing majority of Americans become increasingly open-minded about how they perceive and treat others, persons who are stigmatized today may learn to feel more comfortable in places that had previously been perceived to be unwelcoming. Unfortunately, the path that leads to that wider acceptance is still cluttered with impediments, including the increasingly vocal bigots who recently feel more empowered to display their hate toward marginalized groups of people. Yet, an ever-growing majority of people espouse social justice for persons of color, members of the LGBTQ+ community, persons with disabilities, and religious minorities. Consequently, there is reason to hope that more and more Americans will eventually, in their personal and professional lives, loosely adopt the Damanhurians' cooperative spirit and respect for place. If they do, they will practice a style of placemaking aligned with the five ethical principles (*BASIN*) promoted in this book. We are in desperate need of a future led by mindful, empathetic, and altruistic people who are more place conscious and committed to ethical placemaking. That form of placemaking is most likely to thrive when it is anchored to arrangements supportive of collaborative leadership. Such a future can produce remarkable, welcoming places that enrich personal lives, celebrate the communal spirit, and create places that foster social and environmental justice.

Our long-term future, as is typically the case with any civilization, is rooted in the ideas and actions of younger generations who will eventually shape it. In *Fight: How Gen Z Is Channeling Their Fear and Passion to Save America*, John Della Volpe, the director of polling at the Harvard Kennedy School Institute of Politics, makes a convincing case that the Gen Z cohort is currently a powerful force committed to altering our social, cultural, political, and environmental landscape.[6] Although "place" is not central to how Volpe frames his observations, he alludes to how young people's activism will affect some of the places that matter to us, such as planet earth, schools, and neighborhood streets.

Younger generations may indeed rally the rest of us to "save America," but the older generations must step up or step aside.

Most notably, older generations who manage the key social institutions in the United States and other democratic nations are best positioned to reshape the social infrastructure that can facilitate and nurture young people's leadership and activism. Professionals in fields like urban planning, geography, sociology, architecture, and others are especially well suited to help young people develop their place consciousness and understanding of how the *CART* processes associated with place affect their everyday lives and communities of all types and sizes. Helping young people "see" more clearly how place properties affect them individually and collectively within their groups of significance can be empowering. So, too, cultivating young people's *MEAL* life skills will encourage them to be thoughtful and compassionate when contributing to ethical placemaking.

We must support young people developing a deeper appreciation for the ecology of place-based relations while fostering their opportunities to play an active role in all kinds of placemaking activities. Older adults in positions of power need to ensure that young people have a meaningful seat at the decision-making tables related to community development, schools, churches, and other organizations when placemaking initiatives are debated and implemented. Stakeholders, young and old, have much to gain by establishing productive intergenerational partnerships that embrace the spirit of ethical, collaborative placemaking. Ultimately, our world will be in better hands when we more effectively nurture young people's place consciousness and ability to engage in constructive placemaking for themselves and others.

Notes

Introduction

1 Thomas R. Hoschschild, Jr., "'Our Club': Place-Work and the Negotiation of Collective Belongingness," *Journal of Contemporary Ethnography* 36, no. 6 (2010): 619–45.
2 Allan R. Pred, "Place as Historically Contingent Process: Structuration and the Time-Geography of Becoming Places," *Annals of the Association of American Geographers* 74, no. 2 (March 1984): 279–97.
3 Yi-Fu Tuan, *Space and Place: The Perspective of Experience* (Minneapolis: University of Minnesota Press, 1977), 177.
4 Tuan, *Space and Place*, 6.
5 Edward Relph, *Place and Placelessness* (London: Pion, 1976; repr. 2008), preface.
6 Wilfred M. McClay, "Why Place Matters," in *Why Place Matters: Geography, Identity, and Civic Life in Modern America*, ed. Wilfred M. McClay and Ted V. McAllister (New York: New Atlantis Books, 2014), 4–5.
7 Mark A. Wyckoff, "Definition of Placemaking: Four Different Types," MSU Land Policy Institute, 2014, https://www.canr.msu.edu/uploads/375/65814/4typesplacemaking_pzn_wyckoff_january2014.pdf.
8 Mathew Carmona, Steven Tiesdell, Tim Heath, and Taner Oc, *Public Places – Urban Spaces: The Dimensions of Urban Design* (London: Routledge, 2010).
9 Sarah Williams Goldhagen, *Welcome to Your World: How the Built Environment Shapes Our Lives* (New York: Harper, 2017), 17.
10 Goldhagen, *Welcome to Your World*, 275.
11 Thomas F. Gieryn, *Truth Spots: How Places Make People Believe* (Chicago: University of Chicago Press, 2018), 3.
12 Gieryn, *Truth Spots*, 18–19.
13 Tom L. Beauchamp and James F. Childress, *Principles of Biomedical Ethics*, 6th ed. (New York: Oxford University Press, 2009); Stephen C. Taylor, "Health Care Ethics," Internet Encyclopedia of Philosophy, https://www.iep.utm.edu/h-c-ethi/#SH2d; "Principles of Good Practice," Community Development Society, accessed November 18, 2022, https://cdsociety.org/about/#aboutprinciples;

"Towards Shared International Standards for Community Development Practice," International Association for Community Development, https://www.iacdglobal.org/wp-content/uploads/2018/06/IACD-Standards-Guidance-May-2018_Web.pdf.
14. Edward Relph, "Spirit of Place and Sense of Place in Virtual Realities," *Techné* 10, no. 3 (Spring 2007): 19.
15. Jenny Odell, *How to Do Nothing: Resisting the Attention Economy* (Brooklyn: Melville House, 2019).
16. Odell, *How to Do Nothing*, 180.
17. Goldhagen, *Welcome to Your World*, 196.
18. bell hooks, *Belonging: A Culture of Place* (New York: Routledge, 2009).
19. K.L. Wolf, S. Krueger, and K. Flora, "Place Attachment and Meaning – A Literature Review," *Green Cities: Good Health*, College of the Environment, University of Washington, 2014, www.greenhealth.washington.edu.
20. Tara Westover, *Educated: A Memoir* (New York: Random House, 2018), 327.
21. Jay Reeves, "Move to Rename 'Bloody Sunday' Bridge Has Critics in Selma," *Associated Press*, July 3, 2020, https://apnews.com/article/us-news-ap-top-news-selma-racial-injustice-john-lewis-08b23b2f805c0d73e6dfc82b1e01e1f9; Todd Prater, "Attempt to Change Edmund Pettus Bridge Name Fails in State Session," *Selma Sun*, April 22, 2022, https://selmasun.com/news/attempt-to-change-edmund-pettus-bridge-name-fails-in-state-session/article_2400ae16-bcd0-11ec-bb22-27d4dcb1723b.html.
22. "The Question of Palestine," United Nations, accessed January 5, 2024, https://www.un.org/unispal/history/.
23. Janet Donohoe, *Remembering Places: A Phenomenological Study of the Relationship between Memory and Place* (Lanham, MD: Lexington Books, 2014).
24. Donohoe, *Remembering Places*, xiv.
25. Noa Gedi and Yigal Elam, "Collective Memory – What Is It?" *History and Memory* 8, no. 1 (1996): 30–50.
26. Maurice Halbwachs, *On Collective Memory* (Chicago: University of Chicago Press, 1992).
27. Eviatar Zerubavel, *Time Maps: Collective Memory and the Social Shape of the Past* (Chicago: University of Chicago Press, 2003).
28. hooks, *Belonging*, 63.
29. hooks, *Belonging*, 71.
30. Jeff Malpas, *Place and Experience: A Philosophical Topography*, 2nd ed. (New York: Routledge, 2018), 13.
31. David Seamon, *Life Takes Place: Phenomenology, Lifeworlds, and Place Making* (New York: Routledge, 2018), 190.
32. William Marsiglio, *Chasing We-ness: Cultivating Empathy and Leadership in a Polarized World* (Toronto: University of Toronto Press, 2023).
33. William Marsiglio, Kevin Roy, and Greer Litton Fox, "Situated Fathering: A Spatially Sensitive and Social Approach," in *Situated Fathering: A Focus on Physical and Social Spaces*, ed. William Marsiglio, Kevin Roy, and Greer Fox (Lanham, MD: Rowman & Littlefield), 3–26.
34. I considered incorporating outer space into my typology, but decided to focus primarily on earthly settings. I briefly refer in Chapter 2 to how space-oriented transport technologies and hubs are creating new ways of thinking about our experience with place beyond earth. For some reflections on how wealthy space barons are defining place away from earth, see Mary-Jane Rubenstein, *Astrotopia: The Dangerous Religion of the Corporate Space Race* (Chicago: University of Chicago Press, 2022).

35 Lynne C. Manzo, "For Better or Worse: Exploring Multiple Dimensions of Place Meaning," *Journal of Environmental Psychology* 25, no. 1 (2005): 67–86.
36 Christian Picciolini, *Breaking Hate: Confronting the New Culture of Extremism* (New York: Hachette Books, 2019).
37 Maria Lewicka, "Place Attachment: How Far Have We Come in the Last 40 Years?" *Journal of Environmental Psychology* 31, no. 3 (2011): 207–30.
38 Claudia F. Nisa, Jocelyn J. Bélanger, and Birga M. Schumpe, "On Solid Ground: Secure Attachment Promotes Place Attachment," *Journal of Environmental Psychology* 70 (2020): 101463.
39 Goldhagen, *Welcome to Your World*, 270.

1. Framing Properties

1 Russell Stover, "Memoir," *Twenty-Niner Newsletter*, 29th Division Association, in *D-Day: As They Saw It*, ed. Jon E. Lewis (New York: Carroll and Graf, 2004), 104–5, cited in Tom Matthews, "D-Day: First Hand Accounts," Historic Newspapers, updated November 20, 2020, https://www.historic-newspapers.com/blog/d-day-first-hand-accounts/.
2 D-Day, Omaha Beach, June 6, 1944, Vol. 1, Shawn/Michael Productions, May 31, 2014, YouTube video, 59:08, https://www.youtube.com/watch?v=12fV2Qul7jI; D-Day, Omaha Beach, June 6, 1944, Vol. 2, Shawn/Michael Productions, September 25, 2014, YouTube video, 1:03:20, https://www.youtube.com/watch?v=TobitDsyEEQ.
3 Jeff Malpas, *Place and Experience: A Philosophical Topography*, 2nd ed. (New York: Routledge, 2018), 12.
4 Mark Johnson, *The Body in the Mind: The Bodily Basis of Meaning, Imagination, and Reason* (Chicago: University of Chicago Press, 1987), xxxviii.
5 Jakob von Uexküll, *Umwelt und Innenwelt de Tiere* (Berlin: J. Springer, 1909).
6 Ed Yong, *An Immense World: How Animal Senses Reveal the Hidden Realms around Us* (New York: Random House, 2022), 6.
7 Yong, *An Immense World*, 8.
8 Janet Donohoe, *Remembering Places: A Phenomenological Study of the Relationship between Memory and Place* (Lanham, MD: Lexington Books, 2014), 22.
9 The energies we put into building the personal attributes that facilitate a healthy sense of we-ness need not, and often should not, be expressed nonstop in the company of someone else. We ultimately build productive forms of we-ness by maximizing both together time as well as solitary time.
10 Liz Osborun, "Snowiest Cities in United States," Current Results: Weather and Science Facts, accessed February 5, 2023, https://www.currentresults.com/Weather-Extremes/US/snowiest-cities.php.
11 Liz Baker, "Buffalo's Snowbound Residents Turn to a Facebook Group for Help from Their Neighbors," NPR, December 29, 2022, https://www.npr.org/2022/12/29/1145882657/buffalos-snowbound-residents-turn-to-a-facebook-group-for-help-from-their-neighb.
12 Eric Klinenberg, *Heat Wave: A Social Autopsy of Disaster in Chicago* (Chicago: University of Chicago Press, 1995).
13 Taylor Dotson, *Technically Together: Reconstructing Community in a Networked World* (Cambridge, MA: MIT Press, 2017).
14 Ray Oldenburg, *The Great Good Place: Cafés, Coffee Shops, Bookstores, Bars, Hair Salons, and Other Hangouts at the Heart of a Community* (New York: Marlowe, 1999), 16.

15 Sonia Narang, "Mexicans and Americans Bond over a Giant Baby and a Border Wall," The World, September 15, 2017, https://theworld.org/stories/2017-09-15/mexicans-and-americans-bond-over-giant-baby-and-his-border-wall.
16 "Paper & Glue," MSNBC, video, 1:34:00, 2021, https://www.nbc.com/paper-glue/video/paper-glue/8000005142.
17 David J. Chalmers, *Reality+: Virtual Worlds and the Problems of Philosophy* (New York: Norton, 2022).
18 Germaine R. Halegoua, *The Digital City: Media and the Social Production of Place* (New York: New York University Press, 2019), 17.
19 Kate W. Read, "Queering the Brothel: Identity Construction and Performance in Carson City, Nevada," *Sexualities* 16, no. 3/4 (2013): 467–86.
20 Coral Murphy Marcos, "'The Beaches Belong to the People': Inside Puerto Rico's Anti-gentrification Protests," *The Guardian*, July 23, 2022, https://www.theguardian.com/us-news/2022/jul/23/puerto-rico-beach-anti-gentrification-protests.
21 Mariah Espada, "Influencers, Developers, Crypto Currency Tycoons: How Puerto Ricans Are Fighting Back against the Outsiders Using the Island as a Tax Haven," *Time*, April 19, 2021, https://time.com/5955629/puerto-rico-tax-haven-opposition/.
22 Bad Bunny, "El Apagón – Aquí Vive Gente (Official Video) | Un Verano Sin Ti," September 16, 2022, YouTube video, 22:53, https://www.youtube.com/watch?v=1TCX_Aqzoo4.
23 Bad Bunny, "El Apagón."
24 Leslie Kern, *Feminist City* (Toronto: Between the Lines, 2019), 13.
25 Aarian Marshall, "The Pink Transit Tax: Women Spend More Than Men to Get Around NYC," *Wired*, November 12, 2018, https://www.wired.com/story/nyc-public-transportation-pink-tax-gender-gap/.
26 Daphne Spain, *Gendered Spaces* (Chapel Hill: University of North Carolina Press, 1992).
27 Spain, *Gendered Spaces*, 5.
28 Naomi Klein, *How to Change Everything: The Young Human's Guide to Protecting the Planet and Each Other* (New York: Atheneum, 2021).
29 Carl Zimmer, "The Lost History of One of the World's Strangest Science Experiments," *New York Times*, March 29, 2021, https://www.nytimes.com/2019/03/29/sunday-review/biosphere-2-climate-change.html.
30 Mark Nelson, "Biosphere 2's Lessons about Living on Earth and in Space," *Space, Science & Technology* 2021 (January 2021): 1–11, 2.
31 Mark Nelson, *Pushing Our Limits: Insights from Biosphere 2* (Tucson: University of Arizona Press, 2018), ix.
32 Nelson, *Pushing Our Limits*, xiv.
33 Lyle Therese A. Hilotin-Lee, "Child Abuse Background and History," FindLaw, May 25, 2023, https://www.findlaw.com/family/child-abuse/child-abuse-background-and-history.html; James Garbarino, "The Price of Privacy in the Social Dynamics of Child Abuse," *Child Welfare* 56, no. 9 (1977): 565–75.

2. Types of Places

1 Saylee Padwal, "90 Day Fiancé: Armando & Kenneth's Relationship Timeline," Screenrant, May 25, 2021, https://screenrant.com/90-day-fiance-armando-rubio-kenneth-relationship-timeline/.
2 Robert Mcfarlane, *Underland: A Deep Time Journey* (New York: Norton, 2019).

3 For an account of the Australian Aboriginal people's experience with colonialization and environmental justice issues, see David Schlosberg, Lauren Rickards, and Jason Byrne, "Environmental Justice and Attachment to Place: Australian Cases," in *The Routledge Handbook of Environmental Justice*, ed. Ryan Holifield, Jayajit Chakraborty, and Gordon Walker (London: Routledge, 2018), 591–602.
4 Richard Fisher, "The Unseen 'Slow Violence' That Affects Millions," BBC, January 31, 2021, https://www.bbc.com/future/article/20210127-the-invisible-impact-of-slow-violence.
5 Kangjae Jerry Lee, Mariela Fernandez, David Scott, and Myron Floyd, "Slow Violence in Public Parks in the US: Can We Escape Our Troubling Past?" *Social & Cultural Geography* 24, no. 7 (2023): 1185–1202.
6 Xiao Xiao, KangJae Jerry Lee, and Lincoln R. Larson, "Who Visits US National Parks (and Who Doesn't)? A National Study of Perceived Constraints and Vacation Preferences across Diverse Populations," *Journal of Leisure Research* 53, no. 3 (2022): 404–25.
7 Jonathan Haidt, *The Anxious Generation: How the Great Rewiring of Childhood Is Causing an Epidemic of Mental Illness* (New York: Penguin, 2024).
8 "Our Story," GROW HUB, accessed January 13, 2023, https://www.grow-hub.org/our-story/.
9 "The 'Troubled Teen' Industry," National Youth Rights Association, accessed March 7, 2022, https://www.youthrights.org/issues/medical-autonomy/the-troubled-teen-industry/; Sulome Anderson, "When Wilderness Boot Camps Take Tough Love Too Far," *The Atlantic*, August 12, 2014, https://www.theatlantic.com/health/archive/2014/08/when-wilderness-boot-camps-take-tough-love-too-far/375582/#.
10 Jenny Odell, *How to Do Nothing: Resisting the Attention Economy* (Brooklyn: Melville House, 2019), 122.
11 Odell, *How to Do Nothing*, 122.
12 Jeremy Rifkin, *The Empathic Civilization. The Race to Global Consciousness in a World in Crisis* (Cambridge: Polity, 2009).
13 Peter Somerville, "Homelessness and the Meaning of Home: Rooflessness or Rootlessness?" *International Journal of Urban and Regional Research* 16, no. 4 (1992): 529–39; see also Sophie Watson and Helen Austerberry, *Housing and Homelessness: A Feminist Perspective* (London: Routledge and Kegan Paul, 1986).
14 Joshua J. Mark, "Native American Concept of Land Ownership," World History Encyclopedia, October 17, 2023, https://www.worldhistory.org/article/2296/native-american-concept-of-land-ownership/.
15 John Brinckerhoff Jackson, *A Sense of Place, a Sense of Time* (New Haven, CT: Yale University Press, 1994).
16 Jackson, *A Sense of Place*, 67.
17 Feona Attwood, "Inside Out: Men on the 'Home Front,'" *Journal of Consumer Culture* 5, no. 1 (2005): 97.
18 Sarah Pink, *Home Truths: Gender, Domestic Objects and Everyday Life* (Oxford: Berg, 2004), 41; see also Andrew Gorman-Murray, "Materiality, Masculinity and the Home: Men and Interior Design," in *Masculinities and Place*, ed. Andrew Gorman Murray and Peter Hopkins (London: Routledge, 2014), 209–26.
19 Stephen Vider, *The Queerness of Home: Gender, Sexuality, and the Politics of Domesticity after World War II* (Chicago: University of Chicago Press, 2021).
20 Anna Moore, "Fatal Truth: How the Suicide of Alex Reid Exposed the Hidden Death Toll of Domestic Violence," *The Guardian*, March 24, 2021, https://www.theguardian.com/society/2021/mar/24/fatal-truth-how-the-suicide-of-alex-reid-exposed-the-hidden-death-toll-of-domestic-violence.

21 Brandon Andrew Robinson, "Conditional Families and Lesbian, Gay, Bisexual, Transgender, and Queer Youth Homelessness: Gender, Sexuality, Family Instability, and Rejection," *Journal of Marriage and Family* 80, no. 2 (2018): 383–96.
22 Andrew Ross, *Sunbelt Blues: The Failure of American Housing* (New York: Metropolitan Books, 2021).
23 For several exceptions see Brian Taylor, "Unconsciousness and Society: The Sociology of Sleep," *International Journal of Politics, Culture and Society* 6, no. 3 (1993): 463–71; Simon J. Williams, "Sleep and Health: Sociological Reflections on the Dormant Society," *Health: An Interdisciplinary Journal for the Social Study of Health, Illness and Medicine* 6, no. 2 (2002): 173–200; Matthew J. Wolf-Meyer, *The Slumbering Masses: Sleep, Medicine, and Modern American Life* (Minneapolis: University of Minnesota Press, 2016).
24 Robinson, "Conditional Families."
25 Tasha R. Rennels and David F. Purnell, "Accomplishing Place in Public Space: Autoethnographic Accounts of Homelessness," *Journal of Contemporary Ethnography* 46, no. 4 (2017): 490–513.
26 Andrea Elliott, *Invisible Child: Poverty, Survival, and Hope in an American City* (New York: Random House, 2022).
27 Celebration Charter Exhibit "C" Rules, April 13, 2022, https://celebration.fl.us/wp-content/uploads/Celebration-Charter-Exhibit-C-Rules-March-2020-updated-13-Apr-2022.pdf.
28 *The Bubble: A Documentary Film about Celebration, Florida,* directed by Philip B. Swift, video, 59:00, 2013, https://www.amazon.com/gp/video/detail/B00EPQRB7U/ref=atv_dp_share_cu_r.
29 Evan V. Symon, "6 Bizarre Realities of Life in a Town Owned by Disney," *Cracked*, January 21, 2017, https://www.cracked.com/personal-experiences-2442-so-perfect-its-creepy-i-live-in-city-designed-by-disney.html.
30 See Jackson, *A Sense of Place,* for an alternative interpretation of the role trailers played in shaping the culture of rural communities and the lives of occupants in New Mexico after World War II.
31 Sonya Salamon and Katherine MacTavish, *Singlewide: Chasing the American Dream in a Rural Trailer Park* (Ithaca, NY: Cornell University Press, 2017), 195.
32 "About FIC," Foundation for Intentional Community, accessed October 9, 2022, https://www.ic.org/foundation-for-intentional-community//; for an assortment of related definitions and a description of the origins of the label, see "What Is an Intentional Community? – 30th Birthday, Day 13," Foundation for Intentional Community, November 13, 2017, https://www.ic.org/what-is-an-intentional-community-30th-birthday-day-13/.
33 Bianca Heyming, "Intentional Communities – 50% Less Hippie Than You'd Expect," TEDx, July 19, 2017, YouTube video, 15:01, https://www.youtube.com/watch?v=EusOgAAlFG0.
34 Russell Flannery, "What Happened to America's Communes?" *Forbes*, April 11, 2021, https://www.forbes.com/sites/russellflannery/2021/04/11/what-happened-to-americas-communes/?sh=359102b5c577.
35 Liz Walker, *EcoVillage at Ithaca: Pioneering a Sustainable Culture* (Gabriola Island, BC: New Society Publishers, 2005); "About Us," Living Tree Alliance: The Kibbutz Reimagined, accessed October 2022, https://livingtreealliance.com/about/.
36 Rebekka Diestelkamp and Michaela Christ, "Making a Difference – Place-making and Negotiating Change: A Study of an Intentional Community in Northern Germany," *GAIA* 31, no. 1 (2022): 29–35.

37 Leslie Kern, *Feminist City* (Toronto: Between the Lines, 2019), 149.
38 Kern, *Feminist City*, 148.
39 Kern, *Feminist City*, 149.
40 Danny Zimny-Schmitt, "Things I Learned Traveling to Every County in America," Medium, November 10, 2023, https://medium.com/@dannyz3143/things-i-learned-traveling-to-every-county-in-america-49f3c87c43a6.
41 Extra Miler Club, https://extramilerclub.com/.
42 Kathryn Edin, H. Luke Shaefer, and Timothy J. Nelson, *The Injustice of Place: Uncovering the Legacy of Poverty in America* (New York: Mariner, 2023), 145.
43 For a timely and incisive analysis of the long historical conditions that ground the most recent iteration of our culture wars, see James Davison Hunter, *Democracy and Solidarity: On the Cultural Roots of America's Political Crisis* (New Haven: Yale University Press, 2024).
44 Mark A. Wyckoff, "Definition of Placemaking: Four Different Types," Michigan State University Land Policy Institute, accessed February 28, 2022, https://www.canr.msu.edu/uploads/375/65824/4typesplacemaking_pzn_wyckoff_january2014.pdf.
45 "William H. Whyte," Project for Public Spaces, January 3, 2010, https://www.pps.org/article/wwhyte.
46 "Placemaking: What If We Built Our Cities around Places?" Project for Public Spaces, 2018, https://uploads-ssl.webflow.com/5810e16fbe876cec6bcbd86e/5b71f88ec6f4726edfe3857d_2018%20placemaking%20booklet.pdf.
47 Thejas Jagannath, "Five of the Best Placemaking Initiatives in the US," Smart Cities Dive, accessed September 18, 2022, https://www.smartcitiesdive.com/ex/sustainablecitiescollective/five-best-placemaking-initiatives-us/991756/.
48 Quincy T. Mills, *Cutting along the Color Line: Black Barbers and Barber Shops in America* (Philadelphia: University of Pennsylvania Press, 2013); Antonio M. Johnson, *You Next: Reflections in Black Barbershops* (Chicago: Lawrence Hill Books, 2020).
49 Frédéric Laloux, *Reinventing Organizations: A Guide to Creating Organizations Inspired by the Next Stage of Human Consciousness* (Brussels: Nelson Parker, 2014).
50 Amna Nawaz and Frank Carlson, "Exonerated but Not Supported, the Wrongfully Convicted Struggle to Heal Their 'Wounds,'" PBS NewsHour, November 19, 2021, https://www.pbs.org/newshour/show/exonerated-but-not-supported-the-wrongfully-convicted-struggle-to-heal-their-wounds.
51 Danielle Kaeble and Lauren Glaze, "Correctional Populations in the United States, 2015" (US Department of Justice, Office of Justice Programs, Bureau of Justice Statistics, 2016).
52 John Irwin, *The Warehouse Prison: Disposal of the New Dangerous Class* (Los Angeles: Roxbury Publishing, 2005).
53 Irwin, *The Warehouse Prison*, 58.
54 Irwin, *The Warehouse Prison*, 59.
55 Irwin, *The Warehouse Prison*, 80.
56 Kaeble and Glaze, "Correctional Populations."
57 G. Caleb Alexander, Matthew Tajanlangit, James Heyward, et al., "Use and Content of Primary Care Office-Based vs Telemedicine Care Visits during the COVID-19 Pandemic in the US," *JAMA Network Open* 3, no. 10 (2020): e2021476.
58 Kechi Iheduru-Anderson, "Reflections on the Lived Experience of Working with Limited Personal Protective Equipment during the COVID-19 Crisis," *Nursing Inquiry* 28, no. 1 (January 2020): e12382.

59 Sophie Hennekam, Jamie Ladge, and Yuliya Shymko, "From Zero to Hero: An Exploratory Study Examining Sudden Hero Status among Nonphysician Health Care Workers during the COVID-19 Pandemic," *Journal of Applied Psychology* 105, no. 10 (2020): 1088–100.

60 Marion Callahan, "What Does School Look like during COVID? Traffic Patterns, No Lockers and 'Big Mask Voices,'" *Bucks County Courier Times*, October 22, 2020.

61 "1969: The Stonewall Uprising," LGBTQIA+ Studies: A Resource Guide, Library of Congress Research Guides, accessed March 8, 2022, https://guides.loc.gov/lgbtq-studies/stonewall-era#:~:text=June%2028%2C%201969%20marks%20the,which%20stretched%20over%20six%20days.

62 Eviatar Zerubavel, *Time Maps: Collective Memory and the Social Shape of the Past* (Chicago: University of Chicago Press, 2003).

63 National Network: Information, Guidance, and Training on the Americans with Disability Act, "What Is the Americans with Disabilities Act (ADA)?" accessed September 18, 2022, https://www.ada.gov/topics/intro-to-ada/.

64 Hanna Rosin, "The Overprotected Kid," *The Atlantic*, April 15, 2014, https://www.theatlantic.com/magazine/archive/2014/04/hey-parents-leave-those-kids-alone/358631/; "The Land: An Adventure Play Documentary," New Day Films, 2015, video, 24:00, https://www.newday.com/film/land.

65 Mark Matousek, "Ex-Carnival, Royal Caribbean, and Norwegian Cruise Line Workers Reveal What It's Really Like to Live at Sea," *Business Insider*, February 7, 2020, https://www.businessinsider.com/cruise-ship-workers-reveal-what-life-is-like-sea-2019-4.

66 "Falling in Love at Sea: Dating on a Cruise Ship," *Life of Iris* (blog), October 27, 2020, https://lifeofiris.com/2020/10/27/dating-on-a-cruise-ship/.

67 Wikipedia, s.v. "Private Spaceflight," accessed June 26, 2024, https://en.wikipedia.org/wiki/Private_spaceflight.

68 *Space Perspective*, accessed June 23, 2024, https://www.spaceperspective.com/.

69 "Space Perspective Co-founder Jane Poynter on Space Tourism: There's a Huge Market Here," FoxBusiness, April 9, 2024, video, 4:13, https://www.foxbusiness.com/video/6350572532112.

70 Jackie Wattles, "Jeff Bezos and Richard Branson Went to Space. What's Next?" CNN Business, July 21, 2021, https://www.cnn.com/2021/07/21/tech/jeff-bezos-richard-branson-space-what-next-scn/index.html.

71 The 2011 novel *Ready Player One*, by Ernest Cline, is another popular book that is often connected with the dystopian themes associated with a world that supports a metaverse.

72 Casey Newton, "Mark in the Metaverse: Facebook's CEO on Why the Social Network Is Becoming 'A Metaverse Company,'" *The Verge*, July 22, 2021, https://www.theverge.com/22588022/mark-zuckerberg-facebook-ceo-metaverse-interview.

73 Gene Park, "Epic Games Believes the Internet Is Broken. This Is Their Blueprint to Fix It," *Washington Post*, September 28, 2021, https://www.washingtonpost.com/video-games/2021/09/28/epic-fortnite-metaverse-facebook/.

74 Andrew Webster, "Tim Sweeney Explains How the Metaverse Might Actually Work," The Verge, May 23, 2023, https://www.theverge.com/2023/3/23/23652928/tim-sweeney-interview-epic-games-fortnite-metaverse.

75 Mrwhosetheboss, "The Metaverse Could Be a Problem," November 21, 2021, YouTube video, 18:12, https://www.youtube.com/watch?v=RgJwPco3wew.

76 Marques Brownlee, "Who Cares about the Metaverse?" October 28, 2022, YouTube video, 15:50, https://www.youtube.com/watch?v=CqkhjL3WvWQ.

77 Matthew Ball, *The Metaverse: And How It Will Revolutionize Everything* (New York: Liveright, 2022), 29.

78 Adi Robertson and Jay Peters, "What Is the Metaverse, and Do I Have to Care?" The Verge, October 4, 2021, https://www.theverge.com/22701104/metaverse-explained-fortnite-roblox-facebook-horizon.
79 Robertson and Peters, "What Is the Metaverse?"
80 Webster, "Tim Sweeney."
81 *Second Life*, accessed July 24, 2022, https://secondlife.com/.
82 Edd Gent, "What Can the Metaverse Learn from Second Life? Creator Philip Rosedale Says a Virtual Reality Internet Is Still Some Way Off," IEEE Spectrum, January 26, 2024, https://spectrum.ieee.org/metaverse-second-life.
83 Ball, *The Metaverse*, 17. For economic projections of how significant the metaverse is likely to become, see "Metaverse Market Insights," Skyquest, June 2024, https://www.skyquestt.com/report/metaverse-market#:~:text=Metaverse%20Market%20size%20was%20valued,period%20(2024%2D2031). For a qualified assessment of how quickly the metaverse will grow, see Kellen Browning and Mike Isaac, "Apple Is Stepping into the Metaverse. Will Anyone Care?" *New York Times*, June 2, 2023, https://www.nytimes.com/2023/06/02/technology/apple-metaverse-vr.html.
84 Ball, *The Metaverse*.
85 Quokka Labs, "Exploring the Metaverse: Unveiling a New Era of Immersive Virtual Reality Experiences," *Medium*, December 20, 2023, https://medium.com/@quokkalabs135/exploring-the-metaverse-unveiling-a-new-era-of-immersive-virtual-reality-experiences-772676c90f55.
86 David John Chalmers, *Reality+: Virtual Worlds and the Problems of Philosophy* (New York: Norton, 2022), xvii; for a related discussion of how AI is relevant to the metaverse, see "David Chalmers: From the Matrix to the Metaverse (with a Little Help from AI)," The Institute for Futures Studies, Stockholm, May 2023, YouTube video, 48:12, https://www.youtube.com/watch?v=7s0SzcUnzZo.
87 William I. Thomas and Dorothy S. Thomas, *The Child in America: Behavior Problems and Programs* (New York: Knopf, 1928), 571–2.
88 David Chalmers, "What Should Be Considered a Crime in the Metaverse?" *Wired*, January 28, 2022, https://www.wired.com/story/crime-metaverse-virtual-reality/.
89 Matt Stieb, "Mark Zuckerberg's Metaverse Has a Groping Problem," *New York Magazine*, February 4, 2022, https://nymag.com/intelligencer/2022/02/mark-zuckerbergs-metaverse-has-a-groping-problem.html.
90 Luca Braghieri, Ro'ee Levy, and Alexey Makarin, "Social Media and Mental Health," SSRN, August 22, 2023, https://ssrn.com/abstract=3919760; Nicholas Kardaras, *Digital Madness: How Social Media Is Driving Our Mental Health Crisis – and How to Restore Our Sanity* (New York: St. Martin's, 2022); Nicholas Kardaras, *Glow Kids: How Screen Addiction Is Hijacking Our Kids – and How to Break the Trance* (New York: St. Martin's, 2016); Haidt, *The Anxious Generation*.

3. Attachments

1 "Remembering the Deadly 75-Foot Tidal Wave That Leveled Crescent City in 1964," *Active NorCal*, October 26, 2022, https://activenorcal.com/remembering-the-deadly-75-foot-tidal-wave-that-leveled-crescent-city-in-1964/.
2 Rebecca Solnit, *A Paradise Built in Hell: The Extraordinary Communities That Arise in Disaster* (New York: Penguin, 2009).
3 Melinda J. Milligan, "Interactional Past and Potential: The Social Construction of Place Attachment," *Symbolic Interaction* 21, no. 1 (1998): 1–33.
4 Leila Scannell and Robert Gifford, "Defining Place Attachment: A Tripartite Organizing Framework," *Journal of Environmental Psychology* 30, no. 1 (2010): 1–10.

5 Although Scannell and Gifford refer to these processes as "psychological," it seems more accurate to refer to them as "social psychological" because they are shaped by various social processes related to the way we create symbols that facilitate our meaning-making efforts.
6 Amelia Nierenberg, "Finding a New Home, and New Hope, after Leaving Ukraine," *New York Times*, October 25, 2022, https://www.nytimes.com/2022/09/29/neediest-cases/refugees-ukraine-war-new-york.html.
7 Scannell and Gifford, "Defining Place Attachment."
8 Andrés Di Masso et al., "Between Fixities and Flows: Navigating Place Attachments in an Increasingly Mobile World," *Journal of Environmental Psychology* 61 (2019): 126.
9 Lea Sebastien, "The Power of Place in Understanding Place Attachments and Meanings," *Geoforum* 108 (2020): 204–16.
10 Scannell and Gifford, "Defining Place Attachment," 6.
11 "Community Garden Statistics in 2024 (Latest US Data)," Garden Pals, January 15, 2024, https://gardenpals.com/community-garden/.
12 "Cities with the Largest Number of Community Gardens per 1,000 Residents in the United States in 2022," Statista, https://www.statista.com/statistics/1034254/number-of-community-gardens-per-10-000-residents-by-city-in-the-us/.
13 Sebastien, "The Power of Place," 208.
14 Paul Morgan, "Towards a Developmental Theory of Place Attachment," *Journal of Environmental Psychology* 30, no. 1 (2010): 11–22.
15 Morgan, "Towards a Developmental Theory," 12.
16 Abraham H. Maslov, *Motivation and Personality*, 2nd ed. (New York: Harper & Row, 1970).
17 David A. Snow and Leon Anderson, *Down on Their Luck: A Study of Homeless Street People* (Berkeley: University of California Press, 1993).

4. Rituals

1 Tawfiq Nasrallah, "Saudi Arabia: Muslims Can Virtually Touch Kaaba's Black Stone from Home," Gulf News, December 14, 2021, https://gulfnews.com/world/gulf/saudi/saudi-arabia-muslims-can-virtually-touch-kaabas-black-stone-from-home-1.84388660.
2 "Mina, the City of Tents," Arab News, July 19, 2021, https://www.arabnews.com/node/1896291/saudi-arabia.
3 Samy Magdy, "More Than 1,3000 People Died during Hajj, Many of Them after Walking in the Heat," Associated Press, June 23, 2024, https://apnews.com/article/hajj-heat-deaths-mecca-saudi-arabia-pilgrimage-9f97aae1032b14ada29bbea7108195d3.
4 Roy A. Rappaport, *Ritual and Religion in the Making of Humanity* (Cambridge: Cambridge University Press, 1999), 107.
5 Robert N. Bellah, "Durkheim and Ritual," in *The Robert Bellah Reader*, ed. Robert N. Bellah and Steven M. Tipton (Durham, NC: Duke University Press), 170.
6 Heiner Karst, "Routine versus Ritual. Why Does the Difference Matter?" Lets Talk Coaching, March 22, 2021, https://www.letstalkcoaching.com/8407/routine-versus-ritual-why-does-the-difference-matter.
7 Émile Durkheim, *The Elementary Forms of Religious Life: A Study in Religious Sociology* (New York: Free Press, 1995).
8 "The Journey to Thaipusam: The Piercing, the People and the Passion," *The Straits Times*, January 21, 2024, YouTube video, 32:46, https://www.youtube

.com/watch?v=RKZSPayJl_4; see also Dimitris Xygalatas, *Ritual: How Seemingly Senseless Acts Make Life Worth Living* (New York: Little, Brown Spark, 2022).
9 Xygalatas, *Ritual*.
10 Randall Collins, *Interactional Ritual Chains* (Princeton, NJ: Princeton University Press, 2005).
11 Bellah, "Durkheim and Ritual," 153.
12 Christena E. Nippert-Eng, *Home and Work: Negotiating Boundaries through Everyday Life* (Chicago: University of Chicago Press, 1996), 34.
13 David F. Purnell, *Building Communities through Food: Strengthening Communication, Families, and Social Capital* (Lanham, MD: Lexington Books, 2019), 94.
14 Nina Sevilla, "Food Apartheid: Racialized Access to Healthy Affordable Food," NRDC, April 2, 2021, https://www.nrdc.org/experts/nina-sevilla/food-apartheid-racialized-access-healthy-affordable-food.
15 Jennifer J. Esala, "How Far Would You Drive for Fresh Food? How Some Rural New Hampshire Residents Navigate a Dismal Food Landscape," Carsey Institute, University of New Hampshire, New England Issue Brief No. 25 (Winter 2011), https://scholars.unh.edu/cgi/viewcontent.cgi?article=1127&context=carsey.
16 "Starting a School Garden Program: Overview," Kids Gardening, accessed April 24, 2022, https://kidsgardening.org/resources/create-sustain-a-program-starting-a-school-garden-program-overview/; "School Gardens," Growing Minds Farm to School, accessed April 24, 2022, https://growing-minds.org/school-gardens/.
17 "Inn Transition," Junior League of Miami, accessed October 19, 2022, https://www.jlmiami.org/community/community-projects/inn-transition/.
18 James K. Wellman Jr., Katie E. Corcoran, and Kate Stockly-Meyerdirk, "'God Is like a Drug ...': Explaining Interaction Ritual Chains in American Megachurches," *Sociological Forum* 29, no. 3 (2014): 650–72; Warren Bird and Scott Thumma, "Megachurch 2020: The Changing Reality in America's Largest Churches," Hartford Institute for Religion Research, http://hirr.hartsem.edu/megachurch/2020_megachurch_report.pdf.
19 Bird and Thumma, "Megachurch 2020."
20 Wellman Jr., Corcoran, and Stockly-Meyerdirk, "'God Is like a Drug ...'"
21 Bird and Thumma, "Megachurch 2020."
22 Wellman Jr., Corcoran, and Stockly-Meyerdirk, "'God Is like a Drug ...,'" 662.
23 "1. Attending and Watching Religious Services in the Age of the Coronavirus," Pew Research Center, August 7, 2020, https://www.pewresearch.org/religion/2020/08/07/attending-and-watching-religious-services-in-the-age-of-the-coronavirus/.
24 Nick Galov, "22 Online Church Statistics for 2023, or the Digitization of the Sunday Morning Ritual," Web Tribunal, May 20, 2023, https://webtribunal.net/blog/online-church-statistics/#gref.
25 James Emery White, "The Most Overlooked Place to Plant a Church: Online," ChurchLeaders, November 17, 2021, https://churchleaders.com/pastors/410345-church-online.html.
26 "Civil War Reenactment Events 2023 – The Complete List," LivingHistoryArchive, accessed April 22, 2022, https://www.livinghistoryarchive.com/article/civil-war-events-in-america.
27 "Civil War Reenacting: The Civil War in Four Minutes," American Battlefield Trust, June 3, 2015, YouTube video, 4:23, https://www.youtube.com/watch?v=ZcKGlS7wVuk.
28 B. Brian Foster, *I Don't Like the Blues: Race, Place, and the Backbeat of Black Life* (Chapel Hill: University of North Carolina Press, 2020).

29 Foster, *I Don't Like the Blues*, 85.
30 Foster, *I Don't Like the Blues*, 83.
31 Kechi Iheduru-Anderson, "Reflections on the Lived Experience of Working with Limited Personal Protective Equipment during the COVID-19 Crisis," *Nursing Inquiry* 28, no. 1 (July 2021): e12382.
32 Vibhu Paudyal et al., "Provision of Clinical Pharmacy Services during the COVID-19 Pandemic: Experiences of Pharmacists from 16 European Countries," *Research in Social and Administrative Pharmacy* 17, no. 8 (2021): 1507–17.
33 Matthew Desmond, *On the Fireline: Living and Dying with Wildland Firefighters* (Chicago: University of Chicago Press, 2007).
34 Robert J. Ely and Debra E. Meyerson, "Unmasking Manly Men: The Organizational Reconstruction of Men's Identity," *Academy of Management Proceedings* no. 1 (2006).
35 Arnold van Gennep, *The Rites of Passage*, 2nd ed. (Chicago: University of Chicago Press, 2019).
36 "African American Rites of Passage Academy," Lane Community College, accessed May 20, 2022, https://www.lanecc.edu/community/education-community/rites-passage-summer-youth-academies/african-american-rites-passage.
37 Marnie W. Curry, "Will You Stand for Me? Authentic Cariño and Transformative Rites of Passage in an Urban High School," *American Educational Research Journal* 54, no. 4 (2016): 891.
38 Bellah, "Durkheim and Ritual," 164.
39 Rebecca Solnit, *A Paradise Built in Hell: The Extraordinary Communities That Arise in Disaster* (New York: Penguin, 2009), 166.
40 Solnit, *A Paradise Built in Hell*, 168.
41 Avery Anderson, "Exploring Mardi Gras' Legacy of Discrimination," *The Tulane Hullabaloo*, February 19, 2020, https://tulanehullabaloo.com/52135/arcade/mardi-gras-exploring-a-legacy-of-discrimination/.
42 Olivia Durand, "Mardi Gras Is a Critical American Tradition – Even without Parades," *Washington Post*, February 16, 2021, https://www.washingtonpost.com/outlook/2021/02/16/mardi-gras-is-critical-american-tradition-even-without-parades/.
43 George F. Reinecke, "The National and Cultural Groups of New Orleans," Folklife in Louisiana, accessed May 23, 2022, https://www.louisianafolklife.org/LT/Virtual_Books/Guide_to_State/NOGroups.html.
44 Grounds Krewe, accessed January 20, 2023, https://www.groundskrewe.org/home.
45 Solnit, *A Paradise Built in Hell*, 150.

5. Transitions

1 Sr. Maria Louise Edwards, "2020 Report of the Aguilas del Desierto," accessed April 28, 2022, https://static1.squarespace.com/static/5f88dc3421ff8240066b07c4/t/6075d1af8ff2d36a974b6f60/1618334131572/Aguilas+del+Desierto+Newsletter+-+EN.pdf; "Águilas," The New Yorker Documentary, April 14, 2021, YouTube video, 14:07, https://www.youtube.com/watch?v=a8Kduui1Lag.
2 Colibrí Center for Human Rights, accessed June 26, 2024, https://colibricenter.org/.
3 Carmen Valencia, "'My Brother Was a Fighter': One Man's Mission to Find Peace after His Family Died Crossing the Southern Border," Yahoo News, September 23, 2021, https://news.yahoo.com/my-brother-was-a-fighter-one

-mans-mission-to-find-peace-after-his-family-died-crossing-the-southern-border-191957742.html?guccounter=1.
4 Riordon Frost, *Are Americans Stuck in Place? Declining Residential Mobility in the US*, Joint Center for Housing Studies of Harvard University, May 2020, https://www.jchs.harvard.edu/sites/default/files/harvard_jchs_are_americans_stuck_in_place_frost_2020.pdf.
5 Andrés Di Masso et al., "Between Fixities and Flows: Navigating Place Attachments in an Increasingly Mobile World," *Journal of Environmental Psychology* 61 (2019): 125–33.
6 Arnold van Gennep, *The Rites of Passage*, 2nd ed. (Chicago: University of Chicago Press, 2019).
7 Van Gennep, *The Rites of Passage*, 192.
8 David A. Graham, "The Subway-Crime Death Spiral," *The Atlantic*, April 14, 2022, https://www.theatlantic.com/ideas/archive/2022/04/new-york-subway-shooting-transit-crime-death-spiral/629554/.
9 William I. Thomas and Dorothy S. Thomas, *The Child in America: Behavior Problems and Programs* (New York: Knopf, 1928), 571–2.
10 Jonathan English, "Why Public Transportation Works Better Outside the US," Bloomberg, October 10, 2018, https://www.bloomberg.com/news/articles/2018-10-10/why-public-transportation-works-better-outside-the-u-s; Rick Grahn, Stan Caldwell, and Chris Hendrickson, "Recommended Policies for the 21st Century Trends in US Mobility," Wilton E. Scott Institute for Energy Innovation, Carnegie Mellon University, Summer 2019, https://www.cmu.edu/traffic21/pdfs/21st-century-trends-in-us-mobility-smaller.pdf.
11 "Last to Leave: The Fall of Saigon," January 13, 2012, YouTube video, 18:19, https://www.youtube.com/watch?v=zuYaKVcYLyM.
12 Tara Westover, *Educated: A Memoir* (New York: Random House, 2018), 157.
13 "Recidivism of Prisoners Released in 34 States in 2012: A 5-Year Follow-Up Period (2012–2017)," Bureau of Justice Statistics, US Department of Justice, Office of Justice Programs, July 2021, https://bjs.ojp.gov/bjs_pub/rpr34s125yfup1217/Web%20content/508%20compliant%20PDFs/rpr34s125yfup1217_sum.pdf.
14 Elisa Borah and Brooke Fina, "Military Spouses Speak Up: A Qualitative Study of Military and Veteran Spouses' Perspectives," *Journal of Family Social Work* 20, no. 2 (2017): 144–61; Brenda Elliott, "US Military Spouses' Experiences Transitioning Abroad: A Narrative Analysis," *Nursing Forum* 55 (2020): 703–10.
15 Margaret C. Harrell et al., "Working around the Military: Challenges to Military Spouse Employment and Education," RAND National Defense Research Institute, 2004, https://apps.dtic.mil/sti/pdfs/ADA452563.pdf.
16 Rachel Treisman, "Nearly 100 Confederate Monuments Removed in 2020, Report Says; More Than 700 Remain," NPR, February 23, 2021, https://www.npr.org/2021/02/23/970610428/nearly-100-confederate-monuments-removed-in-2020-report-says-more-than-700-remai.
17 Germaine R. Halegoua, *The Digital City: Media and the Social Production of Place* (New York: New York University Press, 2019).
18 Wesley C. Hogan, *On the Freedom Side: How Five Decades of Youth Activists Have Remixed American History* (Chapel Hill: University of North Carolina Press, 2019).
19 Halegoua, *The Digital City*, 216.
20 Halegoua, *The Digital City*, 216.
21 William Marsiglio, *Stepdads: Stories of Love, Hope, and Repair* (Lanham, MD: Rowman & Littlefield, 2004).

6. Claims, Control, and Decision-Making

1. RFE/RL, "Inside Azovstal: The Ukrainian Metalworks That Has Become a 'Last Stand' Fortress," RadioFreeEurope, RadioLiberty, April 19, 2022, https://www.rferl.org/a/war-mariupol-azovstal-last-stand-ukraine-azov/31811117.html.
2. Anthony Faiola and David L. Stern, "Inside Mariupol's Besieged Steel Plant, a Symbol of Bravery and Terror," *Washington Post*, May 12, 2022, https://www.washingtonpost.com/world/2022/05/12/ukraine-mariupol-steel-plant-last-stand/.
3. Becky Sullivan and Joanna Kakissis, "How a Massive Steel Plant Became the Center of Ukraine's Resistance in Mariupol," NPR, May 5, 2022, https://www.npr.org/2022/05/05/1096880452/mariupol-steel-plant-ukraine-resistance.
4. Pjotr Sauer, Peter Beaumont, and Agencies, "Russian Army Takes Control of Mariupol's Azovstal Steel Plant," *The Guardian*, May 20, 2022, https://www.theguardian.com/world/2022/may/20/russian-army-takes-control-of-mariupols-azovstal-steel-plant.
5. "Why Boycott Wendy's," Boycott Wendy's!, accessed June 20, 2022, http://www.boycott-wendys.org/why-boycott-wendys; "Global Growth Vision," Wendy's, accessed June 20, 2022, https://www.wendys.com/global-growth-vision.
6. Sherry Turkle, *Alone Together: Why We Expect More from Technology and Less from Each Other*, 3rd ed. (New York: Basic Books, 2017).
7. Bayliss Fiddiman, Ashley Jeffrey, and Scott Sargrad, "Smart Investments for Safer Schools," Center for American Progress, December 19, 2018, https://www.americanprogress.org/article/smart-investments-safer-schools/.
8. Nader Issa and Sarah Karp, "As Cops Leave the Chicago Public Schools, a New Model of Resolving Conflicts Takes Shape," *Chicago Sun-Times*, June 16, 2022, https://chicago.suntimes.com/education/2022/6/16/23166422/school-resource-police-officer-sro-cops-cps-public-gage-park-high-school-hyde-park-farragut-curie.
9. Sarah Lindstrom Johnson et al., "Surveillance or Safekeeping? How School Security Officer and Camera Presence Influence Students' Perceptions of Safety, Equity, and Support," *Journal of Adolescent Health* 63, no. 6 (2018): 732–8.
10. Fiddiman, Jeffrey, and Sargrad, "Smart Investments."
11. Snejana Farberov, "Official at Virginia School Warned 6-Year-Old Boy Had Gun Hours before He Shot Teacher," *New York Post*, January 13, 2023, https://nypost.com/2023/01/13/school-official-knew-boy-had-gun-before-teachers-shooting/.
12. Julie Dermansky, "Outraged, New Coalition Emerges against Louisiana's Expanding – and Polluting – Petrochemical Industry," DeSmog, March 28, 2109, https://www.desmog.com/2019/03/28/cancer-coalition-against-death-alley-louisiana-expanding-petrochemical-industry/.
13. Arlie Russell Hochschild, *Strangers in Their Own Land: Anger and Mourning on the American Right* (New York: New Press, 2018).
14. Hochschild, *Strangers in Their Own Land*, 109.
15. Dermansky, "Outraged."
16. Karl F. Seidman, *Coming Home to New Orleans: Neighborhood Rebuilding after Katrina* (New York: Oxford University Press, 2013), 6.
17. Seidman, *Coming Home*, 264.
18. R.W. Kates et al., "Reconstruction of New Orleans after Hurricane Katrina: A Research Perspective," *PNAS* 103, no. 40 (2006): 14656; see also Margery Austin Turner, "Building Opportunity and Equity into the *New*

New Orleans: A Framework for Policy and Action," in *After Katrina: Rebuilding Opportunity and Equity into the New New Orleans* (Washington, DC: The Urban Institute, 2006), https://www.urban.org/sites/default/files/publication/51066/900930-Building-Opportunity-and-Equity-Into-the-New-New-Orleans.PDF; Amy Liu, "Building a Better New Orleans: A Review of and Plan for Progress One Year after Hurricane Katrina," The Brookings Institution Metropolitan Policy Program, https://www.brookings.edu/wp-content/uploads/2016/06/200608_katrinareview.pdf.

19 Nikesha Elise Williams, "Katrina Battered Black New Orleans. Then the Recovery Did It Again," *Washington Post*, August 28, 2020, https://www.washingtonpost.com/outlook/katrina-battered-black-new-orleans-then-the-recovery-did-it-again/2020/08/27/193d2420-e7eb-11ea-bc79-834454439a44_story.html; for an assessment of different areas of New Orleans as of 2021, see Kevin Ambrose, "New Orleans: Then and Now Photos, 16 Years after Katrina," *Washington Post*, August 28, 2021, https://www.washingtonpost.com/weather/2021/08/28/hurricane-katrina-orleans-rebuilt-photos/.

20 *Britannica*, s.v. "Mexican–American War: Invasion and War," updated May 7, 2024, https://www.britannica.com/event/Mexican-American-War/Invasion-and-war.

21 "Treaty of Guadalupe Hidalgo," History, updated September 21, 2022, https://www.history.com/topics/mexican-american-war/treaty-of-guadalupe-hidalgo.

22 "Immigration and Relocation in US History: Land Loss in Trying Times," Library of Congress, accessed June 21, 2022, https://www.loc.gov/classroom-materials/immigration/mexican/land-loss-in-trying-times/.

23 In addition to formal government actions, scores of Indigenous peoples also died because they contracted lethal diseases introduced by Europeans, thereby limiting tribal nations' ability to fight more effectively for their land.

24 "Homestead Act (1862)," National Archives, updated June 7, 2022, https://www.archives.gov/milestone-documents/homestead-act.

25 William Marsiglio, *Chasing We-ness: Cultivating Empathy and Leadership in a Polarized World* (Toronto: University of Toronto Press, 2023).

26 Wikipedia, s.v. "List of Indian Reservations in the United States," accessed December 11, 2021, https://en.wikipedia.org/wiki/List_of_Indian_reservations_in_the_United_States; Wikipedia, s.v. "Indian Reservation," accessed December 11, 2021, https://en.wikipedia.org/wiki/Indian_reservation; "Fact for Features: American Indian and Alaska Native Heritage Month: November 2014," United States Census Bureau, November 12, 2014, https://www.census.gov/newsroom/facts-for-features/2014/cb14-ff26.html.

27 "Nation to Nation: Treaties Between the United States and American Indian Nations," *American Indian* 15, no. 2 (Summer/Fall 2014), https://www.americanindianmagazine.org/story/nation-nation-treaties-between-united-states-and-american-indian-nations.

28 "Mary and Carrie Dann of the Western Shoshone Nation," Right Livelihood, accessed July 5, 2022, https://rightlivelihood.org/the-change-makers/find-a-laureate/mary-and-carrie-dann-of-the-western-shoshone-nation/.

29 "Bush Signs Western Shoshone Payout Bill into Law," Indianz, July 8, 2004, https://www.indianz.com/News/2004/003287.asp; Rebecca Solnit, *Storming the Gates of Paradise: Landscapes for Politics* (Berkeley: University of California Press, 2007).

30 Staff, "For the Western Shoshone Theft Is Theft, Even When by Congress," Indian Country Today, updated September 12, 2018, https://ictnews.org/archive/for-the-western-shoshone-theft-is-theft-even-when-by-congress.

31 Solnit, *Storming the Gates of Paradise*, 48–9.

32. Stephen M. Gavazzi and John N. Low, "Confronting the Wealth Transfer from Tribal Nations That Established Land-Grant Universities," *Beyond Town and Gown*, American Association of University Professors, Spring 2022, https://www.aaup.org/article/confronting-wealth-transfer-tribal-nations-established-land-grant-universities#.YreYSnbMJ9N; Margaret A. Nash, "Entangled Pasts: Land-Grant Colleges and American Indian Dispossession," *History of Education Quarterly* 59, no. 4 (2019): 437–67; Sharon Stein, "A Colonial History of the Higher Education Present: Rethinking Land-Grant Institutions through Processes of Accumulation and Relations of Conquest," *Critical Studies in Education* 61, no. 2 (2020): 212–28.
33. Robert Lee and Tristan Ahtone, "Land-Grab Universities: Expropriated Indigenous Land Is the Foundation of the Land-Grant University," *High Country News*, March 30, 2020, https://www.hcn.org/issues/52.4/indigenous-affairs-education-land-grab-universities.
34. Robert Lee, "Morrill Act of 1862 Indigenous Land Parcels Database," *High Country News*, March 2020; for a description of the project methods see https://www.landgrabu.org/lands.
35. Lee and Ahtone, "Land-Grab Universities."
36. "The US Land-Grant University System: Overview and Role in Agricultural Research," Congressional Research Service, August 9, 2022, https://sgp.fas.org/crs/misc/R45897.pdf.
37. Stephen M. Gavazzi and E. Gordon Gee, *Land-Grant Universities for the Future: Higher Education for the Public Good* (Baltimore: Johns Hopkins University Press, 2018).
38. Richard Rothstein, *The Color of Law: A Forgotten History of How Our Government Segregated America* (New York: Liveright, 2017).
39. Lee and Ahtone, "Land-Grab Universities."
40. Talia Boyd, "Native Perspectives: Land Ownership," Grand Canyon Trust, June 29, 2021, https://www.grandcanyontrust.org/blog/native-perspectives-land-ownership.
41. "Dawes Act (1887)," National Archives, updated February 8, 2022, https://www.archives.gov/milestone-documents/dawes-act.
42. "General Allotment Act, Dawes Act, and Relocation Program Termination Policy," February 26, 2013, YouTube video, 5:50, https://www.youtube.com/watch?v=ToUxjZegcF8; "The Dawes Act of 1887," July 5, 2013, YouTube video, 7:57, https://www.youtube.com/watch?v=eNX7CvOiuIw.
43. Theodore Roosevelt, "The Struggle for Self-Determination," Digital History, accessed June 25, 2022, https://www.digitalhistory.uh.edu/disp_textbook.cfm?smtID=3&psid=720.
44. Ruth Etiesit Samuel, "The Elevation of Caitlin Clark Highlights Sports Media's Misogynoir Problem," *Teen Vogue*, April 19, 2024, https://www.teenvogue.com/story/medias-elevation-of-caitlin-clark-highlights-womens-basketballs-misogynoir-problem.
45. Justin McCarthy, "Record-High 70% in US Support Same-Sex Marriage," Gallup, June 8, 2021, https://news.gallup.com/poll/350486/record-high-support-same-sex-marriage.aspx; Samantha Schmidt, "Americans' Views Flipped on Gay Rights. How Did Minds Change So Quickly? *Washington Post*, June 7, 2019, https://www.washingtonpost.com/local/social-issues/americans-views-flipped-on-gay-rights-how-did-minds-change-so-quickly/2019/06/07/ae256016-8720-11e9-98c1-e945ae5db8fb_story.html; "Americans' Support for Key LGBTQ Rights Continues to Tick Upward," PRRI, March 17, 2022, https://www.prri.org/research/americans-support-for-key-lgbtq-rights-continues-to-tick-upward/.

46 "Mapping Attacks on LGBTQ Rights in US State Legislatures in 2024," ACLU, updated June 7, 2024, https://www.aclu.org/legislative-attacks-on-lgbtq-rights?state=&impact=.
47 Eesha Pendharkar, "Number of Trans Youth Is Twice as High as Previous Estimates, Study Finds," *Education Week*, June 14, 2022, https://www.edweek.org/leadership/number-of-trans-youth-is-twice-as-high-as-previous-estimates-study-finds/2022/06.
48 Jaclyn Diaz, "Florida's Governor Signs Controversial Law Opponents Dubbed 'Don't Say Gay,'" NPR, March 28, 2022, https://www.npr.org/2022/03/28/1089221657/dont-say-gay-florida-desantis.
49 Kristen Schilt and Laurel Westbrook, "Bathroom Battlegrounds and Penis Panics," *Contexts* 14, no. 3 (2015): 26–31.
50 Richard H. Hall, J. Eugene Haas, and Norman J. Johnson, "An Examination of the Blau-Scott and Etzioni Typologies," *Administrative Science Quarterly* 12, no. 1 (1967): 118–39.
51 Barry Holman and Jason Ziedenberg, "The Dangers of Detention: The Impact of Incarcerating Youth in Detention and Other Secure Facilities," Justice Policy Institute, accessed February 11, 2023, https://justicepolicy.org/wp-content/uploads/2022/02/06-11_rep_dangersofdetention_JJ.pdf.

7. Cultivating Place Consciousness to Enrich Society

1 Adrian Shirk, *Heaven Is a Place on Earth: Searching for an American Utopia* (Berkeley: Counterpoint Press, 2022).
2 "About Us," Damanhur Welcome Center, accessed August 12, 2022, https://damanhur.travel/about-us/.
3 Jeff Merrifield, *Damanhur: The Story of the Extraordinary Italian Artistic and Spiritual Community*, 2nd ed. (Santa Cruz: Hanford Mead Publishers, 2006).
4 Engrid Barnett, "The Truth about the Secret Underground Temples of Damanhur," Grunge, February 3, 2023, https://www.grunge.com/883428/the-truth-about-the-secret-underground-temples-of-damanhur/.
5 Merrifield, *Damanhur*.
6 See "Damanhur: For a Culture of Peace," January 24, 2019, YouTube video, 28:41, https://www.youtube.com/watch?v=inFc9_zAPpA.
7 See "Damanhur: For a Culture of Peace."
8 Falco Tarassaco (Oberto Airaudi), *The Synchronic Lines: The Energy Streams of Planet Earth* (Vidracco, Italy: Devodama, 2015).
9 Barnett, "The Truth"; Merrifield, *Damanhur*.
10 Ross Robertson, "Atlantis in the Mountains of Italy," *What Is Enlightenment* no. 36 (April–June 2007), https://s3.eu-central-1.amazonaws.com/wieoldissues/wie_en_weboptimized/EN_issue_36.pdf.
11 Merrifield, *Damanhur*.
12 Barnett, "The Truth."
13 Sarah Williams Goldhagen, *Welcome to Your World: How the Built Environment Shapes Our Lives* (New York: Harper, 2017), 270.
14 Norbert Götz and Janne Holmén, "Introduction to the Theme Issue: 'Mental Maps: Geographical and Historical Perspectives,'" *Journal of Cultural Geography* 35, no. 2 (2018): 157–61.
15 Min Reuchamps, Dimokritos Kavadias, and Kris Deschouwer, "Drawing Belgium: Using Mental Maps to Measure Territorial Conflict," *Territory, Politics, Governance* 2, no. 1 (2014): 30–51; Virpi Kaisto and Chloe Wells, "Mental

Mapping as a Method for Studying Borders and Bordering in Youth People's Territorial Identifications," *Journal of Borderlands Studies* 36, no. 2 (2021): 259–79.
16. See "Mental Mapping and Perception," National Geographic Society, updated January 22, 2024, https://education.nationalgeographic.org/resource/mental-mapping-and-perception/; Jiří Pánek, "From Mental Maps to GeoParticipation," *The Cartographic Journal* 53, no. 4 (2016): 300–7.
17. Brandi Snowden and Nadia Evangelou, "Racial Disparities in Homeownership Rates," Economists' Outlook, National Association of Realtors, March 3, 2022, https://www.nar.realtor/blogs/economists-outlook/racial-disparities-in-homeownership-rates.
18. Richard Rothstein, *The Color of Law: A Forgotten History of How Our Government Segregated America* (New York: Liveright, 2017).
19. Rothstein, *The Color of Law*.
20. Kimberly Fain, "The Devastation of Black Wall Street," JSTOR Daily, July 5, 2017, https://daily.jstor.org/the-devastation-of-black-wall-street/; see also Hannibal B. Johnson, *Black Wall Street: From Riot to Renaissance in Tulsa's Historic Greenwood District* (Fort Worth, TX: Eakin Press, 1998).
21. Eviction Lab, accessed November 20, 2022, https://evictionlab.org/eviction-tracking/.
22. "Billion-Dollar Weather and Climate Disasters," National Center for Environmental Information, National Oceanic and Atmospheric Administration, accessed November 20, 2022, https://www.ncei.noaa.gov/access/billions/time-series.
23. "About NASMM: History," National Association of Move Managers, accessed June 4, 2023, https://www.nasmm.org/about-nasmm/about-nasmm/history/.
24. Paula Span, "Moving Is a Monumental Task for Many Older Americans. These Organizers Can Help," *New York Times*, May 22, 2023, https://www.nytimes.com/2023/05/20/health/elderly-move-managers.html.
25. Tamara L. Sheldon and Crystal Zhan, "The Impact of Natural Disasters on US Home Ownership," *Journal of the Association of Environmental and Resource Economists* 6, no. 6 (2019): 1169–203.
26. "Data and Statistics: Global Trends," UNHCR: The UN Refugee Agency, accessed November 20, 2022, https://www.unhcr.org/en-us/globaltrends.html.
27. Coalition for the Homeless of Central Florida, accessed November 20, 2022, https://www.centralfloridahomeless.org/shelter-programs.
28. *A Word to the Wives*, 1955, posted August 13, 2010, YouTube video, 13:28, https://www.youtube.com/watch?v=q7EN8CkMY0A1955.
29. Sarah Pink, *Home Truths: Gender, Domestic Objects and Everyday Life* (Oxford: Berg, 2004).
30. Ted K. Bradshaw, "The Post-Place Community: Contributions to the Debate about the Definition of Community," *Community Development* 39, no. 1 (2008): 5–16.
31. Robin Means and Simon Evans, "Communities of Place and Communities of Interest? An Exploration of Their Changing Role in Later Life," *Ageing & Society* 32, no. 8 (2012): 1300–18.
32. Daniel Kemmis, *The Good City and the Good Life: Renewing the Sense of Community* (Boston: Houghton Mifflin, 1995).
33. Kemmis, *The Good City*, 15–16.
34. Richard C. Harwood, *Stepping Forward: A Positive, Practical Path to Transform Our Communities and Our Lives* (Austin, TX: Greenleaf, 2019), 117.
35. Lance Freeman, "Displacement or Succession? Residential Mobility in Gentrifying Neighborhoods," *Urban Affairs Review* 40, no. 4 (2005): 463–91.

36 Daniel Putnam, "Gentrification and Domination," *The Journal of Political Philosophy* 29, no. 2 (2021): 167–87.
37 Peter Moskowitz, *How to Kill a City: Gentrification, Inequality, and the Fight for the Neighborhood* (New York: Nation Books, 2018).
38 Chris Michael and Ellie Violet Bramley, "Spike Lee's Gentrification Rant – Transcript: 'Fort Greene Park Is like the Westminster Dog Show,'" *The Guardian*, February 26, 2014, https://www.theguardian.com/cities/2014/feb/26/spike-lee-gentrification-rant-transcript.
39 Stacey Sutton, "What We Don't Understand about Gentrification," TEDxNewYork, January 15, 2015, YouTube video, 13:53, https://www.youtube.com/watch?v=XqogaDX48nI/; Stacey Sutton, "Gentrification and the Increasing Significance of Racial Transition in New York City 1970–2010," *Urban Affairs Review* 56, no. 1 (2020): 65–95.
40 Freeman, "Displacement or Succession?"
41 Freeman, "Displacement or Succession?" 488.
42 Lance Freeman, *There Goes the 'Hood: Views of Gentrification from the Ground Up* (Philadelphia: Temple University Press, 2006).
43 Freeman, *There Goes the 'Hood*, 7.
44 Sutton, "What We Don't Understand about Gentrification."
45 Mark Davidson, "Critical Commentary. Gentrification in Crisis: Towards Consensus or Disagreement," *Urban Studies* 48, no. 10 (2011): 1987–96; Mark Davidson, "Displacement, Space and Dwelling: Placing Gentrification Debate," *Ethics, Place & Environment* 12, no. 2 (2009): 219–34.
46 Kate S. Shaw and Iris W. Hagemans, "'Gentrification without Displacement' and the Consequent Loss of Place: The Effects of Class Transition on Low-Income Residents of Secure Housing in Gentrifying Areas," *International Journal of Urban and Regional Research* 39, no. 2 (2015): 323–41.
47 Sutton, "Gentrification."
48 Sutton, "Gentrification," 90.
49 Richard L. Florida, *The Rise of the Creative Class: Revisited* (New York: Basic Books, 2012); Enrico Moretti, *The New Geography of Jobs* (Boston: Houghton Mifflin Harcourt, 2012); Peter F. Drucker, "The Rise of the Knowledge Society," *The Wilson Quarterly* 17, no. 2 (Spring 1993): 52–71.
50 Miriam Zuk et al., "Gentrification, Displacement, and the Role of Public Investment," *Journal of Planning Literature* 33, no. 1 (2018): 31–44.
51 Lindsay M. Miller, "We Need to Change How We Think about Gentrification," *National Civic Review* 107, no. 4 (Winter 2019), https://www.nationalcivicleague.org/ncr-article/we-need-to-change-how-we-think-about-gentrification/.
52 Marta Gierczyk, "Magic City Killjoys: Women Organizers, Gentrification, and the Politics of Multiculturalism in Little Haiti," *Anthurium* 16, no. 1 (2020): 1–21.
53 Tyeshia Redden et al., "Gainesville's Forgotten Neighborhood: An Examination of Narratives in Planning," *Journal of the American Planning Association* 88, no. 3 (2021): 392–404.
54 Laura Dedenbach et al., "Building the Foundation for Arnstein's Ladder: Community Empowerment through a Participatory Neighborhood Narrative," in *Learning from Arnsteins' Ladder: From Citizen Participation to Public Engagement*, ed. Mickey Lauria and Carissa Schively Slotterback (New York: Routledge, 2020).
55 Dedenbach et al., "Building the Foundation," 292.
56 Redden et al., "Gainesville's Forgotten Neighborhood," 402.
57 Redden et al., "Gainesville's Forgotten Neighborhood," 402.
58 Redden et al., "Gainesville's Forgotten Neighborhood," 402.
59 Gierczyk, "Magic City Killjoys."

60 Germaine R. Halegoua, *The Digital City: Media and the Social Production of Place* (New York: New York University Press, 2019), 30.
61 Halegoua, *The Digital City*, 48.
62 Halegoua, *The Digital City*, 59.
63 Sam Stejskal, "Inside the Political Fight over David Beckham and Jorge Mas's Potential Inter Miami Stadium Development," *The Athletic*, April 27, 2022, https://theathletic.com/3276828/2022/04/27/inter-miami-stadium-freedom-park-jorge-mas-billy-corben-david-beckham/.
64 Anastasia Globa, Beau B. Beza, and Rui Wang, "Towards Multi-sensory Design: Placemaking through Immersive Environments – Evaluation of the Approach," *Expert Systems with Applications* 204 (2022): 117614; see also Anastasia Globa, Beau B. Beza, and Rui Wang, "Sensory Urbanism and Placemaking," in *Intelligent and Informed: Proceedings of the 24th International Conference on Computer-Aided Architectural Design Research in Asia (CAADRIA 2019)*, ed. Matthias Hank Haeusler, Marc Aurek Schnabel, and Tomohiro Fukuda, vol. 2 (Hong Kong: CAADRIA, 2019), 737–46.
65 Amanda Gutierrez, Eric Leonardson, and Norman W. Long, "How Do Soundwalks Engage Urban Communities in Soundscape Awareness?" Paper presented at Invisible Places, April 7–9, 2017, São Miguel Island, Azores, Portugal, http://invisibleplaces.org/2017/pdf/Gutierrez-b.pdf.
66 Robert Lee, "Morrill Act of 1862 Indigenous Land Parcels Database," *High Country News*, March 2020; for a description of the project methods, see https://www.landgrabu.org/lands.
67 "Stepping Out & Stepping Up: The Land-Grant Truth and Reconciliation Project. Stepping Out of Our Comfort Zone & Stepping Up to Our Responsibilities," The Ohio State University, accessed December 10, 2022, https://u.osu.edu/landgranttruth/articles-podcasts-and-videos/.
68 Stephen M. Gavazzi and John N. Low, "Confronting the Wealth Transfer from Tribal Nations That Established Land-Grant Universities," *Beyond Town and Gown*, American Association of University Professors, Spring 2022, https://www.aaup.org/article/confronting-wealth-transfer-tribal-nations-established-land-grant-universities#.YreYSnbMJ9N.
69 GayBarchives, accessed June 26, 2024, http://gaybarchives.com/; see also Rick Karlin and St Sukie de la Croix, *Last Call Chicago: A History of 1001 LGBTQ-Friendly Taverns, Haunts and Hangouts* (Cathedral City, CA: Rattling Good Yarns Press, 2022).
70 Art Smith, correspondence with author, June 19, 2023.
71 "103 David Fischer on His Iconic Gay Bars in St. Pete COCKtail and WETspot and ZAZoo'd, Saint, Back Room," GayBarchives, October 30, 2022, YouTube video interview, 1:03:42, https://www.youtube.com/watch?v=cwS2qxMkm6E.
72 Randy Fair, "Celebrating the History of LGBTQ Safe Spaces: Art Smith and Gay Barchives," Campaign for Southern Equality, November 22, 2020, https://southernequality.org/celebrating-the-history-of-lgbtq-safe-spaces-art-smith-and-gay-barchives/.
73 Leilah Stone, "Queer Spaces Will Always Be Necessary," Metropolis, May 26, 2022, https://metropolismag.com/viewpoints/queer-spaces-will-always-be-necessary/.
74 Bluestockings Cooperative, accessed November 25, 2022, https://bluestockings.com/.
75 Adam Nathaniel Furman and Joshua Mardell, eds., *Queer Spaces: An Atlas of LGBTQ+ Places and Stories* (London: RIBA Publishing, 2022).

76 Japonica Brown-Saracino, *How Places Make Us: Novel LBQ Identities in Four Small Cities* (Chicago: University of Chicago Press, 2018).
77 Rachel Aldred and Katrina Jungnickel, "Constructing Mobile Places between 'Leisure' and 'Transport': A Case Study of Two Group Cycle Rides," *Sociology* 46, no. 3 (2012): 359–74.
78 Marc Tison and Barry Walsh, *Pipe Fiends: A Visual Overdose of Canada's Most Infamous Skate Sport* (Montreal: Média MudScout, 2006).
79 Gerard Kyle and Garry Chick, "The Social Construction of a Sense of Place," *Leisure Sciences: An Interdisciplinary Journal* 29, no. 3 (2007): 209–25.
80 David Hindley, "'More Than Just a Run in the Park': An Exploration of Parkrun as a Shared Leisure Space," *Leisure Sciences: An Interdisciplinary Journal* 42, no. 1 (2020): 85–105.
81 Gerard Kyle et al., "An Examination of the Relationship between Leisure Activity Involvement and Place Attachment among Hikers along the Appalachian Trail," *Journal of Leisure Research* 35, no. 3 (2003): 249–73.
82 Isabel Wilkerson, *Caste: The Origins of Our Discontents* (New York: Random House, 2020).
83 Andrew W. Kahrl, *The Land Was Ours: How Black Beaches Became White Wealth in the Coastal South* (Chapel Hill: University of North Carolina Press, 2016); for an analysis of Black and Puerto Rican mothers' and children's grassroots efforts to make privately controlled Connecticut beaches accessible, see Andrew W. Kahrl, *Free the Beaches: The Story of Ned Coll and the Battle for America's Most Exclusive Shoreline* (New Haven, CT: Yale University Press, 2018).
84 Amy R. Hurd, Denise M. Anderson, and Tracy Mainieri, *Kraus' Recreation and Leisure in Modern Society*, 12th ed. (Burlington, MA: Jones & Bartlett Learning, 2022).
85 Andrew T. Kaczynski and Karla A. Henderson, "Environmental Correlates of Physical Activity: A Review of Evidence about Parks and Recreation," *Leisure Sciences: An Interdisciplinary Journal* 29, no. 4 (2007): 315–54; Penny Gordon-Larsen et al., "Inequality in the Built Environment Underlies Key Health Disparities in Physical Activity and Obesity," *Pediatrics* 177, no. 2 (2006): 417–24.
86 David Scott, "Economic Inequality, Poverty, Park and Recreation Delivery," *Journal of Park and Recreation Administration* 31, no. 4 (2012): 5–6.
87 "The City Project," Community Partners, accessed December 18, 2022, https://communitypartners.org/success-story/the-city-project/.
88 Adriana Campelo et al., "Sense of Place: The Importance for Destination Branding," *Journal of Travel Research* 53, no. 2 (2014): 154.
89 Campelo et al. "Sense of Place," 154.
90 Campelo et al. "Sense of Place," 155.
91 Campelo et al. "Sense of Place," 162.
92 Greg Richards, "From Place Branding to Placemaking: The Role of Events," *International Journal of Event and Festival Management* 8, no. 1 (2017): 8–23, 10.
93 Organisation for Economic Co-operation and Development, *Tourism and the Creative Economy* (Paris: OECD Publishing, 2014), 14.
94 Ann Markusen and Anne Gadwa, *Creative Placemaking* (Washington, DC: National Endowment for the Arts, 2010), 3, https://www.arts.gov/sites/default/files/CreativePlacemaking-Paper.pdf.
95 Tom Boellstorff, *Coming of Age in Second Life: An Anthropologist Explores the Virtually Human* (Princeton, NJ: Princeton University Press, 2008).

96 Quentin Jones, "Virtual-Communities, Virtual Settlements and Cyber-Archaeology: A Theoretical Outline," *Journal of Computer-Mediated Communication* 3, no. 3 (1997): 6.
97 Rodney Harrison, "Excavating *Second Life*: Cyber-Archaeologies, Heritage and Virtual Communities," *Journal of Material Culture* 14, no. 1 (2009): 80.
98 Harrison, "Excavating *Second Life*," 91.
99 Bruno de Andrade, Alenka Poplin, and Ítalo Sousa de Sena, "Minecraft as a Tool for Engaging Children in Urban Planning: A Case Study in Tirol Town, Brazil," *International Journal of Geo-Information* 9, no. 3 (2020): 170; "A Country in the Making: Learning about Architecture, Geography, Culture and National Heritage through *Minecraft*," Minecraft Education, accessed February 12, 2023, https://education.minecraft.net/en-us/blog/a-country-in-the-making-learning-about-architecture--geography--culture-and-national-heritage-through-minecraft.
100 Daniel Plunkett, "On Place Attachments in Virtual Worlds," *World Leisure Journal* 53, no. 3 (2011): 168–78.
101 T.E. Bosch, "Memory Studies, A Brief Concept Paper" (working paper, University of Leeds, School of Media and Communication, Media, Conflict and Democratisation [MeCoDEM], January 2016, ISSN 2057–4002), http://eprints.whiterose.ac.uk/117289/.
102 Nikil Saval, *Cubed: A Secret History of the Workplace* (New York: Anchor Books, 2014); "Nikil Saval," Senator Biography, Pennsylvania State Senate, accessed July 14, 2024, https://www.legis.state.pa.us/cfdocs/legis/home/member_information/senate_bio.cfm?id=1921.
103 Frederick Winslow Taylor, *The Principles of Scientific Management* (New York: Harper & Brothers, 1911); William Henry Leffingwell, *Scientific Office Management* (Chicago: A.W. Shaw, 1917).
104 Saval, *Cubed*, 33–4.
105 Saval, *Cubed*, 249.
106 Saval, *Cubed*.
107 "Inside the $5 Billion Apple Headquarters," Tech Vision, September 12, 2020, YouTube video, 5:54, https://www.youtube.com/watch?v=FzcfZyEhOoI; "Inside Google's Massive Headquarters," Tech Vision, November 18, 2020, YouTube video, 6:30, https://www.youtube.com/watch?v=Z-pT0XDYvDM; "Facebook Is Building a City for Its Employees," Tech Vision, September 26, 2020, YouTube video, 5:33, https://www.youtube.com/watch?v=f1fbuOkxugs.
108 Matt Cain, "Top 10 Emerging Technologies in the Digital Workplace," *Forbes*, November 2, 2016, https://www.forbes.com/sites/gartnergroup/2016/11/02/top-10-emerging-technologies-in-the-digital-workplace/?sh=1c3984691e48.
109 Andy Lantz, "Top 5 Trends to Watch in the Future of Work," RIOS, September 24, 2021, YouTube video, 2:05, https://www.youtube.com/watch?v=swjJ_EuYutc&t=5s.
110 WELL, accessed June 26, 2024, https://www.wellcertified.com/.
111 International Workplace Studies Program, Cornell University, accessed June 26, 2024, https://iwsp.human.cornell.edu/.
112 "Disability Impacts All of Us," Disability and Health Promotion, Centers for Disease Control and Prevention, updated May 15, 2023, https://www.cdc.gov/ncbddd/disabilityandhealth/infographic-disability-impacts-all.html.
113 Priyanka Anand and Purvi Sevak, "The Role of Workplace Accommodations in the Employment of People with Disabilities," *IZA Journal of Labor Policy* 6, no. 12 (2017): 1–20.
114 Theresia Degener, "Disability in a Human Rights Context," *Laws* 5, no. 3 (2016): 35.

115 Kathy Padkapayeva et al., "Workplace Accommodations for Persons with Physical Disabilities: Evidence Synthesis of the Peer-Reviewed Literature," *Disability and Rehabilitation* 39, no. 21 (2017): 2134–47.
116 Padkapayeva et al., "Workplace Accommodations," 2137; see also "2010 ADA Standards for Accessible Design," ADA, US Department of Justice, Civil Rights Division, September 15, 2010, https://www.ada.gov/law-and-regs/design-standards/2010-stds/.
117 "OSHA at 50: 50 Years of Workplace Safety and Health," Occupational Safety and Health Administration, US Department of Labor, accessed December 30, 2022, https://www.osha.gov/osha50.
118 Jeff Brown, "Nearly 50 Years of Occupational Safety and Health Data," *Beyond the Numbers* 9, no. 9 (2020), US Bureau of Labor Statistics, https://www.bls.gov/opub/btn/volume-9/nearly-50-years-of-occupational-safety-and-health-data.htm.
119 Laura Kesy and Stephen Pegula, "Census of Fatal Occupational Injuries Commemorates 20 Years of Occupational Safety and Health Data," *Beyond the Numbers* 3, no. 23 (2014), US Bureau of Labor Statistics, https://www.bls.gov/opub/btn/volume-3/census-of-fatal-occupational-injuries-commemorates-20-years.htm.
120 For information about OSHA standards and citations following inspections, see "Top 10 Most Frequently Cited Standards," Occupational Safety and Health Administration, accessed June 27, 2024, https://www.osha.gov/top10citedstandards.
121 "Health Hazards Evaluations – About the Program," The National Institute for Occupational Safety and Health (NIOSH), Centers for Disease Control and Prevention, accessed December 30, 2022, https://www.cdc.gov/niosh/hhe/about.html.
122 Centers for Disease Control and Prevention, "Heat-Related Deaths among Crop Workers: United States, 1992–2006," *Morbidity and Mortality Weekly Report* 57, no. 24 (2008): 649–53.
123 Michelle Tigchelaar, David S. Battisti, and June T. Spector, "Work Adaptations Insufficient to Address Growing Heat Risk for US Agricultural Workers," *Environmental Research Letters* 15, no. 9 (2020): 094035, https://iopscience.iop.org/article/10.1088/1748-9326/ab86f4.
124 Hannah Hickey, "Agricultural Pickers in US to See Unsafely Hot Workdays Double by 2050," UW News, April 28, 2020, https://www.washington.edu/news/2020/04/28/agricultural-pickers-in-us-to-see-unsafely-hot-workdays-double-by-2050/.
125 Erica Chavez Santos et al., "The Effect of the Participatory Heat Education and Awareness Tools (HEAT) Intervention on Agricultural Worker Physiological Heat Strain: Results from a Parallel, Comparison, Group Randomized Study," *BMC Public Health* 22, no. 1 (2022): 1746.

Epilogue

1 Norbert Götz and Janne Holmén, "Introduction to the Theme Issue: 'Mental Maps: Geographical and Historical Perspectives,'" *Journal of Cultural Geography* 35, no. 2 (2018): 157–61.
2 William Marsiglio, *Chasing We-ness: Cultivating Empathy and Leadership in a Polarized World* (Toronto: University of Toronto Press, 2023).
3 Sarah Williams Goldhagen, *Welcome to Your World: How the Built Environment Shapes Our Lives* (New York: Harper, 2017).

4 Scholarly Community Encyclopedia, s.v. "Night Vision Device," updated October 13, 2022, https://encyclopedia.pub/entry/29146#:~:text=The%20first%20military%20night%20vision,the%20first%20devices%20in%201935.
5 Cary Funk, Brian Kennedy, and Elizabeth Podrebarac Sciupac, "Public Opinion on the Future Use of Brain Implants," Pew Research Center, July 26, 2016, https://www.pewresearch.org/science/2016/07/26/public-opinion-on-the-future-use-of-brain-implants/.
6 John Della Volpe, *Fight: How Gen Z Is Channeling Their Fear and Passion to Save America* (New York: St. Martin's, 2022).

Index

90 Day Fiancé (reality show), 61–3
9 to 5 (1980 movie), 304

Action Office (Propst), 303
action settings
  concept of, 13–14
  creating unique, 109, 301, 314, 316, 320
  place attachments from, 119, 247, 260, 289–90, 308–9
  politics of placemaking and, 265, 270, 274, 282, 322
affordances, 13, 29
  technology and, 48, 284
Afghanistan, war in, 132, 189
Aguilas del Desierto (Eagles of the Desert), 176–8
Ahtone, Tristan, 238–9
altruism, 282, 324
  examples of, 124–5, 215
  as *MEAL* life skill, 9, 11, 251, 258, 262–3, 319–20
Americans with Disabilities Act (ADA), 106, 307
architecture, 22, 234, 271, 279, 325
  Damanhurian, 256, 258
  influence of building, 98, 218, 227–8, 297, 305, 320–1

LGBTQ+/feminist, 76, 289
  quality places, creation of, 7, 92–3, 231, 300
  workplace, 300, 308
Aristotle, 39–40
Arizona, 58, 231
  desert crossing, 176–8
art, 192
  leisure places for, 108, 203, 297
  we-ness through, 46, 172, 254, 284
attachments
  as *CART* process, 10–11, 25–6, 29, 81, 120, 261–2, 314–16
  changes in, 133–4, 204–6
  digital technologies and, 47–8, 116
  human hardwiring for, 9, 19, 106, 125, 133
  memories/experiences and, 125–7, 129–30, 279
  place (*see* place attachment)
  social interactions and, 119, 125–32, 223, 264, 288–90
augmented reality (AR)
  technologies, 113–16, 321
  shaping embodied experiences, 47, 158, 305
Austin (homeless father), 81–2

352 | Index

autonomy, 271–3
  as *BASIN* principle, 10, 29, 258, 262–3, 277, 319
  design/initiatives to increase, 269–70, 293, 295, 306–8
  place-based, 50, 171, 187

Ball, Matthew (*The Metaverse*), 113
Baltimore, Maryland, 272–3
BASIN principles (beneficence, autonomy, social and environmental justice, inclusive collaboration, nonmaleficence)
  concept of, 10–11
  in placemaking, 29, 258, 262–3, 316, 319, 324
basketball courts, 105–7
beaches, 63, 123
  access to, 54, 92, 291–2
  Normandy, 33–8, 40, 126, 189
  protection of, 52–3, 284
Bellah, Robert, 145, 150, 171
belonging. *See* group belonging
beneficence, 10, 29, 258–63, 277–8, 293, 307, 319
Bermuda, 236–7
bioregionalism, 72–3
biosphere consciousness, 73, 319
  discourse on, 57, 59, 102, 314
  experiments, 58–9
Black Lives Matter (BLM) movement, 2, 26, 287
Black people, 14, 187
  barbershops, 94–5, 287
  Clarksdale blues scene and, 160–2
  gentrification, facing, 53–4, 275–7, 279
  homeownership, 266
  police oppression against, 2–3, 220
  poverty, 53, 130
  restrictions on recreational spot access, 290–2
  segregation of, 130
  we-ness and, 105, 287, 294
  white racism against, 173–4, 229, 267, 291–2
blue-collar work, 130, 301
  place attachments in, 308–10
  place-based symbolism of, 4, 83, 87, 302
  See also white-collar work
blues music, 160–2
blue states, 63, 88. *See also* red states
Bluestockings, 289
borders
  artwork featuring, 45–6
  crossing, 4, 177–9
  as cultural markers, 16, 90, 159, 179, 182–3, 260
  Ukrainian defense of, 92, 213
  US-Mexico, 16, 45–6, 176–9, 231
  we-ness across, 45–6
Boys & Girls Clubs, 154, 208
built environment
  calls for more thoughtful, 7–8, 11, 300–1, 305–12, 320–3
  community impacts of, 8, 102, 108, 286
  dynamic nature of, 65–6, 91, 274, 278
  health impacts of, 8, 108, 300, 308–10
  mobilizing around access to, 108, 291
  place-based interactions/memories in, 125, 129, 197
  rituals and, 143
  simulations, 283
Bürolandschaft (Quickborner), 302–4, 312

"cancer alley" (Louisiana), 16, 223–6
Capitol (US), insurrection, 28, 135
Carnival, 172–3
CART processes (claims, attachments, rituals, and transitions), 325

concept of, 10–11, 312, 314–15
influence on place-based
  experiences, 29, 81, 249, 257,
  316–18
models of, 119–20, 261–3
Catholicism, 156, 172, 190
Celebration, Florida (*The Bubble*), 83–5
Chalmers, David (*Reality+*),
  116–17, 321
Chicago, 94, 121, 220
  heat wave in, 44, 175
childhood
  labor in, 15
  nature relationships in, 18, 65–71
  place-based memories of, 84,
    126–7, 150–1, 206, 229
  varying experiences in, 191–2, 199,
    222, 237, 246
children, 315
  decisions made for, 56, 99, 101,
    185, 270
  designing/modifying places for,
    6–8, 48, 60, 155, 194–5
  foster, 82, 222
  homelessness and, 77, 80, 82
  leisure activities of, 44, 65–71,
    105–8, 290, 294–5
  parental care/conflict, 21, 50, 69,
    77, 109–10, 246–8, 267
  place attachment for, 128, 138, 191,
    196–200
  protection of, 179, 211, 213, 225–6
  sharing rituals with, 72, 159, 163,
    168, 196
  transitions with, 183, 196, 222–3
  See also parenting
cities
  connections to, 88, 264
  cultural exchange between, 124–5
  gendered organization of, 55–6
  gentrification of (*see* gentrification)
  needing destinations, 93–4
  placemaking in, 268, 272–5, 298
  smart, 47, 281–2
  thoughtful design of, 7, 93, 228
  transitions in, 83, 228–9, 274
  wealth/access disparities in, 137,
    153, 292
City Project, The, 294–5
civic culture, 273
civil rights movement, 16, 235,
  287, 291
Civil War reenactments, 89, 158–9
claims over place
  asserting, 4, 54, 75, 203, 215–19,
    243
  as CART process, 10–11, 29, 81,
    119–20, 251, 260–2, 314–15
  contested, 213–16, 226–32, 234–6,
    317
  control of, 48–9, 74, 218, 237
  elements of, 207–10
  embodied experiences and, 4, 91,
    213–16, 322
  gendered, 24–5, 75, 107, 114, 270
  groups mobilizing for, 203, 214–19,
    227–9, 243–4
  Indigenous, 67, 75, 232–5, 241, 244,
    285–6
  individual vs. group, 217–18
  instability of, 231–5, 274
  leverage in, 245–9
  mutually negotiated, 235–7
  permanency of, 221–6
  physical/social scope, 218–21,
    228–9
  place attachment and, 28, 37, 155,
    207–10, 215, 260
  property-based, 49, 75, 208,
    241, 257
  rituals and, 168, 174–5, 215
  transitions and, 52, 209, 229–30
  US-Mexico, 231–2, 235
  virtual, 114, 116, 219–21
  wartime, 91–2, 213–16
Clark, Caitlin, 243

Clarksdale, Mississippi, 160–2
climate
  change/crisis, 57, 143, 228, 284, 310–11
  cultural, 220, 243
  experiences influenced by, 43–4, 106, 109
Coalition Against Death Alley (CADA), 225–6
collaboration. *See* inclusive collaboration
collective effervescence, 147–8, 157
collective identities
  claiming places and, 49–50, 128–9, 205
  expressions of, 304, 322
  Indigenous, 232, 241
  memories (*see* collective memories)
  place attachments forming, 26, 134–5
  regional, 159
collective memories
  concealing/purging of, 267
  concepts of, 17–18
  forging of, 41–2, 102, 119, 300
  place-based, 315, 317
Collins, Randall, 148–9, 157
colonialism, 53, 90
  Indigenous communities versus, 67, 232, 238–40
communes, 85–7
communities, 239, 317
  attachment to, 119–20, 129, 218, 261
  coming together of, 46, 123–5, 257, 286
  embodied experiences in, 4–8, 79, 91, 120
  gentrification of (*see* gentrification)
  homelessness in (*see* homelessness)
  influence on well-being, 21, 223–5, 322, 325
  in/stability of, 52–3, 264
  intentional, 76, 85–7
  meaningfulness of, 63, 126–7
  organizing to protect, 91, 108, 224–5
  placemaking in, 60, 76, 92, 251, 265–6, 271–3, 283–5
  poverty/disparities in, 89–90, 198, 265–6, 290–5
  rituals in, 155, 160
  spiritual, 253–4
  symbolism of, 83
  thought (*see* thought communities)
  varying definitions of, 85–7
  virtual, 299
community gardens, 137, 155
community groups, 70
  mobilizing for community betterment, 21, 108, 227, 264, 271–3
  rituals of, 146, 154–5
  as social domain, 29, 259, 299, 316, 319
concentration camps, 5, 78, 103
Confederacy, 89, 105, 159, 202
consciousness of place (*see* place consciousness)
contested scenarios, 8
  colonial expansion and, 231–5, 241–2, 244
  concept of, 226, 245
  examples of, 227–30, 236
COVID-19 pandemic
  health care in, 99–100, 164–6
  lack of choice amid, 98–100, 164–6
  mobilities in, 184, 186
  place-based rituals affected by, 26–7, 143, 156–8, 164
  political polarization and, 21, 26–7, 88
  schools and classrooms in, 100–1, 229
  sense of belonging amid, 21, 26–7, 101–2, 288
  workplace changes in, 164–6, 300–1
Crescent City, California, 123–5
cruise ships, 109

Daley, Yvonne (*Going Up the Country*), 86
Damanhur, 87, 253–9, 324
Dann, Mary and Carrie, 233
Dawes Act, 241–2
D-Day attack, accounts of, 34–7
deep dyadic we-ness, 9
  attachment to place and, 92–5, 119, 133, 178, 182, 242
  forging, 15, 23, 26, 170–1, 188, 255, 304
  limitations on, 99
  place-based evolution of, 54, 62, 70, 104, 143, 198, 317
  virtually mediated, 135, 322
  See also dyadic we-ness
digital places/placemaking, 281
  metaverse experiences of, 113–18, 322–3
  process and performance in, 204–6, 322–3
  ritual-focused, 158, 322
  transitioning between organic and, 42, 46–8, 101, 120, 318, 322–3
  work-related, 304–5
Di Masso, Andrés, 132, 180–1
disability. *See* people with disability
discourses, public, 109
  biosphere consciousness and (*see* biosphere consciousness)
  embodied experiences influenced by, 6, 48, 67, 87–9
  gendered, 59–60, 87, 106–8
  influence of place-based, 17, 42, 57–60, 101
  as place property, 48, 62, 120, 149, 318
  on schools, 101, 170
  social movement shifting of, 238, 244, 287
  in virtual spaces, 47, 117–18
Disney World, 77, 83–4
Donohoe, Janet (*Remembering Places*), 17, 41

Durkheim, Émile (*The Elementary Forms of Religious Life*), 147–8
dyadic we-ness, 15, 23, 66, 69–70, 94, 109, 152, 178. *See also* deep dyadic we-ness

elderly people, 99, 183, 211
  care for, 6, 43, 165, 247–8
  See also grandparents
Elliott, Andrea (*Invisible Child*), 81
embodied experiences, 36, 301
  CART processes and, 11
  enhancing, 320, 323
  place-based shaping of, 4, 19–21, 38–42, 76, 91
  virtual reality versus, 46–7
  See also proprioception
empathy, 57
  group placemaking and, 217–18, 220, 282–4, 295, 324
  as *MEAL* life skill, 9–13, 251, 258, 262–3, 319–20
  place-based experiences and, 15, 125, 178
  Ukrainians' wartime, 213–17
  virtual spaces and, 115, 284
  workplace, 308–12
environmentalism, 50, 57, 65
environmental justice,
  as *BASIN* principle, 10, 29, 262–5, 272–7, 319
  CART processes and, 10–11, 121, 251, 263
  consciousness of place and, 19, 158, 284
  MEAL life skills and, 10–11, 251, 263
  place-based struggles for, 16–17, 293–5
  VR technology, 284
  workplaces and, 305–7
Environmental Protection Agency (EPA), 224–5

356 | Index

exchange of goods and services, 21, 184
　sites for, 94–6, 215
　virtual, 114
experience-in-place, 22

Facebook, 112, 205, 304
firewalking
　high school, 168–70
　Mauritian, 147
food
　apartheid, 153
　buying, 62, 153–4
　fast, 216
　growing/raising, 86, 137, 154–5
　insecurity, 78, 153–4, 212–13
　preparing/sharing, 23, 80, 149, 151–4
　unhealthy, 97, 153
Foster, B. Brian (*I Don't Like the Blues*), 160–2
fraternities, 167, 174, 197
Freeman, Lance (*There Goes the 'Hood*), 276

Gainesville, Florida, 70, 79, 81–2, 88
　health and fitness center in, x, xii
　neighbourhood planning in, 279–80, 285, 314
gangs
　belonging, sense of place-based, 15, 167–8, 175
　claiming of territory, 168, 221
　recruitment, 168, 179
　rites of passage/rituals, 167–8, 171
　social media use, 221
Garcia, Robert, 294
Gardner, Chris, 81
Gavazzi, Stephen (*Land-Grant Universities for the Future*), 103–4, 239, 285–6
Gee, E. Gordon (*Land-Grant Universities for the Future*), 239
gender identity
　assumptions/attitudes about, 40–1, 55, 172
　discourses (based) on, 25, 59–60, 87, 243
　rituals and, 166–7, 172–3
　social justice issues of, 169, 202, 244
　varying performances of, 51, 114, 172
　virtual spaces and, 114, 117
　we-ness based on, 25, 55, 95, 169, 287–9
　See also LGBTQ+ community
gendered places/placemaking
　assumptions about, 55, 75–7
　home-related, 74–7, 270
　leisure, 106–7, 117, 287
　properties, 42, 120, 318
　urban planning and, 55–6, 59–60, 280
　work-related, 59–60, 166, 303–4
genocide, 225
　US legacy of Indigenous, 16, 102, 232
gentrification
　as contentious issue, 68, 180, 205, 274–8
　movements to counter, 52–4, 203, 274–5, 280–1, 297–8
　racism in, 52–4, 274–9
　women amid, 278, 280–1
Gen Z, 69, 324
George Floyd
　memorial to, 1, 8, 221
　murder of, 2–3, 126
Gierczyk, Marta, 280–1
Gieryn, Thomas (*Truth Spots*), 8, 19
Gifford, Robert, 128, 132
Goldhagen, Sarah Williams (*Welcome to Your World*), 7–8, 13, 29, 258–9
Graham, David, 186
grandparents, 277
　transitions for, 197, 266
　visiting, 19, 150–1

group belonging
  desire for, 9, 11, 28, 128, 158–9
  in five social domains, 29–30, 132–4, 264–5
  influential forces of, 26–7, 42, 181, 260
  in nature, 18
  negotiations of, 41, 89, 215, 317
  place attachments and, 14–15, 133–4
  places shaping notions of, 4–5, 13, 20–5, 64, 76
  public spaces and, 92, 94, 102–3, 299
  rituals and, 146, 149–50, 156–7, 171
  sports and, 162–3, 316
  transitions and, 54–5, 179, 199
  workplaces and, 305, 316
GROW HUB (Growing Real Opportunities to Work – Harvest of Urban Business), 70
gyms, 108, 207
  gendered dynamics in, 106–7
  place attachments to, x, xii, 180, 209–10
  social rituals in, 13, 154, 163–4
  workplace, 13, 304

Haidt, Jonathan (*The Anxious Generation*), 69
Hajj, the, 140–4, 146–7, 156
Halegoua, Germaine (*The Digital City*), 47, 204–5, 281–2
Harwood, Richard, 273
health care, 11, 311
  amid COVID-19: 99–100, 164–6
  institutional, 96–7, 168–9
  virtual/telehealth, 99, 165, 184
Hitler, Adolf, 49, 103–4
Holocaust Memorial Museum, 103–4, 197
homelessness, 186
  children and, 77, 80, 82
  family experiences of, 80–2
  individual experiences of, 183, 248

non-dwelling placemaking/transitions, 82–3, 185, 265, 269
  varying definitions of, 77–8
  we-ness amid, 79–83, 139, 152
homeownership, 83, 95–6, 180, 183, 266–7, 269
homeplaces
  concept/dimensions of, 15, 73–4, 82, 193
  contrasting experiences of, 15, 76–7, 101
  as gendered, 76, 271
  instability of, 81–2, 248
  middle-class vs. working-class notions of, 75–6
  privacy and, 74–5, 79
  roots and, 14, 74, 76
  sharing of, 67, 74–6, 101, 271
  voluntary vs. involuntary occupancy, 78
hooks, bell (*Belonging*), 14, 18–19
Hochschild, Arlie (*Strangers in Their Own Land*), 224
housing, 79, 133
  co-, 86–7
  crisis, 53–4, 77, 279
  prison, 98
  racial discrimination and, 130, 228, 265–7, 292
  transitions, 155, 180, 269
  See also gentrification; homeplaces

ideational we-ness, 99, 322
  concept of, 9, 182, 317
  experiences of, 15, 90–2, 133–5, 143, 314
  nurturing, 23, 73, 94–5, 144, 178, 198
  placemaking and, 54, 92, 119, 129, 239, 286
  rituals and, 143–4, 156, 163, 170–1, 243, 255
  stripping of opportunities for, 188, 242
  workplace, 303–4, 308

identities, 158
  collective (*see* collective identities)
  discrimination based on, 77, 244, 287
  embodied expression of, 63, 76
  gender/sexual, 25, 76, 244, 287–9
  individual/personal, 23, 26, 134, 137, 322
  place attachments and, 18, 26, 54, 134–6, 158
  place-based shaping of, 4, 13, 37–8, 134, 151
  territorial, 89–91, 223, 260
  transformations in, 22, 27, 170
  transitions and, 181, 209
  virtual expression of, 135–6, 184, 322
  workplace, 303–4
immigrants, 83, 177
  discrimination facing, 68, 90, 177–8, 269
  European, 67, 104, 232
  place attachment, 127, 222
  undocumented, 173, 183, 311
inclusive collaboration,
  as *BASIN* principle, 10, 29, 258, 262–3, 277, 319
  community placemaking and, 272–3, 279, 293, 296
  virtual, 283, 300
  workplace, 306–7
Indigenous people, 173, 292, 341n23
  dispossession of, 67–8, 232, 238–44, 275, 285–6
  land-grant universities, 238–40, 285–6
  mobilizing of, 203, 234
  relationships with land/nature, 72, 75, 193–5, 232–4, 240–4
  reservations, 16, 194, 232–3
  teachings of, 193–6
industrialization, 67, 94, 131, 167, 214, 270
  post-, 60, 278
injustice
  place-based challenging of, 16, 202, 238, 285–7
  poverty and, 89, 294
  in public parks, 68, 292–3
Inouye, Daniel K., 233
Instagram, 45, 205, 221
institutions, 168–9, 232
  abandonment of certain communities, 44, 229, 238, 307
  challenges with navigating, 51, 101–2
  influence on placemaking, 6, 78, 136, 229, 264, 314, 317
  lack of choice in, 51, 97
  land-grant (*see* land-grant universities)
  norms of, 170, 267, 324–5
  place properties of, 42, 120, 261, 318
  spatial, 56
  variations among, 96, 237
intentional communities, 85–7
International WELL Building Institute (IWBI), 305–6
International Workplace Studies Program, 306
interstitial spaces, 51
Irwin, John (*The Warehouse Prison*), 98–9
Israel, 16

Jackson, John Brinckerhoff, 75
Jacobs, Jane (*The Life and Death of Great American Cities*), 93
Jeannette, Pennsylvania, 83
Jensen (homeless father), 81–2
Jewish people, 5, 103, 4, 287
Johnson, Mark (*The Body in the Mind*), 38
JR (border wall artwork), 45–6
Junior League of Miami, 155–6
justice
  environmental (*see* environmental justice)

lack of (*see* injustice)
racial (*see* racial justice)
social (*see* social justice)
studies of neighborhood, 279–80, 290–5
systems of criminal, 96, 198 (*see also* police)

Kahrl, Andrew (*The Land Was Ours*), 291–2
Kamome (Japanese boat), 123–5
Kemmis, Daniel (*The Good City and the Good Life*), 272
Kern, Leslie (*Feminist City*), 55–6, 87
Kidd, Ricky, 97–8
Klinenberg, Eric (*Heat Wave*), 44
Kraus, Richard, 292

land-grant universities, 238–40, 285–6
landmarks, 21
  national, 102, 214
  place properties of, 120, 264, 317
  remembrance through, 102, 104
  rituals and, 142, 149
  social protest/persecution, 16, 102, 214
  See also monuments
Lantz, Andy, 305
Latinx people, 173, 277, 294
  cultural values, 62, 169
  youth, 169, 220
leadership, 224, 307
  business, 92, 108, 113, 124, 160
  collaborative, 284, 293, 308
  community, 70, 92–3, 108, 272–3, 279, 293
  cultivating, 155, 217–18, 282, 325
  Indigenous, 232, 286
  as *MEAL* life skill, 9–11, 214–15, 242, 251, 258–63, 319–20
  placemaking, 19, 107–8, 155–7
  political/national, 28, 53, 92, 160, 186, 214, 227
  for social change, 19
  we-ness and, 124–5, 156–7
  workplace, 166, 306
Lee, Robert, 238–9
Lee, Spike, 275
Leffingwell, William Henry (*Scientific Office Management*), 301
leisure spots
  branding destination initiatives, 297
  community debates over, 108, 160–2, 293–6
  competitive vs. cooperative approaches in, 21, 48, 107, 221–2, 284, 316
  creative placemaking, 146–7, 298
  discourse about, 60, 160–2, 243
  experiences in, 25, 105, 126–7, 243, 258, 264
  influence on well-being, 21, 63, 120, 293–6, 317, 320
  place-based rituals in, 146, 149, 155, 159–60
  as social domain, 10, 29, 174, 259–62, 265, 316–19
  varying/privileged access to, 105–6, 108–10, 267, 290–5
  virtual, 70, 115, 184, 298–300
  we-ness in, 106–8, 174, 294–5
leverage
  concept of, 245–7
  expressions of power, 49, 148–9, 232, 243–5, 271
  loss of, 248–9
  of we-ness, 10, 154, 203, 251, 315
LGBTQ+ community, 207
  bars, 16, 102, 206–7, 287–9
  claims to places, 76–8, 102, 243–4, 287–9
  collective identity, 9, 62, 74, 324
  social movements of, 26, 102, 243, 324
  youth, 77–8, 244
Lincoln, Abraham, 67, 232, 238

Little Haiti (Miami), 280, 297
Los Angeles, 94, 294
Louisiana, 4, 16, 223–5
Louv, Richard (*Last Child in the Woods*), 68–9

Macfarlane, Robert, 64–5
MacTavish, Katherine (*Singlewide*), 84–5
MAGA (Make America Great Again) movement, 90–1, 149
Malpas, Jeff (*Place and Experience*), 20
Manzo, Lynne, 22, 24, 65
maps of danger, 87–8
Mardi Gras, 172–4
Maslov, Abraham, 138
McClay, Wilfrid, 6
MEAL life skills (mindfulness, empathy, altruism, leadership)
    application of, 10–11, 242, 262–3, 282
    concept of, 9, 319–20
    cultivating, 29, 251, 258, 308, 312, 325
meaning, place-based, 138–9, 154, 296–8
    action settings and, 13, 36, 247, 274, 314
    assigning, 8, 18, 130–1, 178–9, 269–70
    claims of, 4–5, 54, 91, 193, 208, 255
    complexity of, 25–6, 84, 113, 215
    conflicts over, 16, 91, 192, 202, 226
    consciousness of (*see* place consciousness)
    distinctive, 8, 59, 96
    embodiment and, 38–40, 103, 290
    expanding, 6, 62, 202, 230
    of home, 6, 59, 63, 74, 263–4
    memories and, 125–8
    natural settings and, 72, 131, 284
    people shaping, 25, 109, 161, 207, 234–5
    rituals and, 26, 128, 144–9, 158, 168–70, 301
    symbolic (*see* symbolism)
    as transformative, 17, 22, 27–8, 103, 136, 203
    transitions and, 180–2, 188–9, 201
    virtual, 113, 116–17, 135, 300
    we-ness and, 10, 20, 151, 259, 273–4, 286
Mecca, pilgrimage to, 140–4, 146–7
megachurches, 156–8
memorial sites, 124
    9/11: 159
    conflict over, 1–3
    rituals and, 130, 159
    symbolism of, 5, 214
    we-ness experiences at, 102–4, 214
memories, 156
    collective (*see* collective memories)
    discursive construction of, 17, 65, 220
    place-based building of, 41, 272
Merrifield, Jeff, 257
Meta (formerly Facebook), 112, 114
metaverse, 120, 264, 317
    concepts of, 21, 47, 112–14, 184
    experiences with, 117–18, 135, 261
    participation in creating, 114–17, 298, 321
    we-ness in, 113–17
Mexico
    border with US, 16, 45–6, 176–9, 231
    claims over place, 231–2, 235
    war with US, 231, 235
migration, 112, 180
    southern border, 176–9
military, 67, 175
    families, 200–1
    place-based experiences in, 51, 96, 132
    we-ness in, 52, 92, 132
Millet, Dean, 223–4
Milligan, Melinda, 125
mindfulness, 170, 324
    connection with nature and, 72–3

as *MEAL* life skill, 9–11, 251, 258, 262–3, 282, 319–20
place consciousness and, 38, 118, 125, 137
placemaking and, 58, 274, 284, 310
Minecraft, 298–9
mnemonic communities, 18
mobile home industrial complex, 84–5
monuments, 93, 299
American national, 67, 102
Confederate, 89, 105, 202
Indigenous, 234–5
See also landmarks
Moskowitz, Peter (*How to Kill a City*), 274–5
moteliers, 77–8
Muir, John, 67–8
multisensory design, 76, 283
Munger, Harley, 123
Muslims, 156
Mecca pilgrimage, 140, 143–4, 146–7

Nannette, 190–1
nationalism, 90–1, 175
white (*see* white nationalism)
national parks, 88
creation of, 67, 294
racialized legacy of, 67–8, 291
natural disasters
changes and tensions after, 52, 175, 227–9
displacement from, 112, 129, 180, 189, 200, 268–9
we-ness amid, 16, 55, 123–5, 228
nature
accessibility (or lack) of, 68–9, 105
discourse on, 59, 65, 210, 224
dyadic we-ness in, 69–70, 152
individual connection with, 14, 18, 52, 65–6
meaningfulness of, 63, 119, 194, 210
place-based significance of, 21, 120, 264, 317
racialized/class-based access to, 67–8, 267–8
rituals in, 72, 144, 170
Nazism, 5, 34, 37, 103–4, 212, 237
neighborhoods, 183
block parties in, 7, 51
changing design of, 43–5, 52–3, 95, 180, 275–9
discourse about, 60, 84–5, 279–80
gentrification of (*see* gentrification)
lower-income/poorer, 44, 75–6, 150, 265, 275–6, 294–5
mobilizing to support, 30, 137, 203, 227–9, 274–81, 324
natural spaces in, 105
place attachments to, 4, 14, 25, 92, 129–30
power to shape, 25, 204, 236, 298–9
physical conditions of, 41–4, 75
segregated, 18–19, 266
transitions between, 200–1, 222
watch/protection programs, 6–7
we-ness in, 44–5, 125–7, 152–4, 236, 315
See also Participatory Neighborhood Narrative (PNN); suburbs
Nelson, Mark, 58–9
nested places, 3, 37, 182, 264
Nevada, 51, 231, 233
New Orleans, 223, 274
Mardi Gras, 172–4, 223,
post-Hurricane Katrina, 227–30
New Zealand, 296
Nippert-Eng, Christena, 151
nonmaleficence, 10, 258–63, 273, 278, 292, 319
Normandy (northern France), 33–4, 36–8, 126, 189
Northern states, 291
regional identities, 88–9

Northern states (*continued*)
    See also blue states; red states; Southern states

Odell, Jenny (*How to Do Nothing*), 12, 72–3
Oldenburg, Ray (*The Great Good Place*), 45
Operation Neptune, 33–4, 37
Ortiz, Ely and Rigoberto, 177

Palestine, 16
parenting, 77, 86, 206, 222
    concerns about kids' safety, 69, 101, 107–8, 179, 229–30
    conservative upbringing by, 15, 191, 244
    control over kids' activities, 99, 107–8, 244
    nature, relations with, 65, 163
    power relationships/discipline, 50, 246–8, 270
    rituals, 163, 167
    single/divorced, 183, 196–7
    use of technology, 69, 246–7
    wealth gaps in, 266–8, 270
    See also children
Participatory Neighborhood Narrative (PNN), 279–80, 314–15
people with disability, 41
    accessing preferred leisure/sport experiences, 70, 106, 108, 206–7, 243
    legislation and conventions for, 106, 307
    social justice for, 307–8, 324
    use of virtual technologies, 118, 141
    workplace issues for, 306–8
person-process-place (PPP) framework, 128–32
    See also place attachment
Pink, Sara (*Home Truths*), 76

place
    affective aspects of, 4–5, 13, 25, 129
    conceptualizations of, 3–5, 27–8
    consciousness of (*see* place consciousness)
    distorted sense of, 6, 37, 118, 201, 267, 280
    dynamic nature of, 2, 9–10, 65–6, 75, 93, 101, 314
    properties of (*see* properties of place)
    as socially constructed (*see* social construction of places)
    space versus, 3–4
place attachment, forging of, 242
    concept of, 14, 25–6, 85, 208, 217
    goal-based motives for, 132–3, 136–7, 139
    identity and self-perception and, 134–6, 159, 196
    life course continuity, 137–8, 206
    memories and, 116, 127–8, 208–9, 315
    negative, 14–16, 208–9
    notions of home and, 83, 95–6, 162, 196
    person-place-process framework and, 128–9, 131
    physical or social features of, 131–2
    survival as factor in, 138–9, 196
    transitions as factor in, 132–3, 180–1, 189, 204
    virtual, 47–8, 116, 299–300
    we-ness and, 127–8, 152, 159, 162–3, 290
place consciousness, 295
    CART processes affecting, 11, 120, 312, 319–21
    collective, 155–8, 231, 263
    concepts of, 12, 127
    Damanhurians', 256, 259

deepening/heightening, 10–11, 73, 118–20, 154, 284, 321
  enhanced placemaking and, 28, 31, 59, 259–64, 301, 324
  transitions and, 184, 199
placemaking
  BASIN principles in, 29, 258, 262–3, 316, 319, 324
  in cities, 268, 272–5, 298
  collaborative, 272–3, 279, 293, 296, 316
  community/public space, 60, 76, 92–3, 251, 265–6, 271–3, 283–5
  creative, 146–7, 298
  domestic, 75–6, 267
  empathy and, 217–18, 220, 282–4, 295, 324
  gendered (*see* gendered places/placemaking)
  homelessness and, 82–3, 185, 265, 269
  institutional influence on, 6, 78, 136, 229, 264, 314, 317
  mindfulness in, 58, 274, 284, 310
  politics of, 265, 270, 274, 282, 322
  virtual (*see* digital places/placemaking)
place-work, 2, 80–1, 131
planning, urban
  gendered, 55, 60, 280–1
  gentrification and (*see* gentrification)
  place attachment and, 282, 325
  placemaking and, 271, 278, 293, 320–1
  Participatory Neighborhood Narrative (PNN), 279–82, 314–15
  value-based land-use decisions, 92–4, 282, 293
  VR technology and, 283–4, 299
playgrounds, 155
  adult, 94

adventure/nature-based, 52, 66, 107–8
  expectations of experiences at, 8, 48
police, 7, 95
  demands to reform, 2, 8
  public clashes with, 16, 102, 173
  school presence, 219–20
  violence, 2–3, 173
Porters (Gainesville neighborhood), 279–80, 285, 314
poverty, 48, 66, 180, 198
  displacement and, 53, 68, 265
  hazardous work and, 216, 311
  home insecurity and (*see* homelessness)
  placemaking and, 292–5
  racism and, 131, 161–2, 228, 266
  rural, 89–90
  urban, 44, 81
power
  over vs. with, 49–50, 247, 308
  shared, 42, 49–50, 101, 120, 318
primary groups, 10, 29
  placemaking and, 265–7, 299, 316, 319
  rituals and, 146, 150–4, 259, 265
prisons, 15
  institutional conditions of, 51, 78, 96–9, 175, 245
  lifelong influence of, 97–8
  Nazi, 5, 103
  symbolic meaning of, 8, 48
  transitions to and from, 197–9
  warehouse, 98–9
Promise Keepers, 22–3
properties of place
  awareness of, 119, 182, 249, 322, 325
  discourse and, 57–60, 120, 149
  expectations of, 127, 317–18
  gendered, 55–7, 120
  institutional/cultural conditions, 51, 96, 101, 120

properties of place (*continued*)
  organic/digital, 42, 47–8, 101, 120, 318
  physical conditions, 42–6, 120, 133–4, 149, 256
  public/private, 42–3, 50–1, 62, 79, 120, 318
  rituals and, 150–2, 174, 180
  shared power, 42, 49–50, 101, 120, 318
  social structural, 42, 48–9, 96, 120, 170, 241, 318
  stability, level of, 51–5, 120, 222–3
  symbolic, 48, 120, 147–9, 256
  temporal, 222–3
  we-ness and, 51, 62, 109–10, 146, 261
property
  alteration for placemaking, 6, 95–6, 236, 276
  claims to, 232, 236, 241, 248
  Indigenous versus Western/colonial notions of, 74–5, 215–16, 232, 241
  neighborhood design and, 43–4, 137
  rituals, 150, 152
  transitions, 182, 203, 208
proprioception, 40–1, 320
Propst, Robert, 303
Proust's Principle, 37–8
psychodrama retreat, 23–4
public spaces
  concept of, 92–3
  debates over use of, 2, 27, 219
  legislation on, 51
  place consciousness and, 21, 119, 120, 264, 317
  placemaking in, 79–80, 92, 144, 267, 289, 292
  as quality places, 7, 93
  rituals/symbolism in, 154, 175, 202
  transitions to/from, 63
  withdrawal from, 45, 161
Puerto Rico, anti-gentrification movement in, 52–4, 274–5, 297

Purnell, David (*Building Communities Through Food*), 80–1, 152, 154
Putin, Vladimir, 49, 91, 213–14
Putnam, Daniel, 274

Queer Spaces: An Atlas of LGBTQIA+ Places and Stories (Furman and Mardell), 289

racial justice
  place-based vocalizations for, 2, 8
  struggles for, 16, 285–7, 292
racial segregation, 19, 90, 130–1, 240, 266–7, 292
  we-ness amid, 162, 172, 291
racism, 161
  community planning/housing, 240, 266–7, 279–80, 292
  Mardi Gras/New Orleans, 172–3, 228
  presence in US, 2–3, 19, 131, 267
Rappaport, Roy, 144–5
recreational spots, 58, 130
  building in lower–income neighborhoods, 294
  change in use of, 52
  conservationist movement and, 67–8
  inequitable access to, 67–8, 108, 290–4
  placemaking with, 108, 198, 292–5
  we-ness and, 154, 159, 293–5
red states, 63, 88. *See also* blue states
refugees, 180, 183
  camps for, 78, 222
  Ukrainian, 91, 112
Relph, Edward, 5, 12
reunions, 24, 150
Richards, Greg, 297–8
Rifkin, Jeremy, 57, 73
Rikuzentakata, Japan, 123–4
rites of passage, 166, 168–70, 181, 258
  phases of, 167

rituals
- as *CART* process, 10–11, 119–20, 261–3, 312, 314–18
- children and, 72, 159, 163, 168, 196
- claims to place, 168, 174–5, 215
- collective effervescence, 147–8, 157
- concepts of, 144–6
- amid COVID-19: 26–7, 156–8, 164
- gendered, 166–7, 172–3
- group belonging and, 89, 146, 149–50, 156–7, 171
- ideational we-ness and, 143–4, 156, 163, 170–1, 243, 255
- leisure spot, 146, 149, 155, 159–60
- nature-based, 72, 144, 170
- place-based meaning and, 26, 128, 144–9, 158, 168–70, 301
- in primary groups, 146, 150–4, 259, 265
- as property of place, 150–2, 174, 180
- in public spaces, 154, 175, 202
- routines versus, 145–6

Robertson, Ross, 256–7
Roosevelt, Theodore, 67–8, 242
Rosedale, Philip (*Second Life*), 115
Ross, Andrew (*Sunbelt Blues*), 77
Rothstein, Richard (*The Color of Law*), 240, 266
rural places, 63, 98, 138
- experiences in, 14–15, 18–19, 65–6, 88–90
- isolation/poverty in, 153, 160–2, 207
- perceptions of, 87, 105, 191, 196
- placemaking in, 160–2, 272
- struggles against development projects, 52–3
- we-ness in, 290

Russia, invasion of Ukraine, 91, 129–30, 185, 211–15. *See also* Ukraine

Salamon, Sonya (*Singlewide*), 84–5
Saval, Nikil (*Cubed*), 301–3

Scannell, Leila, 128, 132
schooling and classrooms, 91
- claiming of place, 209–10, 218–20, 228–30, 243
- COVID-19 and, 26–7, 100–1, 165, 229
- gentrification and, 276, 278
- home-based, 15, 101, 165, 191–2
- place attachment, 24, 126–7, 130–1, 209–10, 264
- policy impacts, 90, 229–30, 244, 247
- power to make decisions on, 25, 99, 218–20, 325
- properties of place, 42–3, 51, 56, 109, 112
- rituals in, 154–5, 163, 168–70, 194–5
- safety concerns, 56, 100–1, 219–20
- thoughtful design of, 8, 21, 193–4, 254, 258, 289, 293–4
- transitions, 183–7, 190–5, 197–200, 222
- we-ness in, 124, 134, 155, 239

Scott, David, 293–5
Seamon, David (*Life Takes Place*), 20
Second Life, 115, 298–9
Seidman, Karl (*Coming Home to New Orleans*), 227–8
Seinfeld, 95, 204
sense of place, 6–7, 12, 47–8, 54, 83, 157
senses, physical
- differences in, 39–40, 260
- heightened place-based, 36, 125
- mindfulness of, 38, 118, 302, 321
- technological change and, 113–14, 125, 283–4, 323
- *See also* multisensory design; umwelt

sleep, 138
- influence of place on, 71–2, 76, 314
- insecurity, 78–80
- we-ness and, 144, 209

smart cities, 47, 281–2

Smith, Art (GayBarchives), 288
Smith, Will and Jaden (*The Pursuit of Happyness*), 81
social construction of places
　analysis of, 11, 31, 234
　consciousness of, 8–9, 204, 282
　life experiences mediated through, 31, 36, 221
　notions of home in, 72–3
　virtual places and, 112, 135, 321
social ecology, community, 11, 85, 205–6
social justice
　as *BASIN* principle, 10, 29, 258, 262–5, 272–7, 319
　CART processes and, 10–11, 121, 251, 263
　consciousness of place and, 19, 104, 108, 158, 256
　gentrification and, 274–5
　Indigenous people and, 285–7
　MEAL life skills and, 10–11, 251, 263
　place-based struggles for, 16–17, 216
　placemaking and, 42, 169, 274, 290–4, 324
　sports/leisure places and, 104, 108, 293–5
　workplaces and, 305–7
social media, 6
　minimizing face-to-face encounters, 12, 69, 109, 118, 323
　place-based mobilizing through, 220–1
　sense of place and, 47–8, 54, 118, 135, 205
　we-ness and, 27, 196
social networks, xii, 115–16, 277
　ideal, 12–13
soldiers, 199, 323
　place-based forging of we-ness, 36, 38, 92, 131–2
　psychological trauma, 24, 35–6, 104, 126

transitions to/from safety, 183, 189, 201, 211–13
solidarity, social, 92
　rituals as reinforcing, 156, 160, 166–7, 171–5
Solnit, Rebecca (*A Paradise Built in Hell*), 172, 175, 234
Somerville, Peter, 74–5
sororities, 133–4, 167, 174, 197
soundwalks, 284–5
Southern states, 176
　experiences in, 19, 87–8
　racist/Confederate history, 16, 158, 173, 291–2
　regional identities, 4, 89–90, 160–2, 183
　See also blue states; Northern states; red states
space travel, 110–12
Spain, Daphne (*Gendered Spaces*), 56–7
sports, 51
　disabled access to, 70, 106, 108, 206–7, 243
　gendered participation in, 243–4
　group belonging, 162–3, 200, 316
　philosophy about, 107, 130, 200
　rituals/placemaking and, 160–2, 290–7
　as social domain, 10, 29, 120, 259, 262, 316, 319
　social justice and, 104, 108, 293–5
　stadiums, gathering in, 8, 14
　team fandom, 10, 83, 162–3, 183, 205
Stephenson, Neal (*Snow Crash*), 112
Stepping Out & Stepping Up (SOSU), 286
Stone, Leilah, 289
Stonewall Inn, 102, 289
Stover, Russell, 34–5
suburbs, 40, 69, 87, 265, 272
　dampening social life in, 7, 44–5
Sutton, Stacey, 276–7, 279

Sweeney, Tim (Epic Games/*Fortnite*), 113, 114–15
symbolism, 318
  assignment of place-based, 48–9, 100, 126, 213–14, 256–8
  of blue-collar work, 4, 83, 87, 302
  collective identity/narrative, 76, 100, 138, 162, 167, 197–9, 244
  of home, 15, 76, 79, 270
  Indigenous land-based, 232, 241–2
  of places, 2–5, 13, 27, 59, 94, 170–1, 178
  properties of place, 42, 48, 62, 120, 147–9, 256, 318
  rituals and, 26, 128, 142–9, 156–8, 168–70, 301
  shared meaningful, 17, 25–6, 74, 130, 174
  social movements and, 26, 102
  of transitions, 181, 189, 200, 208
  we-ness and, 9, 22, 109–12, 243, 285
  workplace, 268–9, 301, 303

Taylor, Dorothy Mae, 173
Taylor, Frederick Winslow, 301–3
technology, 59, 257
  affordances, 48, 284
  AR/VR: 46–7, 113–17, 135, 158, 283–4, 305
  communications, 63, 147, 158, 179
  institutional, 98, 101
  mediated experiences, 204–5, 219, 283, 298–9, 321–3
  metaverse, 112–14, 317–19
  nature/dyadic connections and, 67, 69–70, 141, 282–3
  in parenting, 69, 246–7
  smart city, 47, 281–2
  telehealth, 99, 165, 184
  transitions through, 179–80, 184, 196
  urban planning, 283–4, 299
  workplace, 166, 300–5, 308

third places, xii, 154, 203
  decline of, 45, 94–5
  television portrayals of, 95
Thomas, W.I. and Dorothy Swain, 117, 186
thought communities
  concept of, 9, 271
  engagement in rituals, 146, 156–9
  place attachment and, 285, 287–9
  social domain of, 10, 29, 251, 259, 316, 319
TikTok, 205, 221
trailer parks, 84–6
transitions
  aspects of, 27
  children and, 183, 196, 222–3
  in cities, 83, 228–9, 274
  homelessness and, 82–3, 185, 265, 269
  life, 116, 167, 179–82, 254, 268
  meaningful place-based, 180–2, 188–9, 201
  military, 183, 189, 201, 211–13
  neighborhood, 200–1, 222
  organic/digital, 42, 46–8, 101, 120, 318, 322–3
  place attachment and, 132–3, 180–1, 184, 189, 199, 204
  placemaking claims, 52, 209, 229–30
  relationships, 62–3
  school-based, 183–7, 190–5, 197–200, 222
  symbolism of, 181, 189, 200, 208
  technologically mediated, 179–80, 184, 196
transit systems, 56, 65, 108, 139
  (lack of) investment in, 185–7, 278
  safety concerns on, 87, 186–7
trauma, 177, 248
  confronting/surviving, 19, 24, 193
  place-based, xi, 19, 36, 78, 129
Trump, Donald, 9, 45, 89, 135, 149–50

truth spots, 8, 34, 102
Tuan, Yi Fu (*Space and Place*), 4
Turkle, Sherry, 219

Uexküll, Jakob von, 39
Ukraine
    Azovstal steel plant shelter, 211–15, 227
    displacement from, 91, 112, 129–30, 185
    place attachment in, 52, 91–2, 112, 211–15
    war in, 91, 139
umwelt, 39–40, 320, 323
underland, 64–5
urbanism, 45, 229
urban places, 4, 47, 229
    designing, 7, 92–4, 261, 271–3, 279–81, 299–300
    gendered experiences of, 55–6, 60, 87–8
    gentrification (*see* gentrification)
    place attachment to, 14, 63, 183, 196
    planning in (*see* planning, urban)
    poverty in, 44, 81
    rituals in, 168
    place consciousness, 40, 87, 320–1
    soundwalks in, 284–5
    See also cities; smart cities

van Gennep, Arnold (*The Rites of Passage*), 167, 181–2
vehicles, transportation, 108, 184–5, 188–9, 264
Vider, Stephen (*The Queerness of Home*), 76
virtual reality (VR)
    shaping embodied experiences, 46–7, 113–18
    technology, 113–17, 135, 158, 283–4, 305
Volpe, John Della (*Fight*), 324

we-ness
    from art, 46, 172, 254, 284
    across borders, 45–6
    cultivating, 15, 104, 134, 144, 162, 272, 305–8
    disaster responses and, 16, 55, 123–5, 228
    dyadic (*see* deep dyadic we-ness; dyadic we-ness)
    forms of, 9–10
    gender identity and, 25, 55, 95, 169, 287–9
    homelessness and, 79–83, 139, 152
    ideational (*see* ideational we-ness)
    in leisure spots, 106–8, 174, 294–5
    meaningful place-based, 10, 20, 151, 259, 273–4, 286
    metaverse experiences of, 27, 113–17, 196
    military, 36, 38, 52, 92, 131–2
    nature-based, 69–70, 152
    neighborhood, 44–5, 125–7, 152–4, 236, 315
    place attachment, 127–8, 152, 159, 162–3, 290
    properties of place and, 51, 62, 109–10, 146, 261
    amid racism, 162, 172, 291
    rituals and, 143–4, 156, 163, 170–1, 243, 255
    in schools, 124, 134, 155, 239
    spontaneous, 9–10, 46, 94–5, 119, 304
    symbolism and, 9, 22, 109–12, 243, 285
Western Shoshone Nation, 233–4
Westover, Tara (*Educated*), 15–16, 191–2
white-collar work, 301–4, 309. *See also* blue-collar work
white nationalism, 9, 24–5, 50, 174
Whyte, William H. (*Street Life Project*), 93

Wilkerson, Isabel (*Caste*), 291
women, 25, 143, 167, 207
  claims over place, 24–5, 75–6, 107, 115, 134, 211, 270
  discourse about, 40–1, 59–60, 87, 106–8, 270–1
  domestic violence support for, 155–6
  gentrification and, 53, 278, 280–1
  leisure activities and places, 105–7, 243
  metaverse experiences, 117–18
  properties of place and, 55–7, 120
  sports participation, 243–4
  urban planning and, 55–60, 87–8, 173, 280–1
  workplace experiences, 303–4
  See also gendered places/placemaking
Word to the Wives, A (1955 film), 270–1
workplaces
  agricultural, 239, 308–12
  architecture, 300, 308
  blue-collar (*see* blue-collar work)
  collaborative, 284, 293, 306–8
  amid COVID-19: 164–6, 300–1
  digital, 304–5
  experiences of people with disabilities in, 306–8
  empathy in, 308–12
  fitness centers in, 13, 304
  gendered dynamics in, 59–60, 166, 303–4
  group belonging in, 303–5, 308, 316
  leadership, 166, 306
  safety concerns at, 216, 308–11
  symbolic meaning in, 268–9, 301, 303
  technology in, 166, 300–5, 308
World War II, 33–4, 103–4, 212, 236, 303
Wyckoff, Mark, 7

Xygalatas, Dimitris (*Ritual*), 147–8

Yong, Ed (*An Immense World*), 40–1, 283
youth
  activism, 324–5
  biosphere/place consciousness, 72–3, 84, 293, 295
  collaborative time in nature, 69–73
  LGBTQ+, 77–8, 244
  metaverse experiences, 118, 299
  placemaking by, 154, 207, 267–8
  police and detention system involvement, 220, 247
  racism and, 131, 220, 267
  we-ness and, 50, 72–3, 105, 207

Zelenskyy, Volodymyr, 92, 213–14
Zerubavel, Eviatar, 17–18
Zimny-Schmitt, Danny, 88–9
Zuckerberg, Mark, 112, 114, 116

www.ingramcontent.com/pod-product-compliance
Ingram Content Group UK Ltd.
Pitfield, Milton Keynes, MK11 3LW, UK
UKHW022012160225
455131UK00002B/2/J